PEOPLE AND WORK

PEOPLE AND WORK

Edited by
Geoff Esland, Graeme Salaman and Mary·Anne Speakman
at The Open University

Holmes McDougall, Edinburgh
in association with
The Open University Press, Milton Keynes

First published 1975 by

Holmes McDougall
Allander House
137-141 Leith Walk
Edinburgh

in association with

The Open University Press
Walton Hall
Milton Keynes

Designed by Lewis Eadie

Cover illustration by Jim Proudfoot

Set in Plantin 110, 10 on 12pt

Printed in Great Britain by
Holmes McDougall, Perth

ISBN 0 7157 1471-6

ACKNOWLEDGEMENTS

The editors and publishers are grateful to the following for permission to reproduce copyright material in this book:

Heinemann Educational Books Ltd., London
Fontana Paperbacks, London
Cambridge University Press, London
Sociological Review, London
Macmillan Publishing Co. Inc., New York
John Wiley and Sons Inc., New York
Harper and Row, Publishers, Inc., New York
Daedalus, Journal of the Academy of Arts and Sciences, Boston, Mass.
Social Research, New York
Plenum Publishing Corporation, New York

The editors and publishers have made every effort to trace the copyright of the material used in this book and in any case where they have been unsuccessful, apologise for any accidental infringement of copyright.

CONTENTS

INTRODUCTION

This selection of readings has been compiled for the use of Open University students following the course People and Work[1]. *As such, it represents one component of a guided course of study which includes correspondence texts, set reading, tutorials and radio and television programmes. Our selection of articles has obviously been substantially influenced by the issues and topics contained in the course. Nevertheless, in producing this book, we have kept in mind a much larger group of readers who are interested in the sociology of work.*

One of the obvious characteristics of the sociological treatment of work is that it is dispersed through many of the specialities within sociology—for example, the sociology of the professions, occupational sociology, industrial sociology, and, of course, sociological theory. In constructing the Reader we felt increasingly that this feature of sociological activity had resulted in the fragmentation of those questions about work and economic life which had been so central in the ideas of the early social theorists. We have tried, therefore, to avoid the established sociological demarcations and to include a number of relevant areas of theory and research. The selection of readings is essentially concerned with the politics of work, *by which is meant the ways in which forms of work relate to structures of power and interest in societies. We have been particularly concerned to situate accounts of work activity and experience in the wider context of the economic and political structures within which employment occurs. Thus, we have included material on the relationships between work and identity or consciousness; we also look at the processes by which people are guided or coerced into certain kinds of work; and a number of papers consider the political aspects of work organization and the implications of certain occupations assuming positions of dominance in society. More detailed discussion of these questions is contained in the introductions to each of the four sections and also the opening article.*

1. *People and Work* is a third-level course produced jointly by the Faculties of Social Sciences and Educational Studies at The Open University.

8

In preparing the book we have been greatly helped by the suggestions and assistance of the People and Work *Course Team: David Boswell, Peter Braham, Richard Brown, Ben Cosin, Roger Dale, Alan Fox, Peter Hamilton, Terry Johnson, Theo Nichols, Ken Patton, Gwynn Pritchard, David Weeks, Janet Woollacott and Vincent Worth.*

We are also particularly grateful to Barbara Kehoe, and Susan Charlton for their assistance and to Jacky Korer and Tom Gregersen for their help with the detailed editing.

SECTION ONE
WORK
AND
SOCIETY

INTRODUCTION Graeme Salaman

The articles included in this section may, at first sight, appear somewhat
disparate and incongruous. They are, however, in their various ways, all
contributions to an underlying argument. Because of its thematic
significance this argument needs some exposition.

The argument asserts the *importance* of work, and in particular, its
importance to those who do it. All the most interesting and valuable
sociological accounts and discussions of work have been characterized by
a compassionate concern for those who are condemned, by virtue of
their location within the productive process, and the division of labour,
to what Gouldner has recently described as the awareness (and experience) '. . . that work, as many know it, is nothing less than the wasting
of life'.[1] But for many people work represents not simply the lack of
opportunities for creativity and self development, but has more definite
and damaging consequences—to health, family life, identity, and life
chances.

A useful way of understanding variations in work activities and
rewards, and their origins, is through the concept *class*. Class refers not
only to the varying amounts of economic power of groups within an
economic system, but also to the differences in experiences and life
chances that follow from positions within that economic and productive
system. These positions, of course, reflect the possession, or lack of
possession, of marketable resources. ' . . . "Class situation" . . . we may
express . . . briefly as the typical chance for a supply of goods, external

---

1. Alvin Gouldner, 'The Unemployed Self' in Ronald Fraser (ed.) *Work, Volume
Two: Twenty Personal Accounts*, Penguin, Harmondsworth, 1969, p. 346.

living conditions, and personal life experiences, in so far as this chance is determined by the amount and kind of power, or lack of such to dispose of goods or skills, for the sake of income in a given economic order.'[2]

For most people (certainly all those except the owners of capital) 'disposal of goods and skills' (and of sheer labour power) occurs at work, and work events, deprivations and conditions must count heavily among the 'personal life experiences' that are associated with levels of market power. Certainly the levels of reward (in the widest sense) which accompany different sorts of work determine the 'chance for a supply of goods, external living conditions', etc.

Variations in the levels and sorts of deprivations or rewards associated with various kinds of work reflect the market capacity—the 'worth'—of the people involved, given the priorities and interests of a a capitalist society. Furthermore the differences in life chances that are related to these work deprivations and opportunities demonstrate the conflict of interest intrinsic to such a form of economic and social arrangement.

But some writers have argued not only that these class-based differences in work rewards and costs are no longer evident, but, even more seriously, that various changes in Britain and other capitalist societies have resulted in a post-industrial society, a new, and less capitalist form of capitalism. This Reader, and this section of the Reader, will not support this view: on the contrary the survival of the essential features of capitalism, with their implications for the distribution of life chances, especially as these are represented by work events and deprivations, will be argued.

To understand work in any society it is necessary to understand the nature of that society. Whether or not a society is a capitalist one (and the question of the utility and applicability of that concept) is an important consideration in any analysis of work events and arrangements. After all class is not simply a way of describing structured differences in life chances; it is also a method of understanding the nature of a society and economy. As Giddens has remarked, a class society ' . . . is not simply a society in which there happen to be classes, but one in which class relationships provide the key to the explication of the social structure in general'.[3] An important part of this 'explication of the social structure in general' is the way in which events and life chances are determined by market capacity and market forces, but also important is the way in which through their experience of these events, decisions and deprivations (many of which happen at and through work) men begin to develop

2. From *Max Weber*, H. H. Gerth & C. W. Mills (trans. & eds.), Routledge & Kegan Paul, London, 1948, p. 181.
3. Anthony Giddens, *The Class Structure of the Advanced Societies*, Hutchinson, London, 1973, p. 127.

a consciousness of their interests and their opposition to those who employ them. In this case class becomes, as E. P. Thompson puts it, ' . . . not a thing, (but) . . . a happening'.[4]

Obviously then, the importance of work is not restricted to its personal significance, but also extends to the political implications of work events and deprivations.

Political in the sense that through work experiences people can begin to resist what they regard as deprivations and injustices at work, and in the wider sense that through such experiences and resistance they may begin either to develop radical political attitudes, or to behave in a 'disruptive' manner. But work has a further political dimension: it is clear that work involves a great deal of inequality. Work varies in its deprivations and delights, its opportunities and its monotony, its dangers and its costs. Some of these differences are discussed by Wedderburn and Craig in their article. Inequality is, at least potentially, political, since it constitutes a possible basis of schism, and dissension. But one of the striking things about work inequalities, even when they involve the sort of dramatic and severe work event described by Parker in his article, is that they are surrounded by legitimating ideologies which assert the necessity for some men to control others, and for work-based rewards to vary. Furthermore the decisions and events which result in large-scale deprivations—such as lay-offs, redundancies, bankruptcies, etc.—are constantly being 'depoliticized': they are represented as the inevitable results of technological change, market fluctuations, the need for improved efficiency, or reduced costs, or 'streamlining' and 'modernization', and so on. But these apparently value-free criteria, these technocratic, instrumentality rationalities, are not devoid of political, and societal interests; on the contrary, they serve to advance the interests of some groups at the same time as they assert their impartiality. Shroyer has argued that the structures of knowledge and evaluation that lie behind areas of decision-making when they are ' . . . construed as "technical problems" requiring information and instrumental strategies produced by technical experts' have become ' . . . a new form of legitimating power and privilege'.[5] One important way in which this has been achieved is that the use of such apparently inevitable, and immutable (and generally accepted) rationality ' . . . removes the total social framework of interests in which strategies are chosen, technologies applied, and systems established, from the scope of reflection and rational reconstruction'.[6]

4. E. P. Thompson, *The Making of the English Working Class*, Penguin, Harmondsworth, 1968, p. 939.
5. Trent Schroyer, 'Toward a Critical Theory for Advanced Industrial Society' in H. P. Dreitzel (ed.) *Recent Sociology*, No. 2, Macmillan, New York, 1970, pp. 210, 212.
6. See below. Jürgen Habermas, 'Technology and Science as "Ideology" '.

The articles included in this section relate to this underlying background argument of the importance and utility of class in understanding work arrangements and experiences and ideologies as follows. The first article, by Esland and Salaman, attempts to delineate the main features of early sociological approaches to the study of work. The theories of Marx, Weber and Durkheim are considered and certain common themes suggested. The authors argue that these early social theorists shared an interest in the way in which forms of work arrangement and types of work experience related to types of society, and the role of attitudes, values and ways of thinking in mediating this relationship. They suggest that this broad interest in what they call the politics of work has tended to become dissipated by more recent specializations in the sociology of work. And the article ends with an attempt to rediscover the sorts of problems and issues which inspired the early theorists, and which still require urgent analysis.

The articles by Wedderburn and Craig, and Blackburn, in their various ways, argue for the empirical utility of the concepts class and capitalism. Wedderburn and Craig supply interesting and much-needed data on the nature of work differences and deprivations. All too often these differences had merely been asserted (or denied) without empirical referent. These authors introduce an empirical, concrete note into the discussion. Blackburn's article constitutes a rejoinder to those theorists who had argued that capitalist societies have changed qualitatively, or indeed, that they have been replaced by a new form of society — industrial society. Although not directly about work, Blackburn's empirical answer to these arguments supplies a useful reminder of the societal framework within which, at least in Britain, work occurs.

Like the other contributions, Habermas's article is entirely within the tradition established by the early social theorists. Habermas describes the political implications and basis of the structure of knowledge and values which lies behind industrial planning, work and decision-making, and which has many implications for work events and structures. Habermas argues for the essential interest-based nature of knowledge, even that knowledge which is increasingly presented as neutral, and value-free, and which operates to legitimate societal power structures and the decisions which emanate from them. It is this sort of knowledge that inspires and legitimates work arrangements and work events although by its apparent technical, rational nature this function is disguised. Nevertheless, ' . . . it is . . . an apologetic standard through which (the) . . . relations of production can be justified as a functional institutional framework.'[7] Hence its importance for any understanding of work, and its context.

7. See below Jürgen Habermas, 'Technology and Science as "Ideology"'.

Child and Parker, in their two articles, describe in detail two different ways in which men's lives and livelihoods can be adversely affected by work events. Furthermore both writers locate the events they describe within a societal and economic context. They attempt to illuminate personal distress and anxiety, as it stems from work, against a background of social and economic change. Parker supplies a wealth of useful empirical data on the extent, nature, causes and consequences of redundancy—an event which, for those concerned, carries enormous significance. Child analyses alterations in the role of foremen and relates these to changes in organization, and organizational ideology. Of particular interest is Child's discussion of the manner in which changes in the foremen's traditional roles influence their sense of identification with, or alienation from, the interests and ideologies of management. For all its focus on work and work roles in organizational settings Child's interest in this 'boundary role, lodged ambiguously between the two traditionally defined "sides of industry" at a major watershed in the class system', and his attempt to discover variations in class indentifications and the perspectives they generate, places this article firmly within a class-based interest in work.

1. TOWARDS A SOCIOLOGY OF WORK Geoff Esland and Graeme Salaman

This article will attempt to delineate what we take to be some important and useful aspects of a sociology of work; in so doing we will consider work from the point of view of varieties of sociological theory and then move on to look at how far current work in the various sub-disciplines of sociology that are concerned with work employ or ignore the approaches and insights of this theoretical background. The article concludes with a consideration of one direction in which the sociology of work could usefully proceed.

For the early sociological theorists work was an enormously important social activity which played a central part in their analyses of society and social change, but by no means all recent work on the topic reflects (or even notices) its early theoretical significance. The theories of Marx, Durkheim and Weber in relation to work are centred on the dialectic between types of work experience, organization, and economic structures, and societal stability or change, as mediated by ideational factors of various kinds. Secondly, many of the classic sociological writings on work were inspired by an unmistakeable concern for the directions of social and economic change, and compassion for those who seemed likely to suffer from these changes. But a great deal of recent research on work shows no such concern. Indeed in the case of much of this work humanitarianism and compassion have been replaced either by bland empiricism or by a concern for practical (i.e. managerial) problems and outcomes. Thirdly, the sweep, and unity of the early theorists' approach to the study of work—as evidenced in the way in which such writers as Marx, Durkheim and Weber and, later, C. Wright Mills, located that treatment of work within theories and philosophies of society—has tended to disintegrate into highly discrete, narrow and recondite studies carried out under a variety of rubrics deriving from various sociological sub-disciplines and esoteric specialities.

We shall argue that this sociological specialization—this way of doing sociological work—is an important part of the reason for the trivialization of the sociology of work. We shall suggest instead that it should be seen in the context of a politically and structurally sensitive sociology of culture.

Work in sociological theory

But a brief summary of the early theorists' approaches to the study of work is

---

1. Original article. Copyright © 1975 The Open University, Milton Keynes. Geoff Esland and Graeme Salaman are Lecturers in Sociology at the Open University.

appropriate. First, however, we must be clear about what we mean by work. Work does not refer to particular types of activity: for one man may willingly and enthusiastically indulge in an activity which for another man is his work. Work is essentially a means of earning a livelihood. It should be obvious therefore that a thorough-going sociology of work—as developed by the early sociological theorists—would inevitably be concerned with the relationship between this activity and the social structures within which it occurred, and the impact and significance of this activity for the individuals concerned. After all in any society except the most simple, earning a living will invariably depend upon a complex and specialized division of labour, upon economic factors, and upon technology.

Marx's interest in work occupies a central place in his analysis of capitalism. Under capitalism the members of one class sell their labour to those who, through their ownership of capital are able to buy the labour of the propertyless and to extract profit from the arrangement. This profit, created by labour, is employed to finance further arrangements of the same sort. The profit is created by work— but work done under certain sorts of social (and finally political) conditions—i.e. the private ownership of the means of production. Work carried out under these conditions serves to constantly recreate the conditions themselves—that is, it produces and reproduces the power of the owners of capital since the labour of the propertyless creates profit, and therefore further capital.

But although work in capitalist society plays a central part in re-creating that form of society it also has an important role in destroying and transcending that society. This consequence of work is discussed through the two notions of alienation and class consciousness. Through these concepts Marx explores the meaning and significance of work in a capitalist society and the potential implications of such work for the stability of this type of society.

By alienation Marx refers to a separation, a detachment of the worker from his work, the products of his labour, his colleagues and himself. Alienation describes, in part, the separation of the worker from the value of his product through the expropriation of surplus value and the use of this profit to create further forms of expropriation. This concept is also used, however, to describe the process (inherent in capitalism with its emphasis on the market and profit) whereby the labourer becomes a commodity for sale.

Broadly speaking, by class consciousness Marx means the awareness among workers of their shared interests, and their opposition to the interests of the capitalists, and a determination to the revolutionary abolition of the capitalist system. Such a consciousness on the part of the working class would act, Marx maintained, as the impetus for revolutionary change within capitalist society, and the factors that produce such consciousness (like the situation which is the subject of the consciousness) are intrinsic to the capitalist mode of production. They are important for our purposes because they operate through the work situation. Marx argued that the developing nature of capitalism, with its periodic crises, its tendency to cause a relative widening of the differences between capitalist and proletariat, and the existence of a 'reserve army' of unemployed, would, together with other factors, lead to the development of class consciousness. The other factors include the concentration of the workers and their employment in large, homogeneous, organizational work forces.

One significant development in Marxist analysis has been the recognition of the transition from entrepreneurial capitalism to the welfare capitalism of the corporate state. This process is particularly important in so far as it has created a number of service occupations—in teaching, welfare, accountancy and the mass media—which, in a sense, have become the secondary agents of the capitalist ethic. The ways in which these occupations embody and transmit capitalist principles are central to the structuring of consciousness in societies which have become dependent on a belief in consumption and economic growth.

Durkheim's interest in work, although drastically different from that of Marx, can be seen to share certain common features—notably a concern for establishing the relationship between work and the stability of the social structure within which it occurs. Durkheim's main interest in work is in exploring the relationship between the nature of work activities, their specialization and inter-dependence, and the integration of the society. He writes,

> We are thus led to consider the division of labour in a new light . . .
> the economic services that it can render are picayune compared to the
> moral effect it produces, and its true function is to create in two or
> more persons a feeling of solidarity. In whatever manner the result is
> obtained, its aim is to cause coherence among friends and to stamp
> them with its seal![1]

Durkheim argues that the form of division of labour operative within a society serves to achieve the integration of that society. In traditional forms of society the division of labour is extremely simple—and consists of hardly more than differences of function allocated on a sexual or age basis. But in modern societies the division of labour is highly specialized and differentiated. These differences relate to the integration of these societies. Durkheim argues that the form of the division of labour is directly related to the nature and extent of societal integration. He writes, for example,

> It would serve not only to raise societies to luxury, . . . it would be a
> condition of their existence. Through it, or at least particularly through
> it, their cohesion would be assured.[2]

Durkheim admits that the division of labour *can* produce what he calls pathological effects—i.e. it can result in disintegration, and reduced solidarity. It might be suggested that such a possibility must be admitted in the face of the evident conflicts and crises that characterized late nineteenth-century European societies. But Durkheim maintains that although these are 'normal' they are pathological: in the main the highly complex division of labour that characterizes modern societies shows evidence of previous forms of solidarity and produces a new, interdependent type. The 'pathologies' result from the fact that the division of labour is characterized by *anomie*. Durkheim attributes the obviously negative and disruptive features of modern societies to the fact that the division of labour

1. Emile Durkheim, *The Division of Labour in Society*, The Free Press, New York, 1964, p. 56.
2. *Ibid*, p. 63.

is not entirely in line with the distribution of peoples' abilities and talents.

> For the division of labour to produce solidarity, it is not sufficient,
> then, that each have his task; it is still necessary that *this task be
> fitting to him.* . . . if the institutions of classes or castes sometimes give rise to
> anxiety and pain instead of producing solidarity, this is because the
> distribution of social functions on which it rests does not respond . . .
> to the distribution of natural talents.[3]

For our purposes the most interesting and relevant aspects of Weber's writings are those that discuss the ideas and mental principles that characterize, or are prevalent in, capitalist societies.

In the *Protestant Ethic and the Spirit of Capitalism* Weber attempts to explain the relationship between protestantism and capitalism by isolating and delineating the beliefs and doctrines that characterize protestantism, and assessing their impact on the believer. He argues that one result of these beliefs is the production of capitalist actions. Weber defined capitalist action as

> . . . one which rests on the expectation of profit by the utilization of
> opportunities for exchange, that is on (formally) peaceful chances of
> profit.[4]

However modern capitalism differs from earlier forms in that it involves the ' . . . rational capitalistic organization of (formally) free labour'.[5] Of course Weber also regarded various other factors as important, such as the separation of the family from business activity, and the freedom from economic restriction and regulation, and the use of double-entry book-keeping which permitted the capitalist to assess and monitor the profitability of his various ventures. Needless to say these calculations could only take place in terms of money, which supplies a general standard of assessment, a reliable and consistent rule.

However for our purposes the interesting feature of Weber's work on capitalism is the emphasis he places on the nature and role of rationality under capitalism. As Freund has remarked, in capitalist society Weber saw rationality not simply as a principle of action with specific characteristics (see below) but also as an all-pervasive feature of life. He says:

> It exerts a permanent action, developing and transcending itself cease-
> lessly . . . the rationality of the West has taken the form of a progressive
> intellectualization of life; it has tended to strip the world of charm and
> poetry; intellectualization means disenchantment . . . the world becomes
> increasingly the artificial product of man, who governs it much as one
> controls a machine. Hence . . . the formidable ascendancy of technology.[6]

3. *Ibid*, p. 375.
4. Max Weber, *The Protestant Ethic and the Spirit of Capitalism*, Allen and Unwin, London, 1930, p. 17.
5. *Ibid*, p. 21.
6. Julien Freund, *The Sociology of Max Weber*, Penguin, London, 1968, pp. 143–4.

Other writers have elaborated on such a conception of rationality as a feature of modern life (see Berger, Berger & Kellner) and the role of such a world view, such a system of priorities and criteria, as controlling ideologies. In his writing on rationality Weber makes a distinction between 'formal' and 'substantive' rationality. 'Formal' rationality is used to ' . . . describe the extent of quantitative calculation or accounting which is technically possible and which is actually applied'.[7] Clearly in this sense modern capitalism and bureaucracy are characterized by a remarkable degree of institutionalized formal rationality. By 'substantive' rationality Weber means,

> . . . the degree in which a given group of persons . . . is or could be adequately provided with goods by means of an economically oriented course of social action. This course of action will be interpreted in terms of a given set of ultimate values no matter what they may be.[8]

In other words Weber distinguishes between attempts to systematically assess the efficiency or success of an action, (which is greatly assisted by the existence of money which supplies a method of measurement) and the values and ultimate ends which are employed. Substantive rationality refers to

> . . . a relation to the absolute values or to the content of the particular given ends to which it is oriented.[9]

Weber also employed the concept rationality when discussing the development of bureaucracy. Bureaucracy, which Weber regarded as a central feature of capitalism, is based upon legal authority, which means that a person's authority and decisions (and others' obedience to the decisions) follow from impersonal norms and rules which are designed within a system of commitment to rational action and predictability. While conscious of the inefficiences of bureaucracy Weber stressed that this type of organization only really developed within capitalism and was central to the development of that form of economic organization—supplying precision, calculability, lucidity, etc. The bureaucratic form of organization

> . . . compares with other organizations exactly as does the machine with the non-mechanical modes of production.[10]

The great advantage of the bureaucratic mode of operation lies in its *impersonality* (it discharges business 'without regard for persons'), and its emphasis on 'calculable rules'. He writes,

> Its specific nature, which is welcomed by capitalism, develops the more perfectly the more the bureaucracy is 'dehumanized', the more

7. Max Weber, *The Protestant Ethic and the Spirit of Capitalism*, Allen and Unwin, London, 1930, p. 184–5.
8. *Ibid.*, p. 185.
9. *Ibid.*, p. 185.
10. From *Max Weber*, H. H. Gerth & C. W. Mills (trans. & eds.), Routledge & Kegan Paul, London, 1948, p. 214.

completely it succeeds in eliminating from official business love, hatred, and all purely personal, irrational, and emotional elements which escape calculation.[11]

The three theorists whose work has been sketched in above have supplied us with a rich vocabulary with which to discuss work activity and experience in capitalist society. Although each writer's approach is integrated into a particular and idiosyncratic analysis of society and social process it is nevertheless possible to see in their disparate writings on work certain common themes and insights.

First these authors display a concern for the people involved in the work processes and social and economic structures they talk about.

The humanitarianism of the early theorists is evident in their approaches to the subject itself. This is particularly evident in the case of Marx, whose theory of capitalist society centres on a concern for a type of economic order that is based upon the intrinsic and systematic exploitation of one group for the benefit of another. As John O'Neill has pointed out,

> Marx's critique of political economy is essentially a humanist critique of *the absence of man* and his world-alienation produced through the subjectivization of the principle of property.[12]

A profound sympathy for the sufferings and deprivations that attend the emergence and development of capitalism can be discerned in the writings of the early theorists. And this compassion is reflected in the attempt to uncover the economic and social features and tendencies which produce the disturbing consequences. They attempt to show how the consequences experienced by the individual—anomie, alienation, dehumanizing, disenchanting bureaucratic rationalities, etc.—are systematically related to social structure and social change. They achieve what C. Wright Mills regarded as one of the main features of the sociological imagination—the linking of history and personal biography.

Secondly these theorists' approach to the study of work is *sociological*, that is, it is centrally concerned with investigating the relationship between work activities (and their significance for the people concerned) and the larger social processes and events. Not only, as we have seen, do they attempt to locate work experiences within a context of social and economic change, they also consider the impact of these work experiences and activities *for the stability of the social system itself*. Again this is most evident in Marx's analysis of work experience in terms of the development of class consciousness, but it is also a central feature of Durkheim's investigation of the relationship between a complex, differentiated and highly specialized division of labour and the survival (in some form) of social integration and solidarity. We have seen that the views of Marx and Durkheim on the relationship between work and social integration conflict, but the questions they raised were surprisingly similar: how do industrial/capitalist forms of production and division of labour relate to the persistence or instability of society?

11. *Ibid.*, pp. 215–6.
12. J. O'Neill, 'For Marx Against Althusser' in *The Human Context*, Vol. 6, No. 2, 1974, pp. 385–98.

Both theorists discuss this question in terms of the ideas, consciousness, sentiments or moralities that develop under certain forms of productive arrangements. Both, in short, have recourse to a sociology of knowledge.

Marx, Weber and Durkheim are furthermore concerned with the *politics of work*. Their analyses of varieties of work arrangements and the values and priorities that are associated with them and their 'political' significance display a considerable interest in the socio-political arrangements that lie behind them. Not only do they consider work in terms of its relationship to socially significant, (supportive or disruptive) bodies of knowledge and morality, but they also necessarily, pay considerable attention to the personal work experiences and events which influence, and are mediated by, these ideas and values. They consider work in terms of its capacity to generate conflict and/or consensus in society at large and in smaller contexts of organizations or occupations.

It is our contention that these two views of work which can be clearly discerned in the work of the early theorists, despite their differences, have ceased to inspire, or be evident in, more recent analyses that pass as contributions to the sociology of work. To demonstrate this it is necessary to take a brief overview of this field of academic activity.

Current state of the sociology of work

The most obvious feature of current sociological analyses of work activities and processes is their sub-division and differentiation. There are now a number of sociological sub-disciplines which are concerned, in one way or another, with work: industrial sociology, occupational sociology, the sociology of the professions, itself fragmented into the sociology of medicine and education, and others (the sociology of industrial relations, or of class structures). This sociological differentiation is an understandable consequence of the development of the discipline during the last 100 years. But unfortunately it has also been associated with a differentiation of approach and interest that has, we argue, resulted in a loss of interest in those issues that inspired the early sociologists.

This loss of inspiration is displayed in two ways: on the one hand the sociology of work has become so differentiated, specific and inward-looking that much of it has lost the political concerns of the early theorists' work—and the close links between work, economy and stability/change and the mediating role of ideational factors, characterizing their work have tended to be overlooked. Secondly, the sub-division of the sociology of work has resulted in each sub-discipline concentrating its attention on some aspects of the topic, at the expense of others, and has led each speciality to consider its demarcated subject matter in terms of a particular selection of theoretical approaches and insights.

Industrial sociology for example is, quite naturally, concerned with the sociological discussion of industrial institutions, roles and processes; that is, this sociological sub-discipline approaches the study of work (when it deals with this topic) through

... the study of the social system of the factory and of the influences external to the factory which affect that system.[13]

These authors continue to emphasize that

> industrial sociology is important because industrial structure and processes shape every aspect of human life and are deeply embedded in the social fabric of societal and personal choices.[14]

Now such a subject matter would seem to lead directly to the sorts of issues and problems that the early sociologists studied. And Parker and his colleagues note that

> The classical social theorists provided important leads into the significant questions and areas of analysis in industrial society.

But they add,

> These concerns have not been treated equally in the development of industrial sociology.[15]

Although industrial sociology has shown some tendency to focus on practical, managerial problems and interests (a tendency which is reflected in the theoretical development of the speciality, as much as in the actual topics studied) nevertheless this speciality has shown an awareness of the issues raised by the classic social theorists, notably in the many studies that document the human and social costs of various types of work and work organization, and that measure work-based differences between class groups.[16] For our purposes the most interesting and relevant aspects of industrial sociology are those studies, which play a significant part in British industrial sociology, that consider varieties of work activities, circumstances and events and their relationship to class-conscious attitudes and cultures.[17]

However, not surprisingly in view of the basic orientation of industrial sociology—i.e. towards industrial institutions, etc.—this sub-discipline tends to lose sight of non-industrial work, non-industrial organizations such as schools, government bureaucracies, etc., and the importance of occupational or professional cultures and loyalties. Like the other sociological specialities that study work the academic focus and context of the sub-discipline result in an interest in some sorts (industrial) of work but not others.

Occupational sociology on the other hand focusses attention not on industrial

13. Tom Lupton, *The University Teaching of the Social Sciences: Industrial Sociology*, UNESCO, 1961, quoted in S. R. Parker, R. K. Brown, J. Child and M. A. Smith, *The Sociology of Industry*, Allen and Unwin, London, 1972.
14. S. R. Parker, et al, *The Sociology of Industry*, Allen and Unwin, London, 1972, p. 21.
15. *Ibid.*, p. 17.
16. E.g. John H. Goldthorpe, David Lockwood, Frank Bechhofer and Jennifer Platt, *The Affluent Worker: Industrial Attitudes and Behaviour*, Cambridge University Press, Cambridge, 1968.
17. See D. Lockwood, *The Blackcoated Worker*, Allen and Unwin, London, 1958.

relations and behaviour within factories, or on the institutions of industrial societies, but on occupations. Nosow and Form argue that this 'vital' sub-discipline involves five substative fields:

> . . . the social nature of work and related phenomena such as leisure, play, recreation, retirement and unemployment. The second is concerned with the analysis of occupational structure . . . . A third major theme, the study of individual occupations, commonly deals with the institutional complex of the occupations. . . . The fourth is the analysis of how the occupational structure and individual occupations articulate with other segments of society . . . a fifth theme is the study of a particular occupation to highlight an important problem in the broader society.[18]

Many of those who study work through this approach with its associated fields, themes, concepts, problematics and theories seem to believe that a sociology of work is synonymous with a sociology of occupations. Such a view must involve an odd conception of occupation, for surely not all work involves an occupation. An occupation consists of a body of skills and techniques shared by people with some shared occupational culture and some conception of themselves as members of their occupation. In this sense many people have no occupation—they just work for a particular organization or firm. Just as industrial sociology usually concentrates on work in industrial settings, occupational sociology is limited to work which is done by members of established and demarcated occupations. Both overlook the work of significant portions of the population.

The sociology of occupations tends, on the whole, either to emphasize the subjective interactionist aspects of occupations and occupational cultures—through such notions as career, identity, role, socialization, etc., or to adopt a consensual conception of larger societal processes and events. There is of course a close relationship between these two features of the speciality. They are nicely demonstrated by Pavalko in his introduction to the *Sociology of Occupations and Professions:*

> Sociologists who study work diverge on many points, but a fundamental assumption running through their interest in the topic is that occupations are *social roles.* . . . Defining occupations as social roles immediately suggests a number of analytic problems. Why do individuals decide to enter one rather than another occupational role ? How are occupational roles learned ? What are the personal and social consequences of performing one rather than another occupational role ? How does the behaviour expected of occupational roles conflict with behaviour expected in other (e.g. family) roles ?[19]

Now these may or may not be interesting questions. But if they are typical of the issues that emerge from a commitment to studying work through the con-

18. Sigmund Nosow and William H. Form, *Man, Work and Society,* Basic Books, New York, 1962, p. 3.
19. Ronald Pavalko, *Sociology of Occupations and Professions,* Peacock, Illinois, 1971, p. 3.

ceptual and theoretical equipment of the sociology of occupations, then it is immediately obvious that they are one-sided. The issues that preoccupied the early theorists, the concern for varieties of work experience and their relationship to the structure of society and its stability or change have been replaced by a view of work as a scripted performance in a societal scenario. The nature of work roles, their inter-relationships with other, non-work roles, and their impact on incumbents' identities have replaced an interest in the nature of work *activity* and the differences in rewards and deprivations that are systematically related to the structure of society and which may, through their impact on people's conception of their interests vis-a-vis those of others, lead to social and political change. On the whole occupational sociology, with its emphasis on *occupation* rather than *work*, its commitment to a consensual model of society and focus on occupational *roles* with all the barrage of concepts that typically follow that conceptual orientation, seems unlikely to be able to consider the sorts of issues raised by the early theorists.

In connection with the difference in selected topics and theoretical orientations of industrial sociology and occupational sociology it is interesting to compare the treatment of work cultures and knowledge in the two specialities. While industrial sociologists study the ways in which different sorts of work and market situations within industrial enterprises are related to bodies of shared attitudes, values and ideas that in turn influence the political and social philosophies and perceptions of those concerned, occupational sociologists usually appear to sacrifice any interest in, or awareness of, the organizational or industrial contexts of work or the societal or political consequences of work-based bodies of knowledge in favour of a fascination for the esoteric and bizarre cultures that are associated with certain occupations, and a concern for understanding the ways in which these occupational cultures are transmitted and maintained. (Through such concepts as 'role', 'self', 'identity', 'socialization', 'reference group', etc.)

Unquestionably there is room for such investigations employing this interactionist approach, and it is possible to think of a few significant contributions of this sort (e.g. Polsky's *Hustlers, Beats and Others*) but it seems unfortunate that attention should be attracted away from an attempt to relate all sorts of work experiences to the development of politically and socially significant structures of knowledge, culture and consciousness as a result of a focus on occupationally transmitted cultures. Many people do not belong to occupations, and most of the significant ideas and attitudes that are influenced by and related to work experiences are not cultures in the sense of *occupational* cultures. Is the class consciousness of an assembly-line worker an occupational culture? Is it made more or less available and obvious via the sorts of concepts associated with this sociological sub-discipline?

Now this is not to deny that the concept occupation, and a sociological investigation of occupational phenomena *needs* to be irrelevant to the sorts of concerns and interests first developed by the early social theorists. The concept occupation, is potentially useful for exploring certain sorts of work-based knowledge and values, with their implications for shared parochial, or class-based conceptions of interest. The relationship between class and occupational consciousness is an extremely important one that requires analysis. And the relationship between occupational activity, power and culture and social structure and process needs study. But these issues are rarely explored, and they are unlikely to be illuminated by a sociology of occupations that is largely restricted to the internal world of occupational cultures and the processes whereby these are transmitted and maintained.

The unfortunate manner in which the sociology of occupations has moved away from a consideration of work in society is nicely illustrated by a table in an introductory text book by Lee Taylor, entitled *Occupational Sociology*. This table speaks for itself. It seems highly unlikely that any of these areas of study contain work that is significantly related to the issues and areas that preoccupied Marx, Weber and Durkheim: the focus on occupation has resulted in a distinctive bias.

Major Areas of Subject Matter in Occupational Sociology Articles, 1946-52 and 1953-59

| | Per Cent | |
Area Studied	1946–52	1953–59
Career	23.2	12.9
Occupational status and mobility	14.1	21.0
Ethnic group and occupations	13.6	8.2
Working force	10.7	8.2
Occupational role and personality	8.5	16.4
Occupational images	6.8	5.1
Occupational comparisons	3.9	5.1
Methodology	3.9	7.7
Client-professional relations	2.8	1.0
Occupational culture and ethics	2.3	9.8
Miscellaneous	10.2	4.6
Total Per Cent	100.0	100.0
Total Number of Articles	177	195

Source: Erwin O. Smigel, *et. al.*, "Occupational Sociology: A Re-examination,' *Sociology and Social Research* 47 (July 1963), 475.

It is normal in sociology (as elsewhere) to make a distinction between ordinary occupations and professions. The sociology of professions, because of its subject matter, differs in various ways from the sociology of occupations. But in most cases these points of difference take the speciality no nearer to a sociology of work. With some interesting and valuable exceptions (Johnson, T., Freidson, E., McKinley, J.)[20] the sociology of professions is concerned with the same issues that fascinate and motivate the professionals themselves—i.e. what is a profession and how is it that members become fully committed to the defining body of values and expertise? It is true that there have been some attempts to relate the nature and existence of professions to the structure of society, but as other have

20. Terence Johnson, *Professions and Power*, Macmillan, London, 1972, Eliot Freidson, *Professional Dominance*, Atherton, New York, 1970 and John B. McKinley, 'On the Professional Regulation of Change' in Paul Halmos (ed.), *Professionalization and Social Change*, University of Keele, 1973, pp. 61–84.

pointed out the most influential of these assumes a highly functional approach and accepts the social importance and necessity of the professions and the orientations and priorities they apparently employ.

It is rare in the sociology of the professions that the issues raised by the early theorists are apparent. All too often the sociological investigation of the relationship between professions and society, the development of the division of labour and the structure and stability of society have been replaced by a concern for delineating the characteristics of professions or for analysing the 'alienation' and dissatisfaction of professionals employed in bureaucracies. As Johnson has noted,

> The sociology of the professions received much of its initial impetus from two fundamental questions. The first concerned the extent to which professional occupations could be regarded as a unique product of the division of labour in society. The second question posed the problem: do professions perform a special role in industrial society, economic, political or social?[21]

But, he continues, these questions have been transformed into,

> . . . a largely sterile attempt to define what the special 'attributes' of a profession are. These definitional exercises litter the field.[22]

Another speciality with some claim to an interest in work is that field of academic activity known as the sociology of organizations. Here again we find that all too often a sociology of organizations has been replaced by what is described as organisation theory. This latter creature is explicitly oriented towards researching the on-going practical problems of organizational members—particularly senior ones. Apart from some influential and famous exceptions this speciality too loses sight of *sociology* in its fascination with *organizations*. The analysis of organizational events rarely looks beyond the organization to the society outside, and the reliance on such concepts as organizational structure, organizational roles, and rules, organizational cultures, cliques and groups, inevitably predispose towards a loss of interest in extra-organizational determinants of activity and a lack of concern for the relationship between the organization and society. It is odd that in organizational studies there is rarely any mention of workers. Apparently it is felt that workers are more appropriately studied by industrial sociology. The sociology of organizations looks at managers, professionals in bureaucracies, foremen (occasionally), administrators, bureaucrats.

Similarly within the sociology of organizations there is remarkably little interest in the work that organizational members do. There is a great deal of attention paid to the ways in which members are controlled, and to the nature of and inter-relationships between elements of *organizational structure*. But the day-by-day work that is done by organizational members in their locations within this

---

21. Terence Johnson, *Professions and Power*, Macmillan, London, 1972, p. 10.
22. *Ibid.*, p. 10.

structure gets scant attention. And this is odd because a large proportion of people whose work is studied by industrial sociologists and occupational sociologists work in organizations. And a great deal of, say, the consciousness of conflicting interests that develops between workers and management and is described in an industrial sociology study occurs within organizations. But you would never think so to read most sociology of organizations. Similarly the alienation, deprivation, frustration and boredom suffered by those who do dull and monotonous work under the control of assembly line or supervisor are experienced within organizations. But this rarely appears in this speciality.

The reasons for this are not hard to find. They are, firstly, that on the whole the sociology of organizations has adopted a highly formalistic, structural perspective on its subject matter, which tends frequently to be inspired by management problems and interests; and secondly, this speciality restricts its explanation of the behaviour of organizational members to events and circumstances within the organization itself. The behaviour, say, of workers, is explained in terms of their roles, or their esoteric and fascinating work-group sub-cultures, and the activity of executives and managers follows from their knowledge of and commitment to the goals of the organization (or from their informal cliques). But that workers' behaviour is also influenced by their position within the society and community, and that it might be determined by their conceptions of their shared interests, or that the organization's goals might have important implications for societal, political events, is rarely acknowledged. As with the sociology of occupations and professions there is an excessive emphasis on the structural contexts within which work occurs and insufficient attention to the issues that would normally follow a sociological approach. We are not merely arguing, as Albrow has done, that there is '... need ... for sociologists to study organizations as societies'.[23] although we concur with this suggestion. We are also maintaining that there is a need for sociologists to study organizations (occupations, professions) in *society*; in terms of the ways in which these work structures and organizations are systematically related to economic, political and social structures, and their implications for stability or change in these structures.

One important way, as we have seen, of investigating this relationship is by considering the ways in which work activities and experiences influence the development of politically relevant knowledge and values among those involved, and the ways in which work experiences and events are defined by generally accepted logics of rationality, instrumentality, and professional authority. A sociology of work-based and relevant knowledge could shed a great deal of light on the relationship between position within the economic order and attitudes towards that order, and on the nature of legitimating ideologies.

New directions

One important consequence of the fragmentation of work as a subject of study

23. Martin Albrow, *Bureaucracy*, Macmillan, London, 1974, p. 410.

in sociology has been the depoliticizing of some of its major aspects. Questions of legitimacy and power, if they arise at all, are usually limited to the organizational contexts of work, or to intra-occupational issues of hierarchy and control,—for example, questions of supervision within industry, or case studies of control and conflict within particular industrial enterprise. There has been relatively little consideration of the cultural context within which work occurs—the structure of various definitions and 'rationalities' that supply the legitimations of work events, inequalities and experiences, or which undermine radical, alternative value systems. In particular the role of specific occupations in developing and dis-seminating imperialistic logics and rationalities needs to be investigated. Similarly, little has been done since Mills' work to produce critical perspectives on the major cultural conditions under which specific types of work activity occur and are legitimated. Nor has there been enough consideration of the re-lationships between the various apparatuses of the state in relation to work. This is not to deny that in the recent developments of Marxist theory in particular there have been significant contributions to the analysis of the structural organ-ization of work. Nevertheless, the contexts in which these developments have taken place have been primarily philosophical and exegetical and at a level of abstraction which makes difficult a view of work as both everyday practice and the actualization of cultural and productive forces in society.

For instance, in a good deal of the discussion of the class structure, alien-ation, and the ownership and control of capital, the relationship between material work reality and the diversity of work cultures and 'world images' is often treated as problematic. As Goldthorpe and Lockwood argue,

> from a sociological standpoint what is in fact of major interest is the variation in which groups differently located in the social structure actually experience and attempt to meet the needs which at a different level of analysis may be attributed to them all.[24]

A recent conference on the class images of traditional workers (oriented around Lockwood's 1966 paper) constantly discovered the 'ambivalence' of the class imagery of workers. It has been noted that conceptions of class and power vary. During industrial disputes a sense of class conflict at work and in society is very much more sharply drawn than during 'normal' working periods. Similarly, during times of non-confrontation, people's conception of their employing organization can be 'inconsistent': Beynon for example, draws attention to the fact that factory production rests upon the acceptance of a cooperative model of production, at the same time as involving day-by-day experiences which belie this view. As he says:

> The contradiction of factory production, and the source of contra-dictory elements within class consciousness, is rooted in the fact that the exploitation of workers is achieved through collective, coordinated activities within both the factory and society generally.[25]

24. John H. Goldthorpe, et al., *The Affluent Worker: Industrial Attitudes and Behaviour*, Cambridge University Press, Cambridge, 1968, p. 178.
25. Huw Beynon, *Working for Ford*, EP Publishing, Wakefield, 1975, p. 102.

More importantly perhaps, the daily political exercise of cultural domination—both the forms it takes, and the extent of its enforcement—is taken for granted or subsumed under the logic of capitalist organization, and instrumental rationales of efficiency.

The result has been described by Mannheim:

> The fundamental tendency of all bureaucratic thought is to turn all problems of politics into problems of administration . . . behind every law that has been made there lie the socially fashioned interests and the *Weltanschauungen* of a specific social group.[26]

For example the pervasiveness of 'cost-effective' logic among both managers and trade unionists hinders the development of a radical conception of industrial events such as redundancy or accidents.[27] Similarly as Taylor et al., recently argued, the extension of legal controls to incorporate industrial-relations activity previously subject only to negotiated rules constitutes an example of the enlargement of an occupational (in this case legal) mandate—a feature which is applicable to other occupations.[28]

Part of the reason for the intellectual concentration in sociology on theories of structure rather than theories of structured action is the insistence of some Marxist analysis that consciousness is a dependent variable in relation to the material structures and institutions of production. This has led to an unwarranted assumption that inter-subjectivity and everyday action do not need to be explained except in relation to a set of 'scientifically determined' structures. One of the chief consequences of this approach is that it denies the power of technological culture to *act back on* the creation and use of technological instruments. This is particularly important where the instruments have become psychological or operational as they have in many areas of work experience and organization. The scientization of programmes designed to improve worker motivation and output, and the rendering of labour as cost in the grammar of accountancy, have come to be regarded as so self-evidently necessary that the subjugation of existence which is involved is brushed aside. To extend Habermas's point about the rationality of advanced industrial societies, the scientization of the practices and conditions of employment has become a specific form of unacknowledged political domination. As such this process warrants serious consideration for the ways in which it becomes translated into concrete terms of power and control. Winkler in his research into company directors draws attention to the tendency of directors to conceive of workers almost exclusively as a commodity. He documents

> . . . the triumph in the boardroom of accountancy over economics and social psychology, not to mention more humanistic considerations . . . . For all the directors labour was simply a cost to be minimized.[29]

26. Karl Mannheim, *Ideology and Utopia*, Harcourt, Brace, New York, 1936, p. 105.
27. See below Theo Nichols, 'The Sociology of Accidents and the Social Production of Injury'.
28. E.g. Thomas Szasz, *Ideology and Insanity*, Penguin, Harmondsworth, 1974.
29. See Jack Winkler, 'The Ghost at the Bargaining Table: Directors and Industrial Relations', British Journal of Industrial Relations, Vol 12, No. 2, July 1974. (pp. 191-212)

Similarly C. Wright Mills, writing in *White Collar*, has reminded us of the power of manipulation when it is embodied in the abstractions and legitimized processes of modern bureaucracies:

> In the movement from authority to manipulation, power shifts from the visible to the invisible, from the known to the anonymous. And with rising material standards, exploitation becomes less material and more psychological.[30]

Mills also notes the important role of occupations and occupational ideologies, in supplying legitimations of existing structures of power and interest.

As he demonstrates in *The Professional Ideology of Social Pathologists*, the rationalization of occupational practice during the past century has led to conceptions of social order and legitimacy becoming embedded in the ideologies of particular occupations.[31] This is especially true of the occupational adjuncts to managerialism, and of the various correctionalist occupations such as social work and psychiatry and of mass-media occupations. Cultural domination in its various forms then becomes contingent on the politics of work practice, and the presentation of a case to the public—lay and professional—which emphasizes the occupation's social utility, and right to legislate for others. This is particularly true and significant for those occupations which have gained a societal mandate to process, treat, classify, diagnose, cure and counsel 'problem' individuals.[32]

It is obviously important and valuable to investigate the material nature of work—the 'work' and 'market' situations and the various work experiences and circumstances that are systematically related to the market power of those who sell, or buy, labour and expertise. It is also important to understand the relationship between such events, and people's definition of them. But one of the major weaknesses, in our view, of an historical materialist analysis of economic production which ignores the active and generative power of culture and consciousness is that it fails to take seriously the view that so-called material structures are themselves cultural products and become transmuted into the meanings and inter-subjectivity of everday life. Questions relating to power, therefore, which are normally viewed as problems of structure, or work conditions or social placement then become converted into aspects of cultural hegemony and the capacity of some social groups (not necessarily the most prestigious) to define the realities of others. Baritz's article, *The Servants of Power*,[33] is a good example of the way of which one particular occupation—academic social science—has produced, and been rewarded for producing, knowledge which is highly instrumental for managerial control and utilization of labour. Brown[34] has documented a similar process with respect to the Tavistock school of industrial sociology.

This view is consistent with the recent 'critical theory' of Habermas and Schroyer in their analysis of advanced industrial society. One of the central

30. C. Wright Mills, *White Collar*, Galaxy, New York, 1956, p. 110.
31. C. Wright Mills, 'The Professional Ideology of Social Pathologists' in *American Journal of Sociology*, vol. 49, 1943.
32. See below e.g. David Ingleby, 'The Psychology of Child Psychology'.
33. See below L. Baritz, 'The Servants of Power'.
34. Richard Brown, 'The Tavistock's Industrial Studies' in *Sociology*, Vol. 1, No. 1, 1967, pp. 33–60.

elements of their argument is that technology and science have become the dominant ideological force in contemporary society. Not only does it shape the working conditions of a large part of the population but it also provides a legitimating substructure of taken-for-granted knowledge for what Illich calls addictive consumer thinking. The class structure has been maintained through the absorption into work processes of a technological logic which operates both in the material structures of machinery and as a form of 'technological consciousness'. The resistance of advanced societies to fundamental changes in their class structure owes much to the *total socialization* of people into an inevitabilized sense of social placement, and a social progress dependent on it. As Habermas puts it:

> Paradoxically . . . this repression can disappear from the consciousness of the population because the legitimation of domination has assumed a new character: it refers to the 'constantly increasing productivity and domination of nature which keeps individuals living in increasing comfort.[35]

Social domination is then rooted in the self-evident worthwhileness of improvements in what the rhetoric of mass-media politics portrays as the 'standard of living'. A great deal of recent work confirms the salience of 'instrumental' orientations to work.[36] Furthermore many writers have noted that such goals have also become dominant among trade unionists—with important consequences for their incorporation into the capitalist system.[37] Giddens notes that unlike struggles over control, which are political since they '. . . involve attempts on the part of working-class associations to acquire an influence over . . . the "government" of industry', struggles over ' . . . *the modification of market capacity to secure scarce economic rewards*'[38] represent a partial encapsulation of conflict.

'Technocratic consciousness' is alienating in that it renders invisible the political nature of its control. As Schroyer has suggested,

> Wherever scientism permeates a scientific establishment, it functions as a social a priori that uncritically permits the extension of an exploitive instrumental rationalization. That is, it contributes to the generation of decision-making whose 'rationality' is instrumental effectiveness and efficiency. Such mechanisms work against a broader mode of rationalization that would maximize the participation and individuation of affected people.[39]

Such conclusions are far from being the abstractions they appear to be. There

35. See below. Jürgen Habermas, 'Technology and Science, as "Ideology" '.
36. See Goldthorpe, et al., *The Affluent Worker: Industrial Attitudes and Behaviour*, Cambridge University Press, Cambridge, 1968 and Geoffrey Ingham, 'Organizational Size, Orientation to Work and Industrial Behaviour', *Sociology*, Vol. 1, No. 3, 1967, pp. 239–58.
37. See Alan Fox, *A Sociology of Work in Industry*, Collier-Macmillan, London, 1971 and Michael Mann, *Consciousness and Action Among the Western Working Class*, Macmillan, London, 1973.
38. Anthony Giddens, *The Class Structure of the Advanced Societies*, Hutchinson, London, 1973, p. 205.
39. Trent Schroyer, 'Toward a Critical Theory for Advanced Industrial Society' in H. P. Dreitzel (ed.), *Recent Sociology*, No. 2, Macmillan, New York, 1970, p. 211.

have been a number of recent studies which demonstrate the dispossession which is involved when techniques of rational planning are converted into tangible regimes of work or redundancy.[40] Further, as Berger et. al., have argued, the 'carriers of technocratic consciousness' extend well beyond the primary organizations of economic production.[41] Their operations are buttressed by the cultural apparatuses of the mass media and education and by the operations of the state departments involved in economic and manpower planning. As sociologists engaged in the fields of education and deviance and work are currently finding, a critical sociology concerned with the questioning of contemporary forms of domination and alienation has to take on increasingly the enormously self-evident legitimacy of applied positivism and technologized control just as workers who attempt to move from economism to conflict over control and authority within the enterprise have to be prepared, in their attack on managerial 'rights', to question the whole system of inter-connected legitimations and assumptions of which any particular 'right' is a part. An awesome task. The combination of rational planning with politically neutralized bureaucracies serving the goal of economic progress has done much to desensitize workers and sociology itself as a way of understanding contemporary society. It is important that the sociology of work regains the political and social awareness that we discussed earlier, and that work activity and experiences should be seen in the context of more comprehensive critiques of capitalist society and mass capitalist culture.

40. See Rod Martin and Bob Fryer, *Redundancy and Paternalist Capitalism*, Allen and Unwin, London, 1973 and Huw Beynon, *Working for Ford*, Penguin, Harmondsworth, 1973.
41. P. L. Berger, B. Berger & H. Kellner, *The Homeless Mind*, Penguin, Harmondsworth, 1973. See particularly ch. 4.

2. TECHNOLOGY AND SCIENCE AS 'IDEOLOGY'
Jürgen Habermas

For Herbert Marcuse on his seventieth birthday, July 19, 1968.

Max Weber introduced the concept of 'rationality' in order to define the form of capitalist economic activity, bourgeois private law, and bureaucratic authority. Rationalization means first of all, the extension of the areas of society subject to the criteria of rational decision. Second, social labor is industrialized, with the result that criteria of instrumental action also penetrate into other areas of life (urbanization of the mode of life, technification of transport and communication). Both trends exemplify the type of purposive-rational action, which refers to either the organization of means or choice between alternatives. Planning can be regarded as purposive-rational action of the second order. It aims at the establishment, improvement, or expansion of systems of purposive-rational action themselves.

The progressive 'rationalization' of society is linked to the institutionalization of scientific and technical development. To the extent that technology and science permeate social institutions and thus transform them, old legitimations are destroyed. The secularization and 'disenchantment' of action-orienting world-views, of cultural tradition as a whole, is the obverse of the growing 'rationality' of social action.

Herbert Marcuse has taken these analyses as a point of departure in order to demonstrate that the formal concept of rationality—which Weber derived from the purposive-rational action of the capitalist entrepreneur, the industrial wage laborer, the abstract legal person, and the modern administrative official and based on the criteria of science as well as technology—has specific substantive implications. Marcuse is convinced that what Weber called 'rationalization' realizes not rationality as such but rather, in the name of rationality, a specific form of unacknowledged political domination. Because this sort of rationality extends to the correct choice among strategies, the appropriate application of technologies, and the efficient establishment of systems (with *presupposed* aims in *given* situations), it removes the total social framework of interests in which strategies are chosen, technologies applied, and systems established, from the scope of reflection and rational reconstruction. Moreover, this rationality extends only to relations of possible technical control and therefore requires a type of action that implies domination, whether of nature or of society. By virtue of its

---

2. Reprinted from *Toward a Rational Society* by Jurgen Habermas by permission of Heinemann Educational Books Ltd., London. Copyright © 1971. (pp. 81-122)

structure, purposive-rational action is the exercise of control. That is why, in accordance with this rationality, the 'rationalization' of the conditions of life is synonymous with the institutionalization of a form of domination whose political character becomes unrecognizable: the technical reason of a social system of purposive-rational action does not lose its political content. Marcuse's critique of Weber comes to the conclusion that

> the very concept of technical reason is perhaps ideological. Not only the application of technology but technology itself is domination (of nature and men)—methodical, scientific, calculated, calculating control. Specific purposes and interests of domination are not foisted upon technology 'subsequently' and from the outside; they enter the very construction of the technical apparatus. Technology is always a historical-social *project:* in it is projected what a society and its ruling interests intend to do with men and things. Such a 'purpose' of domination is 'substantive' and to this extent belongs to the very form of technical reason.[1]

As early as 1956 Marcuse referred in a quite different context to the peculiar phenomenon that in industrially advanced capitalist societies domination tends to lose its exploitative and oppressive character and become 'rational', without political domination thereby disappearing: 'domination is dependent only on the capacity and drive to maintain and extend the apparatus as a whole'.[2] Domination is rational in that a system can be maintained which can allow itself to make the growth of the forces of production, coupled with scientific and technical progress, the basis of its legitimation although, at the same time, the level of the productive forces constitutes a potential in relation to which 'the renunciations and burdens placed on individuals seem more and more unnecessary and irrational'.[3] In Marcuse's judgement, the objectively superfluous repression can be recognized in the 'intensified subjection of individuals to the enormous apparatus of production and distribution, in the deprivatization of free time, in the almost indistinguishable fusion of constructive and destructive social labor.'[4] Paradoxically, however, this repression can disappear from the consciousness of the population because the legitimation of domination has assumed a new character: it refers to the 'constantly increasing productivity and domination of nature which keeps individuals . . . living in increasing comfort.'[5]

The institutionalized growth of the forces of production following from scientific and technical progress surpasses all historical proportions. From it the institutional framework draws its opportunity for legitimation. The thought that relations of production can be measured against the potential of developed productive forces is prevented because the existing relations of production present themselves as the technically necessary organizational form of a rationalized

1. H. Marcuse, 'Industrialization and Capitalism in the Work of Max Weber' in J. J. Shapiro (trans.) *Negations: Essays in Critical Theory*, Beacon Press, Boston, 1968, pp. 223f.
2. H. Marcuse, 'Freedom and Freud's Theory of the Instincts' in J. J. Shapiro and S. M. Weber (trans.) *Five Lectures*, Beacon Press, Boston, 1970, p. 16.
3. *Ibid.*, p. 3.
4. *Ibid.*, p. 3.
5. *Ibid.*, p. 3.

society. Here 'rationality', in Weber's sense, shows its Janus face. It is no longer only a critical standard for the developmental level of the forces of production in relation to which the objectively superfluous, repressive character of historically obsolete relations of production can be exposed. It is also an apologetic standard through which these same relations of production can be justified as a functional institutional framework. Indeed, in relation to its apologetic serviceability, 'rationality' is weakened as a critical standard and degraded to a corrective *within* the system: what can still be said is at best that society is 'poorly programmed'. At the stage of their scientific-technical development, then, the forces of production appear to enter a new constellation with the relations of production. Now they no longer function as the basis of a critique of prevailing legitimations in the interest of political enlightenment, but become instead the basis of legitimation. *This* is what Marcuse conceives of as world-historically new.

But if this is the case, must not the rationality embodied in systems of purposive-rational action be understood as specifically limited? Must not the rationality of science and technology, instead of being reducible to unvarying rules of logic and method have absorbed a substantive, historically derived, and therefore transitory a priori structure? Marcuse answers in the affirmative. . . .

Weber's 'rationalization' is not only a long-term process of the transformation of social structures but simultaneously 'rationalization' in Freud's sense: the true motive, the perpetuation of objectively obsolete domination, is concealed through the invocation of purposive-rational imperatives. This invocation is possible only because the rationality of science and technology is immanently one of control: the rationality of domination.

Marcuse owes this concept, according to which modern science is a historical formation, equally to Husserl's treatise on the crisis of European science and Heidegger's destruction of Western metaphysics. From the materialist position Ernst Bloch has developed the viewpoint that the rationality of modern science is, in its roots, distorted by capitalism in such a way as to rob modern technology of the innocence of a pure productive force. But Marcuse is the first to make the 'political content of technical reason' the analytical point of departure for a theory of advanced capitalist society. Because he not only develops this viewpoint philosophically but also attempts to corroborate it through sociological analysis, the difficulties inherent in this conception become visible. I shall refer here to but one ambiguity contained in Marcuse's own conception. . . .

If the phenomenon on which Marcuse bases his social analysis, i.e. the peculiar *fusion of technology and domination*, rationality and oppression, could not be interpreted otherwise than as a world 'project', as Marcuse says in the language of Sartre's phenomenology, contained in the material a priori of the logic of science and technology and determined by class interest and historical situation, then social emancipation could not be conceived without a complementary revolutionary transformation of science and technology themselves. In several passages Marcuse is tempted to pursue this idea of a New Science in connection with the promise, familiar in Jewish and Protestant mysticism, of the 'resurrection of fallen nature.' This theme, well-known for having penetrated into Schelling's (and Baader's) philosophy via Swabian Pietism, returns in Marx's *Paris Manuscripts*, today constitutes the central thought of Bloch's philosophy, and, in reflected forms, also directs the more secret hopes of Walter Benjamin, Max Horkheimer, and Theodor W. Adorno. It is also present in Marcuse's thought:

> The point which I am trying to make is that science, *by virtue of its own method* and concepts, has projected and promoted a universe in which the domination of nature has remained linked to the domination of man—a link which tends to be fatal to this universe as a whole. Nature, scientifically comprehended and mastered, reappears in the technical apparatus of production and destruction which sustains and improves the life of the individuals while subordinating them to the masters of the apparatus. Thus the rational hierarchy merges with the social one. If this is the case, then the change in the direction of progress, which might sever this fatal link, would also affect the very structure of science—the scientific project. Its hypotheses, without losing their rational character, would develop in an essentially experimental context (that of a pacified world); consequently, science would arrive at essentially different concepts of nature and establish essentially different facts.[6]

In a logical fashion Marcuse envisages not only different modes of theory formation but a different scientific methodology in general. The transcendental framework within which nature would be made the object of a new experience would then no longer be the functional system of instrumental action. The viewpoint of possible technical control would be replaced by one of preserving, fostering, and releasing the potentialities of nature: 'there are two kinds of mastery: a repressive and a liberating one.'[7] To this view it must be objected that modern science can be interpreted as a historically unique project only if at least one alternative project is thinkable. And, in addition, an alternative New Science would have to include the definition of a New Technology. This is a sobering consideration because technology, if based at all on a project, can only be traced back to a 'project' of the human species *as a whole*, and not to one that could be historically surpassed.

Arnold Gehlen[8] has pointed out in what seems to me conclusive fashion that there is an immanent connection between the technology known to us and the structure of purposive-rational action. If we comprehend the behavioral system of action regulated by its own results as the conjunction of rational decision and instrumental action, then we can reconstruct the history of technology from the point of view of the step-by-step objectivation of the elements of that very system. In any case technological development lends itself to being interpreted as though the human species had taken the elementary components of the behavioral system of purposive-rational action, which is primarily rooted in the human organism, and projected them one after another onto the plane of technical instruments, thereby unburdening itself of the corresponding functions. At first the functions of the motor apparatus (hands and legs) were augmented and replaced, followed

6. H. Marcuse, *One Dimensional Man*, Beacon Press, Boston, 1964, pp. 166f.
7. *Ibid.*, p. 236.
8. Arnold Gehlen, 'Anthropologische Ansicht der Technik' in H. Freyer, et al., (eds.) *Technik in technischen Zeitalter*, Düsseldorf, 1965.

by energy production (of the human body), the functions of the sensory apparatus (eyes, ears, and skin), and finally by the functions of the governing center (the brain). Technological development thus follows a logic that corresponds to the structure of purposive-rational action regulated by its own results, which is in fact the structure of *work*. Realizing this, it is impossible to envisage how, as long as the organization of human nature does not change and as long therefore as we have to achieve self-preservation through social labor and with the aid of means that substitute for work, we could renounce technology, more particularly *our technology*, in favour of a qualitatively different one.

Marcuse has in mind an alternative *attitude* to nature, but it does not admit of the idea of a New Technology. Instead of treating nature as the object of possible technical control, we can encounter her as an opposing partner in a possible interaction. We can seek out a fraternal rather than an exploited nature. At the level of an as yet incomplete intersubjectivity we can impute subjectivity to animals and plants, even to minerals, and try to communicate with nature instead of merely processing her under conditions of severed communication. And the idea that a still enchained subjectivity of nature cannot be unbound until men's communication among themselves is free from domination has retained, to say the least, a singular attraction. Only if men could communicate without compulsion and each could recognize himself in the other, could mankind possibly recognize nature as another subject: not, as idealism would have it, as its Other, but as a subject of which mankind itself is the Other.

Be that as it may, the achievements of technology, which are indispensable as such, could surely not be substituted for by an awakened nature. The alternative to existing technology, the project of nature as opposing partner instead of object, refers to an alternative structure of action: to symbolic interaction in distinction to purposive-rational action. This means, however, that the two projects are projections of work and of language, i.e. projects of the human species as a whole, and not of an individual epoch, a specific class, or a surpassable situation. The idea of a New Science will not stand up to logical scrutiny any more than that of a New Technology, if indeed science is to retain the meaning of modern science inherently oriented to possible technical control. For this function, as for scientific-technical progress in general, there is no more 'humane' substitute.

Marcuse himself seems to doubt whether it is meaningful to relativize as a 'project' the rationality of science and technology. In many passages of *One-Dimensional Man*, revolutionizing technological rationality means only a transformation of the institutional framework which would leave untouched the forces of production as such. The structure of scientific-technical progress would be conserved, and only the governing values would be changed. New values would be translated into technically solvable tasks. The *direction* of this progress would be new, but the standard of rationality itself would remain unchanged:

> Technics, as a universe of instrumentalities, may increase the weakness as well as the power of man. At the present stage, he is perhaps more powerless over his own apparatus then he ever was before.[9]

9. H. Marcuse, *One Dimensional Man*, Beacon Press, Boston, 1964, p. 235.

This sentence reinstates the political innocence of the forces of production. Here Marcuse is only renewing the classical definition of the relationship between the productive forces and the production relations. But in so doing, he is as far from coming to grips with the new constellation at which he is aiming as he was with the assertion that the productive forces are thoroughly corrupted in their political implications. What is singular about the 'rationality' of science and technology is that it characterizes the growing potential of self-surpassing productive forces which continually threaten the institutional framework *and at the same time*, set the standard of legitimation for the production relations that restrict this potential. The dichotomy of this rationality cannot be adequately represented either by historicizing the concept or by returning to the orthodox view: neither the model of the original sin of scientific-technical progress nor that of its innocence do it justice.

The difficulty, which Marcuse has only obscured with the notion of the political content of technical reason, is to determine in a categorially precise manner the meaning of the expansion of the rational form of science and technology, i.e. the rationality embodied in systems of purposive-rational action, to the proportions of a life form, of the 'historical totality' of a life-world. This is the same process that Weber meant to designate and explain as the rationalization of society. I believe that neither Weber nor Marcuse has satisfactorily accounted for it. Therefore I should like to attempt to reformulate Weber's concept of rationalization in another frame of reference in order to discuss on this new basis Marcuse's critique of Weber, as well as his thesis of the double function of scientific-technical progress (as productive force and as ideology). I am proposing an interpretative scheme that, in the format of an essay, can be introduced but not seriously validated with regard to its utility. The historical generalizations thus serve only to clarify this scheme and are no substitute for its scientific substantiation.

By means of the concept of 'rationalization' Weber attempted to grasp the repercussions of scientific-technical progress on the institutional framework of societies engaged in 'modernization.' He shared this interest with the classical sociological tradition in general, whose pairs of polar concepts all revolve about the same problem: how to construct a conceptual model of the institutional change brought about by the extension of subsystems of purposive-rational action. Status and contract, *Gemeinschaft* and *Gesellschaft*, mechanical and organic solidarity, informal and formal groups, primary and secondary groups, culture and civilization, traditional and bureaucratic authority, sacral and secular associations, military and industrial society, status group and class—all of these pairs of concepts represent as many attempts to grasp the structural change of the institutional framework of a traditional society on the way to becoming a modern one. Even Parsons' catalog of possible alternatives of value-orientations belongs in the list of these attempts, although he would not admit it. Parsons claims that his list systematically represents the decisions between alternative value-orientations that must be made by the subject of any action whatsoever, regardless of the particular or historical context. But if one examines the list, one can scarcely overlook the historical situation of the inquiry on which it is based. The four pairs of alternative value-orientations,

> *affectivity* versus *affective neutrality*,
> *particularism* versus *universalism*,
> *ascription* versus *achievement*,
> *diffuseness* versus *specificity*,

which are supposed to take into account *all* possible fundamental decisions, are tailored to an analysis of *one* historical process. In fact they define the relative dimensions of the modification of dominant attitudes in the transition from traditional to modern society. Subsystems of purposive-rational action do indeed demand orientation to the postponement of gratification, universal norms, individual achievement and active mastery, and specific and analytic relationships, rather than to the opposite orientations.

In order to reformulate what Weber called 'rationalization', I should like to go beyond the subjective approach that Parsons shares with Weber and propose another categorial framework. I shall take as my starting point the fundamental distinction between *work* and *interaction*.

By 'work' or *purposive-rational action* I understand either instrumental action or rational choice or their conjunction. Instrumental action is governed by *technical rules* based on empirical knowledge. In every case they imply conditional predictions about observable events, physical or social. These predictions can prove correct or incorrect. The conduct of rational choice is governed by *strategies* based on analytic knowledge. They imply deductions from preference rules (value systems) and decision procedures; these propositions are either correctly or incorrectly deduced. Purposive-rational action realizes defined goals under given conditions. But while instrumental action organizes means that are appropriate or inappropriate according to criteria of an effective control of reality, strategic action depends only on the correct evaluation of possible alternative choices, which results from calculation supplemented by values and maxims.

By 'interaction', on the other hand, I understand *communicative action*, symbolic interaction. It is governed by binding *consensual norms*, which define reciprocal expectations about behavior and which must be understood and recognized by at least two acting subjects. Social norms are enforced through sanctions. Their meaning is objectified in ordinary language communication. While the validity of technical rules and strategies depends on that of empirically true or analytically correct propositions, the validity of social norms is grounded only in the intersubjectivity of the mutual understanding of intentions and secured by the general recognition of obligations. Violation of a rule has a different consequence according to type. *Incompetent* behavior, which violates valid technical rules of strategies, is condemned per se to failure through lack of success; the 'punishment' is built, so to speak, into its rebuff by reality. *Deviant* behavior, which violates consensual norms, provokes sanctions that are connected with the rules only externally, that is by convention. Learned rules of purposive-rational action supply us with *skills*, internalized norms with *personality structures*. Skills put us in a position to solve problems; motivations allow us to follow norms. The diagram below summarizes these definitions. They demand a more precise explanation, which I cannot give here. It is above all the bottom column which I am neglecting here, and it refers to the very problem for whose solution I am introducing the distinction between work and interaction.

	Institutional framework: symbolic interaction	Systems of purposive-rational (instrumental and strategic) action
action-orienting rules	social norms	technical rules
level of definition	intersubjectively shared ordinary language	context-free language
type of definition	reciprocal expectations about behaviour	conditional predictions conditional imperatives
mechanisms of acquisition	role internalization	learning of skills and qualifications
function of action type	maintenance of institutions (conformity to norms on the basis of reciprocal enforcement)	problem-solving (goal attainment, defined in means-ends relations)
sanctions against violation of rules	punishment on the basis of conventional sanctions: failure against authority	inefficacy: failure in reality
'rationalization'	emancipation, individuation; extension of communication free of domination	growth of productive forces; extension of power of technical control

In terms of the two types of action we can distinguish between social systems according to whether purposive-rational action or interaction predominates. The institutional framework of a society consists of norms that guide symbolic interaction. But there are subsystems such as (to keep to Weber's examples) the economic system or the state apparatus, in which primarily sets of purposive-rational action are institutionalized. These contrast with subsystems such as family and kinship structures, which, although linked to a number of tasks and skills, are primarily based on moral rules of interaction. So I shall distinguish generally at the analytic level between (1) the *institutional framework* of a society or the sociocultural life-world and (2) the *subsystems of purposive-rational action* that are 'embedded' in it. Insofar as actions are determined by the institutional framework they are both guided and enforced by norms. Insofar as they are determined by subsystems of purposive-rational action, they conform to patterns of instrumental or strategic action. Of course, only institutionalization can guarantee that such action will in fact follow definite technical rules and expected strategies with adequate probability.

With the help of these distinctions we can reformulate Weber's concept of 'rationalization'.

The term 'traditional society' has come to denote all social systems that generally meet the criteria of civilizations. The latter represent a specific stage in the evolution of the human species. They differ in several traits from more primitive social forms: (1) A centralized ruling power (state organization of political power in contrast to tribal organization); (2) The division of society into socioeconomic classes (distribution to individuals of social obligations and rewards according to class membership and not according to kinship status); (3) The prevalence of a central world view (myth, complex religion) to the end of legitimating political power (thus converting power into authority). Civilizations are established on the basis of a relatively developed technology and of division of labor in the social process of production, which make possible a surplus product, i.e. a quantity of goods exceeding that needed for the satisfaction of immediate and elementary needs. They owe their existence to the solution of the problem that first arises with the production of a surplus product, namely, how to distribute wealth and labor both unequally and yet legitimately according to criteria other than those generated by a kinship system.[10]

In our context it is relevant that despite considerable differences in their level of development, civilizations, based on an economy dependent on agriculture and craft production, have tolerated technical innovation and organizational improvement only within definite limits. One indicator of the traditional limits to the development of the forces of production is that until about three hundred years ago no major social system had produced more than the equivalent of a maximum of two hundred dollars per capita per annum. The stable pattern of a precapitalist mode of production, preindustrial technology, and premodern science makes possible a typical relation of the institutional framework to subsystems of purposive-rational action. For despite considerable progress, these subsystems, developing out of the system of social labor and its stock of accumulated technically exploitable knowledge, never reached that measure of extension after which their 'rationality' would have become an open threat to the authority of the cultural traditions that legitimate political power. The expression 'traditional society' refers to the circumstance that the institutional framework is grounded in the unquestionable underpinning of legitimation constituted by mythical, religious or metaphysical interpretations of reality—cosmic as well as social—as a whole. 'Traditional' societies exist as long as the development of subsystems of purposive-rational action keep within the limits of the legitimating efficacy of cultural traditions.[11] This is the basis for the 'superiority' of the institutional framework, which does not preclude structural changes adapted to a potential surplus generated in the economic system but does preclude critically challenging the traditional form of legitimation. This immunity is a meaningful criterion for the delimitation of traditional societies from those which have crossed the threshold to modernization.

The 'superiority criterion', consequently, is applicable to all forms of class society organized as a state in which principles of universally valid rationality (whether of technical or strategic means-ends relations) have not explicitly and

10. See G. E. Lenski, *Power and Privilege: A Theory of Social Stratification*, McGraw, New York, 1966.
11. P. L. Berger, *The Sacred Canopy*, Doubleday, New York, 1967.

successfully called into question the cultural validity of intersubjectively shared traditions, which function as legitimations of the political system. It is only since the capitalist mode of production has equipped the economic system with a self-propelling mechanism that ensures long-term continuous growth (despite crises) in the productivity of labor that the introduction of new technologies and strategies, i.e. innovation as such, has been institutionalized. As Marx and Schumpeter have proposed in their respective theories, the capitalist mode of production can be comprehended as a mechanism that guarantees the *permanent* expansion of sub-systems of purposive-rational action and thereby overturns the traditionalist 'superiority' of the institutional framework to the forces of production. Capitalism is the first mode of production in world history to institutionalize self-sustaining economic growth. It has generated an industrial system that could be freed from the institutional framework of capitalism and connected to mechanisms other than that of the utilization of capital in private form.

What characterizes the passage from traditional society to society commencing the process of modernization is *not* that structural modification of the institutional framework is necessitated under the pressure of relatively developed productive forces, for that is the mechanism of the evolution of the species from the very beginning. What is new is a level of development of the productive forces that makes permanent the extension of subsystems of purposive-rational action and thereby calls into question the traditional form of the legitimation of power. The older mythic, religious, and metaphysical worldviews obey the logic of interaction contexts. They answer the central questions of men's collective existence and of individual life history. Their themes are justice and freedom, violence and oppression, happiness and gratification, poverty, illness, and death. Their categories are victory and defeat, love and hate, salvation and damnation. Their logic accords with the grammar of systematically distorted communication and with the fateful causality of dissociated symbols and suppressed motives. The rationality of language games, associated with communicative action, is confronted at the threshold of the modern period with the rationality of means-ends relations, associated with instrumental and strategic action. As soon as this confrontation can arise, the end of traditional society is in sight: the traditional form of legitimation breaks down.

Capitalism is defined by a mode of production that not only poses this problem but also solves it. It provides a legitimation of domination which is no longer called down from the lofty heights of cultural tradition but instead summoned up from the base of social labor. The institution of the market, in which private property owners exchange commodities—including the market on which propertyless private individuals exchange their labor power as their only commodity—promises that exchange relations will be and are just owing to equivalence. Even this bourgeois ideology of justice, by adopting the category of reciprocity, still employs a relation of communicative action as the basis of legitimation. But the principle of reciprocity is now the organizing principle of the sphere of production and reproduction itself. Thus on the base of a market economy, political domination can be legitimated henceforth 'from below' rather than 'from above' (through invocation of cultural tradition).

If we suppose that the division of society into socioeconomic classes derives from the differential distribution among social groups of the relevant means of production, and that this distribution itself is based on the institutionalization of relations of social force, then we may assume that in all civilizations this institutional framework has been identical with the system of political domination: traditional authority was political authority. Only with the emergence of the capitalist mode of production can the legitimation of the institutional framework be linked immediately with the system of social labor. Only then can the property order change from a *political relation* to a *production relation*, because it legitimates itself through the rationality of the market, the ideology of exchange society, and no longer through a legitimate power structure. It is now the political system which is justified in terms of the legitimate relations of production: this is the real meaning and function of rationalist natural law from Locke to Kant. The institutional framework of society is only mediately political and immediately economic (the bourgeois constitutional state as 'superstructure').

The superiority of the capitalist mode of production to its predecessors has these two roots: the establishment of an economic mechanism that renders permanent the expansion of subsystems of purposive-rational action, and the creation of an economic legitimation by means of which the political system can be adapted to the new requisites of rationality brought about by these developing subsystems. It is this process of adaptation that Weber comprehends as 'rationalization'. Within it we can distinguish between two tendencies: rationalization 'from below' and rationalization 'from above'.

A permanent pressure for adaptation arises from below as soon as the new mode of production becomes fully operative through the institutionalization of a domestic market for goods and labor power and of the capitalist enterprise. In the system of social labor this institutionalization ensures cumulative progress in the forces of production and an ensuing horizontal extension of subsystems of purposive-rational action—at the cost of economic crises, to be sure. In this way traditional structures are increasingly subordinated to conditions of instrumental or strategic rationality: the organization of labor and of trade, the network of transportation, information, and communication, the institutions of private law, and, starting with financial administration, the state bureaucracy. Thus arises the substructure of a society under the compulsion of modernization. The latter eventually widens to take in all areas of life: the army, the school system, health services, and even the family. Whether in city or country, it induces an urbanization of the *form* of life. That is, it generates subcultures that train the individual to be able to 'switch over' at any moment from an interaction context to purposive-rational action.

This pressure for rationalization coming from below is met by a compulsion to rationalize coming from above. For, measured against the new standards of purposive rationality, the power-legitimating and action-orienting traditions—especially mythological interpretations and religious worldviews—lose their cogency. On this level of generalization, what Weber termed 'secularization' has two aspects. First, traditional worldviews and objectivations lose their power and validity *as* myth, *as* public religion, *as* customary ritual, *as* justifying metaphysics, *as* unquestionable tradition. Instead, they are reshaped into subjective belief systems and ethics which ensure the private cogency of modern value-orientations (the 'Protestant ethic'). Second, they are transformed into constructions that do both at once: criticize tradition and reorganize the released material of tradition according to the principles of formal law and the exchange of equivalents (rationalist natural law). Having become fragile, existing legitimations are replaced by new ones. The latter emerge from the critique of the dogmatism of traditional interpretations of the world and claim a scientific character. Yet they retain legitimating functions, thereby keeping actual power relations inaccessible to analysis and to public consciousness. It is in this way that ideologies in the restricted sense first came into being. They replace traditional legitimations of power by appearing in the mantle of modern science and by deriving their justification from the critique of ideology. Ideologies are coeval with the critique of ideology. In this sense there can be no prebourgeois 'ideologies'.

In this connection modern science assumes a singular function. In distinction from the philosophical sciences of the older sort, the empirical sciences have developed since Galileo's time within a methodological frame of reference that reflects the transcendental viewpoint of possible technical control. Hence the modern sciences produce knowledge which through its *form* (and not through the subjective intention of scientists) is technically exploitable knowledge, although the possible applications generally are realized afterwards. Science and technology were not interdependent until late into the nineteenth century. Until then modern science did not contribute to the acceleration of technical development nor, consequently, to the pressure toward rationalization from below. Rather, its contribution to the modernization process was indirect. Modern physics gave rise to a philosophical approach that interpreted nature and society according to a model borrowed from the natural sciences and induced, so to speak, the mechanistic worldview of the seventeenth century. The reconstruction of classical natural law was carried out in this framework. This modern natural law was the basis of the bourgeois revolutions of the seventeenth, eighteenth, and nineteenth centuries, through which the old legitimations of the power structure were finally destroyed.

By the middle of the nineteenth century the capitalist mode of production had developed so fully in England and France that Marx was able to identify the locus of the institutional framework of society in the relations of production and at the same time criticize the legitimating basis constituted by the exchange of equivalents. He carried out the critique of bourgeois ideology in the form of *political economy*. His labor theory of value destroyed the semblance of freedom, by means of which the legal institution of the free labor contract had made unrecognizable the relationship of social force that underlay the wage-labor relationship. Marcuse's criticism of Weber is that the latter, disregarding this Marxian insight, upholds an abstract concept of rationalization, which not merely fails to express the specific class content of the adaptation of the institutional framework to the developing systems of purposive-rational action, but conceals it. Marcuse knows that the Marxian analysis can no longer be applied as it stands to advanced capitalist society, with which Weber was already confronted. But he wants to show through the example of Weber that the evolution of modern society in the framework of state-regulated capitalism cannot be conceptualized if liberal capitalism has not been analyzed adequately.

Since the last quarter of the nineteenth century two developmental tendencies have become noticeable in the most advanced capitalist countries: an increase in state intervention in order to secure the system's stability, and a growing inter-dependence of research and technology, which has turned the sciences into the leading productive force. Both tendencies have destroyed the particular constel-lation of institutional framework and subsystems of purposive-rational action which characterized liberal capitalism, thereby eliminating the conditions relevant for the application of political economy in the version correctly formulated by Marx for liberal capitalism. I believe that Marcuse's basic thesis, according to which technology and science today also take on the function of legitimating political power, is the key to analyzing the changed constellation.

The permanent regulation of the economic process by means of state inter-vention arose as a defense mechanism against the dysfunctional tendencies, which threaten the system, that capitalism generates when left to itself. Capitalism's actual development manifestly contradicted the capitalist idea of a bourgeois society, emancipated from domination, in which power is neutralized. The root ideology of just exchange, which Marx unmasked in theory, collapsed in practice. The form of capital utilization through private ownership could only be main-tained by the governmental corrective of a social and economic policy that stabil-ized the business cycle. The institutional framework of society was repoliticized. It no longer coincides immediately with the relations of production, i.e. with an order of private law that secures capitalist economic activity and the corresponding general guarantees of order provided by the bourgeois state. But this means a change in the relation of the economy to the political system: politics is no longer *only* a phenomenon of the superstructure. If society no longer 'auto-nomously' perpetuates itself through self-regulation as a sphere preceding and lying at the basis of the state—and its ability to do so was the really novel feature of the capitalist mode of production—then society and the state are no longer in the relationship that Marxian theory had defined as that of base and superstructure. Then, however, a critical theory of society can no longer be constructed in the exclusive form of a critique of political economy. A point of view that methodically isolates the economic laws of motion of society can claim to grasp the overall structure of social life in its essential categories only as long as politics depends on the economic base. It becomes inapplicable when the 'base' has to be compre-hended as in itself a function of governmental activity and political conflicts. According to Marx, the critique of political economy was the theory of bourgeois society only as *critique of ideology*. If, however, the ideology of just exchange disintegrates, then the power structure can no longer be criticized *immediately* at the level of the relations of production. . . .

Since the end of the nineteenth century the other developmental tendency characteristic of advanced capitalism has become increasingly momentous: the scientization of technology. The institutional pressure to augment the produc-tivity of labor through the introduction of new technology has always existed under capitalism. But innovations depended on sporadic inventions, which, while economically motivated, were still fortuitous in character. This changed as technical development entered into a feedback relation with the progress of the modern sciences. With the advent of large-scale industrial research, science, technology, and industrial utilization were fused into a system. Since then, industrial research has been linked up with research under government contract, which primarily promotes scientific and technical progress in the military sector. From there information flows back into the sectors of civilian production. Thus technology and science become a leading productive force, rendering inoperative the conditions for Marx's labor theory of value. It is no longer meaningful to calculate the amount of capital investment in research and development on the basis of the value of unskilled (simple) labor power, when scientific-technical progress has become an independent source of surplus value, in relation to which the only source of surplus value considered by Marx, namely the labor power of the immediate producers, plays an ever smaller role.

As long as the productive forces were visibly linked to the rational decisions and instrumental action of men engaged in social production, they could be understood as the potential for a growing power of technical control and not be confused with the institutional framework in which they are embedded. However, with the institutionalization of scientific-technical progress, the potential of the productive forces has assumed a form owing to which men lose consciousness of the dualism of work and interaction.

It is true that social interests still determine the direction, functions, and pace of technical progress. But these interests define the social system so much as a whole that they coincide with the interest in maintaining the system. *As such* the private form of capital utilization and a distribution mechanism for social rewards that guarantees the loyalty of the masses are removed from discussion. The quasi-autonomous progress of science and technology then appears as an independent variable on which the most important single system variable, namely economic growth, depends. Thus arises a perspective in which the development of the social system *seems* to be determined by the logic of scientific-technical progress. The immanent law of this progress seems to produce objective exigencies, which must be obeyed by any politics oriented toward functional needs. But when this semblance has taken root effectively, then propaganda can refer to the role of technology and science in order to explain and legitimate why in modern societies the process of democratic decision-making about practical problems loses its function and 'must' be replaced by plebiscitary decisions about alternative sets of leaders of administrative personnel. This technocracy thesis has been worked out in several versions on the intellectual level.[12] What seems to me more important is that it can also become a background ideology that penetrates into the consciousness of the depoliticized mass of the population, where it can take on legitimating power. It is a singular achievement of this ideology to detach society's self-understanding from the frame of reference of communicative action and from the concepts of symbolic interaction and replace it with a scientific model. Accordingly the culturally defined self-understanding of a social life-world is replaced by the self-reification of men under categories of purposive-rational action and adaptive behavior. . . .

In consequence of the tendencies that have been discussed, capitalist society has changed to the point where two key categories of Marxian theory, namely class struggle and ideology, can no longer be employed as they stand.

12. See H. Schelsky, *Der Mensch in der wissenschaftlichen Zivilisation*, Cologne-Opladen 1961, J. Ellul, *The Technological Society*, Knopf, New York, 1967 and A. Gehlen, 'Über Kulturelle Kristallisationen' in *Studien zur Anthropologie und Soziologie*, Berlin, 1963; 'Über Kulturelle Evolution' in M. Hahn and F. Wiedmann (eds.) *Die Philosophie und die Frage nach dem Fortschritt*, Munich, 1964.

It was on the basis of the capitalist mode of production that the struggle of social classes as such was first constituted, thereby creating an objective situation from which the class structure of traditional society, with its immediately political constitution, could be *recognized* in retrospect. State-regulated capitalism, which emerged from a reaction against the dangers to the system produced by open class antagonism, suspends class conflict. The system of advanced capitalism is so defined by a policy of securing the loyality of the wage-earning masses through rewards, that is, by avoiding conflict, that the conflict still built into the structure of society in virtue of the private mode of capital utilization is the very area of conflict which has the greatest probability of remaining latent. It recedes behind others, which, while conditioned by the mode of production, can no longer assume the form of class conflicts. . . .

If the relativization of the field of application of the concept of ideology and the theory of class be confirmed, then the category framework developed by Marx in the basic assumptions of historical materialism requires a new formulation. The model of forces of production and relations of production would have to be replaced by the more abstract one of work and interaction. The relations of production designate a level on which the institutional framework was anchored only during the phase of the development of liberal capitalism, and not either before or after. To be sure, the productive forces, in which the learning processes organized in the subsystems of purposive-rational action accumulate, have been from the very beginning the motive force of social evolution. But, they do not appear, as Marx supposed, *under all circumstances* to be a potential for liberation and to set off emancipatory movements—at least not once the continual growth of the productive forces has become dependent on scientific-technical progress that has *also* taken on functions of *legitimating political power*. I suspect that the frame of reference developed in terms of the analogous, but more general relation of institutional framework (interaction) and subsystems of purposive-rational action ('work' in the broad sense of instrumental and strategic action) is more suited to reconstructing the sociocultural phases of the history of mankind. . . .

Marx, to be sure, viewed the problem of making history with will and consciousness as one of the *practical* mastery of previously ungoverned processes of social development. Others, however, have understood it as a *technical* problem. They want to bring society under control in the same way as nature by reconstructing it according to the pattern of self-regulated systems of purposive-rational action and adaptive behavior. This intention is to be found not only among technocrats of capitalist planning but also among those of bureaucratic socialism. Only the technocratic consciousness obscures the fact that this reconstruction could be achieved at no less a cost than closing off the only dimension that is essential, because it is susceptible to humanization, *as* a structure of interactions mediated by ordinary language. In the future the repertoire of control techniques will be considerably expanded. On Herman Kahn's list of the most probable technical innovations of the next thirty years I observe among the first fifty items a large number of techniques of behavioral and personality change:

> *30.* new and possibly pervasive techniques for surveillance, monitoring and control of individuals and organizations;

33. new and more reliable 'educational' and propaganda techniques affecting human behaviour—public and private;
34. practical use of direct electronic communication with and stimulation of the brain;
37. new and relatively effective counterinsurgency techniques;
39. new and more varied drugs for control of fatigue, relaxation, alertness, mood, personality, perceptions, and fantasies;
41. improved capability to 'change' sex;
42. other genetic control or influence over the basic constitution of an individual. [13]

A prediction of this sort is extremely controversial. Nevertheless, it points to an area of future possibilities of detaching human behavior from a normative system linked to the grammar of language-games and integrating it instead into self-regulated subsystems of the man-machine type by means of immediate physical or psychological control. Today the psychotechnic manipulation of behavior can already liquidate the old fashioned detour through norms that are internalized but capable of reflection. Behavioral control could be instituted at an even deeper level tomorrow through biotechnic intervention in the endocrine regulating system, not to mention the even greater consequences of intervening in the genetic transmission of inherited information. If this occurred, old regions of consciousness developed in ordinary-language communication would of necessity completely dry up. At this stage of human engineering, if the end of psychological manipulation could be spoken of in the same sense as the end of ideology is today, the spontaneous alienation derived from the uncontrolled lag of the institutional framework would be overcome. But the self-objectivation of man would have fulfilled itself in planned alienation—men would make their history with will, but without consciousness.

I am not asserting that this cybernetic dream of the instinct-like self-stabilization of societies is being fulfilled or that it is even realizable. I do think, however, that it follows through certain vague but basic assumptions of technocratic consciousness to their conclusion as a negative utopia and thus denotes an evolutionary trend that is taking shape under the slick domination of technology and science as ideology. . . .

A new conflict zone, in place of the virtualized class antagonism and apart from the disparity conflicts at the margins of the system, can only emerge where advanced capitalist society has to immunize itself, by depoliticizing the masses of the population, against the questioning of its technocratic background ideology: in the public sphere administered through the mass media. For only here is it possible to buttress the concealment of the difference between progress in systems of purposive-rational action and emancipatory transformations of the institutional framework, between technical and practical problems. And it is necessary for the system to conceal this difference. Publicly administered definitions extend to *what* we want for our lives, but not to *how* we would like to live if we could find out, with regard to attainable potentials, how we *could* live. . . .

13. H. Kahn and A. J. Wiener, 'The Next Thirty-three Years: A Framework for Speculation' in D. Bell (ed.) *Toward the Year 2000: Work in Progress*, Daedalus Library, Boston, 1969, pp. 8of.

3. THE NEW CAPITALISM   Robin Blackburn

The traditional aim of socialist thought has been to become nothing less than the self-awareness of capitalist society. In a society profoundly ignorant of itself, it was the task of socialists to comprehend the principles on which the society worked. By discovering the real nature of capitalism, they were attempting to recapture an economic system that had escaped social control.

Today this intellectual task remains as formidable as ever, because capitalist society is by the law of its own nature in a continual state of restless transformation. The true character of capitalism has to be rediscovered by each new generation. And at this point it is necessary to ask whether capitalism has not changed so much since the classic period that we are now really confronted with an altogether different type of society. It is this possibility that I wish to examine. My conclusion will be that today we confront a radically *new* form of capitalism, but that the most novel features of neo-capitalism, far from mitigating or abolishing the fundamental contradiction of capitalism, rather pose this contradiction *in a purer and more dramatic manner*.

What defines capitalist society is its property system. Though private property has not been abolished in any legal sense, it is frequently argued that the private ownership of the 'means of production' has somehow been drained of real social significance. It is said that modern companies are controlled by professional managers with little reference to the interests of the 'capitalists' who formally own them. It is also claimed that the growth of Government intervention—through the creation of a public sector, welfare services and the introduction of economic planning—reduces still further the traditional importance of private wealth. The first transformation infuses industry with a new sense of social responsibility, the second ensures the supremacy of social justice. The two complementary theories provide an account of the economic structure of society which is comprehensive enough to provide an alternative to the traditional socialist account. The true political economy of the new capitalism may be less comforting than these theories suggest; at least a confrontation with them can enrich socialist theory itself.

The managers' revolution

In Britain, the view that capitalism has been overtaken by a managerial revolution

---

3. Reprinted from *Ideology in Social Science* by R. Blackburn by permission of Fontana Paperbacks, London. Copyright © 1972. (pp. 164-86)

is most systematically expounded in two books by C. A. R. Crosland, *The Future of Socialism*[1] and *The Conservative Enemy*.[2] It also appeared in the Labour Party document *Industry and Society*.[3] In the United States a variant of the managerialist thesis has recently been developed by J. K. Galbraith (1972) in his book *The New Industrial State*.[4] The major point of reference for the prophets of the managerial revolution is the classic capitalism of the nineteenth century—and it is usually Marx's account of this classic model they invoke and contrast to their own analysis of the contemporary reality. In this classic epoch, the entrepreneur united in his person the functions of manager and owner. What has occurred since that date is what is called a 'decomposition of capital' with a consequent separation of ownership and control. Nowadays most large companies have a great many nominal owners—12,000 in the typical large British company. The theorists of the managerial revolution argue that it is impossible for all these owners to exercise any real control over the company they own. They are, in fact, forced to delegate this power to the paid managers of the company. These managers may have only a minimal shareholding in the company, or at any rate, a shareholding which only represents a tiny fraction of the total. These changes are re-inforced by the increasing technical complexity of management which delivers still further power into the hands of the managers. Naturally, these changes in control lead, so the argument runs, to changes in company policy. According to optimistic variants of the theory there is an increasing emphasis upon the welfare of the company employees and a growing indifference to high dividends. The interest of the manager lies in harmonious work relations and in the long-term growth of the company, not in dividend maximization. . . . The reasoning behind these assertions can be shown to be fundamentally deficient in describing the character of *any* modern capitalist society, and even a corrected scheme cannot be applied without further modification to the specifically British variant of modern capitalism. These deficiencies can be considered under the following three headings.

A. THE SOCIAL UNITY OF MANAGERS AND OWNERS

The sociological critique of the managerial revolution thesis is now fairly well established. . . . One fact which all research encounters is that those who actually direct and manage the modern capitalist enterprise are usually important shareholders in their own right even if they have much less than a controlling proportion of the shares in the company. . . . Those directors or managers who have no important share holding are still likely to be tied to their owners by their social aspirations and values, by a respect for the institutions of property and by a common social background. However, as we shall see, capitalism has surer guarantees of managerial behaviour than these ideological bonds would in themselves provide.

B. ECONOMIC LOGIC OF THE MARKET

Marx himself never considered that the capitalist entrepreneur, in any real sense, *controlled* the economy as a whole, nor that any individual capitalist controlled,

1. C. A. R. Crosland, *The Future of Socialism*, Jonathan Cape, London, 1956.
2. C. A. R. Crosland, *The Conservative Enemy*, Jonathan Cape, London, 1962.
3. *Industry and Society: Labour's Policy on Future Public Ownership*, Labour Party, London, July 1957.
4. J. K. Galbraith, *The New Industrial State*, Deutsch, London, 1972.

except in a very secondary sense, even his own enterprise. . . . In their daily actions men in a capitalist society produce and reproduce a certain type of economy; but this economy, which conditions the actions of the capitalist as well as of the worker, is not subject to *their command*.

Marx emphasised the *anarchy* of capitalist production. 'Anarchy' was used in a double sense. Firstly, it referred to the fact that the ultimate goal of capitalism as a system was the accumulation of capital and the making of profit, whereas the only goal of the socialist economy would be the satisfaction of human needs. Secondly, it referred to the fact that the actual mechanisms of the capitalist economy—the market system—were not subordinated to human control. This compounded anarchy afflicted the traditional capitalist economy with endemic imbalance—in particular, with the wild cycle of boom and slump. At the level of the enterprise the autonomy left to the entrepreneur was the ability to interpret, more or less successfully, the dictates of the market and to exploit, more or less successfully, the labour power he purchased. Thus, the workings of the law of value ensured that his enterprise could only survive if it corresponded to some demand effective within the market. Moreover, he was constrained to supply that demand in a manner which yielded him a return on his capital that did not fall too far below the average. If he made a loss, he might find himself in the bankrupt's court or, at best, his capital would begin to dwindle and he would gradually cease to be a capitalist.

If this analysis was correct, then the 'control' of modern capitalist economies will only be different to the extent that the working of the law of value through the capitalist market has been modified. The market has been and is being modified considerably (some of the implications of this will be explored later), but the 'managerial revolution' is not an important modification of the market mechanism, if indeed it modifies it at all. Even at the enterprise level the initiative in the hands of the manager is to subordinate, with greater or less efficiency, his company to the changed market situation. That the modern manager 'controls' any more than the traditional entrepreneur is in this sense quite mistaken. The sanction of the take-over raid becomes under the new conditions a powerful deterrent to company policy not directed towards market demands. . . . Improved methods of interpreting the market only make the manager's subordination to it more complete.

Crosland claimed, however, that the ultimate goals of profit-making and capital accumulation had been modified by increased social responsibility in those companies where ownership and control are most clearly separated. The only admissible evidence on this point would be observed differences in managerial behaviour. . . .

Moreover, it is by no means clear that the motives of the modern manager are so different from those of his predecessor. It is frequently claimed that the modern manager is growth-orientated: but was the idea of growth for its own sake of capital accumulation instead of profit consumption, really so foreign to the nineteenth-century captain of industry ? Marx himself certainly did not think so: 'Accumulate! Accumulate! That is Moses and all the prophets', he wrote. . . . Indeed, it is likely that in many cases the modern manager can *less* afford to ignore the need for profit distribution than the capitalist who manages his own firm. All studies agree that the manager of the modern company must allow for a certain minimum dividend even during the most inappropriate periods. By contrast such companies as Beaverbrook Limited, which was owner-managed, went for decades without any increase in dividends despite booming profits.

Turning to observable differences in behaviour between professionally managed and owner-managed firms, the two criteria most often cited by advocates of the managerial revolution are the extent of dividend distribution and the degree of concern shown for the welfare of the worker and the community. Where company paternalism is concerned, however, this can certainly not be claimed as an invention of those companies where ownership is divorced from management. To this day, the most striking examples of company concern for employee 'welfare' occur in the owner-managed concerns (in Britain, the chocolate companies; in Italy, Olivetti; in Japan, Matsushita). It is true that company paternalism is now more generally prevalent than before, but this is due to factors other than the simple rise of professionally-managed industry: for example, to the pressure of the trade unions and the greatly increased productivity of modern industry. Above all, the manager of both types of company today faces a shortage of skilled workers at a time when they are increasingly vital to the productive process. A multiplicity of fringe benefits and welfare schemes can become a market necessity, a device for tying the skilled worker to a particular factory. If, as is sometimes the case, company paternalism is too prodigal for its market situation, then the company will be weakened as a result. The recent takeover of an Olivetti division is a case in point.

As for dividend policy, the significance of the differences between owner-managed and professionally-managed firms is equally often misinterpreted. It is argued, for instance, that the tendency for manager-run companies to plough back profits and give smaller dividends is a visible mark of concern for growth. But the long-run operation of the market will ensure that if the manager does not distribute much of the profit to the shareholders then the rise in the value of the company brought about by re-investment of profits in the company will result in a rise of share values. These capital gains can be converted for the individual into (untaxed) current income. During certain periods this has been an attractive option given the prevailing tax structure. Some idea of how attractive this can be, is suggested by the fact that the average director's shareholding, worth £28,000 when the Oxford Institute survey was carried out over ten years ago, *would now be worth about £60,000 even if he has purchased no additional shares*. The owner-managed company is less in a position to take advantage of escalation in share values—if share gains are realized to any extent (by selling company shares) then the owner-managers will gradually cease to be the dominant owners. In other words, in a capitalist economy, growth can never be opposed as a goal to capital accumulation and profit-making. . . .

If there is a difference between the logic of professionally-managed and owner-managed companies, it is that the former more exactly reflects the rationality of the market. The manager has less freedom to make decisions which answer to a purely personal whim or obsession. As professionally-managed companies come to dominate industry and commerce, artificial rigidities, preventing the free flow of capital in response to market pressures, disappear. Even where the new managers re-invest a very high proportion of the companies' profits, they must always estimate the 'opportunity cost' of such investments: that is, they must ensure that their return on capital compares satisfactorily with the return typical of the rest of the economy. . . .

The responsible modern manager will probably aim at a 'fair' profit rather than a short-term maximization, but in doing this he will neither be ignoring the pressures of the market nor be acting so differently from his nineteenth-century predecessors. Dividends cannot be too low or it will be difficult to attract share-buyers in future, and the 'responsible' manager will, presumably, wish to see a wide safety margin between his company and the take-over raid or the bankruptcy court. If he judges wrongly then these two regulators will ensure that resources are not deployed inefficiently in market terms. . . .

But within the international economy it is impossible to evade the operation of the market. Relative decline is the price of too much caution, tradition or comfort. In the decade of the fifties, the rate of profit in British industry fell by about one quarter; J. R. Sargent[5] has persuasively argued that this fact is directly related to technical stagnation and the decline of Britain's international industrial and trading position.

Many proponents of the managerialist thesis maintain that the large size of the modern corporation renders it virtually invulnerable to bankruptcy or take-over. The bankruptcy of Rolls-Royce in 1971, the travail of Penn Central or such routine events as the Greyhound Corporation's take-over of Armour in 1970, show that enterprises of very considerable size are by no means immune to these sanctions. Between 1964 and 1969 there were no fewer than 855 acquisitions of manufacturing or mining firms with assets of over $10 million in the United States.[6] . . . Although a typical large corporation today supplies about one half of the funds it needs for investment this by no means frees it from financial restraints or the fear of take-over. If it is to grow and compete satisfactorily that other half of its funds which it raises externally will be vital to it. If it raises a bank loan rather than issuing new shares this will in no way allow it to escape the necessary financial scrutiny. The lack of self-sufficiency of the modern corporation is evident enough from the fact of widespread interlocking directorships between financial and other industrial and commercial enterprises. The existence of banking directors on the boards of industrial and commercial companies does not signal a return to the days of classical finance capital but it does demonstrate their dependence on proper financial criteria when issuing shares or raising credit.

To deny that a managerial revolution has occurred is not to refuse all significance to the facts on which the theory was based. One of the more significant changes which have occurred in the train of the so-called managerial revolution is a change in the forms of property income. What appears in one perspective as a 'decomposition' of capital appears in another as a more effective means for its accumulation. The retention and re-investment of profits by the modern company continually increase the value of its shares—and as capital gains they are untaxed or only lightly taxed. . . .

5. J. R. Sargent, *Out of Stagnation*, Fabian Society, London, 1963.
6. J. R. Felton, 'Conglomerate Mergers, Concentration and Competition' in *American Journal of Economics and Sociology*, July, 1971.

The question of the evidence for or against the managerialist thesis has always been a vexed one. From the beginning the managerialists have felt secure in the belief that all research pointed in the direction of a substantive separation of 'ownership' and 'control'. The simple fact that corporation executives were not the same people as the majority of controlling shareholders was solidly established by Adolf Berle and G. C. Means in 1934 in their work *The Modern Corporation and Private Property*.[7] But as the discussion so far has sought to show, it is the interpretation of these facts which is in question, rather than the facts themselves. Indeed there is now a whole new body of evidence which quite undermines the theory of a managerial revolution and which tends to support the types of argument against it which I have outlined above. . . .

Thus a study of the objectives of 25 large British companies based on replies to a searching questionnaire produced the following conclusion: 'None of the companies had any doubts that their primary objective was to be efficient and profitable and that being socially responsible would serve no useful purpose if it hindered these overall company goals.'[8]

A study of a sample of corporations in the North of England conducted by Theo Nichols arrives at the following judgement of the ownership control issue:

> We do not doubt that they (managers) have certain immediate economic
> interests which are in conflict with the maximization of shareholders'
> welfare. We do think, however, that in the long run moral, economic
> and legal considerations (and an as yet unascertainable mixture of all three)
> make it probable that they will satisfy shareholder expectations. There
> seems little reason to consider them, or the economic system they govern,
> as the manifestation of a 'post-capitalist' society.[9]

Critics of those who uphold the managerialist thesis have often complained that the managerialists have furnished precious little hard evidence that the professional manager acts in a significantly different way with respect to profit maximization than the owner-manager. . . . Unless and until they do this convincingly the proponents of the managerial revolution theory will be the flat-earthers of economics and sociology.

C. THE DECOMPOSITION OF MANAGEMENT

Finally, the technical dimension of contemporary management must be considered. One of the claims of the managerial revolution is that the technical complexity of modern management is a major factor conferring autonomy on the managers who are professionally trained in skills that lay owners cannot hope to acquire. The truth today is that the whole trend of modern technology is tending to undermine the omnicompetence of the top manager. The 'decomposition of capital' is being followed by a 'decomposition' of the managerial function. Hardly

7. A. Berle and G. C. Means, *The Modern Corporation and Private Property*, Harcourt Brace, London, 1934.
8. Barbara Shenfield, *Company Boards*, Allen and Unwin, London, 1971, p. 164.
9. T. Nichols, *Ownership, Control and Ideology*, Allen and Unwin, London, 1969, p. 153.

had the manager been hailed as the executor of a successful revolution than, as a pure type, he began to disappear. For in modern industry, whole departments of specialists are entrusted with one or other managerial function (marketing, operations research, investment allocation, process control, etc.). . . .

If the decomposition of the managerial function is scrutinised then it soon becomes apparent that it is the very specialization of the expert that constitutes the real limit on his power. The sphere of competence of the specialist is very strictly defined by his own particular skill. Rewards and sanctions descend downwards in a hierarchical manner inhibiting the development of group solidarity among those on the same level. We have seen that top management is constrained by the context of capitalist competition to maximize profits and to accumulate capital. The performance of each department can be evaluated in terms of its contribution to these overall goals. Increasingly sophisticated procedures in cost accounting enable top management to develop criteria for subordinating every aspect of company operations to financial control. The head office of a large corporation will employ an armoury of checking devices to ensure that its constituent divisions and departments contribute fully to the profit potential of the resources the corporation commands. Often competition between different divisions of the same corporation or the possibility of contracting out functions performed inside the corporation serve as a lever exercised by the head office over its outlying parts. Only in a company with most incompetent management will really important decisions about investment policy, product range, output, price, size of labour force, etc., escape proper central audit. The financial department will, of course, tend to have a decisive say in nearly all questions. However, the power residing with the financial expert is one which he derives from the context of the capitalist market itself and must exercise on behalf of the ultimate owners of the corporation.

The rise of the conglomerate corporation in the sixties showed how the problems of the 'pure' accumulation of capital had outgrown the boundaries of company organization based on a particular plant or even branch of industry. Nobody who charted the rise of the multi-product conglomerate and its subsequent vicissitudes could imagine that top management or the so-called 'technostructure' could stand in the way of capital's thirst for profit. The opening or closing of a plant, the hiring and firing of technicians of every type, must reflect finely calculated profit expectations. Any manager who ignores this imperils his own personal position and exposes his company to the competition of its rivals or to the predatory activities of the take-over expert.

It is the essence of capitalist organization that the 'dead' stored up labour of the past represented by capital dominates the living labour that propels the accumulation process forward. It is the company's task to organize as efficiently as possible the labour time that it has purchased. If each plant is to earn an adequate return on capital then the labour employed by it must be exploited as efficiently as possible. It is the task of management to so organize its plant that the value of what the workers produce exceeds by as much as possible the sum laid out in buying labour time and other factors of production. It is clear that this aim can only be achieved by maintaining an authoritarian structure within the factory, and throughout the company, which prevents either workers or technicians from controlling the productive organism of which they are the motor force. The labour of the worker or technician is purchased from him on an individual basis yet its power to create value resides in its collective, co-operative character. Capital reaps the reward of profit only because it insists on controlling and organizing the fruits of organized, co-operative labour. . . . To imagine that the personnel manager, production manager or supervisor has any choice other than to extract surplus value as efficiently as possible from his labour force is quite absurd. That is to say that they seek to raise the value of what the worker produces as much as possible above the cost of hiring him. While the production managers are concerned with extracting profitable labour from the work-force, the marketing and sales managers are concerned with realizing these profits by actually selling the goods the workers have produced. Harmonizing these different functions and bringing them into line with the financial criteria of an average or above average rate of return on capital is the job of top management. Within each of these functions there will be some room for the initiative of the particular managerial skill involved. But none of these agents of capitalist rationality are sovereigns of the economic process. In a more or less limited period of time they must all account for their actions in the only terms which count in the capitalist context: a good rate of return on capital.

Neo-capitalism and class struggle

The essential feature of neo-capitalism is not so much a modification of the internal structure of companies as a modification of the national economic framework as a whole. In Britain the first really important intervention by the State in the national economy was produced by the exigencies of war production during the First World War. But State intervention only became generalized with the use of Keynesian techniques of regulating aggregate demand. This in itself was worth any number of managerial revolutions in its impact on the workings of a capitalist economy. . . .

In the typical neo-capitalist economy, the ultimate goals of capitalism are not changed, but increasingly rational methods are employed to attain these goals— the accumulation of capital and the making of profits. Of course, the ultimate irrationality of these goals continually and endemically contaminates the 'rational' means being used to pursue them. The cycle of boom and slump is checked but other imbalances continually manifest themselves. In the last American recession, unemployment increased to over seven million; the loss of production even in boom years runs to many millions of dollars with some four million workers remaining permanently unemployed. Meanwhile, within the capitalist world as a whole, vast populations in the underdeveloped countries are pauperized by the anarchic movements of world commodity prices. Within nearly every advanced country itself, heavily populated regions are mysteriously condemned to stagnation and decay (N.E. England, Northern Ireland, Scotland, Massif Central, Southern Italy, Wallonia, Kentucky, etc.). Whole industrial sectors in each country are neglected or retarded and a persistent imbalance between public and private goods manifests itself. The relation of the capitalist economy to the natural environment is predominantly one of wasteful plunder in the pursuit of private profit: rivers are polluted, dust bowls are created, the air is contaminated and precious resources are squandered. The cluttered sprawl of most capitalist cities is a vivid testimony to the absence of any ultimate control over the workings of the system. But, despite all this, rationality of a kind is being, and has been, introduced. But a certain increase in the intelligibility of the capitalist system has been introduced at the same time.

It has been a main contention of Marxist writing that a socialist society would be distinctive above all in its *transparency*. Bourgeois society is essentially opaque. The movements of the economy remain obscure and unsuspected by even the most expert. In a socialist society men would restore to themselves that control over the society they create which capital has confiscated from them. A certain premonition of the transparency of socialist society seems to haunt neo-capitalism. It does this by giving added lucidity to the workings of the economy. Above all, it increases *the visibility of exploitation* produced by capitalist social relations. . . .

The most critical field of State intervention in the advanced capitalist economy is that of incomes policies. The attempt to regulate the overall levels of profits and wages is potentially the most explosive development of all those which constitute the new form of capitalism. Marxists have often suggested that the real relations of production were in many ways much less visible in capitalist society than they had been in pre-capitalist societies. The serf could not fail to know that he actually gave a part of his labour time or his crop to his feudal lord, whatever notions he might have held to justify this. By contrast, in the classic capitalist society the very anarchy and alienation of the productive process obscured the worker's vision of his relation to the capitalist—he knew that he was *bossed* but not necessarily that he was *exploited*. . . . Rises in the *absolute* level of wages have obscured the remarkable fact that the relative shares of profits and wages have displayed a 'historical constancy' since the end of the nineteenth-century (though periods of depression necessarily involve low profits).[10] The factor income of capital has usually withstood the assaults of organized labour. It is this which suggests that the effectiveness of the labour movement as a 'countervailing power' is severely limited. Comparing different countries it can be seen that wage increases and the provision of welfare services are not uniquely correlated with the strength of the labour movement. Some notable forms of welfare provision have been created under the political influence of the labour movement (the health service in Britain, insurance and holidays in France, pensions in Sweden). But on the other hand certain spectacular recent increases in wages have occurred in countries where organized labour is comparatively weak (e.g. Japan). Capitalism contains an armoury of measures to combat labour's attempt to reduce the rate of exploitation: speed-up, 'productivity deals', intensification of labour, inflation, tax increases, welfare cuts, etc. But if these measures have to be supplemented by an incomes policy the capitalist state will usually be driven to challenge the rights of organized labour. . . .

10. N. Kalder, 'The Theory of Capital' in F. Lutz and D. Hague (eds.) *The Theory of Capital*, International Economic Association, London 1961.

The introduction of attempts to coordinate incomes unintentionally makes possible a return to something like the pre-capitalist visibility of exploitation but in a more universal context.

In the 1960s nearly every European capitalist government sought to introduce some form of wages or incomes policy. This seemed the only way to contain inflation and prevent declining price competitiveness in international markets. Even though these attempts to control wages did not necessarily lead to a slower rate of increase of wage rates they were to be followed by increasingly militant economic class struggle. The strike statistics for these countries follow a rising curve after the mid-sixties reaching a peak in France in 1968, in Italy in 1969 and in Britain in 1970. . . .

In the long run, the confrontation between trade unions and the capitalist state which any attempt to control or plan incomes must involve can only bring into question the nature of capitalist social relations and the workings of capitalist political institutions. For a certain period the political implications of such a confrontation will not be understood by any working-class movement that is dominated by a purely trade unionist or reformist ideology. But whatever the stage of the political development of a given working-class movement, it is likely that the application of incomes policies will render more palpable the fundamental class antagonism between workers and capitalists, creating favourable conditions for intervention by revolutionary workers' organizations. Moreover, the sharp expression of class contradictions at a national and even international level also poses the question of the contradiction between the increasingly social nature of the forces of production and the still private character of appropriation via capitalist property relations. These two types of contradiction are likely to be most explosive where they coincide most clearly. *The modern working class with all its skills and its capacity for social co-operation is, after all, the vital component of the forces of production.* In the broader class struggles of an imperialist world challenged from without and divided within, capital finds that it can only maintain its economic position by weakening its political position. The more it seeks to contain its own contradictions the more it unifies and radicalizes its real antagonist: a working class capable of destroying it because it is the bearer of a superior form of social co-operation.

4. RELATIVE DEPRIVATION IN WORK Dorothy Wedderburn and Christine Craig

Inequality and deprivation are multi-dimensional. Nowhere is this more apparent than in the work situation. Employers and employed stand in different and unequal relationships to one another both of power and of command over resources. This results in the more obvious inequalities—those of wealth and income—between capital owners and employees. And if this appears to beg the question of who are the 'owners' or 'employers' in modern capitalist society it cannot be denied that there is a vast gulf between the wealth and power of top managers and lower level employees. In fact, the employing enterprise is a hierarchy where income differences are paralleled by other dimensions of economic inequality which may extend to differences in the regularity and dependability of income, and in the nature and extent of fringe benefits. There are also less tangible inequalities which relate to the content of work, to the kind of social relationships which people are involved in at work, and to the exercise of power. There are varying degrees of constraint imposed by the rules which govern working life. Jobs vary widely in their degree of interest and responsibility, they vary in the opportunities afforded for the development of individual potentialities and in the opportunities which they provide for upward mobility.

Some of these inequalities lend themselves easily to documentation and measurement, others less so. Few attempts have been made to relate one dimension of inequality to another, or to examine how far deprivation in one sphere is accompanied by deprivation in another. Yet because of the importance of work in our society these inequalities permeate many other aspects of an individual's life. In what follows we first review the data which is available about inequality at work . . .

The range of inequalities at work

Official studies in the sixties suggested that there had been some improvement in the position of manual workers compared with non-manual workers in respect of fringe benefits such as occupational pension schemes and the provision of sick pay by employers, which can be viewed as part of the total package of remuneration. Yet there remained wide differences between occupational groups, and between the public and the private sector. In 1971 it was estimated that 87 per cent of male non-manual workers were members of occupational pension schemes compared with only 56 per cent of manual workers (in fact, a decline in manual

---

4. Reprinted from *Poverty, Inequality and Class Structure* by D. Wedderburn, Ed., by permission of Cambridge University Press, London. Copyright © 1974. (pp. 141-54)

worker membership since 1967, when it was 64 per cent).[1] Moreover, there were considerable differences in the basis of treatment under these schemes. Any scheme which calculates benefits as a percentage of 'normal' earnings will, of course, reflect existing earnings' differentials between different occupational groups. But 59 per cent of the occupational pension schemes for manual workers provided a pension calculated as a fixed sum per year of membership of the scheme. In contrast, 85 per cent of the non-manual schemes were salary service schemes and provided pensions based upon final salary or salary in the last years of service.

Such surveys, however, did not examine differentiation within the very broad headings of manual and non-manual. Moreover, they were carried out across industries or occupational groups so they did not cast any light on the differences in the position of different occupational groups employed by the same employer. More data is now available which does enable some such comparisons to be made over a diverse range of employment conditions. There are two main sources. The first is an enquiry carried out at the Department of Applied Economics, Cambridge, into the differences in the terms and conditions of employment of manual and non-manual employees in manufacturing industry.[2] Secondly, data are available from the Department of Employment's New Earnings Survey[3] which has been conducted annually since 1968. The following discussion draws on both these sources.

The Cambridge study was carried out in two stages. First, in 1968, a postal questionnaire was sent to a random sample of establishments which employed more than one hundred workers, in manufacturing industry. (This is henceforth referred to as the 1968 postal enquiry.) The sample was stratified by industry group, size of establishment and region. Information was collected about the formal employment conditions of 'typical' male employees aged between 35 and 40, with five years' service, in each of the following six categories:

1. Semi-skilled or production worker (operatives).
2. Foreman in the plant or works, or plant supervisor.
3. General routine clerical worker.
4. Draughtsman, or technician of similar grade.
5. Professionally qualified employee, a member of middle management.
6. Work's manager or member of senior management.

The main object was to discover differences between these categories. Standardization in respect of age and length of service was introduced to overcome any problems which might arise from the fact that employment conditions are frequently related to these two variables. For example, entitlement to sick pay or holidays may increase with length of service. These six occupational categories

1. Ministry of Labour, *Sick Pay Schemes: A Report*, HMSO, London, 1964 and Government Actuary, *Occupational Pension Schemes, 1971*, Fourth Survey, HMSO London, 1972.
2. C. Craig, *Men in Manufacturing Industry*, Mimeographed, Cambridge, 1969; and C. Craig, 'Terms and Conditions of Employment of Manual and Non-manual Workers': Final Reports to S.S.R.C.', unpublished, Cambridge, 1971 and D. Wedderburn, 'Inequality at Work', *New Society*, vol. 15, 1970.
3. Department of Employment and Productivity, *New Earnings Survey, 1968*, HMSO, London, 1970 and Department of Employment and Productivity, *New Earnings Survey, 1970*, HMSO, London, 1971.

were selected to represent the broad strata in the occupational hierarchy of firms, where, it was hypothesized, there would be a greater homogeneity of employment conditions within the strata than between them. The enquiry covered most terms and conditions of employment other than the level of pay; for example, hours, holidays, sick pay, pension schemes, attendance, length of notice of dismissal, disciplinary measures and promotion opportunities.

The replies to this postal enquiry described the formal (or official) terms and conditions of employment, i.e. those which were part of the firms' written rules and agreements. But there is considerable scope for variation in the interpretation of formal rules. There are areas where management discretion plays an important part, for example, in the granting of time off for domestic reasons, and the period for which sickness absence with pay is granted. In the case of such things as disciplinary measures and promotion possibilities, even where formally agreed procedures exist, custom and practice have considerable influence. Such matters cannot be studied by means of a postal questionnaire. Supplementary data was therefore obtained from case-studies of 26 companies which had participated in the postal enquiry—(henceforth referred to as the case studies). These suggested that the manual/non-manual gap is certainly wider than is shown by a study of official terms and conditions.

Table 1 presents a summary of some of the main findings from the postal enquiry which relate to formal terms and conditions of employment. In all these

Table 1 Terms and conditions of employment (percentage of establishments where the condition applies)

Selected conditions of employment	Operatives	Foremen	Clerical workers	Tech-nicians	Management Middle	Senior
Formal sick pay scheme available	46	65	63	65	63	63
Sick pay provided for more than 3 months	49	58	55	57	65	67
Coverage by formal pension scheme	67	94	90	94	96	95
Pension calculated as fixed amount per year of service	48	18	16	14	13	12
Holidays, excluding public holidays, of 15 days or more a year	38	71	74	77	84	88
Choice of time at which holidays taken	35	54	76	76	84	88
Time off with pay for domestic reasons	29	84	84	86	92	93
Period of notice of dismissal in excess of statutory requirements	13	29	26	29	53	61
Clocking on to record attendance	92	33	24	29	2	4
Pay deduction as penalty for lateness	90	20	8	11	1	—
Warning followed by dismissal for frequent absence without leave	94	86	94	92	74	67

Source: Craig, Men in Manufacturing Industry.

areas there is a sharp contrast between the manual workers (operatives) on the one hand, and non-manual grades on the other, and in every case the manual conditions are less favourable. The sharpest contrast is between operatives and senior management. Only 35 per cent of operatives had any choice about the time when they took their holiday, compared with 88 per cent of senior management. Only 29 per cent of operatives were likely to be given time off with pay for domestic reasons such as a death in the family, or illness of a wife compared with 93 per cent of senior management. On the other hand, 46 per cent of operatives were covered by a formal sick pay scheme compared with 63 per cent of senior management. There is in fact, overall, a greater similarity of treatment between the grades in respect of the more purely 'economic' aspects of the terms of employment, such as sick pay and pension schemes, than in aspects controlling working hours and behaviour such as holidays, attendance recording and certain disciplinary penalties.

But there is also evidence of some differentiation within the non-manual strata. It is small in respect of the traditional fringe benefits, but there is a discernible break in respect of other items like periods of notice, choice of holiday time and disciplinary measures. Here foremen, clerical workers and technicians have less favourable conditions than management grades. In one or two areas even, like record attendance and choice of holiday time, the conditions of foremen are rather closer to those of operatives than to other non-managerial grades, presumably reflecting both the physical proximity of the foremen and operatives on the production process and also the demands of production itself. But by and large the findings suggest that the terminological distinction which many firms make, between 'operatives' (hourly paid), 'staff' and 'management' do reflect objective differences of employment. Because of this we shall in further discussion mostly reduce our six categories to the three of 'manual workers', 'staff' and 'management'. At the same time we should note that the *big* divide in employment conditions still falls between operatives or manual workers on the one hand, and non-manual grades, staff and management, on the other.

Table 1 shows some of the main differences in the kind of treatment given to the different occupational groups across industry, but does not show the extent to which employers gave equality of treatment to the different groups within their own firms. Table 2 shows that uniformity was the exception, and that in all cases where there was differentiation, the manual workers had the least favourable conditions. The postal enquiry (a reasonably representative sample of manufacturing industry) did not produce a single firm where all occupations were treated uniformly for all terms and conditions. The subsequent case studies suggested that the true picture was of even greater inequality. For example, although 42 per cent of establishments stated on their questionnaires that the canteen facilities were the same for all grades, we found in the case studies that in many firms it was customary for different occupational groups to use different facilities; and among the firms where penalties for bad time-keeping were officially the same for all (17 per cent of the establishments), there were certainly many where the penalties were less likely to be enforced for non-manual workers.

Evidence from both the postal enquiry and the case-studies led to the conclusion that manual workers were in every case more closely bound by discipline than were staff. Sometimes this was because of the exigencies of the production system itself, but it also reflected a widespread belief among management that manual workers were less responsible than staff and less identified with the company. Discipline, therefore, tended to be stricter for manual workers than for staff, immediate penalties more severe, and the amount of discretion allowed both to the employees and their supervisors much more limited. In the case of discipline there was a heavy reliance upon the 'rules' to control manual workers; for staff, there was personal consideration, even in some cases counselling and guidance. Even where formal disciplinary agreements existed for all grades, they were more frequently invoked for manual workers and at earlier stages. Precisely because there was more flexibility and discretion for staff recourse to

Table 2 Summary of the degree of uniformity of treatment of different occupational groups

	Percentage of establishments where the condition of employment is the		
	Same for all grades	Least favourable for operatives: Same for non-manual grades	Least favourable for operatives and differ- ences between non- manual grades[b]
Sick pay schemes	16	49	27
Pension schemes	31	52	10
Holidays	19	27	41
Canteen facilities[a]	42	11	33
Penalties for lateness	6	52	33
Penalties for bad time keeping	17	23	50

[a] 'Least favourable' in this context means 'separate'. No data was available to judge the quality of the canteen.
[b] Some establishments could not be fitted into these three categories and have been omitted.
Source: Craig, *Men in Manufacturing Industry.*

formal procedures was less necessary. But, where both operatives and categories of staff were organized in trade unions and had procedure agreements, the use of the procedure was seen as more advantageous to the manual workers than to the staff. The case studies do suggest, however, that this position might be changing with the growth of white-collar trade unionism among some grades, a point to which we return below.

Control of attendance and standards of required behaviour is one aspect of the employment situation where a very sharp line is drawn between manual and non-manual workers. Physical working conditions are another. It requires little documentation to establish that manual workers as a group are exposed to worse noise levels, extremes of temperature, noxious smells, and enjoy lower standards of amenities such as lavatories and canteens. A very important consequence of the conditions in which they work is the greater physical risk to which manual workers are exposed. To the risk of loss of life or severe disablement from acci- dents at work must be added the risk of contracting industrial disease.

Manual workers also spend much longer in these less favourable physical conditions. They have, on average, shorter holidays and a longer working week than most non-manual workers, and are more likely to have to work 'unusual' hours. Data from the Department of Employment's New Earnings Survey (henceforth referred to as the NES) show that whereas in 1970 60 per cent of non-manual grades were working less than 38 hours a week, more than 65 per cent of manual grades were working more than 40 hours; and a quarter were working more than 50 hours a week including overtime. The NES also showed that no less than 22 per cent of manual grades received shift payments compared with only 4 per cent of non-manual workers. Shift working interferes with normal family and social life. It may be, as the National Board for Prices and Incomes Report[4] argued, that manual workers select themselves in such a way that for those who work shifts the advantages of, for example, higher pay and free time during the day more than compensate for the disadvantages. But this only serves to underline the relative deprivation of manual workers many of whom have to make this kind of choice between various desired ends when non-manual workers are not forced to.

Table 3   Make up of pay[a] by occupational group—Men (percentages)

	All manual occupations		Some non-manual occupations				All non-manual occupations	
			Managers		Technicians			
	Of total pay	Of employees paid this way	Of total pay	Of employees paid this way	Of total pay	Of employees	Of total pay	Of employee paid this way
Basic pay	69.1	97.6	91.5	99.8	93.0	100.0	91.3	99.4
Overtime pay	16.4	63.6	0.7	6.1	4.8	27.5	2.8	19.0
Shift and other premium payments	3.0	21.7	0.1	0.6	0.6	5.0	0.3	3.6
Payment by result	6.9	18.7	–	0.2	–	0.2	0.1	0.2
Bonus	3.3	31.4	4.5	32.6	0.9	15.8	2.2	21.4
Commission	0.2	1.3	2.8	9.9	0.1	0.5	2.5	7.6

[a] Excluding holiday, sick pay and miscellaneous pay.
Source: Department of Employment, *New Earnings Survey, 1970* (HMSO, 1971).

The 1968 postal enquiry and the NES data on the make-up of pay provide a vivid illustration of another dimension of inequality between manual and non-manual workers. This is in the extent to which earnings are predictable and dependable. The Cambridge postal enquiry showed that while 90 per cent of manual workers suffered deductions from pay if they were late to work, only a minority of staff and virtually no management were treated in this way. It also showed that if there are, for example, domestic emergencies and time has to be taken from work, the vast majority of manual workers would lose pay while the great majority of non-manual workers would not. In the NES survey 16 per cent

4. National Board for Prices and Incomes, *Hours of Work, Overtime and Shift Working*, HMSO, London, 1970.

of all manual workers had lost money, i.e. been paid for less than their basic hours compared with only 3 per cent of the non-manual grades. This included loss of pay as a result of voluntary absenteeism, which is heavier among manual than non-manual workers and where it might be argued the manual worker is deliberately making a choice. As we have seen, however, in the advent of domestic crisis he has no choice but to be absent and lose pay. The manual worker is also far more dependent upon overtime and payment by results which are also important in making earnings irregular and fluctuating. In 1970 only 70 per cent of the total take-home pay of manual workers was derived from their basic pay compared with over 90 per cent of the pay of non-manual workers.

Actual level of earnings is of course central to any discussion about occupational differences, and earnings capacities do still vary greatly despite a widespread belief that differentials between manual and non-manual groups have narrowed considerably in the post-war period. Routh's[5] historical survey has, in

Table 4   Distribution of earnings by industry and occupation, April 1970 (full-time men paid for a full week)

Selected occupations	Median earnings £ per week	As percentage of the median			
		Lowest decile	Lower quartile	Upper quartile	Highest decile
Manufacturing industry					
Manual	28	69	83	120	142
Non-manual	32	65	80	127	170
All industries and services					
Unskilled worker	22	69	82	123	149
Semi-skilled worker	26	69	82	121	144
Skilled worker	27	71	83	121	145
Foreman or supervisor	31	72	85	118	137
Clerk—routine or junior	19	76	86	120	144
Clerk—intermediate	23	75	86	117	138
Technician—laboratory	26	67	80	128	156
Draughtsman	31	74	87	116	131
Engineer—mechanical	37	61	78	125	154
Accountant	40	48	73	130	163
Works, production, manager	40	67	80	126	156
Marketing, advertising, sales manager	49	62	80	127	161

Source: Department of Employment, *New Earnings Survey, 1970* (HMSO, 1971).

fact, established a remarkable stability over a fifty-year period, but data from the 1970 NES shed some light on why the popular view persists. As Table 4 shows, in 1970 the median earnings of adult male non-manual workers in manufacturing industry were some 17 per cent higher than those of all manual workers. In all industries (that is both service and manufacturing) the median earnings of most

5. G. Routh, *Occupation and Pay – Great Britain*, 1906-1960, Cambridge University Press, Cambridge, 1965.

of the specific occupations within the non-manual group were also higher than those in the manual group. Foremen, draughtsmen, mechanical engineers and managers all had higher earnings than even skilled manual workers. But the median earnings of a routine male clerical worker were only £19 a week compared with the £27 of a skilled manual worker, and a laboratory technician was earning the same as a semi-skilled worker. If we examine not only the dispersion of earnings *between* occupational groups, but also *within* them, it is clear that the spread of earnings among non-manual workers was much greater than among manual workers (see the decile and quartile intervals in Table 4). It is therefore not difficult for *some* non-manual workers to find *some* manual workers earning more than themselves, even though this is not typical of the groups as a whole.

But Table 4 data relate to the averages of all workers in an occupational group irrespective of age or length of service. There are other aspects of life-time earnings which suggest that manual workers may be even more relatively deprived, for the earnings progression of the two categories of workers is very different (Table 5). The manual worker typically has a longer working life. He leaves school earlier. It is the case that compared with a young non-manual worker, age for age, he may earn more in his early years partly because the young non-

Table 5   Median earnings by age, April 1970 (Full-time men paid for a full week. All industries and services: £ per week)

Age group	Manual	Non-manual
15–17	8.9	8.6
18–20	16.5	13.7
21–4	23.7	21.9
25–9	26.0	28.4
30–9	27.4	34.4
40–9	26.9	35.6
50–9	24.8	34.0
60–4	22.6	28.9
65 and over	19.4	23.1
All ages	24.8	30.3

Source: Department of Employment, *New Earnings Survey, 1970* (HMSO, 1971).

manual worker may be employed in training positions (so, too, of course will the manual worker serving an apprenticeship), but also because the young manual worker can exert effort to increase his earnings through working overtime or extra piece-rate payments. Non-manual occupations, however, are typically associated with payment systems carrying with them increments paid at least over a salary range, even though the content and nature of the job do not change. This type of progression is particularly common in public employment. It also exists in private industry but there it is more usual to award pay rises as 'merit' increases, so that the level of pay is determined by management's judgement of the quality of the individual.[6]

6. National Board for Prices and Incomes, *Salary Structures*, HMSO, London, 1969.

Such pay progression is relatively rare for manual workers, who are more likely to find their earning abilities declining after the mid-forties because they are less able to expend the physical effort required to sustain them. Nor can manual workers expect much pay progression as a result of promotion to higher positions in a career structure whereas this is quite typical of the experience of a non-manual worker. For manual workers we can say, then, that higher pay over time comes in the main from increased effort or longer hours. In the short run it is seen to come, most importantly, from the results of collective action through membership of a trade union. Higher pay for the non-manual worker is in the main the result of incremental salary scales, personal assessment of his merit by the employer and by the possibilities of a 'career'—that is promotion to more responsible, highly paid, positions (although, as we note below, this situation may be changing).

The case-study material underlined the fact that few manual workers have opportunities to progress in the sense of crossing the manual/non-manual line. In certain kinds of production processes it may be possible to move from jobs with lesser to greater skill, but all would lie within the same general spectrum of manual work. The most common promotion would be to that of the position of foreman. Increasingly, however, the opportunities for promotion, where they exist, lie with the technically qualified men and the case-studies show some examples of the replacement of the traditional shop-floor foreman by a technically qualified man. In other words, the opportunities for upward mobility for the manual worker are being narrowed even further. But promotion prospects in non-manual occupations also vary. Foremen of the traditional kind promoted from the shop floor cannot expect to go much further, and the case-studies also revealed extremely limited career opportunities for routine clerical workers.

Other surveys have quantified the extent to which overall security of employment differs for different occupational groups.[7] This situation may be changing somewhat. It certainly appears that in the 'shake-out' of labour in 1971–72 companies were concerned to reduce overheads as much as they were to cut back on immediate production costs, although the unemployment rate for non-manual workers remained lower than for manual workers. Technological change, in particular computers, may also have some long-term impact on white collar employment, by reducing the number of routine clerical jobs. These are trends which should be watched for the future. In the meantime, manual and non-manual occupations remain fairly sharply differentiated both in respect of security and in the periods of notice given when dismissal does occur. The law specifies minimum periods of notice which are the same for all grades of worker, but the 1968 postal enquiry revealed that in only 13 per cent of establishments were operatives normally entitled to more than the legal minimum period of notice, compared with a quarter where clerical workers, and a half where other non-manual grades received more than the legal minimum. Thus despite the laying down of a legal minimum floor which is the same for all, old inequalities are reasserting themselves.

7. S. R. Parker, G. C. Thomas, N. D. Ellis and W. McCarthy, *Effects of the Redundancy Payment Act*, HMSO, London, 1971, p. 97 and A. I. Harris, *Labour Mobility in Great Britain*, (assisted by Rosemary Clausen), HMSO, London, 1966, p. 64.

The Cambridge enquiry was one of the first to try to document systematically inequalities in the relational aspects of work. But the information it obtained about the application of disciplinary procedures and promotion prospects can do little more than indicate a vast area of inequality which deserves further attention. In particular it is important to know more, first, about the way in which the actual work task itself is experienced and second about the experience of power.

It does not require very sophisticated analysis to see that the job of a surgeon, or even of a production manager is more intrinsically interesting and rewarding than that of a lathe operator or of an oven-man on a biscuit production line. But there are no systematic methods yet available by which jobs may be ranked according to the degree of interest afforded. How can one compare the interest of the work of an invoice clerk with that of a panel operator? It is possible to identify characteristics of the work task which are valued, such as variety, autonomy, freedom from mechanical or physical constraints, high levels of informational and judgemental inputs. But no scaling system has been devised to embrace the total range of occupations in modern society. And to ask workers to rate their own jobs according to the degree of interest afforded confounds the problem because their judgements can be seen to depend upon their initial expectations.

One possible approach to an objective measure at the moment is to ask people whether they would choose the same kind of work if they were beginning their life over again, or if they would continue in the same kind of job if they inherited enough money to live comfortably. Blauner summarizes the results of a number of such studies which show:

> Higher percentages of satisfied workers are usually found among professionals and businessmen. In a given plant, the proportion satisfied is higher among clerical workers than among factory workers, just as in general samples it is higher among middle class than among manual working-class occupations. Within the manual working class, job satisfaction is highest among skilled workers, lowest among unskilled labourers and workers on assembly lines.[8]

Equally important, but no less difficult to establish is the experience of power in the work situation. The Cambridge study certainly indicated that there was a hierarchy running from manual workers to management, in which rules governing behaviour at work became progressively more relaxed. The opportunity to exercise discretion in the performance of the work itself also varies, although here the manual/staff distinction, at least, is certainly too crude, because craftsmen are likely to have far more discretion than routine clerical workers. But there is also the dimension of power to influence decisions or to control the actions of other people in the organization. Studies such as those of Tannenbaum[9] based on people's perception of power again suggest a familiar

8. R. Blauner, 'Work Satisfaction and Industrial Trends in Modern Society' in R. Bendix and S. M. Lipset (eds.) *Class, Status and Power*, The Free Press, London, 1967, 2nd. edn., p. 475.
9. C. G. Smith and A. S. Tannenbaum, 'Organizational Control Structure: A Comparative Analysis' in A. S. Tannenbaum (ed.) *Control in Organizations*, McGraw Hill, New York, 1968.

hierarchy from manual workers through various levels of management. But with the complexity of modern organizations this hierarchy is no longer a simple pyramid and one is left asking uncomfortable questions about whether the position of the routine clerical worker in a sales department is very different in respect of 'power' from that of the production worker.

Lockwood has distinguished between 'market situation'

> that is to say the economic position narrowly conceived, consisting of source and size of income, degree of job-security, and opportunity for upward occupational mobility

and 'work situation'

> the set of social relationships in which the individual is involved at work by virtue of his position in the division of labour.[10]

Together, he argued, these two situations comprise what Marx understood as class position. This review of the current position in Britain suggests that manual workers' 'market situation', despite some changes, remains inferior in most respects to that of most non-manual workers. The non-manual group, however, is extremely heterogeneous and there are some occupations where security of employment, and opportunities for promotion seem more akin to those of manual workers. Similarly in respect of the 'work situation'—that is the nature of the work task, the experience of work constraints and the experience of power—it is possible to generalize and say that non-manual workers are better off than manual workers, but there are many differences within the non-manual group. To summarize it might be said that the overall picture is one of considerable inequality in all aspects of the employment relationship; where the traditional dividing line between manual and non-manual occupations still represents a fairly sharp break in conditions: but where some differentiations within the non-manual group are also important.

10. D. Lockwood, *The Blackcoated Worker*, Allen and Unwin, London, 1966, p. 155.

5. THE INDUSTRIAL SUPERVISOR John Child

Many among the older generation of British supervisors wistfully recall the days when becoming a foreman, the archetypical industrial supervisor role, was a mark of considerable advancement. To be able to say, in the words of the song, 'I've got the foreman's job at last', was to have crossed a significant social and political divide in the earlier period of British industrial society. Those were the days when half-mythical figures such as 'Jumbo' Prentice, the bowler-hatted foreman, ran engineering shops single-handed, enjoying unquestioned authority among their men and a secure status in the community.

During the course of the nineteenth century, the foreman's role had gradually become integrated into the complex monitoring and control systems of organized industry. However, his command over labour, which dated from the earlier role of labour contractor, was still unquestioned by employers. The view of supervision which prevailed in the last quarter of the century was summed up in a British text on 'Workshop Management' published in 1878. According to Frederick Smith, its author, the foreman

> should always let the workman see that . . . his will is to be supreme in the workshop. An employer should not unduly interfere between the foreman and his men . . . actual engaging and discharging should be the work of the foreman *only*.[1]

These precepts were still being followed at the Swindon railway works shortly before the First World War broke out.[2] The foreman's power was clearly evident. Every morning it was normal for a crowd of men to gather outside the works seeking a job. They lined up, and the foremen would walk up and down inspecting them. After each man subserviently asked for a job, a foreman would give his answer—'yes' or 'no'. Who was taken on was in practice often a matter of personal connection or favouritism. It was also the prerogative of the foreman to dismiss workers, and at that time the company had become increasingly ruthless in its dismissal of older and sick employees. In most departments some of the men lived in rooms or houses rented from their foremen. The foreman's power and status was in this way further enhanced through being a rentier. The fore-

1. Frederick Smith, *Workshop Management: A Manual for Masters and Men*, Wyman, London, 1878.
2. Alfred Williams, *Life in a Railway Factory*, Duckworth, London, 1915.

5. Original article. Copyright © 1975 Holmes McDougall Ltd., Edinburgh. John Child is Professor of Sociology at the University of Aston Management Centre.

man at Swindon maintained a distinctive social standing as an authority figure at work and as a minor property-owning member of the lower middle class within the community. This picture was probably reasonably typical of its time.

Today, the industrial supervisor's distinctive and apparently secure standing has all but evaporated. Although in the construction industry in any large British city it is still possible to find the 'labour master' dealing as an entrepreneurial and rentier foreman in the old style with lower intelligence labour, this type of role is not found in the general run of industry. Some have suggested that under certain conditions, such as the automation of production processes[3] or the development of autonomous working groups,[4] there will be little if any role for the foreman at all. The 'end of management' which Fletcher[5] has predicted from his studies of middle and junior managers, has already begun to enter into many foremen's minds as a distinct possibility. This helps to account for the rapid increase in supervisory unionization in recent years. We have had a number of supervisors' strikes in Britain, for example in civil airline maintenance. The supervisor's traditional commitment to company and management now appears to be the exception rather than the rule. The Institute of Supervisory Management, which stands for the recognition of supervision as a full part of management, has in recent years through its journal been complaining anxiously that there is a 'dire need' to clarify the supervisor's role.[6]

This change over the years is symbolized in modes of foremen's dress. The bowler hat reflected a widely adopted behavioural norm of foremen as an occupational group. It was almost aggressively displayed and almost universally recognized. At times it became a source of protection, as in the shipyards where according to lore a steel-lined version would protect the wearer from bolts dropped from a great height! Otherwise, however, the bowler hat was a non-functional symbol of unquestioned authority. Today's supervisor has far less distinction of dress. Perhaps just the long coat, but that is usually issued by the company and carefully fitted into a company-designated system of graduated distinctiveness in clothing, in which the foreman comes near to the bottom of the status hierarchy.

It is worth taking a closer look at how supervision has undergone this dramatic change within the space of only some sixty years, because it adds a further dimension to the sociology of industrial development. This historical canvas will have, of necessity, to be painted in broad sweeps, postponing a closer look at variations between different types of supervisors and their jobs for subsequent sections which deal with the contemporary scene.

Changes in the industrial supervisor's role

In the period before the First World War, the industrial supervisor (or foreman)

3. E. R. F. W. Crossman, *Automation and Skill*, DSIR, HMSO, London, 1960 and James C. Taylor, 'Some Effects of Technology in Organizational Change', *Human Relations*, 24, 1971, pp. 105–23.
4. Jon Gulowsen, 'A Measure of Work-Group Autonomy' in Louis E. Davis and James C. Taylor (eds.) *Design of Jobs*, Penguin, Harmondsworth, 1972.
5. Colin Fletcher, 'The End of Management' in John Child (ed.) *Man and Organization*, Allen and Unwin, London, 1973.
6. The Institute of Supervisory Management, *The Supervisor*, December 1971.

was typically 'the man in charge'. He generally had the sole power of hiring and firing, since personnel standards did not exist outside of a few firms such as Cadbury's and other 'enlightened' companies, while union power was not widespread. We have seen a British example of what that power meant, and this was paralleled by the situation in America at the same time. Sayles and Strauss quote an old-timer on American foremen:

> In the old days the foreman used to be King—he really *was* a big shot —he'd walk down the plant floor like he really owned the place and you better do what he wanted fast—or you'd be looking for another job.[7]

As well as exercising this unconstrained control over labour, the foreman would also normally deal personally with matters of planning and allocating work, work methods, quality, safety and wages.

The relationship of foremen to other groups in the enterprise was relatively simple and unambiguous at this time. He had pretty well sole control of workers. In many companies, the average size of which was much smaller than today, there was no-one between the foreman and the owner-manager; sometimes there would just be a works manager. So the relationship upwards was also relatively straightforward. There was no question of equality or similar standing with the owner or 'the Master'—no concept of the foreman belonging to a management team. In fact, the concept of management barely existed then. So the foreman knew where he stood and there was a general acceptance of his status; this is a most important contrast to his position in industry today. Diagrammatically, we can summarize the foreman's organizational position some sixty years ago as:

Figure 1   The foreman in charge.

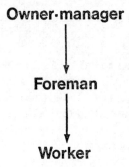

The foreman was a man in the middle (to use a more recent description), but since the main flow of power and authority was downwards, he did not often feel caught between two opposing forces.

During the inter-war years a noticeable change began to take place, which had been foreshadowed by developments in a few firms even before the 1914–18

7. L. R. Sayles and George Strauss, *Human Behaviour in Organizations*, Prentice-Hall, Englewood Cliffs, N. J., 1966, 2nd edn., p. 413.

war. In the first place, the theme of 'homes fit for heroes' and a resolve to improve upon the social and industrial conditions prevailing before the war was accompanied not only by the short-lived Whitley Council movement but also by an insistence on the part of many commentators that the foreman's treatment of employees must be reformed. The foreman (and this was to be repeated after the Second World War) was to a large degree singled out as the culprit for the industrial unrest and hostility to employers which prevailed at the time. This sharp change of emphasis is examined in more detail in my study of British Management Thought;[8] it was summed up at the time by John Lee who described the supervisor's new role as 'the leader, the guide, the farther-seer . . . (who) will realize that his control must be rather radiation than domination'.[9]

Secondly, there was in this period the early development of management as a specialized force in industry with a sense of its separate, even quasi-professional identity. It brought in train a series of new techniques to deal with many of the activities previously left to the foreman—techniques of selection, welfare, quality control, production planning, maintenance, work study, and so forth. Frederick W. Taylor had advocated, as part of his programme of scientific management,[10] the breaking up of the foreman's job into specialized tasks ('functional foremanship' he called this), each of these tasks becoming the responsibility of a new functional department. This left just the leadership or human-relations role to foremen. Although most companies rejected Taylor's functional foremanship in the form he precisely laid down, they have since that time effectively followed the same principle through increasingly investing in specialized personnel, quality, work study, production planning and other departments which have severely impinged on the status of the foreman by relieving him of major segments of his former role. This process helps to account for the stress on the foreman's human relations and leadership functions ever since the post-World War I period. It sometimes became the case that foremen had little else left to do. The foreman's position therefore became more insecure as the number of managerially legitimated activities on which he could base his role decreased. Any resulting sense of anomie would be exacerbated by his lack of training in the field of human relations which was left to him.

During the late 1930s, both in Britain and the United States, trade-union membership grew markedly among shop-floor workers, and with the advent of relatively full employment in the 1940s the power of labour was considerably enhanced. Gone were the days when workers depended upon the foreman for holding on to their job, and when workers' loyalties would attach to him alone. Instead, his ability to enforce his authority on the shop floor was now uncertain, not to be taken for granted, while his very position of leadership was being challenged by workers' own chosen and union-accredited representatives, the shop stewards. Indeed, the stewards' basis of authority, frames of reference for action, ideological justification and (sometimes) even their training were often more adequate than those of foremen.

8. John Child, *British Management Thought*, Allen and Unwin, London, 1969.
9. John Lee, *Management: A Study of Industrial Organization*, Pitman, London, 1921.
10. Frederick W. Taylor, *The Principles of Scientific Management*, Harper, New York, 1911.

These trends had advanced sufficiently in the United States for Roethlisberger to state in 1943 that the industrial supervisor (particularly the production
foreman in a unionized plant) had become the 'man in the middle'.[11] The foreman was expected to satisfy the requirements for production placed upon him by
management and the demands of his workforce which was now often unionized.
Further, he was subject to pressures and constraints placed upon him by specialized staff—pressures for his department to maintain quality standards, to
prevent strikes or to reduce absenteeism, or constraints imposed in the form of
day-to-day interference with the shop floor and an increasing volume of procedures and form-filling routines. How could he satisfy all these various parties
at once, each of them cutting away at the basis of his former authority? And what
a contrast to the day still within living memory when he alone had the say within
his shop or section! Fletcher has summarized this view of what had happened in
dramatic terms:

> Industrial supervisors, classically foremen, are men in the middle.
> Wedged between workers and management they represent both to each
> other and neither to themselves. Supervisors are constantly torn by
> competing demands and loyalties. They have come up from the ranks
> but are not part of management. Nevertheless, they are the voice of the
> front office that is heard on the shop floor. These strains are
> exacerbated by the continuous whittling away of their power and status
> by management and machine. The supervisor is robbed of the capacity
> to withstand the strain of his position. The middle is simply no man's
> land and supervisors sustain the scars of industrial conflict.[12]

Since the time that the man-in-the-middle thesis was first formulated to
encapsulate the essence of the foreman's position, this latter has been weakened
yet further. As collective bargaining has become more widely established so
increasingly the foreman has been by-passed in labour negotiations even over
quite local and limited issues. Shop stewards have tended to take matters
straight to the level of works manager or its equivalent where they discern that
the real source of power to negotiate lies. On management's side, the raising of the
locus of negotiation with labour above the foreman's head has often been part and
parcel of a centralization of personnel policies. This was an attempt to maintain
consistency in the face of union attempts to force changes in conditions by
picking off individual segments of the firm. The foreman therefore began to find
himself held responsible for maintaining good labour relations in his department
while scarcely being a party to the setting of their basic parameters.

The centralization of labour negotiations within plants and companies has
also been a concomitant of their increasing size, and the enlargement of management hierarchies and staffs. This has increased the 'distance' between industrial
supervisors and management in two respects. First, supervisors are further
removed from the levels at which decisions affecting the shop floor and departments are made. Second, along with the growth of management superstructures

---

11. F. J. Roethlisberger, *Management and Morale*, Harvard University Press,
    Cambridge, Mass., 1943.
12. Colin Fletcher, 'Men in the Middle: a reformulation of the thesis', *Sociological
    Review*, 17, November, 1969, pp. 341.

has come an ideology of expertise and so-called 'professionalism' which excludes the foreman without formal qualifications from the expectations of promotion he could previously entertain. As companies recruit more of their managers from among graduates, holders of professional qualifications, of HNDs and other diplomas, so the foreman's job becomes more of a dead end. The social distance between managers and industrial supervisors has thus increased sharply in recent years so far as career and life style is concerned. The foreman is even less a part of management in these respects than he used to be. In a review of American middle-managers' jobs, Nealey and Fiedler[13] concluded that the largest gap in the industrial hierarchy today lies between the first-line industrial supervisor and the manager above him.

Many foremen, then, as we look at the present day, could more accurately be considered as 'marginal men' as Wray described American foremen back in 1949. They are excluded from many management decisions while often being held accountable as managers of men—they are 'special victims of the disparity between social norms and social reality'.[14] They are sometimes paid less than the employees over whom they have charge. Their very jobs may be threatened by developments such as work-group autonomy or automation. It is not surprising that when this state of affairs first became clear to foremen in the United States back in the 1940s, many thousands joined the union (the Fireman's Association of America, subsequently banned under the Taft-Hartley Act) and there were a number of foremen's strikes even in key war industries. A similar pattern, including a surge of unionization among foremen, has been apparent during the last ten years or so in Britain.

The way in which foremen have become collectively organized in Britain is itself indicative of their attempt to safeguard a distinctive identity for themselves. The employer-oriented unionism of the old Foreman's Mutual Benefit Society, which excluded membership of conventional economic unions, is dead. The Institute of Supervisory Management, which stands for the incorporation of supervisors into management has never attracted a large membership and today appears to be in decline. On the other hand, foremen have not generally joined the general manual or even the craft unions, of which most were once members and to which their workpeople belong, in spite of the fact that such unions have often established separate sections for foremen and technicians. Instead, they have sought refuge in specifically supervisory unions such as ASTMS.

The marginality of contemporary industrial supervisors is usually analysed with particular reference to their work situation. As Nichols[15] has correctly pointed out, however, the positions which foremen hold in the industrial structure may be paralleled by their ambivalent social perspectives and by the peculiar way in which they are located on the edge of the great class divide. Who foremen adopt as their reference groups today is a question deserving of research. Many foremen, even in the past, may have been without clear social reference

13. Stanley M. Nealey and Fred Fiedler, 'Leadership Function of Middle Management', *The Psychological Bulletin*, Vol. LXX, 1968, pp. 313-29.
14. Donald Wray, 'Marginal Men of Industry: The Foremen', *American Journal of Sociology*, LIV, January, 1949, p. 301.
15. Theo Nichols, 'Labourism and Class Consciousness: The "Class Ideology" of Some Northern Foremen', *Sociological Review*, 22, 1974, pp. 483-502.

Figure 2   The foreman today: a man on the margin?

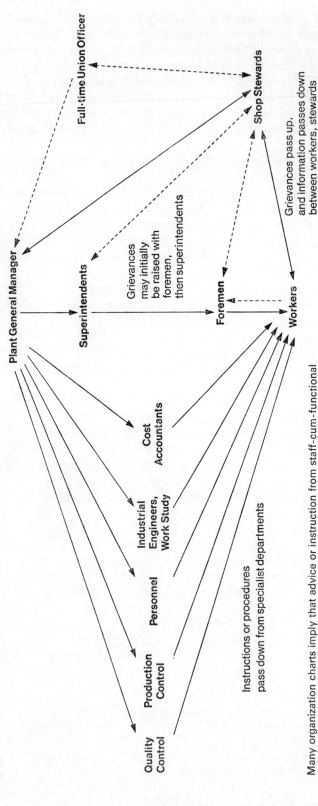

Many organization charts imply that advice or instruction from staff-cum-functional departments such as Personnel pass to the Foremen. Figure 2 portrays the situation as it is often perceived by Foremen and as it not infrequently works in practice. The Foreman is by-passed by staff specialists and by shop stewards. Indeed, his isolation may well be compounded by the frequent contacts developed on specialist issues between stewards and staff such as work-study and personnel. In such instances, the foreman again tends to perceive his role as superfluous. Solid lines in the diagram represent the main flows of communication as foremen often perceive them.

points regarding the education of their children, general life style, modes of speech, dress and so forth. I suggest later on that contemporary foremen divide into a number of contrasting groups in terms of social criteria such as these.

So far as the contemporary work setting of most industrial supervisors is concerned, a diagram cannot do justice to all its complexities. The sketch given in Figure 2 does serve, however, to draw out some of the contrasts between now and some sixty years back when one compares it with the relatively straight-forward and central role of the old-time foreman given in Figure 1. Figure 2 portrays the elements of marginality as foremen tend to perceive this and, as the diagram suggests, it is not uncommon for superintendents (or 'general foremen') to feel they are in a marginal position as well. It is significant that many superintendents have also joined ASTMS.

Contrasting types of supervision

In the preceding historical review, contrast between supervisory jobs and supervisors at a particular point in time was sacrificed in favour of contrast over time. Many questions were necessarily begged. What, in the first place, is industrial supervision and how does it vary? And what about the types of people who become supervisors: what are their origins, aspirations and outlooks towards the job? The following two sections are concerned with these questions, and attempt to illustrate the contrasts that exist within the field of study.

Thurley and Hamblin[16] defined a 'supervisor' as someone who exercises authority by actual 'overseeing', inspection and direction in the area of operations. The term 'industrial supervisor' locates this definition within the field of economic activity, and indeed most research has been carried out on production supervisors within manufacturing industry. Thurley and Hamblin[17] distinguished three levels of authority which were found quite commonly in the five firms they studied:

1. 'The *second-line supervisor* (called supervisor, foreman, senior foreman or shift engineer), directing the supervisory system and linking it with higher management.

2. The *first-line supervisor* (chargehand or foreman), i.e., the man who is regarded by the operatives as their 'immediate boss' and who possesses direct and undisputed formal authority over them.

3. The *semi-supervisor* (leading toolsetter, senior process man, head girl or technical assistant), combining supervisory with operative duties and possessing more informal than formal authority.'

These hierarchical distinctions tend to be drawn more clearly and more formally in larger plants than in smaller ones. In many smaller plants supervision is concentrated into the first-line position performing the functions of all three groups, and it is this position to which the label of foreman is most commonly attached. Thurley and Hamblin's own research was mainly confined to

16. K. E. Thurley and A. C. Hamblin, *The Supervisor and His Job*, DSIR, HMSO, London, 1963.
17. *Ibid.*, p. 5.

first-line supervisors in production departments. The second-line position is quite often designated unambiguously as a management role, but the role and authority of the semi-supervisor is not always so clear. In plants studied by the author in the Midlands, semi-supervisors (leading hands, chargehands and similar) have often performed a key linking function between white foremen and a workforce which contained a heavy immigrant element—in some cases he literally provided the only bilingual link being a coloured person himself.

Hierarchical distinctions between supervisory roles may be, however, of significance over and above their differences in functions performed. The first-line position is most usually identified with being a foreman. If second-line positions, one step up in the hierarchy, are designated as career management posts, then a significant social barrier is likely to reside just above the foreman. If second-line positions are normally open to foremen then some entry into middle management may be permitted and the greatest social distance in the management hierarchy will be further up the line, between middle and higher management. Status, if not hierarchical, distinctions between line foremen and functional specialists may represent an equally wide gulf, as perceived by foremen and probably the specialists themselves.

Thurley and Hamblin's studies represented an important advance. Previously, and this is to some extent even true of today, the literature on supervision had tended to treat the subject indiscriminately, assuming that by and large supervisors had common tasks and problems. For historical reasons already discussed, much of this literature took the view that the essence of all supervisory roles and the locus of most of their problems lay in the 'management of men'—in the human relations aspects of the job. Thurley and Hamblin took the trouble to examine closely the functions actually performed by 137 supervisors in five firms, employing methods of direct observation. Other studies since then have also looked closely at what supervisors actually do, but only with regard to a limited range of hypotheses and variables.

Thurley and Hamblin's studies demonstrated that the tasks and problems dealt with by production supervisors differed considerably from firm to firm. Even within a single firm the jobs of supervisors in different sections or departments could vary greatly. All the supervisors were to some degree involved in doing four basic tasks: planning the work, checking on how it was being processed, dealing with contingencies in production and reporting back to their managers. The precise nature of these basic tasks and their relative importance differed, however, and other tasks also varied quite considerably in their presence and importance. So did the styles of supervision adopted, the amount of time spent on communication, walking around 'keeping an eye on things', and other behaviour.

Thurley and Hamblin attempted an assessment of the factors which appeared to discriminate between different patterns of supervisory activity and behaviour. Their conclusions were only impressionistic and singled out the technology of the work itself, the supervisor's own preferred style (which the authors ascribed to 'training') and the influence of management practice. Fletcher[18] in a study of 22 production foremen in a Merseyside plant found

18. Colin Fletcher, 'Men in the Middle: A Reformulation of the Thesis', *Sociological Review*, 17, November, 1969.

differences between assembly and machine shops (providing a technological contrast) in that foremen in assembly sought more system and procedure, while those in the more complex workflow area of machining sought to have more personal control over dealing with contingencies. Senior foremen expressed relatively more preference for having greater personal control over activities than did more junior foremen. Technology and stratification therefore differentiated among foremen and the problems they experienced.

Supervision is, of course, not confined to production activities. There are supervisors in charge of engineering and craft activities, concerned with electrical maintenance, mechanical maintenance, building maintenance, with tool and die-making, pattern-making and other skilled work. In science-based industries, and in the research sections of many firms, technical supervisors can be found leading a team of specialists or in charge of projects. In this situation, the function of supervision is certainly present but the sophistication of the activities being supervised and the quality of relationship with subordinates are quite different to the relatively routine production situation described by Thurley and Hamblin. Supervision also extends to offices, where the workforce may be predominantly female and where yet another set of expectations as to appropriate styles of super-vision are likely to prevail. Supervision may even be found in technical service groups, where, for example, a works-study engineer may supervise clerks, bonus checkers and junior work-studymen. All in all, supervision varies quite con-siderably with respect to the type of work and technology in question and the kind of employees being supervised. Management practice affecting supervision will also tend to vary according to the situational factors just mentioned, accord-ing to the size of the organization as a whole, and to the work culture of the industry or region in question.

In discussions of supervision, most attention by far has been given to the supervisor's behaviour 'downwards'—towards the employees in his charge. If one looks at his job from the other angle, of relationships with higher manage-ment and staff specialists, one's attention is drawn not so much to questions of the supervisor's style or even how he spends his time, but to the discretion that is afforded to him and the priorities which are set for him to follow. If we adopt this perspective some important differences emerge between different types of supervision.

For instance, engineering and craft foremen generally enjoy a greater freedom of initiative and action than do production foremen—at least in the iron and steel industry studied by Warr and Bird[19] and in the engineering plants colleagues and I have so far investigated in the Midlands. As might be expected, foremen in charge of craft and engineering activities such as maintenance or die and tool-making usually have full discretion over matters such as checking the quality of work done and materials used in their sections, while production supervisors are typically subject to constraints imposed by quality controllers. Craft and engineering foremen tend to be less constrained by rules and pro-cedures laying down how work is to be planned or jobs to be allocated to men and equipment. They often have more discretion in regard to ordering materials

19. P. B. Warr and M. Bird, 'Assessing the Training Needs of Foremen', *Journal of Management Studies*, 4, October, 1967, pp. 332–53.

(where specialist expertise is usually required), storing them and issuing them. Working more independently as they do, craft foremen tend to have more discretion and responsibility for keeping records of work done and records on their employees, and for making written reports. In situations such as I have studied in the Midlands, some craft foremen are able to assume considerably more responsibility than production supervisors by virtue of the fact that they report from plant level to a functional superior at a divisional level as well as operationally to local management. Having two masters enables pressure from one to be appealed against in the court of the other. A further reason for the relative autonomy of craft foremen derives from the traditional non-authoritarian relationship between one apprentice-trained craftsman and another—there are still quite a few managers in engineering who started their careers as apprentices.

The size of an organization can make a considerable difference to the scope of a foreman's job and is thus a contextual influence of some importance. It has been clearly established in several research investigations that larger organizations employ a more extensive range of specialists in activities such as personnel. industrial engineering, quality control and production control.[20] Equally and predictably once specialist staff functions have been set up, larger size tends to beget a more extensive range of operating procedures aimed at regulating the performance of activities throughout the organization. Size is therefore a significant variable for understanding supervision because the discretion which supervisors have in the conduct of their tasks will vary with the system of management, particularly the degree of bureaucratization, that prevails concerning planning and control processes, concerning procedures for selection, discipline, grievances and other personnel matters, concerning standards and procedures for quality and so forth. The greater the degree of bureaucratization, the lower the personal discretion of supervisors, and this substitution of formal rules for personal supervisory control goes hand in hand with the employment of specialists who devise and operate the procedures in question and to whom any exceptions have to be referred. We have seen how this situation developed over time along with growing industrial scale and managerial 'professionalism'. At the present day it particularly characterizes the type of management practice which production supervisors in larger companies and plants are likely to encounter.

Just as the discretion allowed to foremen will vary between different supervisory situations, so will the priorities which foremen attach to their tasks. Thurley and Hamblin noted variations in the balance of activities carried out by production supervisors in different plants and departments. Bell[21] found that such variation was reflected in the importance attached by supervisors to different activities in terms of how much they contributed to their overall performance. For example, production foremen in charge of piecework sections gave top priority to ensuring the supply of tools and materials. In contrast, for craft and engineering foremen getting the right type of recruits assumed greatest significance among the factors they felt contributed to performance. The contrast is

20. John Child, 'Parkinson's Progress: Accounting for the Number of Specialists in Organizations', *Administrative Science Quarterly*, 18, September, 1973, pp. 328–48.
21. Stuart H. Bell, 'The Priorities and Performance of First-Line Supervisors', Thesis submitted in part fulfilment of the MSc in Business Administration, University of Aston, Birmingham, 1974.

explicable in terms of the pressures typically placed upon foremen by workers on piece-rates to maintain an unbroken flow of work and tools, and the technically sophisticated nature of the work carried out in craft and engineering service departments. Craft and engineering foremen tended to attach high priority to communication upward with chief engineers and maintenance superintendents. Among the production foremen communication with their operatives was given much more importance than communicating upwards with management, or indeed communicating laterally. It appeared that the tendency to by-pass production foremen in communication between management and the shop floor was causing them to devalue their links upwards with management.

Differences in priorities between different types of supervision by and large reflect differences in the work roles and relationships characteristically experienced by the foremen concerned. Bell found that the managers in charge of the foremen he studied showed far less variation in their assessments of priorities in their foremen's jobs than did the foremen themselves. This suggests that managers tend to hold to a common stereotype of 'the' foreman's job, which does not fully accord with variations in its practical realities. This stereotype can still be found in many books on supervision which are written for managers and foremen. An aspect of this ideal-typical view of supervision is that foremen are part of management, not only in the functions they perform, but also in their industrial identification. The recent unionization and militancy of foremen have provided a rude shock to this view in recent years, but it may be true nevertheless that, as Roberts, Loveridge and Gennard[22] suggest of technicians, this militancy is displayed only with reluctance. What in fact are the views of the man in the foreman's job today?

Contrasts among supervisors

It has become part of the conventional wisdom of sociology that industrial workers exhibit marked differences in the meanings and priorities they attach to work and in their degree of identification with different parties to the industrial process—management, other workers, the union or simply with the private worlds of home and family. Very little research has been carried out into the same phenomenon among supervisors, but what little there is suggests that any stereotype applied indiscriminately to all would be quite misleading. Equally, there has been little research among supervisors to match the attention given to the place of industrial workers in the class structure, though Nichols has made a start.[23]

In the plant Fletcher[24] studied, three groups of foremen emerged as having different attitudes towards prevailing management practice. Those foremen who expressed least preference for change and were least critical of the prevailing system (the 'Conservatives') were older, less educated, longer serving, less

22. B. C. Roberts, R. Loveridge and J. Gennard, *Reluctant Militants: A Study of Industrial Technicians*, Heinemann, London, 1972.
23. Theo Nichols, 'Labourism and Class Consciousness: The "Class Ideology" of Some Northern Foremen', *Sociological Review*, 22, 1974, pp. 483–502.
24. Colin Fletcher, 'Men in the Middle: A Reformulation of the Thesis', *Sociological Review*, 17, November, 1969.

careerist and more sociable with other foremen than was true of the other two groups. At the other extreme, the 'Revolutionary' group, the most critical of the prevailing system, were 'much younger, more educated, relatively isolated, selective about a small number of friends (many of whom were junior executives) and fundamentally critical of management.'[25] The middle group of 'Radicals' were more sociable than the Revolutionaries, and their promotion had come less rapidly. 'In a sense', commented Fletcher, 'it could be said that whilst Radicals appear to reflect on management practice from a foreman's point of view, Revolutionaries consider themselves practising managers.'[26]

Fletcher's conclusion is particularly instructive for an understanding of how differences in supervisors' perspectives can be generated:

> The key factor would seem to be that for the supervisors conflict increased with their proximity to management. The closer to the executive by position or by identity, then the greater the conflict. Proximity by position means that senior foremen are *higher*, and in this sense *nearer*, the source of the decisions affecting the shop floor, namely the works manager. Proximity by identity means that the supervisor feels closer to management and is *clearer* about mistakes which they might make and of ways of avoiding making them. These two proximities have considerable theoretical significance.[27]

It is quite likely that there are at least four types of supervisor in regard to the identifications they hold and the perspectives these generate. Belonging to one of these types rather than to another will be predicted to a significant degree from a knowledge of the supervisor's social background, level and type of qualification and previous work experience. While the distinctions made in the following classification are derived from my own research and industrial experience, they are not offered in any definitive manner but merely as points of reference for future, much needed, research:

1. the *'time server'*. Typically this is the foreman who has been promoted after serving many years on the shop floor. He has no previous supervisory or managerial experience, or formal qualifications beyond the ONC level. His background is likely to be manual working class. He has little or no aspirations to be promoted beyond the foreman's job, indeed he may not be wholly confident of exercising the limited responsibility he now has. Worker 'demands' are in fact likely to be perceived as the root of his problems. He has inherited a pattern of limited aspiration derived from an impoverished background. He does not see himself as a professional manager. He is worried about being able to cope with industrial change and about his job security. He belongs to a union (in most cases ASTMS) and values his membership as a significant source of job protection. He identifies strongly with other foremen. The 'time server' clearly overlaps considerably with Fletcher's 'Conservative'. It is possible that this type of foreman was promoted in the first place because he was marginally more competent than

25. *Ibid.*, p. 350.
26. *Ibid.*, p. 350.
27. *Ibid.*, p. 351, Fletcher's italics.

his fellows, because of his long service and perhaps because he poses less of a threat to management's position, ideologies and procedures than does the 'frustrated achiever' described shortly.

2. the '*supercraftsman*'. This type of foreman shares some of the characteristics of the time server such as long service. However, while the time server is usually found in routine production sections, the supercraftsman is more typical of maintenance and skilled sections. Compared to the time server, he will have considerable confidence in his technical qualifications (an apprenticeship supplemented by technical diplomas is quite a common combination), and his leadership will be based primarily on his expertise and specialized knowledge. His technical expertise may also give him some aspirations for further promotion. The technical foreman in a science-based context might fall into this category or he may be a 'cadet' (described below).

3. the '*frustrated achiever*'. This foreman will typically have been promoted from the shop floor at quite a young age and he may have some minor technical qualification. Alternatively he may have had some previous experience as a supervisor or even a manager in another firm, often a smaller firm. His background is frequently middle class, and he may well have ambitions one day to leave paid employment and set up on his own account. He is confident in his own ability to assume responsibility, and he is ambitious to enter the management hierarchy. He regards himself as a manager in what he does and he identifies with management more strongly than with other foremen. If he belongs to ASTMS or another union, it is not out of an identification with the labour movement but rather out of a desire for protection or in deference to pressure from colleagues who are members. Job security is, however, less of a dominant concern for this type of foreman, and rates lower in importance than gaining promotion and being given the opportunity to assume responsibility. He is frustrated because he is held back from the opportunity to satisfy these ambitions, and in consequence he is likely to be quite critical of management policy in general and of his immediate superior's performance in particular. In Fletcher's terms, the 'frustrated achiever' might be a 'Radical' or a 'Revolutionary'.

4. the '*cadet*'. This is a type of foreman I have only met so far through personal experience and contact. He is typically a college or university graduate for whom a foreman's job is expected to be just the first rung of a managerial career ladder. He clearly identifies with management rather than with other foremen. He probably does not join a union, and while he may be quite critical of his superiors this is only likely to become deep-seated if he finds his expected promotion is not forthcoming. If that is the case, the cadet may turn into a 'Revolutionary' unless he finds he can readily secure an acceptable job in another firm.

These thumb-nail sketches present a simplified view of reality, but they do point to the quality of variation which one finds among industrial supervisors today. In small-scale pilot studies carried out in the Midlands, I have found considerable differences in, for example, the degree to which foremen identify with management and its view of industrial relations as opposed to expressing sympathy with shop-floor workers. An identification with management, measured on a multi-item scale, was inversely correlated with the strength of a foreman's identification with other foremen. In other words, foremen either tended to identify with the shop floor and other foremen (this characterized the majority) or they identified with management but not other foremen. The contrast is in effect one between the time-serving conservative on the one hand and the frustrated-achiever radical, on the other. The frustrated achievers have so far mostly proved to be low on commitment to the union, to be relatively confident in their handling of the job and its pressures, and to be highly attracted to any prospect of promotion. Its absence leaves them bitter and critical of management. They are not resigned to their fate, whereas the time servers are much more so and are particularly concerned about the long-term security of their positions. In further research it may be found that social differentiations such as these lie at the basis of clique formation among foremen.

In comparing supervisors, I have said nothing so far about two factors: the relevance of a supervisor's sex and the psychological factors which may bear, for instance, upon his (or her) performance and satisfaction. I have been employing the male gender throughout, and the problem is that relatively little is known about female supervisors and the extent to which they compare with their male counterparts. Female non-supervisory employees enter work with quite different personal priorities and motivations. For some employment means the pursuit of life-long career; for others it is to provide savings as quickly as possible when planning to set up home; for yet others employment is just to help provide the little extra after the family has been raised, and to provide an antidote to the boredom of remaining at home on one's own. Brown and his colleagues[28] found that married women are often reluctant to accept supervisory positions, because these do not offer conditions (such as flexible hours and friendly social contacts) which most married women seek from their work.

It is probably true to say of many industrial supervisors today that they experience a profound alienation in the sense that they find their idealized image of the supervisor's role to be unfulfilled in contemporary practice. The alienation is heightened by statements issued formally by managers on the supervisor's place in management, on the information which should be passed to him as of right, on his place in factory consultation and negotiation, on the confidence that is placed in him and so forth (I have a particular company's 'Charter for Supervision' in mind here). For such statements are the 'social norms' which do not match up to social reality. All foremen I have questioned so far, take the view that the foreman should be the first-line of management and a line manager in every respect. But many of them see little of this in the practical realities of their own role.

Alienation can manifest itself at a deep personal level. As Marx argued, estrangement from one's role in a social system leads ultimately to estrangement

28. R. K. Brown, J. M. Kirkby and K. F. Taylor, 'The Employment of Married Women and the Supervisory Role', *British Journal of Industrial Relations*, II, 1964, pp. 23–41.

from oneself. How far supervisors have travelled along this road is hard to tell. At a less fundamental level, the foremen colleagues and I have interviewed could recall certain events which had given them considerable personal satisfaction. These were mainly occasions on which they had done a particularly good job, made a successful innovation, had praise from management; for some the most satisfying event had been the occasion of their promotion to foremanship. By far the most frequent cause of dissatisfaction had been the actions of management—being by-passed, not backed-up—actions which particularly violated their self-conceptions of a foreman's legitimate role. Lack of further promotion created dissatisfaction for some, as did poor relations with operatives. This division of emphasis between sources of satisfaction and dissatisfaction largely accords with the results of other studies of supervisors[29] and they conform broadly to Herzberg's two-factor theory of motivation.[30]

Within the context of a general level of alienation (which for reasons previously given is especially predictable for production supervisors in large bureaucratically organized plants), it appears that supervisors can experience relative satisfaction with certain events and dissatisfaction with others. This may depend on their personal expectations regarding what they can reasonably hope to achieve from their jobs—indeed, most commentators would conceive of satisfaction as a function of how far expectations are met by actualities, which places it at a more immediate level of consciousness than alienation.

The probability of being able to do a good job—a strong motivating factor—brings various psychological factors into consideration which distinguish one supervisor from another. For example, there is reason to believe that the supervisor who has a more flexible personality will be able to cope with pressures and contingencies bearing upon him with less personal stress and more objective success than will the man with less flexibility. Bell[31] also found that personally flexible managers and supervisors were more successful in reaching agreement on performance priorities. There was reason to believe that the supervisor's own level of performance was determined by the extent to which such agreement was reached.

What of the future?

This is a question very much on the minds of many industrial supervisors today. They consider themselves to be casualties of industrial development, and looked at in an historical perspective they have some reason to take this view. Part of the problem is that the same label has continued to be applied to a position that has radically changed. In effect the foreman of yesteryear is the middle manager, even the plant manager, of today. But his label and all that it connotes historic-

29. E.g., M. M. Schwartz, I. Jenusaitis and M. Stark, 'Motivation Factors Among Supervisors in the Utility Industry', *Personnel Psychology*, XVI, 1963, pp. 45–53 and Frederick Herzberg, 'The Motivation to Work among Finnish Supervisors', *Personnel Psychology*, XVIII, 1965, pp. 393–402.
30. Frederick Herzberg, *Work and the Nature of Man*, World Books, Cleveland, 1966.
31. Stuart H. Bell, 'The Priorities and Performance of First-Line Supervisors', Thesis submitted in part fulfilment of the MSc in Business Administration, University of Aston, Birmingham, 1974.

ally, is attached today to a role that is relatively minor, particularly in production departments. The incongruity is made all the more apparent when managements verbalize a stereotype which contains the historical connotations within situations that deny them an empirical validity.

After many years of regarding the industrial supervisor as a training problem ('develop his leadership skills and all will be well'), there are signs that some managements now appreciate how 'problems' of supervision have to be located in their social and organizational contexts. It is, for instance, becoming apparent that alienated supervisors will not only join a union and be prepared to adopt militant tactics; they will also seriously hold up the introduction of changes in technology, employee participation, job enrichment and so forth.[32] These, it becomes clear, are somewhat more than problems of supervisors' leadership of men—they have far more to do with the relation of supervisors to company and management.

Two solutions are today being canvassed in management circles to close the gap between ideology and reality. One is to do away with the problem by doing away with the supervisor—particularly with the first-line foreman. This line of thought points to the development of more sophisticated technologies which will embody much of the control and integrative functions now performed by production foremen; it also points to the development of work group autonomy and self-regulation. The other solution is quite opposite: to attach to the role of supervision a truly managerial authority and responsibility. In this conception, which can be found in Wilfred Brown's Glacier model of organization,[33] the supervisor would become the shop-floor team leader. Lower level staff personnel would report to supervisors on operational matters over which they would proffer advice and information. Shop stewards would be actively discouraged from by-passing supervisors. The supervisor would have managerial responsibility for the performance of his section and a concomitant authority over the choice and disposal of resources, including personnel.

So far, the signs are that most managements will prefer the second line of development, if only because of union strength among supervisors today and because it accords better with directive managerial ideologies. If that line of development is pursued then its long-term consequences may in fact turn out to be similar to the first alternative, because it is likely that a higher calibre of recruit will have to be attracted into the now elevated supervisory job. Entry into supervision would be confined to cadets and technically qualified staff. The supervisor's job may then in effect become merged with middle-management positions such as that of superintendent, for it is hard to see what function would be left for men in this latter position to perform.

These are processes of change that take us some way into the future. What is clear regarding the present is that the once assured identity of the supervisor within the industrial, class and status system is now in considerable doubt. The position of supervisor varies in its content and in the way it matches the purposes of those who fill it. It is a boundary role in more senses than one. It is

32. M. Weir and S. Mills, 'The Supervisor as a Change Catalyst', *Industrial Relations Journal*, 4, Winter, 1973, pp. 61–9.
33. Wilfred Brown, *Exploration in Management*, Heinemann, London, 1960.

lodged ambiguously at the boundary between the two traditionally defined 'sides of industry', at a major watershed in the class system. For some individuals—the cadets—being a supervisor merely represents an excursion to the edges of the lower class, a journey made before settling down to a defined managerial career. For the frustrated achievers it brings them up to a major barrier in the industrial hierarchy still to be overcome. For others—the time servers and many of the supercraftsmen—the role of the supervisor is the highest point which they expect to achieve in a working-class career. The social meaning of industrial supervision to those engaged in it, and its location within the overall system of work, class and community in modern industrial society is a field much deserving of some systematic study.[34]

34. I am greatly indebted to my colleague, John Berridge, for enlightening me from his fund of first-hand knowledge about supervisors in industry. A useful review of the research literature on supervision is provided in K. Thurley and M. Wirdenius, *Supervision, a Reappraisal*, Heinemann, London, 1973.

6. THE EFFECTS OF REDUNDANCY Stanley Parker[1]

Redundancy is one of the great social and economic problems of our time. It means a loss both to the individual worker and to the community. For someone to be deprived of his job through no fault of his own is in many ways a personal tragedy, and if this happens on any widespread scale it is a condemnation of the economic system by which we live.

Redundancy occurs where the whole or main reason for an employee's dismissal 'is that his employer's needs for employees to do work of a particular kind have diminished or ceased.'[2] The causes of redundancy are economic, technological and organizational: the demand for the product or service may fall, jobs may be abolished or reduced by machines, or the employer may find a way of organizing the same output with fewer workers. In recent years legislation in Britain has alleviated the problem for some of the individuals concerned, but it seems that lump-sum payments to those put out of a job often do not adequately compensate for the resulting hardships.

Firms and other employers differ considerably in the generosity and foresight with which they handle their redundancy situations. In some cases the redundancies are forced on them by external conditions, while in others they are part of the price of planned development or change. There *are* alternatives to redundancy, and mostly the initiative for avoiding it is with the employer or the community: redeployment within the firm, in or outside the industry, or to another part of the country; retraining within the firm, industry or a Government Training Centre.

Redundancy has tended to hit some types of employee harder than others, and one of the biggest problems for most people is finding another job not inferior to the one lost. Research shows that this aim is quite often not achieved, and that many post-redundancy jobs involve a failure to make full use of skills or expertise. There is also the more psychological and insufficiently recognized problem of the stigma attached to being made redundant and the resulting loss of a sense of personal worth.

1. The views expressed here are in the author's private capacity and do not necessarily represent those of the Office of Population Censuses and Surveys.
2. Ministry of Labour, *Official Guide to the Redundancy Payments Scheme*, HMSO, London, 1965, pp. 6–7.

6. Original article. Copyright © 1975 Holmes McDougall Ltd, Edinburgh. Stanley Parker is Principal Social Survey Officer, Office of Population Censuses and Surveys.

The size of the problem

The Redundancy Payments Act came into effect on 6 December 1965, as a result of official recognition that an individual should be compensated for the social and economic costs incurred as a consequence of his involuntary redundancy. The Act provided for a lump-sum payment, eligibility for which is based chiefly on age and length of service with the employer. Men under 65 and women under 60 are eligible, provided they have at least two years' continuous service. The amount of payment, up to a maximum of £1,200 is determined by age (service over 41 counts for more than when younger), length of service (a contribution for each year up to a maximum of 20) and level of earnings (earnings above £40 per week do not count towards the payment).

Since the inception of the Act, official figures have been published of the numbers of statutory redundancy payments made, including analyses by certain categories. The annual totals are shown in Table 1. It should be emphasized that these are *not* totals of all persons made redundant: they exclude those made redundant but who did not qualify for or obtain a statutory payment (see below).

Table 1   Statutory redundancy payments 1966–1974[3]

Year	Number of individuals	All employees (000's)	Redundancy as % of all employees	Index of redundancies as percentage of all employees 1966 = 100
1966	138,845	23,209	0.60	100
1967	249,782	22,799	1.10	183
1968	264,491	22,639	1.17	195
1969	250,764	22,564	1.11	185
1970	275,563	22,391	1.23	205
1971	370,306	21,961	1.69	282
1972	289,372	21,650	1.33	222
1973	170,172	22,180	0.77	128
1974	183,618	22,144	0.83	138

It will be seen that, compared with later years, 'paid' redundancies got off to a slow start in 1966. This was partly due to lack of knowledge by both workers and employers of the provisions of the Act. Subsequent fluctuations were to some extent influenced by the economic climate, although the relation between 'paid' redundancy figures, unemployment figures, and other measures of the state of the economy is not a clear one. A peak of 'paid' redundancies was reached in 1971, with a subsequent trough in 1973–4. Towards the end of 1974, however, there were signs that the worsening economic situation was producing a rate of redundancies substantially higher than that during the same period in the previous year.

Table 2 shows that many more men than women have been made redundant, though it must be remembered that there are roughly twice as many men as women in the labour force. Women tend to be employed more often in service

3. Source: Department of Employment.

industries which experience fewer redundancies, though the ratio of women to men made redundant has been rising in recent years. Proportionately more older workers have been made redundant: male workers aged 50–64 represent 32 per cent of the total male labour force aged 20+, but they accounted for 43 per cent of 'paid' redundancies in 1971, 45 per cent in 1972, 47 per cent in 1973 and 44 per cent in 1974. A similar pattern is evident among women up to the maximum 'redundancy' age of 60.

Table 2   Statutory redundancy payments, by age and sex 1971–74

	Men	%	1971 Women	%	Total	Men	%	1972 Women	%	Total
Under 40	103,710	35	27,217	36	130,927	79,199	35	20,984	35	100,183
40–49	64,626	22	22,006	29	86,632	47,370	20	18,258	29	65,628
50–59	72,891	24	25,726	35	98,617	56,570	25	21,383	36	77,953
60–64	56,549	19			56,549	45,608	20			45,608
Total	297,776	100	74,949	100	372,725	228,747	100	60,625	100	289,372
			1973					1974		
Under 40	41,978	32	12,800	34	54,778	50,490	35	14,623	36	65,113
40–49	27,789	21	11,189	29	38,978	30,297	21	11,587	28	41,884
50–59	34,985	27	14,484	37	49,469	36,752	26	14,475	36	51,227
60–64	26,947	20			26,947	25,395	18			25,395
Total	131,699	100	38,473	100	170,172	142,934	100	40,685	100	183,619

Redundancy occurs in all industries, but some have been harder hit than others and there are variations over time in the incidence of redundancy according to type of industry. In the peak year of 1971 the engineering industry accounted for 20 per cent of the 370,000 payments, though by 1974 this had fallen to 14 per cent. On the other hand, the proportion of all redundancies which occurred in white-collar industries has been rising: in 1971 redundancies in the distributive trades were less than 8 per cent of the total, but by 1974 they had risen to 10 per cent.

The figures discussed so far are those of workers who have qualified for and received a statutory redundancy payment. In addition a large but precisely unknown number of people have been made redundant but who did not qualify for or obtain a statutory payment, mostly because they had less than the required two years' service with their employer. An official enquiry in 1969 produced figures which suggested that in 1968 there were a *minimum* of half a million 'unpaid' redundancies, or roughly double the rate of 'paid' redundancies at that time.[4]

There is no way of telling whether the proportion of 'unpaid' to 'paid' redundancies has changed since the official survey was carried out, but there is no doubt that redundancy without statutory payment continues to affect large

4. S. R. Parker, G. C. Thomas, N. D. Ellis and W. McCarthy, *Effects of the Payments Redundancy Act*, HMSO, London, 1971, p. 146.

numbers of workers. 'Unpaid' redundancies mostly involve short-service employees and are associated with those industries, such as construction and shipbuilding, where the short-term nature of projects, leading to frequent changes of employer, is more or less accepted as a fact of industrial life.

The causes of redundancy

The most extensive information about causes of redundancy comes from the official survey quoted above. Managers in over 800 establishments which had experienced redundancy since the Act were asked what was the main cause of their most recent redundancy. Their answers were coded into a number of groups, which in turn were re-grouped into three main types of cause: economic, technological and organizational. The group into which a particular manager's answer fell was determined by his brief account of the redundancy situation in question, and the answer may not always have revealed the whole story of what led to a particular redundancy. Thus technological and organizational changes could themselves be caused by economic pressures. With this qualification, Table 3 shows that economic causes accounted for 53 per cent of the redundancies in the survey, technological causes for 20 per cent, and organizational change for 14 per cent (other causes accounted for up to 13 per cent).

Table 3   Cause of most recent redundancy[5]

	%	%
Fall in product demand/shortage of work	28	
Contract finished/temporary work	14	
Taxation/rising costs/financial difficulty/Government policy	11	
Total economic causes		53
Reorganized work methods	15	
Introduction of new plant/machinery	4	
Change in product	1	
Total technological causes		20
Reorganization by closure of parts of firm	8	
Merger/takeover	3	
Cutting down staff (cause unspecified)	2	
Firm/establishment moved	1	
Total organizational causes		14
Other answers		9
Not answered		4
Total		100
(% base, managers with post-Act redundancies)		(811)

It is not hard to see how each of the three main types of cause results in redundancy. Decline in product demand is the biggest single economic cause: it results in a decrease in revenue which forces a cut-back in expenditure on labour.

5. Source: Parker, et al., *Effects of the Redundancy Payments Act*, HMSO, London, 1971, p. 41.

It is clearly uneconomic to employ people when there is no work for them, though if the decline in demand is believed to be only temporary employees may be retained on full or reduced pay or 'laid off' without pay until demand revives. Also, employers who undertake a project of limited duration cannot always find a similar project on which to continue employing their workers.

Technological causes are chiefly reorganized work methods and the introduction of new plant or machinery. Such measures are frequently taken to cope with the external market situation but they may also involve upheaval in the work situation. The introduction of new plant or machinery quite often eliminates some jobs, though it may create jobs of other kinds. Even if retraining for a new job is offered by the employer, the worker may not agree to this. Workers may choose to be made redundant if the alternative work they may be offered is not suitable to them. Although the Act does not define 'suitable' work, and disputes are sometimes taken to a tribunal to settle, it is generally accepted that alternative work offered must be similar in skill, earnings and location to avoid liability for a redundancy payment.

Reorganization within the firm or other employing body can also lead to redundancy. The uneconomic parts of a business may be closed down or the business itself may cease operations (the official survey under-represented this cause of redundancy because it relied for interviews on contacting representatives of management, nearly all of whom were still in business). Mergers or takeovers usually aim at economies of scale and, while larger organizations often result in more bureaucracy and jobs at top administrative levels,[6] they also result in some redundancy of staff at middle and lower levels.

Research suggests that the cause of redundancy has a significant influence on the way in which it is handled by the employer. In the official survey causes were grouped as a result of factor analysis into 'situation and contingencies' (economic) and 'management action' (technological and organizational). The main contrast is between causes which are to a large extent outside the control of management, and those which are the consequences of deliberate management action. Redundancies caused by 'situation and contingencies' tended to occur in larger establishments in redundancy-prone industries with a low proportion of female workers and where trade unions were recognized. Redundancies caused by 'management action' were found to be associated with various attempts to minimize the harmful effects on employees, such as offering training to save redundancy, having the firm's own redundancy scheme, attempting to place redundant workers with other employers, and giving employees longer than the statutory notice of redundancy.

Alternatives to redundancy

The chief alternatives to redundancy are retraining and redeployment, and these can be implemented by both employing organizations and by state action. Whether retraining or redeployment is undertaken by an employing organization depends, to some extent, on how far in advance the decision to make people

6. John Child, 'Doublethink in our Organized Society', Inaugural Lecture, University of Aston, 2 May, 1974.

redundant is taken, which in turn relates to the cause of the redundancy (see the section above).

When technological or organizational change prompts the redundancy, there is more likely to be time to minimize the effects on workers by seeking to retrain or redeploy them. For example, this was the case with the redundancies resulting from the rationalization of British Rail, which were described by Wedderburn.[7] However, a sudden fall in product demand allows less time for remedial measures to be taken, as was evident in the account of redundancies caused by the cancellation of the guided missile contract with English Electric Aviation.[8]

Although industrial retraining may appear to the outsider to be one obvious solution to redundancy, it is not a course of action that has widespread appeal to workers facing redundancy. Nor are there sufficient retraining facilities available in the country to meet a greater demand. As Daniel[9] points out, formal retraining is an idea and activity that is alien to British working experience. The whole concept of undertaking full-time formal retraining for a completely new occupation is just not acceptable to most industrial workers. Retraining is seen as something abnormal, undertaken only by abnormal people who have something wrong with them.

There is some public provision for retraining redundant workers, but the consensus seems to be that the present facilities are woefully inadequate, given that retraining can be made a more acceptable proposition to the workers concerned. Government Training Centres retrain only a few thousand workers each year: for example, only four of the 2,664 workers displaced at AEI Woolwich underwent government retraining. This situation contrasts with the Swedish one, where retraining plays a large part in closures. There, with a working population one tenth of the UK, ten times as many people are undertaking government retraining.[10]

Redeployment without retraining depends on suitable jobs being available either locally or in another part of the country. If the alternative employment is not within daily travelling distance of home, it also depends on the willingness of workers to move to another part of the country to find or take up a new job. Again, there is survey evidence that moving to a new area does not appeal to more than a minority of redundant industrial workers. Although about half of the sample of non-redundant employees in the official survey said that, if the question of redundancy arose they would be prepared to move home to another area, to take up or look for a new job, the evidence from the survey of redundant workers suggests that a considerably smaller proportion actually do move after redundancy.[11] It is also relevant to note that more publicity of existing schemes may be helpful: in 1969 only 28 per cent of redundant workers claimed to know

7. D. Wedderburn, *Redundancy and the Railwaymen*, Department of Applied Economics, occasional paper no. 4, Cambridge, 1965.
8. D. Wedderburn, *White Collar Redundancy*, Cambridge University Press, Cambridge, 1964.
9. W. W. Daniel, *Strategies for Displaced Employees*, PEP, London, 1970.
10. *Ibid.*, pp. 47–8.
11. S. R. Parker, et al., *Effects of the Redundancy Payments Act*, HMSO, London, 1971, pp. 113–14, 117.

about the transfer schemes run by the Department of Employment for helping people when they have to move because of their jobs.

The handling of redundancy situations

The employer and the employee are both involved in a redundancy situation, in complementary but very different ways. As Catherine Smith[12] puts it,

> To an employer redundancy can be a necessary expedient to further rationalization programmes or to survive a period of economic downturn. To an employee it can be a personal blow from which he may never fully recover.

There are many things that employers can do to alleviate the adverse effects of redundancy on workers. The frequency with which employers took such action according to the survey of 1969, is shown in Table 4.

Table 4   Extent to which employers adopted specific practices regarding redundancies[18]

	%
Gave employees advance warning	77
Gave employees longer than statutory notice	61
Gave employees paid time off to attend interviews with other employers	60
Gave advance notice to the employment exchange	51
Made attempts to place employees with other employers	28
Provided facilities on the premises for employment exchange staff to register employees for other jobs	10
Had scheme for resettling or retraining employees	9
(% base, managers with post-Act redundancies)	(811)

Most employers were reasonably good about giving advance warning, time off for interviews, and so on. Relatively few of them, however, had schemes for resettling or retraining redundant employees, which backs up the criticism that more needs to be done in this direction. Also, it should be realized that giving employees advance warning and long notice of redundancy is not necessarily a good thing from their point of view: it may simply add to their feelings of insecurity.

Employers may make financial provision for redundant workers over and above what the Act requires them to pay, but the survey suggests that in 1969 relatively few of them did. Five per cent of employers had a private redundancy scheme, and 12 per cent made ex-gratia payments. Eight per cent of all employers interviewed claimed to have had a private redundancy scheme, i.e. including those who had not had to use the scheme.

The method by which employees are selected for redundancy is a possible

12. C. M. Smith, 'Redundancy Policies: A Survey of Current Practice in 350 Companies', *British Institute of Management*, 1974.
13. Adapted from S. R. Parker, et al., *Effects of the Redundancy Payments Act*, HMSO, London, 1971, p. 51, Table 2.17.

bone of contention. The main criteria used by employers, according to their own answers, were length of service (usually 'last in, first out'), efficiency at work and skill level. But two-thirds of employers said they made exceptions to their general rules, mostly to nullify the principle of 'last in, first out' by retaining exceptionally efficient, key and skilled workers.

Twenty-two per cent of 'paid' redundant workers said they had the chance of volunteering for redundancy, and the same proportion said their employer made them an offer in writing of alternative employment. Seventeen per cent thought their employer had acted unfairly concerning their redundancy, and many of these thought they were told too late about their redundancy. Very few of those who had the chance of volunteering for redundancy thought their employer had acted unfairly, which indicates that giving people some sense of control over an unpleasant event such as redundancy may help to soften their sense of resentment that it has to happen to them.

Attitudes to being made redundant

According to the official survey, most workers were upset when they were first told about their redundancy, but nearly a third said they didn't mind either way. In response to an open question about the problems that faced them as a result of being made redundant, only 3 per cent said spontaneously that they felt a sense of stigma or insecurity through being out of work. It is in this area that the sample survey seems to be an inadequate method of measuring the true extent of the psychological effects of redundancy. The subject is no doubt for many people a painful one, about which they are unlikely to wish to talk freely in response to standardized questions put by an interviewer. To understand the full impact of redundancy on people's self-image and sense of worth, we need to turn to some case studies which have given greater prominence to this question.

Daniel discusses what he calls the emotional impact of redundancy. Except perhaps for the toughest and most insensitive individuals, the involuntary severing of employment 'is at least a deep personal shock and can assume the proportions of a natural disaster in people's minds'.[14] People who are secure in their jobs, who have qualities and qualifications that are in demand and the personal skills and experience to exploit that demand, may fail to understand what a terrible blow redundancy often is to the industrial worker and indeed to other types of worker. They may not sufficiently appreciate that security is often the most prized characteristic of a job and that those made redundant may be ignorant of the opportunities that are open to them and unfamiliar with the process of job seeking and finding.

Redundancy creates insecurity, uncertainty and fear because it is something over which the individual has virtually no control and is inconsistent with his own experience and expectations, for all but those with the most casual attachment to their jobs. Daniel expands on this theme:

A man's job is not only his main or only source of income, but is also a

14. W. W. Daniel, *Strategies for Displaced Employees*, PEP, London, 1970, p. 8.

major source of identity, in the home, in the community, and in society generally. It is not surprising, given the economic, social and psychological value attached to jobs, that every major closure and redundancy tends to develop its own folklore or set of myths about the effects on people's lives; about people who were 'never the same men again'; who become bored, bitter and listless and who 'just went to pieces and died because he had nothing to live for', after the closures. Such myths do not have to be literally true, although they may well be so in some cases, to illustrate and demonstrate people's states of mind and the meaning that jobs have for them. [15]

When 1,500 men were made redundant in Liverpool after English Electric's merger with GEC one of them described the impact on himself and his mates. 'Some of the men were in tears . . . it isn't just the job or the money. That isn't what it's all about. It's one's life, you see. The men with me were like brothers to me.' [16] Commenting on the effect of redundancy on a man and his family, Anne Allen wrote, 'A man *is* his job. Take away his occupation and you chip away his identity. Take away his ability to keep his family and you diminish his man-hood. . . . It takes a lot of resilience to hang on to the knowledge that it is the system that is wrong, not you, when nobody wants to employ you.' [17]

The worst effects of redundancy are felt by those who are unable to get another job, perhaps for a long period, and, in the case of older men, redundancy sometimes becomes premature retirement. But even for the man who can walk into another job the day after he is made redundant there is a period of insecurity before he knows whether he can get another job equivalent in all main respects (pay, status, interest, skill, etc.) to the one he lost. Furthermore, there is often a mixture of helplessness and resentment because the change has been externally imposed rather than personally initiated.

Experience after redundancy

How much of a problem is it for redundant workers to get another job? How long do they take to do so? How does the new job compare in important respects with the one lost? To what extent does the lump-sum compensation payment help? Answers to these and similar questions were obtained in the official survey carried out in 1969. The detailed picture may have changed somewhat since then, but it has probably not changed in such a way as to invalidate the broad findings of the survey.

Five out of six 'paid' redundant workers eventually found other employment. Among 'unpaid' redundant workers, who tended to be younger and to work in more 'mobile' industries, the proportion was slightly higher. Age was the biggest single factor influencing success in finding another job: 97 per cent of those aged under 40 at the time of 'paid' redundancy succeeded in finding another job, but only 47 per cent of those aged 60–64. [18] Type of industry also made a big differ-

15. *Ibid.*, p. 9.
16. G. Sereny, 'The Lost Men of Industry', *Daily Telegraph Magazine*, 10 July, 1970.
17. A. Allen, *Sunday Mirror*, 11 July, 1971.
18. S. R. Parker, et al., *Effects of the Payments Redundancy Act*, HMSO, London, 1971, p. 89.

ence: 95 per cent of workers redundant in construction jobs found other work, but only 55 per cent in coal mining. The industrial variation affected the regional variation: from 94 per cent successful among those interviewed in the East and South to 71 per cent in the North.

The average time taken by redundant workers in the sample to start another job was 8 weeks, but this average hides considerable individual variations. Nearly half started another job within two weeks of being made redundant, but 18 per cent took more than three months. (The average time taken to start other jobs by those changing employment for reasons other than redundancy was four weeks.) Again, there were industrial and regional differences: ex-miners averaged 14 weeks, while workers in the East and South took only six weeks.

One of the main aims of making redundancy payments is that this is said to give workers longer to look around for the right job and reduce their chance of having to take an unsuitable stop-gap job. Although those who received higher redundancy payments did take longer to start a new job, part of the explanation is that both size of payment and difficulty of finding a job of any kind increase with age.

Table 5 Comparative occupational level after redundancy[19]

First job after redundancy	Senior mgrs.	Junior mgrs.	Prof. & tech. higher	lower	Clerical	Skilled	Semi-skilled	Unskilled
	%	%	%	%	%	%	%	%
Senior managers, &c	31	9	2	2	—	—	—	—
Junior managers, &c	15	25	—	—	—	1	—	1
Prof. & tech. higher	3	—	62	4	1	—	—	—
Prof. & tech. lower	1	2	—	70	3	1	1	—
Clerical & allied	15	7	10	10	84	1	2	5
Skilled manual	5	5	—	6	1	74	8	4
Semi-skilled manual	1	5	—	2	1	6	42	12
Unskilled manual	18	33	10	6	8	13	42	74
Self-employed	8	11	14	—	2	4	3	3
Not answered	3	3	2	—	—	—	2	1
Total	100	100	100	100	100	100	100	100
(% base, who found a post-redundancy job)	(78)	(55)	(42)	(50)	(157)	(458)	(245)	(470)

A serious problem facing many redundant workers is how to find another job at the same skill or occupational level. Table 5 shows that many of them fail to solve this problem and accept a job at a lower skill or occupational level. About two-fifths of redundant semi-skilled workers moved to unskilled jobs, and even after a second or subsequent change many of them continued to have unskilled jobs. A particularly notable feature of the findings on this question is that relatively few redundant managers obtained post-redundancy employment

19. Source: Parker, et al., *Effects of the Payments Redundancy Act*, HMSO, London, 1971, p. 100, Table 3.38.

at the same occupational level, and many of them took unskilled manual jobs. Skilled workers seemed to suffer least in this respect: if they had to take a less skilled job after redundancy they often succeeded in getting back to a skilled job after their second or subsequent change.

In 1969 job changing after redundancy did not, according to the survey, generally increase earnings. Whereas non-redundant job changers made an average gain of over £2 a week, redundant job changers averaged a slight loss. Pension rights and fringe benefits were more often lost than gained by redundant workers. In line with the often lower skill level of their post-redundancy job, only 15 per cent felt that they used more skill than previously, while 50 per cent felt that they used less skill. Losses in job satisfaction after redundancy outnumbered gains by about three to one. Perhaps the clearest summary indication of the uncompensated loss was the fact that 51 per cent of workers interviewed would have preferred to have kept their old job and not to have had the redundancy money. Only 36 per cent preferred their present job.

Conclusion: alleviating the problem

Besides the Redundancy Payments Act certain other government provisions have been made to help the redundant worker. The Contracts of Employment Act, passed in 1963 and amended in 1972, gives workers the legal right to a minimum notice of dismissal, increasing with length of service. Many workers use their redundancy payment to meet their living expenses while unemployed, and this is supplemented by the earnings-related unemployment benefits introduced in 1966. Of less direct benefit to workers are the provisions of the 1964 Industrial Training Act, the main objectives of which were to see that an adequate amount of training is provided, to improve its quality, and spread the costs of training fairly across each industry.

It is reasonable to ask whether everything is being done that can be done to avoid redundancy and to mitigate its worst effects on workers when it cannot be avoided. On the first question, views about whether redundancy is avoidable are related to what is seen as its cause. Thus although about half of the trade-union officers in the official survey thought that redundancy among their members was to some extent avoidable, they more often thought this in relation to redundancies caused by takeovers and the ending of contracts and less often in relation to those caused by fall in product demand. Trade-union officers appeared more willing to accept that employers sometimes cannot avoid redundancies caused by external factors, and their main opposition was to redundancies which they believed it was within the employer's power to avoid by prudent planning.

The Redundancy Payments Act remains the main piece of legislation which has aimed at alleviating the problem of redundancy. Its economic objectives were to allow managements greater flexibility in their manpower policies and to encourage the movement of labour into industries where it was most needed. Its main social objectives was to compensate workers for the loss of their jobs in order to make mobility more acceptable to them. In the introduction and interpretation of the official survey report, the authors claim that 'the findings of this survey indicate that the Act has broadly achieved its objectives in both the economic and social spheres.[20] Daniel, however, disagrees with this conclusion, and he believes that 'redundancy payments are playing what little part they can (in national manpower policies) but that this is very little and we need much more besides.'[21] While the proportion of money spent on redundancy payments in relation to that spent on Government retraining has probably changed in favour of the latter since 1971, it is still no doubt true that more comprehensive manpower policies are needed to encourage constructive alternatives to redundancy.

20. N. D. Ellis and W. E. J. McCarthy in S. R. Parker, et al., *Effects of the Payments Redundancy Act*, HMSO, London, 1971, p. 21.
21. W. W. Daniel, 'Shake Up for the Shake Out', *Guardian*, 19 November, 1971.

SECTION TWO
OCCUPATIONAL STRUCTURE AND PLACEMENT

INTRODUCTION   Mary-Anne Speakman

As the articles in the first section of this Reader have shown, to understand work activities and experiences it is necessary to understand the nature of the society within which those activities and experiences occur. This section of the Reader attempts to provide a framework within which the kinds of work that people are engaged in and the meaning that that work has for people can be located. It is concerned with the occupational structure at a societal level and changes in the distribution of and necessity for different types of work over time in Western capitalist societies. One issue arising from a discussion of occupational structure is that of placement—how do individuals come to choose and enter a particular type of employment from the potential range of options? The latter two articles discuss this question from a perspective definitely within the class framework posed in Section I, arguing that occupational placement is determined by the individual's position within a stratified society.

The first article by Bell summarizes some of the changes that have occurred in the occupational structure of the USA since the 19th Century—an historical pattern fairly typical of other Western countries. He documents with supporting empirical evidence the decline of the agricultural workforce and the concomitant rise of blue-collar labour and the urbanization of work locations with the movement towards a consumer-manufacturing oriented economy. This has been followed by a decrease in the proportion of workers engaged directly in production, but an increase in white-collar manpower, especially in the tertiary sector of service trades and in the professional and technical categories. Bell describes present society as the 'post-industrial society'—one based on services rather than on direct production. 'If an industrial society is defined by the quantity of goods as marking a standard of living, the post-industrial society is defined by the quality of life as measured by the services and amenities . . . which are now deemed desirable and possible for everyone.' (p. 104) Such changes in the distribution of occupations reflect not only changes in the dominant requirements of society but also 'to the extent that occupation determines other modes of behaviour . . . it is a revolution in the class structure of society as well'. (p. 103) The historic shifts in the profile of the occupational structure have, in this connection, posed problems for the trade-union movement and Bell goes on to delineate some of these problems and suggests that issues of conflict within the labour field may become more rancorous within a post-industrial economy but not necessarily along class-based divisions.

One area that has received the attention of researchers concerned with the occupational structures of societies is that of the overall supply of labour, and the article by Braham is an example of a particular case study of immigrant labour in Western Europe. One solution to a weak or negative growth of the labour force is to introduce foreign manpower into the economy. In many countries, post-war expansion has encouraged indigenous workers to move into work offering better conditions and payment and this has led to the recruitment of immigrant labour to perform the less desirable, low-wage jobs. In some cases, as in Britain, this has resulted in the existence of a permanent, easily identifiable group of immigrant workers, though the situation may be one of more temporary migration, for 'immigrant workers are prized most of all for their mobility; they can be recruited in time of labour shortage, then encouraged to return home when no longer needed.' (p. 125) The introduction of immigrant labour is of interest in several respects: the opportunities available to immigrants offer a measure of the openness of the occupational structure and the presence of immigrants may also result in increased opportunities for the upward mobility of indigenous workers. Thus the recruitment of an immigrant labour force can have a widespread effect on the social job structure which results in it being even more difficult to solve the original problem of a labour shortage without an even more fundamental change in the distribution of rewards.

The third article turns to the issue of occupational choice and placement and is largely a critique of the developmental psychologistic theories postulated by such writers as Ginzberg and Super. These theories propose that occupational choice and subsequent entry into the labour force is arrived at via a series of stages throughout which an individual's ambitions, abilities and aptitudes come to match his self-concept so that the work chosen will provide the maximum degree of self-actualization and fulfilment. Examining the evidence from studies in the transition-to-work field, Roberts argues that this emphasis of 'free-choice' is misplaced as the structural conditions of a class society largely determine the nature of work likely to be entered by different social groups. The ascriptive nature of the family, followed by a stratified educational system with its differing opportunities for certification leads to different 'opportunity structures' for individuals in different social strata so that a matching of self-concept and ambition with work is an unlikely event for most adolescents. Such a situation has implications for the effectiveness of the careers-guidance service which has tended to adopt the developmental theories as its professional ideology and Roberts concludes his article with recommendations relating to the practical requirements of the careers-guidance clients.

The final article adds support to the view that choice of work is strongly influenced, even determined, by the individual adolescent's position within society, and particularly within the educational system. Ashton argues that 'in the course of their passage through the school, young people acquire different frames of reference that direct them toward different types of occupation'. At different points in their school and work careers, individuals make a series of side-bets that function to commit them to different categories of work: unskilled, skilled, white-collar, etc. The results of school experience can in fact be seen as functional in preparing adolescents for work in a class-stratified alienated society. Most individuals experience a fairly non-traumatic transition from the world of education to that of work: the values, attitudes and affective capacities that are inculcated through the educative process equip individuals to 'fit into' a class society and to recreate, generation by generation, the unequal nature of that society.

7. THE COMING OF POST-INDUSTRIAL SOCIETY Daniel Bell

In *The Communist Manifesto*, which was completed in February 1848, Marx and Engels envisaged a society in which there would be only two classes, capitalist and worker—the few who owned the means of production and the many who lived by selling their labor power—as the last two great antagonistic classes of social history, locked in final conflict. In many ways this was a remarkable prediction, if only because at that time the vast majority of persons in Europe and the United States were neither capitalist nor worker but farmer and peasant, and the tenor of life in these countries was overwhelmingly agrarian and artisan. . . .

Marx's vision of the inexorable rise of industrial society was thus a bold one. But the most important social change in Western society of the last hundred years has been not simply the diffusion of industrial work but the concomitant disappearance of the farmer—and in a Ricardian world of diminishing returns in land, the idea that agricultural productivity would be two or three times that of industry (which it has been in the United States for the last thirty years) was completely undreamed of. . . .

Yet if one takes the industrial worker as the instrument of the future, or, more specifically, the factory worker as the symbol of the proletariat, then this vision is warped. For the paradoxical fact is that as one goes along the trajectory of industrialization—the increasing replacement of men by machines—one comes logically to the erosion of the industrial worker himself. In fact, by the end of the century the proportion of factory workers in the labor force may be as small as the proportion of farmers today; indeed, the entire area of blue-collar work may have diminished so greatly that the term will lose its sociological meaning as new categories, more appropriate to the divisions of the new labor force, are established. Instead of the industrial worker, we see the dominance of the professional and technical class in the labor force—so much so that by 1980 it will be the second largest occupational group in the society, and by the end of the century the largest. This is the new dual revolution taking place in the structure of occupations and, to the extent that occupation determines other modes of behavior (but this, too, is diminishing), it is a revolution in the class structure of society as well. This change in the character of production and of occupations is one aspect of the emergence of the 'post-industrial' society. . . .

---

7. Reprinted from *The Coming of Post-Industrial Society: A Venture in Social Forecasting* by Daniel Bell by permission of Heinemann Educational Books Ltd, London. Copyright © 1974. (pp. 123-64)

Industrial societies—principally those around the North Atlantic littoral plus the Soviet Union and Japan—are goods-producing societies. Life is a game against fabricated nature. The world has become technical and rationalized. The machine predominates, and the rhythms of life are mechanically paced: time is chronological, methodical, evenly spaced. Energy has replaced raw muscle and provides the power that is the basis of productivity—the art of making more with less—and is responsible for the mass output of goods which characterizes industrial society. Energy and machines transform the nature of work. Skills are broken down into simpler components, and the artisan of the past is replaced by two new figures —the engineer, who is responsible for the layout and flow of work, and the semi-skilled worker, the human cog between machines—until the technical ingenuity of the engineer creates a new machine which replaces him as well. It is a world of coordination in which men, materials, and markets are dovetailed for the production and distribution of goods. It is a world of scheduling and programming in which the components of goods are brought together at the right time and in the right proportions so as to speed the flow of goods. It is a world of organization—of hierarchy and bureaucracy—in which men are treated as 'things' because one can more easily coordinate things than men. Thus a necessary distinction is introduced between the role and the person, and this is formalized on the organization chart of the enterprise. Organizations deal with the requirements of roles, not persons. The criterion of *techne* is efficiency, and the mode of life is modeled on economics: how does one extract the greatest amount of energy from a given unit of embedded nature (coal, oil, gas, water power) with the best machine at what comparative price? The watchwords are maximization and optimization, in a cosmology derived from utility and the felicific calculus of Jeremy Bentham. The unit is the individual, and the free society is the sum total of individual decisions as aggregated by the demands registered, eventually, in a market. In actual fact, life is never as 'one-dimensional' as those who convert every tendency into an ontological absolute make it out to be. Traditional elements remain. Work groups intervene to impose their own rhythms and 'bogeys' (or output restrictions) when they can. Waste runs high. Particularism and politics abound. These soften the unrelenting quality of industrial life. Yet the essential, technical features remain.

A post-industrial society is based on services. Hence, it is a game between persons. What counts is not raw muscle power, or energy, but information. The central person is the professional, for he is equipped, by his education and training, to provide the kinds of skill which are increasingly demanded in the post-industrial society. If an industrial society is defined by the quantity of goods as marking a standard of living, the post-industrial society is defined by the quality of life as measured by the services and amenities—health, education, recreation, and the arts—which are now deemed desirable and possible for everyone.

The word 'services' disguises different things, and in the transformation of industrial to post-industrial society there are several different stages. First, in the very development of industry there is a necessary expansion of transportation and of public utilities as auxiliary services in the movement of goods and the increasing use of energy, and an increase in the non-manufacturing but still blue-collar force. Second, in the mass consumption of goods and the growth of populations there is an increase in distribution (wholesale and retail), and finance,

real estate, and insurance, the traditional centers of white-collar employment ·
Third, as national incomes rise, one finds, as in the theorem of Christian Engel, a
German statistician of the latter half of the nineteenth century, that the proportion of money devoted to food at home begins to drop, and the marginal
increments are used first for durables (clothing, housing, automobiles) and then
for luxury items, recreation, and the like. Thus, a third sector, that of personal
services, begins to grow: restaurants, hotels, auto services, travel, entertainment,
sports, as people's horizons expand and new wants and tastes develop. But here a
new consciousness begins to intervene. The claims to the good life which the
society has promised become centered on the two areas that are fundamental to
that life—health and education. The elimination of disease and the increasing
numbers of people who can live out a full life, plus the efforts to expand the span
of life, make health services a crucial feature of modern society; and the growth
of technical requirements and professional skills makes education, and access to
higher education, the condition of entry into the post-industrial society itself.
So we have here the growth of a new intelligentsia, particularly of teachers.
Finally, the claims for more services and the inadequacy of the market in meeting
people's needs for a decent environment as well as better health and education
lead to the growth of government, particularly at the state and local level, where
such needs have to be met.

The post-industrial society, thus, is also a 'communal' society in which the
social unit is the community rather than the individual, and one has to achieve a
'social decision' as against, simply, the sum total of individual decisions which,
when aggregated, end up as nightmares, on the model of the individual automobile and collective traffic congestion. But cooperation between men is more
difficult than the management of things. Participation becomes a condition of
community, but when many different groups want too many different things and
are not prepared for bargaining or trade-off, then increased conflict or deadlocks
result. Either there is a politics of consensus or a politics of stymie.

As a game between persons, social life becomes more difficult because
political claims and social rights multiply, the rapidity of social change and
shifting cultural fashion bewilders the old, and the orientation to the future
erodes the traditional guides and moralities of the past. Information becomes a
central resource, and within organizations a source of power. Professionalism
thus becomes a criterion of position, but it clashes, too, with the populism which
is generated by the claims for more rights and greater participation in the society.
If the struggle between capitalist and worker, in the locus of the factory, was the
hallmark of industrial society, the clash between the professional and the
populace, in the organization and in the community, is the hallmark of conflict in
the post-industrial society.

This, then, is the sociological canvas of the scheme of social development
leading to the post-industrial society. To identify its structural lineaments and
trend lines more directly, let me turn now to the distribution of jobs by economic
sector and the changing profile of occupations in the American economy.

The sectors of work and occupations

Shortly after the turn of the century, only three in every ten workers in the

Daniel Bell

country were employed in service industries and seven out of ten were engaged in the production of goods. By 1950, these proportions were more evenly balanced. By 1968, the proportions had shifted so that six out of every ten were in services. By 1980, with the rising predominance of services, close to seven in every ten workers will be in the service industries. (See Tables 1, 2 and 3.) Between 1900 and 1980, in exact reversal of the proportions between the sectors, there occurred two structural changes in the American economy, one, the shift to services, and two, the rise of the public sector as a major area of employment.

Table 1   Sector distribution of employment by goods and services, 1870–1940 (in thousands)

	1870	1900	1920	1940
Total	12,900	29,000	41,600	49,860
Goods-producing total	10,630	19,620	23,600	25,610
Agriculture, forestry, and fishing	7,450	10,900	11,400	9,100
Manufacturing	2,250	6,300	10,800	11,900
Mining	180	760	1,230	1,100
Construction	750	1,660	2,170	3,510
Service-producing total	2,990	9,020	15,490	24,250
Trade, finance, and real estate	830	2,760	4,800	8,700
Transportation and utilities	640	2,100	4,190	4,150
Professional service	230	1,150	2,250	4,000
Domestic and personal service	1,190	2,710	3,330	5,710
Government (Not elsewhere classified)	100	300	920	1,690

Source: Adapted from *Historical Statistics of the United States: 1820–1940*, series D57–71, p. 74.
Note: The totals do not always add up because of small numbers not allocated, and rounding of figures.

In historic fact, the shift of employment to services does not represent any sudden departure from previous long-run trends. As Victor Fuchs[1] points out, 'For as long as we have records on the industrial distribution of the labor force, we find a secular tendency for the percentage accounted for by the Service sector to rise'. From 1870 to 1920, the shift to services could be explained almost entirely by the movement from agricultural to industrial pursuits; employment in services rose as rapidly as industry and the major increases in services were in the *auxiliary* areas of transportation, utilities, and distribution. This was the historic period of industrialization in American life. After 1920, however, the rates of growth in the non-agricultural sector began to diverge. Industrial employment still increased numerically, but already its *share* of total employment tended to decline, as employment in services began to grow at a faster rate, and from 1968 to 1980, if we take manufacturing as the key to the industrial sector, the growth rate will be less than half of the labor force as a whole.

1. V. Fuchs, *The Service Economy*, National Bureau of Economic Research, New York, 1968, p. 22.

The great divide began in 1947, after World War II. At that time the employment was evenly balanced. But from then on the growth rates began to diverge in new, accelerated fashion. From 1947 to 1968 there was a growth of about 60 per cent in employment in services, while employment in the goods-producing industries increased less than 10 per cent. Despite a steadily rising total output of goods through the 1970s, this tendency will persist. Altogether, the goods-producing industries employed 29 million workers in 1968, and the number is expected to increase to 31.6 million by 1980. However, their share in total employment will drop to less than 32 per cent in 1980, from about 36 per cent in 1968.[2]

Table 2   Sector distribution of employment by goods and services, 1947–68.
Projected to 1980 (in thousands)

	1947	1968	1980	Percentage change 1947–68	1968–80
Total	51,770	80,780	99,600	56	23
Goods-producing total	26,370	28,975	31,600	9.8	9
Agriculture, forestry, and fisheries	7,890	4,150	3,180	(−48)	(−23)
Mining	955	640	590	(−33)	(−9)
Construction	1.980	4,050	5,480	10	35
Manufacturing	15,540	20,125	22,358	29	11
Durable	8,385	11,850	13,275	41	12
Non-durable	7,160	8,270	9,100	15.5	10
Service-producing total	25,400	51,800	67,980	104	31
Transportation and utilities	4,160	4,500	5,000	8	10
Trade (Wholesale and retail)	8,950	16,600	20,500	85.5	23
Finance, insurance, and real estate	1,750	3,725	4,640	113	24
Services (Personal, professional, business)	5.050	15,000	21,000	135	40
Government	5,470	11,850	16,800	117	42
Federal	1,890	2,735	3,000	45	10
State and local	3,580	9,110	13,800	150	52

Source: The US Economy in 1980, Bureau of Labor Statistics Bulletin 1673 (1970). The data for 1968 and 1980 are from Table A–16, p. 49. The figures for 1947 are adapted from chart data in Bulletin 1673 by Lawrence B. Krause.
Note: The figures for 1980 assume a 3 per cent unemployment. At a 4 per cent unemployment, there would be a drop in the labor force of one million (i.e. from 99,600 to 98,600), and this loss is distributed between goods-producing (31,600 to 31,000) and service-producing (67,980 to 67,300) employment.
Figures are not always exact because of rounding.¶

Within the goods-producing sector, employment in agriculture and mining will continue to decline in absolute terms. The major change—and the impetus to new jobs in that sector—will come in construction. The national housing goals for the 1968–78 decade call for the building of 20 million new housing units in the private market and 6 million new and rehabilitated units through public subsidy. These goals are now finally being met, and it is expected that employment in construction will rise by 35 per cent in this decade.

Manufacturing is still the single largest source of jobs in the economy. It grew at 0.9 per cent a year during the 1960s largely because of increased employ-

2. All statistical data in this section are from The U.S. Economy in 1980, U.S. Department of Labor Bulletin 1673 (1970).

Daniel Bell

ment in defense industries—aircraft, missiles, ordnance, communications equipment and the like—which have higher labor components because the work is more 'custom-crafted' than in mass production industries. But the shift away from defense spending—with its consequent unemployment in aircraft, missiles, and communications—means a slower rate of growth for manufacturing in the future. Any increase will appear largely in the manufacture of building materials for housing construction.

To return to the larger picture, the most important growth area in employment since 1947 has been government. One out of every six American workers today is employed by one of the 80,000 or so entities which make up the government of the United States today. In 1929, three million persons worked for the government, or about 6.4 per cent of the labor force. Today, twelve million persons work for the government—about 16 per cent of the labor force. By 1980 that figure will rise to seventeen million, or 17 per cent of the labor force.

Government to most people signifies the federal government. But state and local agencies actually account for eight out of every ten workers employed by the government. The major reason has been the expansion of schooling both in numbers of children and in the amount of schooling and thus of the number of teachers employed. Today about 85 per cent of all pupils complete high school as against 33 per cent in 1947. Educational services have been the area of fastest growth in the country and comprised 50 per cent of state and local governmental activities in 1968 (as measured by employment).

Table 3   Sector distribution of employment by goods and services projected to 1980. Distribution by percentages.

	1947	1968	1980
Total	100	100	100
Goods-producing total	51	35.9	31.7
Agriculture, forestry, and fisheries	15.0	5.1	3.2
Mining	2.1	0.8	0.6
Construction	3.9	5.0	5.5
Manufacturing	30.0	24.9	22.4
Durable	16.0	14.7	13.3
Non-durable	14.0	10.2	9.1
Service-producing total	49	64.1	68.4
Transportation and utilities	8.0	5.5	5.0
Trade (Wholesale and retail)	17.0	20.5	20.6
Finance, insurance, real estate	3.0	4.6	4.7
Services (Personal, professional, business)	10.0	18.6	21.2
Government	11.0	14.6	16.9
Federal	3.5	3.3	3.0
State and local	7.5	11.2	13.9

Source: The US Economy in 1980, Bureau of Labor Statistics Bulletin 1673 (1970); conversion of figures into percentages.

General services were the second fastest growth area for employment between 1947 and 1968, and about 10 per cent of employment in general services is in private educational institutions. Thus education as a whole, both public and private, represented 8 per cent of total employment in the United States. Within general services, the largest category is medical services, where employment rose from 1.4 million in 1958 to 2.6 million a decade later.

The spread of services, particularly in trade, finance, education, health, and government, conjures up the picture of a white-collar society. But all services are not white collar, since they include transportation workers and auto repairmen. But then, not all manufacturing is blue-collar work. In 1970 the white-collar component *within* manufacturing—professional, managerial, clerical, and sales—came to almost 31 per cent of that work force, while 69 per cent were blue-collar workers (6,055,000 white-collar and 13,400,000 blue-collar). By 1975 the white-collar component will reach 34.5 per cent. Within the blue-collar force itself there has been a steady and distinct shift from direct production to non-production jobs as more and more work becomes automated and in the factory, workers increasingly are employed in machine-tending, repair, and maintenance, rather than on the assembly line.

Table 4   Percentage distribution by major occupation group, 1900–1960

Major occupation group	1900	1910	1920	1930	1940	1950	1960
Total	100.0	100.0	100.0	100.0	100.0	100.0	100.0
White-collar workers	17.6	21.3	24.9	29.4	31.1	36.6	42.0
Professional and technical	4.3	4.7	5.4	6.8	7.5	8.6	10.8
Managers, officials and proprietors	5.8	6.6	6.6	7.4	7.3	8.7	10.2
Clerical and kindred	3.0	5.3	8.0	8.9	9.6	12.3	14.5
Sales workers	4.5	4.7	4.9	6.3	6.7	7.0	6.5
Manual workers	35.8	38.2	40.2	39.6	39.8	41.1	37.5
Craftsmen and foremen	10.5	11.6	13.0	12.8	12.0	14.1	12.9
Operatives	12.8	14.6	15.6	15.8	18.4	20.4	18.6
Laborers, except farm and mine	12.5	12.0	11.6	11.0	9.4	6.6	6.0
Service workers	9.0	9.6	7.8	9.8	11.7	10.5	12.6
Private household workers	5.4	5.0	3.3	4.1	4.7	2.6	3.3
Service, except private household	3.6	4.6	4.5	5.7	7.1	7.9	9.3
Farm workers	37.5	30.9	27.0	21.2	17.4	11.8	7.9
Farmers and farm managers	19.9	16.5	15.3	12.4	10.4	7.4	4.0
Farm laborers and foremen	17.7	14.4	11.7	8.8	7.0	4.4	3.9

Source: Computed from Historical Statistics of the United States.
Note: Percentages may not add to 100 because of rounding.

In 1980 the total manufacturing labor force will number about 22 million, or 22 per cent of the labor force at that time. But with the continuing spread of major technological developments such as numerical-control machine tools, electronic computers, instrumentation and automatic controls, the proportion of direct production workers is expected to go down steadily. Richard Bellmann, the Rand mathematician, has often been quoted as predicting that by the year 2000 only 2 per cent of the labor force will be required to turn out all necessary manufactured goods, but the figure is fanciful and inherently unprovable. Automation is a real fact, but the bogey of an accelerated pace has not materialized.[3] But even a steady advance of 2 to 3 per cent in productivity a year, manageable though it may be economically and socially (people are usually not fired, but jobs are eliminated through attrition), inevitably takes its toll. What is clear is that if an industrial society is defined as a goods-producing society—if manufacture is central in shaping the character of its labor force—then the United States is no longer an industrial society.

The changeover to a post-industrial society is signified not only by the change in sector distribution—the places *where* people work—but in the pattern of occupations, the *kind* of work they do. And here the story is a familiar one. The United States has become a white-collar society. From a total of about 5.5 million persons in 1900 (making up about 17.6 per cent of the labor force), the white-collar group by 1968 came to 35.6 million (46.7 per cent) and will rise to 48.3 million in 1980, when it will account for *half* (50.8 per cent) of all employed workers. (See Tables 4 and 5.)

Since 1920, the white-collar group has been the fastest-growing occupational group in the society, and this will continue. In 1956, for the first time, this group surpassed the employment of blue-collar workers. By 1980 the ratio will be about 5:3 in favor of the white-collar workers.

Stated in these terms, the change is dramatic, yet somewhat deceptive, for until recently the overwhelming number of white-collar workers have been women in minor clerical or sales jobs; and in American society, as in most others, family status is still evaluated on the basis of the man's job. But it is at this point—in the changing nature of the male labor force—that a status upheaval has been

Table 5   Occupational distribution by numbers and percentage, 1968 (Actual)—1980 (Projected)

Occupational Group	1968		1980	
	Numbers (Thousands)	Per-centage	Numbers (Thousands)	Per-centage
Total	76,000	100	95,000	100
White-collar workers	35,600	46.7	48,300	50.8
Professional and technical	10,300	13.6	15,500	16.3
Managers and officials	7,800	10	9,500	10
Clerical	12,800	16.9	17,300	18.2
Sales	4,600	6	6,000	6
Blue-collar workers	27,500	36.3	31,100	32.7
Craftsmen and foremen	10,000	13.1	12,200	12.8
Operatives	14,000	18.4	15,400	16.2
Laborers	3,500	4.7	3,500	3.7
Service workers	9,400	12.4	13,100	13.8
Farm workers	3,500	4.6	2,600	2.7

Source: Figures computed from US Department of Labor Bulletin 1673.
Note: Percentages may not add to 100 because of rounding.

3. D. Bell, 'The Bogey of Automation', *New York Review of Books*, 26 April, 1965.

taking place. In 1900 only 15 per cent of American men wore white collars (and most of these were independent small businessmen). By 1940 the figure had gone up to 25 per cent (and these were largely in administrative jobs). In 1970 almost 42 per cent of the male labor force—some twenty million men—held white-collar jobs (as against twenty-three million who wore blue collars), and of these, almost fourteen million were managerial, professional, or technical—the heart of the upper middle class in the United States.

The total blue-collar occupations, which numbered about 12 million in 1900, rose to 27.5 million in 1968 and will rise at a slower rate to 31.1 million in 1980. In 1900, the blue-collar workers formed about 35 per cent of the total labor force, a figure which reached 40 per cent in 1920 and again, after World War II, in 1950, but by 1968 it was down to about 36.3 per cent of the total labor force and by 1980 will reach an historic low of 32.7 per cent.

The most striking change, of course, has been in the farm population. In 1900 farming was still the single largest occupation in the United States, comprising 12.5 million workers and about 37.5 per cent of the labor force. Until about 1930, the absolute number of farmers and farm workers continued to rise though their share of employment began to decline. In 1940, because of the extraordinary agricultural revolution, which shot productivity to spectacular heights, the number of farm laborers began its rapid decline. In 1968, employment on the farms numbered 3.5 million, and this will decline to 2.6 million in 1980; from 4.6 per cent of the work force in 1968 it will fall to 2.7 per cent in 1980.

The service occupations continue to expand steadily. In 1900 there were about three million persons in services, more than half of whom were domestics. In 1968, there were almost 9.5 million persons in services, only a fourth of whom were domestics. The major rises were in such occupations as garage workers, hotel and restaurant workers, and the like. Through the 1970s, service occupations will increase by two-fifths or a rate one and one-half times the expansion for all occupations combined.

The category of semi-skilled worker (called operatives in the census classification) from 1920 on was the single largest occupational category in the economy, comprising more workers than any other group. Semi-skilled work is the occupational counterpart of mass production, and it rose with the increased output of goods. But the introduction of sophisticated new technologies has slowed the growth of this group drastically. Total employment will rise from 14 million in 1968 to 15.4 million in 1980, but the rate of increase is half the increase projected for all employment.

As a share of total employment, the percentage of semi-skilled will slide downward from 18.4 per cent in 1968 to 16.2 per cent in 1980 and will at that time be *third* in size ranking, outpaced by clerical, which will be the largest, and by professional and technical workers. Equally, the proportion of factory workers among the semi-skilled will probably drop. In 1968, six out of every ten semi-skilled workers were employed as factory operatives. Large numbers of them now work as inspectors, maintenance men, operators of material-moving equipment such as powered forklift trucks, and the like. Among the non-factory operatives, drivers of trucks, buses, and taxi-cabs make up the largest group.

The central occupational category in the society today is the professional and technical. Growth in this category has outdistanced all other major occupational groups in recent decades. From less than a million in 1890, the number of these workers has grown to 10.3 million in 1968. Within this category, the largest group was teachers (more than 2 million), the second largest professional health workers (about 2 million), scientists and engineers (about 1.4 million), and engineering and science technicians (about 900,000). Despite the momentary slowdown in the demand for education, and the immediate unemployment in engineering because of the shift away from defense work in 1970–71, requirements in this category continue to lead all others, increasing half again in size (about twice the employment increase among all occupations combined) between 1968 and 1980. With 15.5 million workers in 1980, this will comprise 16.3 per cent of total employment as against 13.6 per cent in 1968. (For a graphic representation of the changes in the occupational categories, see Figure 1.)

Figure 1   Employment trends among major occupational categories,[a] 1947–1968 (actual) and 1980 (projected for a services economy with 3 per cent unemployment).

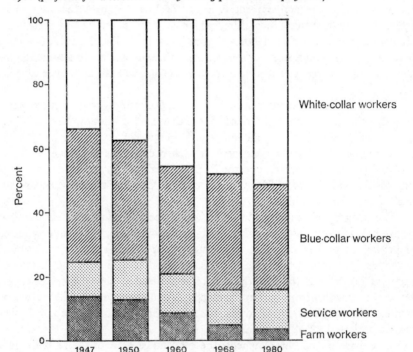

[a] Farm workers include farm managers.

These historic shifts pose a serious problem for the trade-union movement, which in the United States has historically been a blue-collar phenomenon. On the record, the trade-union movement (AFL–CIO plus the major independents) is stronger than it has ever been since the beginning of mass organizing in 1935. In 1970, the total American membership rose to 19,381,000, its all-time high. In the 1960s it gained 2,300,000 members, though the major increase . . . came in the mid-years and the gains of the last two years were only half those of the major period of increase from 1964–66.

Yet this is a superficial way of looking at the problem, for the extraordinary fact is that, as a percentage of the total labor force, the number of members today is *exactly the same* as in 1947; and as a percentage of workers in non-agricultural establishments, the sector where most members are found and most organizing efforts are made, the percentage of union members is *less today* than in 1947. In effect, trade unionism in the United States has made no real advance in nearly quarter of a century. . . .

After the Wagner Act was passed in 1935 and until the end of World War II, union membership made a four-fold gain. In subsequent years, the membership became stabilized. In 1953–54, I wrote a series of studies for *Fortune*[4] and else-where[5] predicting that the labor movement would stop growing, and describing the kind of plateau it would reach. My reasoning was based on the argument that unionism had come to the saturation point in manufacturing and construction simply because it had organized almost all the major employers, and it was too costly to tackle the small units of under a hundred that remained unorganized. There would be an expansion in the distributive trades (teamsters, retail clerks) since these were expanding areas of the labor force, but such gains would be offset by declines in railroad and mining. The unions had shown themselves incapable of organizing the white-collar and technical workers, the only major area for union growth was government employment and this depended on favorable government support.

Union growth in the United States has always been dependent on favorable government support. While it is clear that the upsurge of unionism in the 1930s was indigenous, its *institutionalization* was possible only under the umbrella of the National Labor Relations Board. The union gains could later be consolidated only when the War Labor Board virtually enacted union-shop clauses in collective-bargaining contracts during World War II.

The only real growth in American trade unionism in the last decade has been among government workers, and here the same forces have been at work. In January 1962, President Kennedy issued Executive Order 10988, which encouraged unionism in the federal service. This order gave clear and unequivocal support to public unionism, just as the Wagner Act of 1935 had supported unions and collective bargaining in private business. It declared that 'the efficient administration of the government and the well-being of employees require that orderly and constructive relationships be maintained between employee organizations and management.' In New York City, earlier executive orders by Mayor Robert F. Wagner resulted in the 'breakthrough' of unionism, in 1961, among 44,000 teachers. Similar orders were issued in Philadelphia and other cities with evident results.[6]

4. D. Bell, 'The Next American Labor Movement', *Fortune*, April, 1953.
5. D. Bell, 'Union Growth', in the Proceedings of the Seventh Annual Meeting of the Industrial Relations Research Association, December, 1954.
6. E. M. Kassalow, 'Trade Unionism Goes Public', in *The Public Interest*, No. 14, Winter, 1969.

In 1970, in some measure because of the economic downturn, in other measure because of the facilitating role of government, there began a movement for the unionization of college teachers. The growth of bargaining in the public sector was facilitated by the passage of public employee relations laws or similar measures in 19 states. The prospects for unionization at private institutions were enhanced when the National Labor Relations Board in 1970 assumed jurisdiction at private colleges and universities with gross incomes of more than $1 million a year.

By the end of 1971, collective bargaining agents for professors had been recognized at 133 of the country's 2,500 colleges and universities. These were principally in six states, New York, Michigan, New Jersey, Wisconsin, Illinois, and Massachusetts. But half the total number of the faculty covered were employees of two New York systems, those of the State University and the City University.

In most areas of the country, teachers are organized, but usually in such professional associations as the National Education Association for elementary and secondary school teachers, or the American Association of University Professors. In the past, both have eschewed direct bargaining roles and contented themselves, particularly the NEA, with lobbying activities. In the 1970s, given the competition of teachers' unions, it is likely that both organizations will turn more aggressively to the economic defense of teachers' interests.

In 1956, when the Bureau of Labor Statistics first started collecting data on union membership by industry, 915,000 persons, or 5.1 per cent of a total union membership of 18.1 million, were in government. By the end of 1962, the number had grown to 1.2 million, or 7 per cent of the total membership, and by 1968 union membership had climbed to 2.2 million, or 10.7 per cent of the total membership.

The main push had been in the federal government, where about *half* the employees have been organized. But in the larger area of state and local government, less than 10 per cent of their employees are unionized. . . .

The relatively large advance in government unionism has changed the sector distribution of unionism in the United States. Following the big drive of the CIO, more than half of American unionism was in manufacturing, but that proportion has slowly begun to change in recent years and we can look for greater shifts in the years ahead. . . .

Since 1956, union membership in manufacturing and non-manufacturing has continued to shrink as a proportion of total membership (union membership in manufacturing declined 44,000 between 1968 and 1970), and only membership in the public sector has moved upward. It is estimated that about 60 per cent of manufacturing employment is organized, compared to one-quarter in non-manufacturing and a little less than 20 per cent in government employment.

It is the white-collar field, of course, that is crucial for the future of organized labor, and here trade unionism has done poorly. According to reports from 167 unions and estimates . . . for 22, total white-collar membership in 1968 stood at 3.2 million. This is about 15 per cent of all union members. The highest ratio of white-collar union workers, more than 40 per cent, was in government service, followed by 22 per cent in non-manufacturing and 4 per cent in manufacturing. Sixty-two unions reported a total of 982,000 professional and technical members, but a large proportion of this group consisted of unions exclusively representing professional employees such as actors and artists, musicians, airline pilots, and, of those in government, mainly teachers. The major white-collar areas—in trade, finance, and insurance—remain largely unorganized, as does the entire area of science and engineering technicians and engineers.

Some labor problems of the post-industrial society

... The issues I shall deal with, some of them theoretical in nature, derive largely from the analysis of the changes in the composition of the work force, and the nature of the post-industrial society that I have sketched earlier.

EDUCATION AND STATUS

The most striking aspect of the new labor force is the level of formal educational attainment. By 1980, only 1 in 16 adult workers (25 years and over)—about 5 million—will have had less than 8 years of schooling, while 7 in every 10 adult workers, about 52 million, will at least have completed 4 years of high school. In 1968, by contrast, 1 in 10 (about 7 million) had completed less than 8 years of schooling and 6 in 10 (about 37 million) had completed 4 years of high school.

Many will have gone further. Nearly 1 in 6 persons, 25 years and over (about 13 million) will have completed at least four years of college, as against 1 in 7, or about 8.5 million, in 1968. Moreover, in 1980 about 9.2 million adults, 1 in 8, will have some college training, though less than four years.

Not only is there a much greater degree of educational attainment, but there is also a greater degree of cultural homogeneity. The American labor movement, particularly the blue-collar class, has always had a large component of foreign-born or first-generation workers, many of whom accepted a lower status as a matter of course. In 1950, about 34 per cent of the blue-collar labor force (skilled, semi-skilled and unskilled) were either foreign-born or of foreign or mixed parentage. By 1960, this figure had fallen to 26 per cent. It is likely to fall further.

For the first time, therefore, historically speaking, the American blue-collar labor force is approaching the 'classical' Marxist image of a relatively well-educated, culturally homogeneous force. ...

THE BLACKS

In an essay of almost a decade ago, in which I formulated the theme of the post-industrial society, I wrote: 'Insofar as education is today—and tomorrow—the chief means of social mobility, by charting the school dropout rates and matching them against future skill requirements by education one can sketch a rough picture of class society in the United States thirty years from now. ... By that criterion, thirty years hence, class society in the United States will be pre-dominantly color society.'

The situation today is not as bleak as it was a dozen years ago. Blacks were 4 per cent of the professional and technical group in 1960, but the proportion had almost doubled to 7 per cent in 1970. There were 5 per cent of the clerical group in 1960, and 8 per cent in 1970. Thus, in these key sectors, the pace of gain has been striking. But the total numbers are still small. Only 22 per cent of black males are professional, technical, and clerical, as against 43 per cent of white males. (Thirty-six per cent of black females are professional, technical, and clerical, as against 64 per cent of white females.) Eighteen per cent of black males are unskilled laborers as against 6 per cent of whites, and 18 per cent of black females are domestics as against 3 per cent white.[7]

The single largest group of black workers are semi-skilled (28 per cent of the males, as against 19 per cent of white males). For this group, the problem of better jobs lies with the trade union movement which, while formally accepting the principle of help, has been quite slow, particularly in the construction and skilled trades (14 per cent of blacks are skilled as against 21 per cent of whites) in upgrading black workers. Whether the blacks maintain an alliance with the labor movement, particularly in the political field, depends more on the behavior and response of labor than on that of the blacks. The political independence of the blacks—at least of the top leadership—is one of the realities of the politics of the seventies.

WOMEN

The fact is that a service economy is very largely a female-centered economy—if one considers clerical, sales, teaching, health technicians, and similar occupations. In 1960, 80 per cent of all workers in the goods-producing area were men, and 20 per cent women; conversely, in the services sectors only 54 per cent of all workers were men and 46 per cent women. Looked at along a different axis, 27 per cent of all employed females worked in the goods-producing sector, while 73 per cent of all women worked in the services sector.[8]

The fact that the service industries are so largely unorganized creates a special problem for the labor movement in its relation to women. In 1958, women unionists totalled 3.1 million, or 18.2 per cent of total union membership; by 1968, their number had risen to 3.7 million, or 19.5 per cent of all members. During these 10 years, unions added over 2 million new members to their ranks, and women made up 30 per cent of that increase; since 1958, 600,000 more women in the United States have joined unions.

During those same ten years, however, the number of women in the labor force grew from 32.7 per cent to 37.1 per cent. Thus the ratio of women union members to employed women has declined over the decade from 13.8 to 12.5 per cent. Moreover, most women are grouped into a few unions. A considerable number are blue collar and belong to such unions as the International Ladies Garment Workers, the Amalgamated Clothing, Service Employees (formerly Building Service), the Teamsters and the Auto Workers. The bulk of the others are in communication-workers, teachers, and government-workers unions.

For a variety of sociological reasons, women have been more difficult to organize than men. Fewer women have thought of their jobs as 'permanent', and have been less interested in unions; many female jobs are part-time or 'second

7. Current Population Reports, *The Social and Economic Status of Negroes in the United States*, Series P-23, No. 38, 1970.
8. V. Fuchs, *The Service Economy*, National Bureau of Economic Research, New York, 1968, p. 185.

jobs' for the family, and the turnover of the number of women at work has been much higher than that of men. Since the proportion of women in the labor force is bound to rise—the efforts of women's lib apart—simply because of the expansion of the service industries, the problem for the organized trade-union movement in recruiting more union members will be an increasingly difficult one. . . .

Finally, for more than a hundred years, the 'labor issue' dominated Western society. The conflict between worker and boss (whether capitalist or corporate manager) overshadowed all other conflicts and was the axis around which the major social divisions of the society rotated. Marx had assumed, in the logic of commodity production, that in the end both bourgeoisie and worker would be reduced to the abstract economic relation in which all other social attributes would be eliminated so that the two would face each other nakedly—as would all society—in their class roles. Two things, however, have gone awry with this prediction. The first has been the persistent strength of what Max Weber called 'segregated status groups'—race, ethnic, linguistic, religious—whose loyalties, ties, and emotional identifications have been more powerful and compelling than class at most times, and whose own divisions have overridden class lines. In advanced industrial countries such as Belgium or Canada, no less than in tribal societies such as Africa or communal societies such as India, the 'status groups' have generated conflicts that have torn the society apart more sharply, often, than class issues. Second, the labor problem has become 'encapsulated.' An interest conflict and a labor issue—in the sense of disproportionate power between manager and worker over the conditions of work—remain, but the dispro-portions have shifted and the methods of negotiation have become institutional-ized. Not only has the political tension become encapsulated, there is even the question whether the occupational psychology which Veblen and Dewey made so central to their sociology carries over into other aspects of a man's behaviour as well. (A bourgeois was a bourgeois by day and a bourgeois by night; it would be hard to say this about some of the managers who are executives by day and swingers at night.) The crucial fact is that the 'labor issue' qua labor is no longer central, nor does it have the sociological and cultural weight to polarize all other issues along that axis.

In the next decade, the possible demands for the reorganization of work, the decline in productivity, and the persistent threat of inflation because of the dis-proportionate productivity in the goods and services sectors, the threats of foreign competition, and other issues such as the recalcitrance of some unions on race, or the bilateral monopolies of unions and builders in the construction trades, all may make labor issues increasingly salient and even rancorous. The fact that some unions may even turn from concern with income and consumption to problems of production and the character of work is all to the good. But it is highly unlikely that these will become ideological or 'class' issues, although they may become politicized.

The politics of the next decade is more likely to concern itself, on the national level, with such public-interest issues as health, education, and the environment, and, on the local level, crime, municipal services, and costs. These are all communal issues, and on these matters labor may find itself, on the national level, largely liberal, yet, on the local level, divided by the factious issues that split community life.

But all this is a far cry from the vision of *The Communist Manifesto* of 1848 and the student revolutionaries of 1968. In the economy, a labor issue remains. But not in the sociology and culture. To that extent, the changes which are summed up in the post-industrial society may represent a historic metamorphosis in Western society.[9]

9. All statistical data in the section on The Sectors of Work and Occupations except as otherwise noted, are from *Labour Unions in the United States,* 1969, Bureau of Labor Statistics Bulletin 1665 (1970) and preliminary estimates for 1968-1970 in the BLS release, 'Labor Union and Employee Association Membership, 1970. (Sept. 13, 1971).

8. IMMIGRANT LABOUR IN EUROPE Peter Braham

The volume of immigrant labour

Immigration into various Western European countries is not confined to the post-war period (in the 1920s France actually received more immigrants than the USA). However, since the Second World War, migration into the industrialized countries of Western Europe from the less-developed countries of Southern Europe, and even further afield, has become the largest mass migration since the USA ended unrestricted immigration.

Though immigrants form a substantial proportion of total population in each of the industrialized countries of Western Europe, and a still higher proportion of the labour force, the effects of their presence should not be assessed simply in quantitative terms. Chronic shortages of labour have been filled by a river of immigrants; foreign workers have demonstrated their willingness to fill the jobs abandoned by indigenous workers—where wages and conditions are poor and social status low—and so a large, culturally distinct group has been placed at the foot of the economic ladder. Considerable attention has been focussed on the social problems of immigrants, but immigration is not merely a matter of tangental importance to society as a whole; on the contrary, the consequences of the recent large-scale immigration of workers are of crucial importance to the structure and development of the entire labour force.

In recent years two major flows are distinguishable:
(1) migration of skilled workers, managers and professional personnel between industrialized countries, and sometimes to less-developed regions and
(2) migration of workers from less-developed countries with considerable surplus of labour to industrialized countries with labour shortages.[1]

The vast majority of movements come under (2). Many of these migrants have lived in towns—even if only for a year or two en route—but the majority come from rural backgrounds. They must adjust simultaneously to the city, to a strange country (many cannot speak the language), and, perhaps most difficult of all, to the ordered monotony of the production line and the factory. Attention will be focussed on the need for this immigrant labour, its location and importance, and its impact on the occupational structure of the receiving country.

1. United Nations, 'Economic Survey of Europe in 1965', *Part I The European Economy in 1965*, Geneva, 1966, p. 77.

The numbers of migrant workers have grown beyond all expectations. They are now so numerous that they constitute virtually a tenth state within the European Economic Community, 'a kind of semi-nation' according to the Belgian Minister of Labour. The World Bank recently estimated their number at 9 million (8 million workers plus 1 million dependents), though this figure excludes some 3/4 million Algerians in France and all commonwealth immigrants in Britain. When allowance is also made for illegal and unrecorded immigration the figure exceeds 11 million.[2]

Allowing for the fact that official statistics underestimate the actual flows of immigrant workers, the United Nations Economic Survey concluded that the annual increase in the foreign labour force throughout Europe during the early 1960s might be more than 0.5 million, which was 'almost equal to the entire increase in the employed labour force in Western Europe between 1960 and 1965'.[3] Though this may seem surprising it must be remembered that the increases in population in Western European countries have not necessarily increased the potential labour force. Earlier retirement and the wider availability of secondary and higher education have squeezed the labour force at both ends.

If a weak or negative growth of the labour force constitutes a serious problem it can be met by a variety of policies. For example, labour can be transferred between sectors, rates of economic activity can be improved (perhaps by increasing the percentage of women in employment) or immigrant labour can be imported. Since the post-war expansion—prolonged beyond most expectations—has maintained full employment, and improved education and training have encouraged indigenous workers to move into jobs where pay is better and the conditions more pleasant, both the size of the potential labour force and its distribution between sectors have contributed towards making foreign manpower an essential source of labour supply in many Western European countries. In several countries indigenous labour became so scarce in certain sectors and occupations that recruitment of foreign labour was openly acknowledged as the main means of locating the necessary number of workers.

At first sight, immigrant workers in Britain seem to be in a very different position from that of migrant workers in Europe. Restriction on length of stay in France and Germany depending, not on the wishes of the migrant, but on renewal of residence permit or contract, contributes towards keeping them in inferior jobs and militates against promotion. Foreign workers in Germany, France and Switzerland are mainly *temporary*; their purpose is to earn a good sum of money in the shortest possible period. However, the *impact* of migrants who are considered, and consider themselves, temporary may be similar to that of permanent immigrants; even where most migrants are temporary, the presence of migrants as a group may be permanent. Similar levels of hostility experienced by immigrant workers in Europe and coloured immigrants in Britain reflect the similarity of their position: both constitute easily identifiable groups performing the least attractive jobs.

2. The exact number of immigrant workers living and working in Europe is not known and there is no central office monitoring the issue of work permits. In Britain, even the overall size of the coloured population has to be estimated.
3. United Nations, 'Economic Survey of Europe in 1965', *Part I The European Economy in 1965*, Geneva, 1966, p. 77.

Table 1: *Migrant worker stocks by main receiving countries and by nationality of migrants (1969)*

	Germany	France (1968)	Switzerland	Benelux	United Kingdom	Total
Greeks	174,348	6,100	5,326	7,800		193,574
Italians	340,244	247,540	385,850	91,100		1,064,734
Portuguese	26,379	171,760		16,800		214,939
Spanish	135,546	270,380	89,350	39,900		535,176
Turks	212,951	3,960	6,240	24,500		247,651
Yugoslavs	226,290	32,140	17,155	4,400		279,985
Others	256,301	522,580	131,879	107,900		1,018,660
Total	1,372,059	1,254,460	635,800	292,400	655,000[1]	4,209,719

Source: Ian M. Hume: *Migrant Workers in Western Europe*, Economics Staff Working Paper No. 102, October 1970, International Bank for Reconstruction and Development.
[1]Estimated.

According to the 1966 census, the total estimated coloured population resident in England and Wales*, but born overseas, was as follows:

Area of origin	Born overseas
India†	180,400
Pakistan†	109,600
Ceylon	12,900
Jamaica	188,100
Rest of Caribbean	129,800
British West Africa‡	43,100
Far East§	47,000
Total	710,900

*The numbers for Scotland, published separately in the census, are small.
†Excluding white Indians and Pakistanis.
‡Gambia, Ghana, Nigeria, Sierra Leone.
§Including Hong Kong, Malaya, Singapore.
Source: E.J.B. Rose and associates, *Colour and Citizenship*, London, O.U.P. for I.R.R., 1969.

The need for immigrant labour

Unlike the 1930s and the immediate post-war period, the driving force behind most of the migration into Western Europe has been economic; migrants have come to obtain work and accumulate savings, while employers have needed labour in time of expansion and also to fill particular shortages. The industrial expansion of Europe has required both skilled and unskilled labour. Despite visions of an 'age of automation' (many commentators keep one eye permanently focussed on what appears to be going on in America), widespread mechanization has not eliminated unskilled jobs, and while there has also been a considerable shortage of skilled labour,[4] investment may be modified to make the best of the

4. See Cormac O'Grada, 'The Vocational Training Policy of the EEC and the Free Movement of Skilled Labour', in *Journal of Common Market Studies*, Vol. VIII, No. 2, December, 1969.

available supplies of labour. Though shortages of labour in France, Germany and Britain began to be eased with the arrival of immigrant labour, they seemed only to afflict certain areas and particular industries and were not regarded as generalized and endemic perhaps because, 'with the hopeless unemployment situation of the 1930s still fresh in our minds no-one really believed it (i.e. labour shortage) could last'.[5] That is, labour scarcity could be discounted as a crippling or perennial problem in so far as conditions of strong demand and full employment were not expected to persist indefinitely.

With the exception of France, where permanent immigration was encouraged because it was national policy to boost population, immigration of foreign workers was thought of, when it was considered at all, as a temporary expedient. The 1967 recession in Germany seemed at first sight to demonstrate that this view was correct, that migrant workers were a diminishing necessity. However, the decrease in the number of foreign workers reflected a reduction in recruitment of new immigrants and normally high turnover of immigrant workers, rather than mass dismissals and redundancies of existing workers. Nevertheless, official agencies in Germany would not admit that the recession actually proved the foreign workforce, though reduced, was a permanent fixture.

The free movement of labour between member states was regarded as one of the fundamental innovations of the EEC. It is governed by Articles 48 and 49 of the Treaty of Rome, which one authority has described rather unkindly as 'little more than a liberal capitalist prescription for bringing manpower shortages and surpluses into balance within a given free-trade area'.[6] In any case, the prescription was not sufficient to meet the shortages which developed. At first, millions of Italians moved into the expanding industrial heartland of Europe, but in the mid-1960s Italy, then itself short of skilled labour, began recruiting its own emigrants in Switzerland and Germany. When ad hoc arrangements were then concluded with other poor Mediterranean countries which had labour surpluses, this, in turn, was claimed as something of great general benefit bestowed by the Common Market.

By the end of the 1960s it was quite clear to the Commission of the EEC that excess demand for labour could not be met from within the Market; it looked forward to a more coordinated recruitment of immigrant workers from outside. Quite apart from the problems posed by diminishing indigenous active labour forces, the Commission assumed that 'the presence of a large migrant population will, in any event, always be required because of the unwillingness of community workers to perform certain dirty, difficult or dangerous jobs.'[7]

5. Jan Barentz, 'Migration Labour and Employers', in Hans Van Houte and Willy Melgert (eds.) *Foreigners in Our Community*, Amsterdam, 1973, p. 22.
6. W. R. Böhning, *The Migration of Workers in the United Kingdom and the European Community*, Oxford University Press for the Institute of Race Relations, London, 1972, p. 10.
7. Quoted in *The Guardian*, 30 July, 1974. This prognosis is consistent with Böhning's idea of a 'self-feeding process' of immigration into 'post-industrial societies' (i.e., which have a large semi-automated industrial sector which is declining in relation to the equally large but growing tertiary sector; and a small agricultural sector). If committed to full employment and high economic growth, they will run into endemic labour shortages in low-wage and otherwise undesirable jobs. If unable or unwilling to change the social job structure, labour shortages will be filled by recruiting workers from poor countries with labour surpluses. See *Ibid.*, p. 55.

The underlying shortage of labour is usually revealed in particular sectors and occupations; for example, certain services such as transport and catering, mining, building and construction. Acute undermanning has been largely rectified by recruiting foreign workers who are required to perform the more menial and arduous jobs which might otherwise have been deserted to such an extent that the production of certain goods and services would have been minimal or non-existent. For example, without Irish and West Indian labour, respectively, post-war building programmes and transport services in Britain would have been sharply curtailed.

Post-war Britain had experienced a prolonged shortage of labour which was worsened by considerable emigration, and could not be remedied simply by importing some 120,000 Poles (under a Resettlement Bill) and a further 90,000 European displaced workers.[8] Employers in certain sectors grew desperate, and many tried to recruit workers in Ireland and even further afield. West Indian workers began to appear in the early 1950s, the first of a foreign labour force which held the advantage that its recruitment or entry required no amendment of the very strict Alien Acts. Even so, they were hired only with great reluctance, and when there was little alternative.

A flexible labour force

The immigration from the West Indies into Britain and later from other parts of the 'New Commonwealth' was not spontaneous, rather it arose from the demand for labour.[9] Commonwealth immigrants came to fill the shortages of labour which had developed in certain parts of industry and in certain services, notably transport. Despite heavy immigration, the 1950s and early 1960s were years of full employment. Partly because communications with the West Indies were so good, the level of immigration was extremely responsive to fluctuations in the domestic labour market. However, when immigration control was imposed on commonwealth citizens a movement of workers[10] was solidified into a permanent immigration of workers *and* their families. Though far from perfect in its operation, the working of supply and demand had fuelled the British economy more efficiently than the Commonwealth Immigrants Act has done. Between the implementation of control in July 1962 and December 1969, only 76,630 voucher holders entered, compared with 266,876 dependents (Commonwealth Immigrants Act 1962), and in mid 1969 the total coloured population in England and Wales was estimated at 1,815,000.[11]

In Germany the flow of foreign workers is likewise sensitive to domestic

8. Paul Foot, *Race and Immigration in British Politics*, Penguin, Harmondsworth, 1965, chapter 6.
9. For example, Ceri Peach has shown a close relationship between demand for labour in the U.K. and emigration from the West Indies. Ceri Peach, *West Indian Migrants to Britain*, Oxford University Press for the Institute of Race Relations, London, 1968.
10. Movement as distinct from permanent immigration, since there was a significant turnover of immigrant workers.
11. E. J. B. Rose, et al., *Colour and Citizenship*, Oxford University Press for the Institute of Race Relations, London, 1969, chapter 4.

demand for labour.[12] (Though it must be emphasized that the *size* of the foreign labour force is much less responsive.) Whenever the official German labour offices abroad stopped recruiting workers, the turnover rate was sufficiently high for there to be a significant fall in the total number of foreign workers in employment.[13] The number of foreign workers plus dependents in Germany rose from 500,000 in 1961 to nearly 3 million in 1970,[14] and to 3.3 million in 1973. However, in November 1973 the German Government decided to suspend recruitment of non-EEC workers as a measure to fight the oil crisis, and to protect both indigenous workers and *gastarbeiters* from oil-caused unemployment. All recruiting offices in non-EEC countries were closed indefinitely. The need to protect the German labour force (to say nothing of increasing concern about the actual or threatened increase in the infrastructural expenditure necessary to maintain an immigrant population which includes over one million dependents) and the hope of avoiding having to pay out huge amounts in unemployment benefits have encouraged the Government to seek a drastic reduction in the number of foreign workers.

The oil crisis may well temporarily halt European economic growth and reduce the need for foreign labour, but this is not at all certain. It is widely argued that once the spectre of recession recedes migration of labour will have to be revived. In any event, it is only contemplated to reduce the number of foreign workers in Germany to between 1 and 1.5 million. Their presence is now accepted as a permanent structural phenomenon, because, excepting a major economic crash, few Germans are willing to perform the dirty and arduous jobs done by immigrants. Paradoxically, the British Immigration Acts have removed most of the advantages enjoyed by the Germans. Their consequence has been to trap an *insufficient* supply of labour which cannot be expected to depart in time of economic setback, rather than to let in foreign labour at one time and export it, as surplus to requirements, at another.

A primary value in employing foreign workers is to avoid the constraints of a fully stretched labour force. Employers are in a much better position to utilize labour efficiently if, even though having to tolerate full employment for indigenous workers, they retain the freedom to increase and decrease the number of foreign workers. Contrary to popular opinion, the British balance of migration was in deficit from 1945–57. Between 1958–59 and the advent of immigration control, total net immigration was less than 400,000. The tightness of the labour market and the commitment to full employment compelled many employers to hold on to their workers at all costs, fearful of production bottlenecks should

12. Böhning, 'The differential strength of demand and wage factors in intra-European labour mobility; with special reference to West Germany' in *International Migration*, Vol. VIII, No. 4, 1970, shows that 96 per cent. of variance in the number of new entrants between 1957 and 1968 is explained by changes in domestic demand for labour.
13. Gregory Schmid, 'Foreign Workers and Labour Market Flexibility' in *Journal of Common Market Studies*, Vol. IX, No. 3, March, 1971.
14. *Wirtschaft und statistick* No. 5, 1971, quoted in S. Castles and G. Kosack, *Immigrant Workers and the Class Structure in Western Europe*, Oxford University Press for the Institute of Race Relations, London, 1973, p. 40.

demand for their goods pick up. With emigration effectively offsetting immigration, the total labour force was augmented mainly by the limited increase in rates of economic activity (e.g., women coming into the labour market), giving employers little room for manoeuvre.

It would be accurate to claim that a flexible and plentiful labour supply may tip the balance in a particular situation, and quite wrong to ascribe to it the entire difference in the relative performances of two separate economies. Thus in the long run, wages in Germany have outstripped in real terms those in Britain, while continuing to form a smaller proportion of national income; that is, they constitute a larger share of a smaller 'cake'.

Economic growth cannot be maintained in a liberal-capitalist society if wage increases reduce profits and stifle investment. The initial effect of immigration is to hold down wages, particularly in the poorer paid sectors where migrant labour is concentrated. It was for this reason that the Treasury strongly opposed the Commonwealth Immigration Bill in 1961–62: it argued that by holding down wages in lower-paid jobs immigration helped to maintain the current incomes policy.[15]

It is much easier to understand the frequent hostility of indigenous workers if the effect of easing labour shortages through bringing in foreign workers is to obviate the need for improved pay and conditions. Indigenous workers remaining in unskilled and low-status jobs will be particularly affected, for in the absence of supplies of foreign labour it would eventually have been necessary to pay much more to attract enough local workers. On the other hand, if it is accepted that an economy will function more efficiently with a flexible supply of labour, it might be calculated that it is to the advantage of the local labour force that it is foreigners who are required to be both mobile and expendable. In the German recession of 1966–67, the foreign workforce was reduced by some 400,000 of whom only 30,000 remained to collect unemployment benefit.

The weak market position of immigrant workers

The modern industrial state strives for efficiency in all things, particularly in the utilization of capital and the mobility of labour. Immigrant workers are more adaptable to different working conditions and are more responsive to changes in the pattern of demand for labour than are indigenous workers. Unlike the locals, migrants have few roots in a community and are prepared to travel to find work.

The movements of migrant workers have grown and fluctuated with industry's changing demand for labour. Unless rendered almost impossible by blanket immigration controls, immigrant workers are prized most of all for their mobility; they can be recruited in time of labour shortage, then encouraged to return home when no longer needed. Migrant workers have been seen (and often treated) as units of production, of energy input.

Immigrants have a high rate of economic activity as the immigrant popula-

15. Graham Hallett, 'The Political Economy of Immigration Control' in Charles Wilson (ed.) *Economic Issues in Immigration*, Institute of Economic Affairs, Readings: 5, London, 1970, p. 142.

tion is mostly young and predominantly male;[16] they are very anxious to work and are willing to accept low wages and long hours because such conditions are still preferable to their former existence. Even though many migrant workers may work abroad for very many years, they continue to think in terms of returning home rather than of establishing themselves in their place of work.[17] They hope to earn money quickly, to be saved or sent home to waiting relatives, which motivates them to accept whatever employment is available and so weakens their market position. The reality of an immigrant worker's life is probably most harsh in Germany and Switzerland. The restrictions of a social life overwhelmingly male (Sunday is the worst day, with little else to do but congregate at the local railway station) demonstrate that the sole justification and reason for their presence is *work* and the hope of accumulating some savings.

In this respect, the employment of immigrants in the wool industry of West Yorkshire is most instructive. The night shifts of many of the mills are dependent on immigrant labour.[18] As is the case in many of the foundaries of the Midlands, whole shifts are made up of immigrant workers, providing little or no contact with local workers. The introduction, in this highly competitive industry, of a certain amount of new machinery required less labour but more intensive working. The employers surveyed by Cohen and Jenner doubted whether a rise in wage rates would have been a viable alternative to the employment of immigrants. It was felt that only very large wage increases would have persuaded local labour to perform these jobs, so making such shift work uneconomic. Immigrants were more willing to work the newly required night shifts or a rotating shift system, because their choice of job was limited by discrimination, lack of suitable qualifications and language difficulties. They went on to hypothesize

> that the immigrant newly established in this country is much nearer
> the economist's ideal of economic man. The majority of immigrants are
> single adult males less constrained than the English worker by non-
> economic factors such as socially awkward hours of work and are
> willing to work as long hours as possible to earn as much as possible.[19]

The long-held 'common-sense' view that immigrant workers are concentrated in old, relatively labour-intensive industries should be abandoned. It may be that with a need for increasing productivity to secure a faster return on capital investment, which dictates more semi-continuous working, the potential for employing immigrant labour will be increased.

16. In 1966, 81 per cent. of those born in the 'New Commonwealth' were aged 15–64 compared with 65 per cent. of the British population as a whole. (Source: Commonwealth Immigrants Act, 1962; Control of Immigrants Statistics HMSO; and Annual Abstract of Statistics, 1967, HMSO.) In Germany rates of economic activity are particularly high owing to the policy of organized recruitment which encourages migration of single workers.
17. Paul Siv, 'The Sojourner' in *American Journal of Sociology*, Vol. 58, July, 1952.
18. B. Cohen and P. Jenner, 'The Employment of Immigrants: A Case Study Within the Wool Industry' in *Race*, X, 1, 1968.
19. *Ibid.*, p. 55.

The location of immigrant workers

The impact of immigrant labour is much larger than is indicated by overall figures, because immigrants are concentrated in sectors which—owing to poor conditions and wages—find it very hard to attract sufficient indigenous labour. For example, in Germany, foreign workers account for 7 per cent of total employment, but form a much higher proportion in the secondary (manufacturing) sector. The vast majority of male immigrant workers is in metal production, manufacturing industry, engineering and building.

In Britain, the distribution of immigrant labour is much closer to that of the total labour force, though various nationalities show different concentrations. For example, West Indians are over-represented in metal manufacture, building, transport and light industry; Indians are over-represented in metal manufacture, textiles, transport engineering and electrical work; Pakistanis are concentrated in metal manufacture and textiles; and the Irish are highly concentrated in building work.

Immigrant labour has become important in certain vital industries. With the exception of Britain, immigrants constitute a large minority of the workforce in the European car industry, particularly on the assembly line itself.

Overall figures also reveal little about the distribution of immigrant workers in the social-job structure. In general, they are lodged firmly at the bottom of the economic ladder. The majority are manual workers, mostly unskilled and semi-skilled. Though the longer established immigrant groups (Italians in France and Germany, Poles in Britain) may be very much better off than others, the vast majority of foreign workers endure worse conditions and have inferior jobs than those of the native population.

In France nearly 70 per cent of foreign workers are unskilled or semi-skilled manual workers, though the proportion is even higher among North Africans. Immigrants work principally in industries and occupations where conditions are poor, wages low, and prospects very limited. French workers have deserted certain industries; for example, the building industry, which offers little security, seasonal employment and arduous work, is largely manned by immigrants.

In Britain, though concentrated in unskilled and low-status jobs, the position of immigrants is not quite as extreme as in other European countries. While 26 per cent of the total labour force is classified as semi-skilled or un-skilled, this applies to 42 per cent of Irish males, 50 per cent of Jamaicans and 65 per cent of Pakistanis.[20] The difference is most marked at the divide between non-manual and semi-skilled manual jobs: about 26 per cent of immigrants are in the latter category compared with 14 per cent of the whole population;[21] similarly Cohen found that among Jamaican males living in London, less than one in twenty was in white-collar employment.[22]

It is frequently, and persuasively, argued that without immigrant labour many low-paid and unpleasant jobs would not be performed at all: transport

20. U.K. Census, Economic Activity Tables, Part III, HMSO, London, 1966.
21. *New Society*, 26 June, 1969.
22. B. Cohen, 'Immigrants and Employment' in Simon Abbott (ed.) *The Prevention of Racial Discrimination in England*, Oxford University Press for the Institute of Race Relations, London, 1968.

would be severely affected, rubbish would remain uncollected, road works could not be carried out, and, in Britain, the NHS would collapse. If local labour objected to the recruitment of immigrant labour, management could show quite easily that it would be hired only when local labour was unavailable. Naturally, this was most often the case with low-status, unskilled or semi-skilled jobs—where low pay, unsocial hours or bad conditions repelled indigenous workers.

The situation faced by coloured immigrants is summarized by Daniel,

> It is fair to say that coloured immigrants were often employed only in one type of job . . . and where this was true it was the most menial and unattractive type of job, for which it had been impossible to attract white labour.[23]

The presence of immigrant workers in modern sectors of industry (even though these may well be very vulnerable to the threat of unemployment) does not detract from the principle that immigrants are concentrated in 'suitable' jobs; that is, unskilled or semi-skilled manual jobs (or skilled ones not involving authority over indigenous workers) which have difficulty in attracting labour.

The effect on indigenous workers

Having surveyed 'those in a position to discriminate' the PEP report concluded that applications by coloured immigrants for jobs other than those commonly accepted as 'suitable' would be strongly resisted.[24] The acceptance of immigrant labour is confined to certain areas and is limited by intangible, though effective frontiers. The relative absence of overt conflict owes much to the wish of most immigrants to avoid trouble, hostility and humiliation, so minimizing the amount of direct competition in job applications.

In Western European countries with large numbers of immigrant workers, the differentiation between the immigrant and indigenous workforces shows itself in the growing under-representation of indigenous workers in manual work generally, and in unskilled and semi-skilled jobs in particular. The tendency for the labour market to split into non-competing groups has been most pronounced in Switzerland. Swiss nationals have largely moved out of blue-collar employment to be replaced by foreign workers:

> Between industries, and within industries as between unskilled and semi-skilled and fully skilled jobs, the preference goes to the Swiss, and with it the 'wage drift', or the extent to which earnings rise faster than nominal wage rates through overtime and upgrading.[25]

Radin refers to the infrequent interventions by British trade unions over the hiring of coloured labour.[26] In one case the union was assured that this would not

23. W. W. Daniel, *Racial Discrimination in England*, (Based on the PEP Report), Penguin, Harmondsworth, 1968, p. 120.
24. *Ibid.*
25. C. Kindleberger, *Europe's Post-war Growth—The Role of Labour Supply*, Harvard University Press, Cambridge, Mass., 1967, p. 44.
26. Beryl Radin, 'Coloured Workers and British Trade Unions' in *Race*, VIII, 2, 1966.

adversely affect wages. And thereafter, 'For almost ten years, whenever the bus company wanted to hire additional coloured workers, they negotiated with the union for increases in salary in exchange for new employees.'[27] She concludes that, contrary to the fears of trade unionists, coloured immigrants have not forced down the wages of indigenous workers, and because of the longstanding shortage of labour, most coloured workers receive the same rate for the job as do indigenous workers. However, where immigrants are concentrated in jobs involving arduous work, poor conditions and unsocial hours, trade-union demands or even legislation requiring equal pay for foreign workers does little to halt any tendency for the development of a dual, non-competitive labour market. It is of little consequence that immigrant workers be paid the 'same rate for the job' if few members of the indigenous work force are in these jobs. It is more difficult to improve conditions and wages in occupations with a large number of immigrant workers, and this will inevitably be reflected in the relative position of indigenous workers who remain in these occupations.

It is to be expected that most immigrants will start at the bottom of the economic ladder, and, as immigrants occupy low-level occupations, the indigenous labour force has the opportunity to move out of them. The extent to which this happens is a matter of debate; precise information is rather scarce. One view is that it is thanks to the employment of foreign workers that indigenous workers can get higher-paid jobs and move into white-collar employment. The truth is, perhaps, more complex, though this clearly applies to many indigenous workers: they have taken advantage of conditions of strong demand for labour to move into jobs offering better rewards and prospects, leaving immigrants and the less-advantaged in undesirable jobs. In France, Germany, Switzerland and Britain, immigrant workers are concentrated in the jobs offering the lowest status and the poorest wages, while indigenous workers have tended to move from unskilled and semi-skilled jobs into skilled jobs, and from the factory into the office. Other indigenous workers have benefited not materially, but simply because there is now a new social grouping which is accorded lower social status than their own.

The extent to which large-scale immigration may allow or facilitate the occupational and sectoral mobility of indigenous workers is shown clearly by changes in the distribution of the German labour force between 1960 and 1965:

Sectoral changes in the employment of nationals and immigrants in West Germany between 1960 and 1965. (thousands)[28]

	Nationals	Immigrants	Total
All sectors	658	888	1546
Trade, transport and other services	826	119	945
Commodity-producing sectors	−168	769	601
of which			
metal industry	132	328	460
other manufacturing	−37	230	193
Mining and energy	−128	42	−86
Building and construction	23	164	187

27. *Ibid.*, p. 164.
28. Source: United Nations, 'Economic Survey of Europe in 1965', *Part I The European Economy in 1965*, Geneva, 1966, chapter II, p. 78.

Foreign workers accounted for about 60 per cent of the increase in total numbers employed, but while 90 per cent of them entered the commodity-producing sectors, these areas were being abandoned by indigenous workers who formed nearly 90 per cent of the total employed in newly created jobs in the service sectors.

The trend is far more striking if figures for the self-employed are included:

1960-1965 (thousands)[29]			
	Nationals	Immigrants	Total
All sectors	55	888	943
Trade, transport and other services	785	119	904
Commodity-producing sectors	−730	769	39

The contribution of immigrant workers to the total increase in employment is shown to be overwhelming, and the movement of indigenous workers out of commodity production is on a massive scale.

While in Switzerland immigrant workers have acted very largely as a non-competing group,[30] and Swiss workers have moved out of poorly paid, low-status jobs into skilled and non-manual occupations, in other countries the effect has been less clear cut. Immigration will normally benefit non-competitive groups of workers (or perhaps leave them unaffected), but may affect adversely the position of groups remaining in occupations for which immigrants are recruited. The indigenous remainder may attempt to limit any adverse monetary effects associated with the employment of immigrant labour, perhaps by demanding that immigrants be confined to certain jobs within an occupation, or by insisting that a quota be placed on the proportion of foreigners. Though trade-union organizations may often be weak in these less-skilled sections of the workforce, it may not be too difficult to exert pressure on employers who are often rather reluctant to switch to an unfamiliar, untested source of labour and may wish to placate what remains of their familiar labour force.

David Collard has pointed out that it makes no sense to assess the impact of immigrant labour as if indigenous labour were homogeneous.[31] It is more profitable to examine the extent to which each part of the labour force may be 'substituted' by other elements. On this basis skilled and non-manual labour will be non-competing groups, whilst indigenous unskilled labour will be relatively worse off. Findings of higher levels of prejudice among working-class groups than among middle-class groups give a clue to this structural weakness; immigration on the scale experienced by Britain, France and Germany tends to

29. *Ibid.*
30. Vera Lutz, 'Foreign Workers and Domestic Wage Levels with an Illustration from the Swiss Case' in *Banca Nazionale del Lavoro*, Rome, No. 64, March, 1963.
31. David Collard, 'Immigration and Discrimination: Some Economic Aspects' in Charles Wilson (ed.) *Economic Issues in Immigration*, Institute of Economic Affairs, Readings: 5, London, 1970, pp. 78–9.

diminish the relative incomes and weaken the bargaining position of the less skilled.[32]

The impact of immigrant labour

Once recruited, coloured immigrants in Britain still find it difficult to gain access to skilled jobs; even employees of many years standing may not receive normal promotion. As far as employers are concerned, granting normal promotion and making vocational training easily available to immigrant workers will greatly diminish the benefits of a large amount of cheap labour. Similarly, the attitude of European governments towards immigrant workers has been hardened not only by the changing labour market, but also by the spectre of growing urban ghettoes. When Dr. Patrick Hillery (EEC Commissioner for Social Policy) suggested that the scandalous conditions in which many migrant workers lived within Common Market countries might be remedied by contributions from the EEC Social Fund, it was thought that 'kindness of that sort may soon be found to kill the migrant worker cause'[33] by closing an era when immigrant labour was cheap labour.

At present, hostile attitudes to immigrants underpin discriminatory treatment which tends to maintain the immigrant worker's weak market position and to preserve the cheapness of immigrant labour. As long ago as 1947, Kenneth Little,[34] in his study of immigrants in one part of Cardiff, found that colour was firmly associated with the lowest class. Since a disproportionate number of coloured immigrants are near the foot of the occupational ladder, any tendency to view them as capable only of performing the less-skilled jobs is reinforced.

The expected effect of a shortage of labour would be to raise wages. If these shortages are particularly acute in the less-skilled sections of the labour force, it is inevitable that relative wages in these areas would have to be improved in order to retain existing workers and attract marginal workers. It would not have been surprising if this effect was somewhat delayed as such occupations have long been regarded as low-wage and low-status. However, before this mechanism could operate, supplies of immigrant labour forestalled any dramatic wage adjustments and made it possible to continue to pay low wages, for example, to junior hospital doctors and hospital porters in the NHS.

It is also probable that the injection of a considerable proportion of immigrant workers may reinforce a 'negative' view of certain jobs; for example, London Transport workers or workers on building sites. The result is to empha-

---

32. Immigration has placed the trade unions in an awkward position. It is occasion for only muted surprise that the complete ban imposed by the German government on the recruitment of foreign workers was welcomed by the trade unions as 'correct', while the German employers remained 'doubtful' (they were concerned about the heightened pressure for wage increases when total unemployment was only 1.5% [Report in the *Economist* December 1973]). The unions have been unable to overcome the dilemma (at least with any consistency) that an influx of foreign labour seems to threaten the wages of many of their members, yet opposition to immigration will make it much more difficult to recruit and organize immigrant labour, so making the realization of fears of 'cheap labour' all the more likely.
33. *Economist*, 8 December, 1973.
34. Kenneth Little, *Negroes in Britain: A Study of Racial Relations in English Society*, Routledge & Kegan Paul, London, 1948.

size the divide between jobs which are already sought after and those which are considered undesirable or 'dead-end'; the presence of immigrant workers acts as a kind of 'litmus test' in this respect. Just as improved opportunities in education and training and sustained conditions of full employment allowed indigenous workers to leave undesirable jobs, so the arrival of immigrant workers to remedy the resultant labour shortages made these jobs seem even more undesirable. The outward flow of indigenous workers from low-wage, low-status jobs is likely to be reinforced, leaving immigrant workers and a section of the indigenous work force on the wrong side of a more rigid social-job divide.

The importation of foreign workers cannot provide a permanent solution to this lop-sided occupational structure or to the labour shortages. Yet, barring a severe and prolonged economic crisis and given the initial reasons for the recent mass migration into Western Europe, it tends to become self-perpetuating, even to the extent that some capital investment may be modified to make use of a labour force which is available at low cost, is considered easy to train to perform semi-skilled jobs, and can be persuaded to work long and unsocial hours.

According to James Schwarzenbach, the instigator of several campaigns to curb the number of foreign workers in Switzerland, 'The big businessmen say that Swiss people will not do hard and dirty work any more. I do not want to see Swiss people fall prey to the temptations of the easy life, to earn more for working less . . . it doesn't do us any good to have foreigners come and do our work.'[35] Similar fears have been voiced in the other labour-receiving countries. Even though the situation is much less pronounced in Germany, France and Britain, the pervasive effects of having much of the dirty, arduous and ill-paid labour done by immigrant workers are increasingly worrying. While initial analysis of the arrival of coloured immigrants in Britain was concerned with hostility, ethnicity, rejection and so on, factors which might explain why immigrants were not wanted at work or excluded from many residential areas, it is now more apposite to examine their (reluctant) acceptance in a particular stratum of society, occupying the lowest-status levels and performing the jobs which others do not wish to do. The drying up of supplies of foreign labour, or the decision to limit recruitment perhaps because it is wished to prevent the further growth of a foreign underclass, will produce a serious shortage of workers in the less-skilled and poorer-paid sections of the labour force, especially in jobs such as refuse collection or road mending, where the work is also unpleasant. It will then be necessary to do what was not done previously, that is, to correct the occupational maldistribution by improving pay and conditions in jobs which have been traditionally regarded as being at the bottom of the occupational ladder. There is precious little evidence that this requirement is at last becoming apparent, so it may well prove more difficult to achieve now than it would prior to the era of post-war mass-immigration, which accentuated an already noticeable divide between desirable and less-desirable jobs.

The implications—social and economic—of the presence of so many people, recruited from the less-developed countries to carry out menial and unskilled

35. Quoted in John Goshko, 'The Right to Work (II)', *Guardian* 'Extra', 20 August, 1974.

jobs, have not really been perceived. Their presence is at best seen as an unfortunate necessity, or even a hangover from the misguided and shortsighted policies of previous administrations. If it is accepted as impossible, though desirable, to dispense with the immigrant labour forces, perhaps it is because the industrialized countries are still not prepared to fundamentally overhaul their present occupational structure and accepted distribution of rewards.

9. THE DEVELOPMENTAL THEORY OF OCCUPATIONAL CHOICE: A CRITIQUE AND AN ALTERNATIVE   Kenneth Roberts

At the time when it was emerging earlier in this century, vocational guidance has been described as an aspirant profession in search of a body of theory both to guide its practice and to justify its claims to professional status.[1] During the past twenty years, however, the required theory has apparently arrived in the form of a set of ideas that can be termed 'the developmental theory of occupational choice'. This theory has not only attracted eminent academic sponsorship, but has also been substantially embraced by professionals in the careers-guidance field, both in America where the theory originated, and more recently in Britain. The idiom of this theory has become the conventional wisdom amongst practitioners, enshrined in current textbooks.[2] What follows is intended as a challenge to this contemporary orthodoxy. I shall attempt to show that as a scientific statement purporting to explain how individuals actually enter occupations and respond to their work experiences, the theory's validity is highly questionable, and that basing the practice of occupational guidance upon the theory's premises is likely to have unintended and probably unwelcome consequences.

The developmental theory of occupational choice

For many years problems of occupational choice have attracted the interest of psychologists, sociologists, labour economists and representatives of various other disciplines, but it has always been the psychologists who have made the running. Early ideas in the American vocational-guidance movement were based upon a laudable desire to place square pegs in square holes, and in this atmosphere contributions from differential psychology were warmly received. Frank Parsons[3] was the most renowned articulator of these talent-matching ambitions, suggesting that vocational guidance required the systematic investigation of occupations and a parallel study of individuals' attributes, to be followed by a matching of the two. In this climate psychologists proceeded to investigate the profiles of individuals in various jobs, discriminating between the more- and less-satisfied

1. D. J. Armor, *The American School Counsellor*, Russell Sage Foundation, New York, 1969.
2. For example, J. Hayes and B. Hopson, *Careers Guidance*, Heinemann, London, 1971.
3. Frank Parsons, *Choosing a Vocation*, Houghton Mifflin, Boston, 1909.

9. Original article. Copyright © 1975 Holmes McDougall Ltd, Edinburgh. Kenneth Roberts is Lecturer in Sociology at the University of Liverpool.

and efficient, thus hopefully producing a body of information of direct utility in the guidance process. Such was the 'folk science' that the developmental theory of occupational choice has subsequently replaced.

The developmental theory took coherent shape during the nineteen-fifties, drawing upon existing ideas, the relationships between which had not previously been apparent. It drew upon the established perspectives of developmental psychology including Buehler's[4] suggestion that individuals' life histories, including their occupational histories, could be fruitfully conceptualized as a series of cumulative stages. It drew also upon the work of students of the labour market including Davidson and Anderson[5] who had plotted the career patterns, that is the characteristic movements between jobs, typical amongst individuals in various types of employment. The groundwork of the developmental theory had been further laid by Carter's[6] research amongst out-of-school youth, and his resulting discussion of young people's blundering adjustment to the world of work. The industrial sociologists, Miller and Form,[7] attempted an early synthesis of these ideas to clarify various aspects of occupational behaviour. Then, during the nineteen-fifties, two psychologists, Eli Ginzberg and Donald Super constructed their similar developmental theories of occupational choice.

Condensed statements are inevitably somewhat unjust, but the main elements of the developmental theory can be summarized as follows. It is suggested that individuals' occupational choices, like other attributes such as intelligence and sexuality, develop through a series of identifiable stages. At each stage, it is argued, the direction of an individual's choice will depend upon both psychological factors including his abilities, interests and aptitudes, and upon situational factors such as the family and educational environments that the individual inhabits, upon which his occupational knowledge will depend, and which will offer varying opportunities for individuals to test out maturing self-concepts. Depending upon the object of his occupational choice at any time, it is suggested, an individual will seek appropriate knowledge and experience, eventually in the world of work itself, as a result of which his original choice may be modified. Thus, it is argued, both individuals' occupational choices and careers can be regarded as developing processes, continuing maybe indefinitely but at least until a person enters an occupation that matches and does not subsequently modify his occupational choices

Eli Ginzberg's[8] initial research, amongst high-school and college students, was concerned to identify the stages through which young people's occupational choices evolve. The subjects of his enquiry were drawn from somewhat privileged backgrounds; they were white, middle-class, and educationally successful. They were chosen because 'external environment interfered as little as possible with their freedom to pursue any occupation', and Ginzberg was able to char-

4. C. Buehler, *Der Menschliche Lebenslauf als Psychologisches Problem*, Hirzel, Leipzig, 1933.
5. P. E. Davidson and H. D. Anderson, *Occupational Mobility in an American Community*, Stanford University Press, 1937.
6. H. D. Carter, 'Vocational Interests and Job Orientation', *Appl. Psych. Monogr.*, 2, 1944.
7. D. C. Miller and W. H. Form, *Industrial Sociology*, Harper, New York, 1951.
8. Eli Ginzberg, et al., *Occupational Choice*, Columbia University Press, New York, 1951.

acterize their choices moving through fantasy, tentative and realistic stages, hence onwards towards self-actualization. More recently Ginzberg has applied this conceptual framework in studying the subsequent careers of male and female college graduates.[9]

Donald Super proposed his own names for the stages through which individuals' occupational choices allegedly pass and extended the sequence to cover the whole of individuals' careers.[10] His most original contribution, however, has involved formulating new concepts which prove particularly useful in drawing out the implications of the developmental theory for vocational guidance. For example, Super discusses the 'developmental tasks' that individuals need to accomplish at given stages of vocational development as a pre-condition for successful movement to the next. High-school students, according to Super, amongst other things, need to search for occupational information and gradually extend their self-knowledge. A related concept introduced by Super is 'vocational maturity', which can be scored in a similar way to intelligence, thus indicating how effectively an individual is tackling his developmental tasks. A further concept is 'integrative vocational adjustment' which conceals behind the jargon what Super regards as a point towards which vocational development should lead. Integrative adjustment is the product of vocational behaviour which results in the accomplishment of a task with the greatest degree of long-term satisfaction to the individual. Super is in the process of conducting a longitudinal study of a sample of individuals first contacted whilst at high school,[11] the intention being not so much to test the theory from which it derives as to operationalize its component concepts, including those outlined above, so as to assist the manufacture of a vocational-guidance technology.

Developmental theory and careers guidance

As an explanation of how individuals enter and respond to their occupations the developmental theory, as initially proposed by Ginzberg and Super, was at least a plausible interpretation of the evidence then available. However, its widespread acceptance has probably owed as much to its utility as to the theory's claims to scientific validity.

The theory's implications for careers-guidance procedures are manifold and have led to wide-ranging re-appraisals of former practices.[12] Perhaps most fundamentally, the developmental theory implies that vocational guidance must be a progressive rather than a once-and-for-all process. Under the theory's imprint, guidance can only be construed as a genuinely educational activity, gradually helping to deepen the individual's self-awareness and his knowledge

9. Eli Ginzberg, et al., *Talent and Performance*, Columbia University Press, New York, 1964 and Eli Ginzberg, et al., *The Life-styles of Educated Women*, Columbia University Press, New York, 1966.
10. D. E. Super, *The Psychology of Careers*, Harper, New York, 1957 and D. E. Super and J. P. Jordan, 'Career Development Theory', *British Journal of Guidance and Counselling*, 1, 1973, pp. 3–16.
11. D. E. Super, et al., *Vocational Development: A Framework for Research*, Teachers College, New York, 1957 and D. E. Super and P. L. Overstreet, *The Vocational Maturity of Ninth Grade Boys*, Teachers College, New York, 1968.
12. See J. Hayes and B. Hopson, *Careers Guidance*, Heinemann, London, 1971.

of the world in which he lives. In the guidance process, the adviser or counsellor is called upon to play an essentially supportive role. Effective guidance cannot take the form of simply telling an individual the type of work for which he is best suited. Rather must an adviser attempt to assist the development of a client's self-awareness using counselling, discussions, and encouraging reflection upon the person's performance in situations including school and part-time work. The adviser can also feed information to his client about a range of occupations using media such as literature, films and visits to places of employment. In playing such a role, however, the adviser can never properly act as a decision-maker, but only as a non-directive aid in what is intrinsically a gradual process in which individuals' occupational choices progressively crystallize. Along with these implications, the developmental theory of occupational choice has been substantially embraced by practitioners. And in America, in particular, guidance professionals have been provided with a rationale to guide and justify their activities that they previously lacked.

The history of the vocational-guidance movement in America is a prime example of the growth of a profession prior to the creation of the requisite knowledge-base.[13] Hence, throughout the history of the movement, commentators have been able to point to the lack of theory underlying guidance work, the consequently vague and confused role of the counsellor, and the scant information available about the actual effects, benign or otherwise, of careers guidance.[14] Vocational guidance appeared in America in the early decades of the twentieth century as a result of occupational choice being defined as a public problem. The spread of industrialism and the associated complexity of the occupational structure made job choice an apparent problem in an America whose egalitarian (public) values insisted that every individual's achievements should depend upon his own abilities and efforts. Individuals transparently required information and advice in order to give their efforts a rational direction, and consequently the provision of adequate counselling services became recognized as a hallmark of the satisfactory high school and college.

On account of the society's cultural peculiarities, in Britain occupational choice has more belatedly been recognized as a salient problem. Problems posed by the development of industrialism were earlier treated as problems of selection rather than choice.[15] Assimilating young people into an increasingly complex and specialized occupational structure was treated essentially as a problem of selecting individuals with the appropriate talent for entry into the more prestigious occupations. Hence, until recently, vocational guidance in Britain has been regarded merely as a process of placing individuals in jobs, a routine safely entrusted to semi-trained and low-status personnel. However, recent decades have witnessed profound cultural changes within British society, signified by a

13. D. J. Armor, *The American School Counsellor*, Russell Sage Foundation, New York, 1969.
14. M. R. Katz, 'Theoretical Foundations of Guidance', *Review of Educational Research*, 39, 1969; R. E. Hosford and S. A. Briskin, 'Changes Through Counselling', *Review of Educational Research*, 39, 1969 and H. D. Gelatt, 'Schools Guidance Programmes', *Review of Educational Research*, 39, 1969.
15. R. H. Turner, 'Modes of Ascent through Education: Sponsored and Contest Mobility in the School System', *American Sociological Review*, 25, 1960, pp.855–67.

growing dissatisfaction with an educational system that can only offer failure to many pupils, together with growing demands for wider opportunities and the postponement of formal selection. Hence the recent interest in and expansion of guidance services both within and outside educational institutions. And as in America, the developmental theory of occupational choice has been grasped as offering otherwise absent guidelines.

Needless to say, to indicate how a theory has met a practical need is no criticism of its scientific validity. Indeed, the developmental theory of occupational choice can be regarded as but one illustration of how scientific theories invariably also serve as occupational ideologies. Ginzberg and Super, in the nineteen-fifties, were offering a tentative theory based upon the evidence then available, which is a wholly legitimate exercise. Their efforts, however, have been assimilated as a creed within influential sections of the careers-guidance movement in a way that is comprehensible in terms of professionals' needs, but which the supporting evidence hardly warrants.

A critique of the developmental theory

My objection to the developmental theory is quite simply that it is wrong; that the propositions it contains are inconsistent with the known facts about how individuals enter and respond to their occupations. The theory's main mistake lies in treating individuals' occupational choices as unrealistically central processes in the course of vocational development. Despite the existence of a nominally free labour market, individuals do not typically choose their jobs in any meaningful sense; they simply take what is available. Thus, to predict the type of job a school-leaver will enter, the most relevant information concerns not his aspirations but his educational qualifications and the local job-opportunity structure. Studies conducted in various parts of Britain have rarely found the majority of school-leavers entering jobs reflecting their aspirations. For example, in Carter's[16] Sheffield study only a third of the boys and half the girls obtained the jobs they were aiming for when interviewed prior to leaving school. Similarly in London Joan Maizels[17] found that only a third of the young people she studied obtained jobs exactly like they wanted. In America there is a long history of investigations revealing even higher levels of thwarted ambition.[18]

Once in the labour market, to predict career movements, the most useful information concerns types of jobs individuals currently hold rather than their ambitions. Swift[19] shows, for example, how patterns of job mobility amongst young workers mainly reflect the rewards accruing to stability and mobility in different occupations. Career development only exceptionally represents the

16. M. P. Carter, *Home, School and Work*, Pergamon, Oxford, 1962.
17. Joan Maizels, *Adolescent Needs and the Transition from School to Work*, Athlone Press, London, 1970.
18. H. M. Bell, *Youth Tell their Story*, American Council on Education, Washington, 1938 and R. M. Stephenson, 'Mobility Orientation and Stratification of 1,000 Ninth Graders', *American Sociological Review*, 22, 1957, pp. 204–12.
19. B. Swift, 'Job Orientations and the Transition from School to Work: A Longitudinal Study', *British Journal of Guidance and Counselling*, 1, 1973, pp. 62–78.

unfolding of ambitions. In her London study Maizels[20] found that job movements were more frequently away from than towards her sample's original aims. Likewise in Sheffield, Carter[21] found that job changes during his school-leavers' first year in employment were unrelated to their ambitions expressed whilst still at school. Upon the basis of their study of the American labour force, Blau and Duncan[22] have shown that past jobs are by far the best predictors of future jobs and become increasingly so as individuals progress into their careers. Individuals' occupational choices simply do not play the role in career development attributed by the developmental theory.

Furthermore, as regards the typical industrial worker, his career can hardly be discussed in terms of self-actualization and the implementing of a self-concept. The notion of individuals' ambitions and actual careers gradually moving into harmony is far more an expression of hope than a statement of fact. It is more typical for employees to have to tolerate a lack of fit between their self-concepts and the demands of their occupations. Most workers have to learn to accommodate (and there are various strategies that can be adopted) to whatever jobs are available. Individuals, with whatever hopes and ambitions they may have entertained, have to adapt to the realities of the world of work. For most employees their own ambitions have little opportunity to operate as the dynamic force behind their patterns of vocational development.

The developmental theory of occupational choice typically resembles reality in the case only of those more privileged individuals who are able to make genuine career decisions. Young people in America who graduate from high school and proceed to college can select courses and eventual jobs upon the basis of maturing assessments of their own abilities and interests. And for such individuals their jobs are likely to provide satisfactions and feelings of self-actualization as their careers develop. The subjects of the research upon which Ginzberg grounded his theory were in such fortunate positions. A theory based upon the experience of such individuals, however, is grossly misleading from the point of view of understanding occupational behaviour typical in less privileged sections of the community.

Hence the concepts operationalized by developmental theorists would appear, behind the jargon, to be measuring mainly status and privilege. Research inspired by the developmental theory has produced results generating little confidence that its concepts bear the intended resemblance to reality. For example, Gribbons and Lohnes[23] measured the 'readiness for vocational planning', a concept similar to Super's vocational maturity, of eighth graders. Readiness scores were derived from measures of subjects' knowledge of the educational curriculum, occupations, themselves, and their ability to relate these. Followed up seven years later, however, Gribbons and Lohnes found that their subjects' original scores were not related to different patterns of subsequent

20. Joan Maizels, *Adolescent Needs and the Transition from School to Work*, Athlone Press, London, 1970.
21. M. P. Carter, *Home, School and Work*, Pergamon, Oxford, 1962.
22. P. M. Blau and G. D. Duncan, *The American Occupational Structure*, Wiley, New York, 1967.
23. W. D. Gribbons and P. R. Lohnes, *Emerging Careers*, Teachers College, New York, 1968.

career development. Scores were related, however, to the possession of high aspirations, high educational attainments and enrolment on college preparatory courses.

Comparably, Super himself found that his measures of vocational maturity were related to high educational and subsequently occupational achievements.[24] The impression conjured by the vocational-maturity concept is that the general psychological maturation of the individual's personality will be naturally accompanied by the adoption of increasingly realistic and stable ambitions. Adamek and Goudy's[25] research amongst 372 university students, however, found that the strength of individuals' general self-concepts was unrelated to the stability of their occupational choices. The vocabulary of the developmental theory of occupational choice is as misleading as the theory itself. Rather than enhancing our understanding of occupational behaviour, inspection suggests that its concepts are little more than concealed measures of privilege.

An alternative theory: opportunity structures and career development

To date the developmental theory of occupational choice has faced little serious competition, but, nevertheless, an alternative theory is implicit in a range of ideas about various aspects of occupational behaviour. In the light of the above criticisms it should be clear that an adequate theory explaining how individuals progress into and react to their careers will need to pay more attention than the developmental theory to the various constraints imposed upon participants in the labour force; constraints that operate whatever the aspirations of the individuals involved might be.

There are several bodies of research enquiring into what may be ostensibly unrelated aspects of occupational behaviour and attitudes, that can be combined so as to produce a model of the entry into employment to serve as a rival to the developmental theory. Firstly there is a species of research showing that the directions in which individuals' careers develop are most readily explicable in terms of the opportunities accessible to the individuals concerned. Thus, as comprehensively illustrated in the data assembled by the Crowther Committee,[26] the levels of the occupational hierarchy at which school-leavers enter depend primarily upon their educational achievements. Individuals' aspirations are of secondary importance; no matter how ambitious he may be, a beginning worker is unable to enter the job hierarchy at a level for which he is unqualified. Subsequently when in employment, individuals' career movements are most easily explicable in terms of the opportunities their existing occupations open up. Individuals climb career 'ladders' when they are sufficiently lucky to enter occupations in which progressive careers are available. Swift's[27] British study

24. D. E. Super and P. L. Overstreet, *The Vocational Maturity of Ninth Grade Boys*, Teachers College, New York, 1968.
25. R. J. Adamek and W. J. Goudy, 'Identification, Sex and Change in College Major', *Sociology of Education*, 39, 1966, pp. 183–99.
26. Central Advisory Council for Education, *15–18* (Crowther Report), HMSO, London, 1959.
27. B. Swift, 'Job Orientations and the Transition from School to Work: A Longitudinal Study', *British Journal of Guidance and Counselling*, 1, 1973, pp. 62–78.

provides convincing evidence of this as does Freedman's[28] research based upon the personnel records of five American companies showing that, once hired, individuals' positions and prospects, and consequently their actual career movements, are substantially determined by the 'organizational opportunity structures' in which they become enmeshed.

Secondly we have research concerned with the relationship between education and students' vocational aspirations. Here the weight of the evidence indicates the responsiveness of individuals' ambitions to their educational experiences. Schooling has a profound influence upon its recipients' aspirations, which may not be immediately detected, for its importance lies not so much in whatever explicit vocational guidance may be offered as in a 'hidden curriculum'. In subtle but unmistakable ways, distinct 'climates of expectation' become associated with particular educational institutions and internalized by their pupils.[29] For example, in Britain secondary-modern pupils are expected, and themselves learn, to expect more modest attainments than grammar school pupils.[30] In addition to this, a 'frog-pond' principle invariably operates within educational establishments.[31] Students measure their abilities and accomplishments against their peers', consequently acquiring conceptions of their places in the social pecking order, and as a result of such processes school-leavers' levels of aspiration become related to the streams through which they have passed within their secondary schools.[32] Education may operate as a powerful agent of anticipatory socialization, encouraging the development of realistic aims, or alternatively students may be oriented towards occupations they are unlikely to be able to enter; it depends upon the stage at which educational processes become visibly linked with different destinies.

How specifically students' ambitions are focused depends largely upon the character of the educational courses they are pursuing. Underhill[33] has shown that when college students pursue 'non-vocational' courses, such as in the humanities, occupational choices often change into line with students' already-professed values, whereas when courses have a more specific vocational outlet, as in the cases of medicine, business, and the physical sciences, occupational choices are less likely to fluctuate. Depending upon the flexibility of their connections with processes of occupational recruitment, the specificity of the impact of educational programmes upon individuals' occupational choices will vary, but the type of relationship in question is invariably found.

The third relevant area of research concerns processes of occupational socialization, that is, the ways in which individuals' outlooks are shaped by the

28. M. Freedman, *The Process of Work Establishment*, Columbia University Press, New York, 1969.
29. A. B. Wilson, 'Residential Segregation of the Social Classes and the Aspirations of High School Boys', *American Sociological Review*, 24, 1959, pp. 836–45.
30. See T. Veness, *School-leavers*, Methuen, London, 1962 and D. L. Jayasuriya, *A Study of Adolescent Ambition*, Ph.D. thesis, London, 1960.
31. J. A. Davis, 'The Campus as a Frog Pond', *American Journal of Sociology*, 72, 1966, pp. 17–31.
32. D. Hargreaves, *Social Relations in a Secondary School*, Routledge, London, 1967 and D. N. Ashton, 'The Transition from School to Work', *Sociological Review*, 21, 1973, pp. 101–25.
33. R. Underhill, 'Values and Post-college Career Change', *American Journal of Sociology*, 72, 1966, pp. 163–72.

occupations they have entered. Expressed job choices often appear to be functions rather than determinants of the occupations individuals are in the process of entering.[34] Upon entering employment, whatever their initial dispositions, individuals are subjected to socializing processes making for a reconciliation with the occupational milieux to which they are exposed. In the more intrinsically rewarding occupations, socialization normally involves acquiring a professional identity. For example, medical students gradually begin to think of themselves as doctors and internalize their profession's code of conduct,[35] whilst novice engineers and physiologists learn to value the distinctive rewards that their professions can offer.[36] Polsky's[37] study of poolroom hustlers indicates that equally sophisticated processes of occupational socialization operate in what may be unexpected places. In less-satisfying types of employment, as amongst assembly-line workers,[38] occupational socialization assumes a somewhat different form; the culture of the workplace may teach the novice how to disengage from the task in hand and enjoy secondary gratifications such as the company of his fellows that can make a tedious job tolerable. On-the-job socialization of some form, however, appears to be a universal phenomenon.

If we combine these sources of evidence we have the foundations for an alternative theory of occupational choice with 'opportunity structure' acting as the key concept. Careers can be regarded as developing into patterns dictated by the opportunity structures to which individuals are exposed, first in education and subsequently in employment, whilst individuals' ambitions, in turn, can be treated as reflecting the influence of the structures through which they pass. This model will obviously not apply in all situations. Representations of social behaviour must necessarily attempt to identify key processes within the flux of real life. All theories must inevitably simplify reality and accord prominence to processes considered crucial. In this context, however, the claim I would argue, is that the opportunity-structure theory formulated above offers a more valid indication of the processes involved in the entry into employment as they affect most individuals than the developmental theory, and will therefore offer a more reliable foundation for the practice of careers guidance.

Implications for careers guidance

If accepted, the opportunity-structure theory has its own distinctive implications for careers-guidance practice, contrasting at many points with the guidelines suggested by the developmental theory. Firstly and most fundamentally, there is the implication that guidance must basically be a matter of adjusting the individual to the opportunity structures to which he has access. If careers develop along

34. K. Roberts, 'The Entry into Employment: An Approach Towards a General Theory', *Sociological Review*, 16, 1968, pp. 165–84.
35. R. K. Merton, et al., *The Student Physician*, Harvard University Press, Cambridge, Mass., 1957.
36. H. S. Becker and J. W. Carper, 'The Development of Identification with an Occupation', *American Journal of Sociology*, 61, 1956, pp. 289–98.
37. N. Polsky, *Hustlers, Beats and Others*, Aldine, Chicago, 1967.
38. E. Chinoy, *Automobile Workers and the American Dream*, Doubleday, New York, 1955 and H. Beynon, *Working for Ford*, EP Publishing, Wakefield, 1975.

lines principally set by opportunity structures, then rather than encouraging individuals to develop aspirations primarily upon the basis of conceptions of their own abilities and interests, the guidance process must take the realities of the world of work as its point of departure. In the provision of advice and job information, guidance must be recognized as essentially lubricating more basic processes of occupational selection. Facilitating personal growth and development must be treated as no more than occasional by-products rather than the essential role of careers guidance.

Secondly, the implication is that guidance should be centred around dealing with clients' immediate problems. Rather than being concerned with the provision of general job information and encouraging individuals to crystallize self-concepts, guidance needs to concentrate upon helping individuals to solve the practical problems they face when confronted by the realities of opportunity structures. For example, school-leavers looking for work need information about the jobs actually open to them, rather than global surveys of the occupational structure. Similarly, dissatisfied young workers need information about alternative jobs and realistic advice about what may be the limited satisfactions they can expect to find in the available types of employment. Guidance problems are posed basically by occupational realities as they impinge upon specific groups of individuals, rather than by the internal dynamics of psychological growth.

To practitioners in the careers guidance field these suggestions might appear like a reactionary attempt to turn back the hands of the clock and dismantle 'progress' made during recent decades. The answer to such qualms, however, is quite simply that circumstances tend to usher guidance into playing the type of role in question irrespective of practitioners' inclinations. This is evidenced by Clark's[39] portrait of the latent 'cooling-out function', lowering students' aspirations into line with reality, lurking behind a public image of counselling into the American college, remaining substantially uncontested. Similarly, Kitsuse and Circourel's[40] contrast between the high school counsellor's manifest role of advising students so as to enable them to make their own curricula choices, and his actual role, of filtering students along educational routes leading to occupational opportunity structures that the individuals concerned are judged capable of entering, has provoked no significant challenge.

Ginzberg has recently acknowledged that actual processes of career development are often inconsistent with his theory of occupational choice.[41] He has recognized the limited impact made by counselling with disadvantaged groups, and the importance of the 'constraints' to which non-college sectors of the population are subject. However, rather than radically re-appraising his theory, Ginzberg remains content with only minor modifications and complains that reality is wrong and should be changed into line with his theory's propositions.

If the implications of the opportunity-structure theory appear relatively

39. B. R. Clark, 'The "Cooling-out" Function in Higher Education', *American Journal of Sociology*, 65, 1960, pp. 569–76.
40. J. Kitsuse and A. V. Cicourel, *The Educational Decision-makers*, Bobbs-Merrill, Indianapolis, 1963.
41. Eli Ginzberg, *Career Guidance*, McGraw-Hill, New York, 1971 and Eli Ginzberg, 'Toward a Theory of Occupational Choice: A Restatement', *Vocational Guidance Quarterly*, 1972, pp. 169–76.

unpalatable, this is solely due to the unrealistic expectations of guidance fostered by the recent popularity of the developmental theory. Against this backcloth, defining the careers adviser principally as a servant of the occupational system rather than as an educator essentially concerned with his individual client may appear inhumane yet circumstances inevitably oblige counsellors to act in the stipulated manner. Recommending paying attention to clients' immediate problems may awaken unwelcome memories of the time when vocational guidance was synonymous with crisis counselling, but the fact is that counsellors have to help clients face crises regardless of whether they treat this as an important function. Therefore, through its implications, the opportunity-structure theory suggests not so much a complete re-direction of guidance practices, as a better understanding of their actual significance. And through this better understanding, the prospects are strengthened of careers guidance playing effectively the role that is open to it.

Guidance cannot make jobs more rewarding than they inherently are, nor create otherwise non-existent opportunities for personal growth and development at work. No amount of guidance, whatever its character, will change the realities of work in an industrial society. Discussing guidance as if it could hope to extend to all individuals the opportunities for self-actualization at work currently available for only a few, and widen the horizons of individuals whose scope for occupational choice is presently limited, merely obscures the reality of the situation. Guidance may help individuals to accept more readily opportunities to which they would have to be reconciled in any case. It may also help individuals to cope more effectively than otherwise with specific vocational difficulties as they occur. These are the tasks in terms of which careers guidance can hope to succeed. If it fails to recognize its own limitations, and retains pretensions to more lofty goals, the principal consequence will simply be that careers guidance will aggravate rather than resolve individuals' difficulties in adjusting to the opportunity structures that confront them.

As already pointed out, vocational guidance originally developed largely in the absence of any sound and fully proven knowledge base. Hence the ease with which the developmental theory has been assimilated by practitioners without any convincing evidence of its ability to pay dividends. From what we now know about the effects of vocational guidance, however, two conclusions can be safely drawn. Firstly, research undertaken in both Britain and America, including follow-up studies to examine the consequences of guidance, has indicated that positive though marginal results are normal. For example, in America, Campbell[42] found that, after twenty-five years, comparisons between a counselled group and a control group revealed that the former had recorded higher attainments in terms of occupational status and income though they were still the less-satisfied with various aspects of their lives, suggesting that the conditions initially leading them to seek counselling had not been completely resolved.[43] In Britain before

42. D. P. Campbell, *The Results of Counselling*, Saunders, Philadelphia, 1965.
43. See also J. W. M. Rothney, *Guidance Practices and Results*, Harper, New York, 1958.

the second world war, Heginbotham[44] demonstrated that school-leavers who acted as advised became the more stable and satisfactory employees compared both with an unadvised control group and with individuals who rejected the advice tendered. Such evidence clearly shows that guidance can work.

However, the second conclusion that can be drawn is that the maxim 'the more the better' does not *necessarily* hold in the vocational guidance field. This can be seen by simply comparing the British with the American experience. In Britain enquiry after enquiry over the last twenty-five years has reported school-leavers ill-prepared for their entry into employment, drifting into the labour market armed with little job knowledge and uncertain as to their objectives.[45] The general portrait has been of beginning workers receiving little in the way of systematic vocational guidance and commencing their careers in a state of some confusion. Such enquiries have invariably led to calls for a strengthening of the careers-guidance services. Having school-leavers approach the start of their working lives knowing little about what lies in store for them and without any carefully thought out aspirations has generally been considered intolerable.

However, successive studies of young people in employment have concurrently been reporting a state of scarcely relieved satisfaction and vocational adjustment. Although typically vague, British school-leavers' ambitions have been notably realistic, and no matter what their levels of employment, the majority of young workers have been found content with their attainments, satisfied with their jobs and little inclined to seek new opportunities.[46]

Some investigators themselves have not found the types of jobs available for many young people particularly inspiring. For example, Joan Maizels[47] comments that 'the present requirements of the economic and social structure conflict with the needs of young adolescents to develop and assert their individualities.' She also concludes that 'since few occupations allow for the full use of talents, while a large proportion of jobs for adolescents, as adults, require little technical or other skill, any match achieved is minimal. In many cases it depends upon the capacity of the individual to modify his inclinations, and to function with many of his known and unknown talents dormant.' Consequently Maizels argues a (somewhat utopian) need to give 'a predominantly educational influence to the work environment' so that work will provide all adolescents with opportunities for individual development. However, Maizels is obliged to recognize that few young people, including those she studied, express similar feelings. Such overt vocational discontent that has been recorded among young workers in Britain

44. H. Heginbotham, 'The Development of the Youth Employment Service', in J. H. Leicester and J. A. W. Farndale (eds.) *Trends in the Services for Youth*, Pergamon, Oxford, 1967.

45. G. Jahoda, 'Job Attitudes and Job Choice Among Secondary Modern School Leavers', *Occupational Psychology*, 26, 1952, pp. 125–40 and 206–21; M. D. Wilson, 'The Vocational Preferences of Secondary Modern Schoolchildren', *British Journal of Educational Psychology*, 23, 1953, pp. 97–113; M. P. Carter, *Home, School and Work*, Pergamon, Oxford, 1962; and J. Maizels, *Adolescent Needs and the Transition from School to Work*, Athlone Press, London, 1970.

46. E. G. Sykes, 'School and Work', *Sociological Review*, 1, 1953, pp. 29–47 and M. P. Carter, *Home, School and Work*, Pergamon, Oxford, 1962.

47. J. Maizels, *Adolescent Needs and the Transition from School to Work*, Athlone Press, London, 1970.

has usually appeared more a symptom of general psychological difficulty rather than a specifically occupational problem.[48] In America, in contrast, where counselling has been developing as a normal high-school and college function since the first world war, investigators have uncovered a quite different picture. Young people approach the outset of their careers with generally unrealistic aspirations, and phrases such as 'blundering' and 'floundering' recur in descriptions of out-of-school youth searching for acceptable employment opportunities.[49]

There need be no suggestion that counselling is *the* cause of vocational maladjustment amongst American youth. What can be legitimately argued, however, is that the approaches to counselling that have become increasingly prominent in America, alongside the acclaim attracted by the developmental theory of occupational choice, have done little to relieve the situation. Hence, in Britain, the case for caution, lest, along with the developmental theory, approaches to careers guidance are imported whose consequences are likely to prove both unintended and unwelcome. Although the intentions are quite different, feeding school-leavers with the widest range of job information and broadening their horizons may simply leave the recipients less prepared to acquiesce in the opportunities they eventually find available. Assisting young people to acquire self-knowledge and crystallize related occupational choices may simply leave individuals less adaptable when faced with the constraints of actual opportunity structures. Whilst it may be satisfying to talk about promoting personal growth, in reality no harmony is guaranteed between individuals' aptitudes and occupational requirements. In advanced industrial societies the genuine problem we face is not to ensure that individuals derive the personal fulfilment that jobs can offer, but to reconcile individuals to job opportunities many of which allow little scope for personal development.

For this reason challenging the developmental theory of occupational choice is not exclusively a matter of academic interest. Failing to ground guidance practices upon a valid model of the processes involved in work entry and establishment can only inhibit realization of those benefits that can accrue from careers guidance. Talk of adjusting individuals to often limited opportunities may not be particularly inspiring. Refusal to recognize this as the effective role that guidance can play, however, will not change society for the better. The net result will merely be to leave individuals less adjusted to the world as it is.

48. R. F. L. Logan and E. M. Goldberg, 'Rising 18 in a London suburb', *British Journal of Sociology*, 4, 1953, pp. 323–45 and L. T. Wilkins, *The Adolescent in Britain*, HMSO, London, 1955.
49. K. Roberts, 'The Organization of Education and the Ambitions of School-leavers: A Comparative Review', *Comparative Education*, 4, 1968, pp. 87–96.

10. THE TRANSITION FROM SCHOOL TO WORK: NOTES ON THE DEVELOPMENT OF DIFFERENT FRAMES OF REFERENCE AMONG YOUNG MALE WORKERS[1] D.N.Ashton

In advanced industrial societies, young people spend between ten and fifteen years in educational organizations, isolated from the world of work. They are then obliged to enter different types of occupation that make different demands on their skills and provide different rewards. On *a priori* grounds one would expect this transition to represent a source of more or less serious shock experiences, yet research findings in this field indicate that the transition from school to work is experienced by young people as relatively smooth. This paper is an attempt to provide a first approach toward explaining why it should be experienced in this manner. It will be argued that, in the course of their passage through the school, young people acquire different frames of reference[2] that direct them toward different types of occupation, their experience of which reinforces the frame of reference originally acquired at school. In this way their school experience is functional in preparing them for the world of work.

In an attempt to develop a conceptual framework for the analysis of the processes involved, I have drawn on the published evidence in this field and some findings of the Leicester project. This research, conducted in the Department of Sociology at the University of Leicester, under the direction of Norbert Elias and with which the author was associated, was based on a representative sample of 1,150 young workers of both sexes who left school in 1960 and 1962. There was a response rate of 77 per cent and all the young people were interviewed in their homes. When interviewed, approximately one half of the respondents had had one year's experience of work, while the other half had had three years' experience. The statistical findings and the case studies cited in this

1. This paper developed out of joint work on which the author was engaged with Norbert Elias. His ideas formed an important source of the theoretical framework. I should also like to acknowledge the help and advice given by David Field, Ilya Neustadt and Eric Dunning.
2. Normally the term 'orientations' is used to direct attention toward the various sets of values and attitudes that people acquire and in terms of which they experience work. However, a person's orientation to work is also an integral part of his own self-image, and as I am concerned with the organisation of different self-images and the relationship between these and the different levels at which people experience work, I use the more general term 'frame of reference'. Strictly speaking, such frames of reference are, in most cases, *reinforced* in the school rather than originally acquired there. The argument presented here is not intended to imply that family background, 'sub-cultural' and community values are unimportant in this connection.

10. Extracts from "The Transition from School to Work: Notes on the Development of Different Frames of Reference among Young Male Workers' from the *Sociological Review*, vol. 21, no. 1; February 1973. (pp. 101-25)

paper refer to the 614 males who were interviewed. This material is presented, not in the form of a research report, but as a means of supplementing other available evidence in an attempt to show the usefulness of the adoption of two different perspectives for the analysis of the sociological problem involved.

In an earlier paper it was argued by Keil, Riddell and Green[3] that the problem of adjustment to work should be conceptualized as a process, an approach that has recently been developed in some respects by Haystead[4]. Although primarily concerned with the related problem of occupational choice, Haystead argues that this process should be analysed from the perspective of the young people who are involved. . . .

With reference to the transition from school to work, this experiential perspective can be very useful. It can help us to understand how, through their interaction with others, certain types of youth who enter middle class occupations come to perceive work as a means of 'self-improvement' and 'self-advancement'. Similarly, it contributes to our understanding of how other types of youth, who enter certain working class occupations, come to perceive work as a means of securing immediate monetary rewards. What this perspective cannot help us to understand, is how the socialization process within the two groups differs and gives rise to these differences in the perception of work.

At present this problem is usually resolved by stressing the importance of structural factors or attributes, such as social class, type of school or type of occupation. Yet, given the way in which these 'factors' or 'attributes' are frequently conceptualized—as separate and isolated elements—this merely pushes the problem one stage further back. One still has to ask: what is it about the relationship between that which we refer to as type of school or type of occupation that will enable us to account for the observable differences in the way in which young people experience the world? In order to overcome this problem, types of school, types of occupation and other structural 'factors' will be conceptualized as specific types of configuration; that is, as specific groups of interdependent human beings with distinctive properties. However, the distinctive properties of these configurations can only be established through an analysis of their position and function within the overall social structure. Thus it will be argued here that in order to develop our understanding of how young people acquire different frames of reference, it is necessary to adopt two different yet complementary perspectives.

In the next section of this paper, the movement of young people from school to work will be analysed from a societal perspective. This will enable the properties of the different configurations they form—at school in relation to teachers and other pupils, and at work in relation to employers and other employees—to be established. In the subsequent section, an attempt will then be made to show the way in which the properties of these configurations influence the development of different frames of reference among young males, most of whom, of course,

3. E. T. Keil, D. S. Riddell and B. S. R. Green, 'Youth and Work: Problems and Perspectives', *Sociological Review*, Vol. 14, No. 2, July, 1966.
4. J. Haystead, 'Social Structure, Awareness Contexts and Processes of Choice', *Sociological Review*, Vol. 19, No. 1, February, 1971.

come from backgrounds in the working classes. This will be done by analysing, from the experiential perspective, the movement of two different types of young people through school and work. From this perspective it will also be possible to locate some of the mechanisms by which young people become committed to different types of work through the acquisition of different frames of reference.

When the movement of young people from school to work is analysed from a societal perspective, it is possible to distinguish a number of different channels through which this movement takes place. Each of these consists of a series of positions within the schools and employing organizations, through which young people move and within which most of their direct extra-familial experience of others is confined. For the purpose of this paper it will be sufficient to distinguish two such channels.[5] Both function to commit young people to working class occupations. One leads through the lower streams of the modern or comprehensive school into what I shall call the 'careerless' occupations. The other leads through the higher streams of the modern school and the middle streams of the comprehensive school into occupations that provide the chance of making a 'working class career'. Only a minority of young people move between these channels at any one time.

The distinctive properties of the configurations that form the first of these channels are as follows: within the school, the positions in the lower streams offer few, if any, chances of educational certification to those who enter them; in comparison with the positions in the higher streams they offer few chances for the development of cognitive or manipulative skills beyond an elementary level; they offer few chances of entering positions of authority; and they provide the shortest school career, terminating at the statutory minimum leaving age.[6]

These scholastic positions act as a feeder channel into occupations of a semi-skilled and unskilled type, which provide few, if any, chances of making a career. Unlike other types of occupation that young people can enter, these rarely provide for an hierarchical arrangement of positions where movement is from positions of lower status, income and authority to positions of higher status, income and authority. When movement does take place it is horizontal and discontinuous, between one semi-skilled job and another, rather than vertical and sequential. Such occupations require only a minimal degree of manual dexterity for the performance of work tasks. . . .

With regard to their chances in the market, entrants into these occupations may at the point of entry obtain higher rewards than those in other manual occupations, but the level of their earnings, computed as an average over their

5. This typology is not intended to be exhaustive, merely a first step in the process of conceptualizing the career configurations to be found in advanced industrial societies. On the basis of further research it may be possible to distinguish further types and, within these and those already listed here, a series of sub-types. For example, the channel that leads through the higher streams within the comprehensive school, or alternatively through the grammar school, into those occupations that provide the chance of making a middle-class career. This is distinguished from the working-class career, in part, by the longer career ladder it provides.
6. See M. P. Carter, *Home, School and Work*, Pergamon Press, Oxford, 1962.

working life, is the lowest level of earnings of all occupational groups.[7] Moreover, in part because they provide few chances of advancement, the level of earnings of those who enter them will remain the same throughout their occupational life. The dependent character of these positions within the organization and the low level of skill required for the performance of tasks makes these the most insecure of all occupations. As a consequence, they are awarded the lowest status.

The other channel is that which comprises the 'A' and 'B' streams in the modern school and the middle streams in the comprehensive, which in turn feeds into those occupations that provide the chance for making a working class career. Within the school, these positions offer those who enter them the chance of elementary forms of educational certification or alternatively a 'good school report'; they provide greater opportunity for the exercise and development of cognitive and manipulative skills than is provided in the lower streams; also the pupils who form these streams are given the opportunity of lengthening their school career; and of gaining access to positions of authority within the school.[8]

From these positions young people move into those jobs, usually in the skilled trades, that do provide the chance of making a career, albeit one that is confined within the boundaries of manual work. They do so through the provision of an hierarchical arrangement of positions, whereby those who enter move from positions of lower income, status and authority, to positions of higher income, status and authority. What distinguishes this type of career configuration from others is the relatively short career ladder it forms. It consists of between two and four steps, although the majority of the positions are located on the second step. Most of the entrants into this type of career move from the position of apprentice to that of skilled worker, where they remain. A minority move to the next step, that of the chargehand's position, and of these even fewer reach the ceiling of this career, that of the foreman's position or its equivalent. All may experience vertical movement in the early stages, but subsequently, for the majority, this movement is likely to be horizontal.

Other distinctive properties of this type of configuration are that the work tasks performed are more varied and complex than those found in semi-skilled work. This provides the entrants with the opportunity to exercise and develop their cognitive and manipulative skills. . . .

Partly as a result of their monopolization of these skills, workers in this type of occupation receive a level of income that is, on average, higher than that of careerless workers.[9] Moreover, because these occupations provide the chance of making a career, they also offer the chance of progressively increasing the level of earnings. However, given the structure of this career, only a minority receive a level of earnings which is considerably higher than that received by their fellows. A further consequence of their monopolization of skills is the higher level of job

7. See G. Routh, *Occupation and Pay in Great Britain, 1906–1960,* Cambridge University Press, Cambridge, 1965.
8. See D. H. Hargreaves, *Social Relations in a Secondary School,* Routledge and Kegan Paul, London, 1967 and J. Partridge, *Life in a Secondary Modern School,* Penguin, Harmondsworth, 1968.
9. G. Routh, *Occupation and Pay in Great Britain, 1906–1960,* Cambridge University Press, Cambridge, 1965.

security these occupations offer compared to the careerless. Finally, the remaining distinctive properties of this type of occupation are the fact that they are accorded the highest status of all manual occupations, and the fact that they provide a chance for a minority to improve their status.

In this section, the movement of the young people through both the channels will be analysed from the experiential perspective. An attempt will be made to show how, in the course of their movement, the young people who form these different channels enter into different types of relations with others and face different problems of adjustment. These, it will be argued, give rise to the differences in their frames of reference. . . .

The frame of reference characteristic of many young people who enter careerless occupations is distinguished by its perceptual immediacy, a central concern with the concrete, the here and now, and the absence of any short or long term planning. Work is thought of only in terms of its immediate as opposed to long term rewards. Apart from this concern with the immediate rewards, there is little involvement in work: it is not an area of central interest. Employment is only considered in jobs that require little involvement and make minimal demands on their skills. . . .

How then do these young people acquire this type of frame of reference and how does it function to prepare them for the world of work? The fact that approximately 40 per cent of the young people in our sample entered the same channel as their parents, while the majority of the remainder entered channels adjacent to that of their parents, suggests that the mechanism of social inheritance plays a part. For young people of lower working class parents one would, on the basis of the work of Bernstein, expect this social inheritance to involve the acquisition of a restricted language code.[10] The problems stemming from the use of restricted codes by the children and the predominant use of elaborated codes by teachers, generate a conflict situation intensified by the different values and norms with which both teachers and pupils operate.[11] In short, one would expect social barriers originating from the different life experiences of teachers and pupils to be greater in this channel than in any other.

These barriers are further intensified by the formal organization of the school, which rigidly separates those children destined for some form of educational certification from those who are denied the chance, and by the set of beliefs that function to legitimate the organization. For the process of allocation to the different streams is legitimated, not by reference to the organizational structure of the school, but by what are claimed to be differences in the innate abilities of the children. From the teachers' perspective the allocation of young people to the lower streams is a result of their limited ability. A further set of beliefs frequently held by teachers describes the character of these children as

10. B. Bernstein, *Class, Codes and Control*, Vol. I, Routledge and Kegan Paul, London, 1971.
11. See J. W. B. Douglas, *The Home and the School*, MacGibbon and Kee, London, 1964.

'louts', 'dunces', 'layabouts'. Evidence from recent research in this field[12] suggests that such beliefs are held not only by teachers and others in positions of authority, but also by pupils in higher positions, and that either directly through the teachers or indirectly through such pupils, these derogatory images are communicated to the children in lower streams.

For the young people the process of commitment to semi-skilled and unskilled work starts in the early stages of their movement through the school. In the secondary modern and comprehensive schools their allocation to positions in the lower streams effectively denies them the opportunity to develop their cognitive and manipulative skills beyond a minimal level. In so doing it denies them the opportunity of obtaining any form of educational certification. This commits them to a future in semi-skilled work by denying them the opportunity of developing the requisite skills and obtaining the qualifications necessary for entry into other types of occupation. In addition to these commitments, the young people are further committed through their acquisition of a specific type of self-image.

As they move through the positions in the lower forms, the young people learn to see themselves as 'failures' in the eyes of others and as systematically rejected as inferior by both teachers and pupils in higher positions. . . In this way, by acquiring an image of themselves through their interaction with others as academically incapable, the pupils learn to see those occupations that require some form of educational qualification for entry as beyond their reach. They may regard the apprentice as the one who had done best for himself, but not consider such an occupation as suitable for themselves.

On moving through positions as third and fourth formers, these young people who, as stated earlier are likely to operate with a restricted code, face a situation that reinforces their concern with the here and now. For they move through positions in which, once basic communication skills of a certain kind have been acquired, few opportunities are provided for the further development of cognitive and manipulative skills and few, if any, future rewards are offered for further learning. . . . The problems they face, in the absence of intrinsic interest in the subjects, are those of obtaining some sort of reward or satisfaction in the here and now—problems that are frequently solved in the classroom through 'rule-breaking', and 'messing about'.

Faced with a situation in which there are few incentives for further learning and being in a position in which they are regarded as inferior by others, the main areas of support and reassurance they have as to their own identity is that provided by the peer group. For the values and norms of their peer group offer them support in their counter-rejection of the dominant values transmitted within the school. This rejection of education, and hence of the possibility of entering those occupations that require educational certification, constitutes a process that further commits pupils to semi-skilled work.

In moving through the final stages of their school life, their attitude to school becomes one of increasing hostility. The pupils having lost any incentive to learn, the task for the teachers becomes primarily focused on the problem of maintain-

12. See D. H. Hargreaves, *Social Relations in a Secondary School*, Routledge and Kegan Paul, London, 1967.

ing control. As the school offers no future rewards to these pupils and little support for their identity, then the teachers cannot utilize, as they do for the young people in higher positions, the threat of withdrawing these supports as a sanction; increasingly they resort to the use of physical force. . . .

At the end of their school life, when it comes to making a decision about their 'choice' of job, these young people have already made a series of 'side bets' that commit them to semi-skilled and unskilled work. Moreover, given their self-image as academically inferior, their concern with obtaining rewards in the here and now, and their desire to leave school as soon as possible, jobs of this type have certain attractions. Some may have thoughts about the possibility of an apprentice-ship: dismissing it either because of the poor immediate rewards, such as its low income, or because it is considered to be beyond their reach. For the majority, however, their 'choices', both at this stage and after two or three years' experience of such work, indicate that they are positively attracted to certain aspects of their semi-skilled and unskilled jobs. In entering these there is little or no possibility of their being upwardly mobile through their work, and the longer they remain in it, the more difficult it is to undertake training for skilled work because of the age restrictions on entry.

From the point of view of the young workers both entering and changing jobs within this channel, the kind of requirements that work is expected to satisfy and the kinds of rewards they seek are usually those that can be obtained in the here and now. It is the rewards associated with 'working with machines', 'meeting people', working inside or outside, or obtaining the highest possible income, that are important to them, and hence used as a basis for discriminating between different jobs. As with their situation at school, so once more at work, these young people find again that they move into positions in which the only rewards they can expect are those to be derived from the here and now. In the absence of any future rewards, such as those associated with promotion, factors such as the kind of activity involved in the job, its geographical location and the income it provides become all important. Unlike the young workers in the other occupational channels, the majority do not see themselves as making a career: work is not a means of self-advancement or of proving one's worth. When questioned about what they hoped and expected their jobs to lead to, our inter-viewees would usually reply, 'Don't know', 'I don't bother like that', or 'Nothing'; for given the properties of the type of configuration they form, there is no way, apart from changing their jobs, whereby their future at work can be differentiated from the present. From their perspective, no matter how hard they work or how well behaved they are, this behaviour cannot bring about any change in their present or future situation at work.

For these young people then, their experience of work reinforces the image of themselves transmitted at school: that of young people of limited ability destined for semi-skilled and unskilled jobs. For they are now committed to a future in these careerless occupations. . . .

One of the consequences of the fact that these young people make relatively few job commitments is that they experience little involvement in their work. Once again the parallel with the school situation is evident: the jobs, in making minimal demands on their cognitive and manipulative capacities, provide few opportunities for the development of skills in which the young worker can take pride. . . .

As they experience relatively little involvement in their jobs, their work does not take on the same meaning that it does for those young people who commit themselves to a career. It is not an area in which they can achieve competence within a specific field of occupational activity that will serve to differentiate them from others in similar occupations, nor is it an area in which they can hope to advance themselves in relation to others. Thus, for these young people the fact that they make few commitments to specific jobs and experience little involvement enables them to move freely between jobs. Their decision to enter any one job is far more casual than in the case of other young workers, as in their case they have relatively little to lose should they make a mistake.

Turning now to the frame of reference characteristic of many of the young people in occupations that provide a working class career; this is distinguished by its short-term determinacy. Concern is with the short term future, which does not preclude a concern with the here and now, but nevertheless involves the subordination of immediate to future considerations. The rewards that are sought from work are not only those that can be obtained from the immediate context of the job, but are primarily the short term rewards. Work involves a more differentiated occupational identity in which a distinction is drawn between present and future self. The self is conceived of in relation to skilled work in which there is a correspondingly higher degree of involvement. . . .

How is it possible that these young people come to see themselves and their world of work in such different terms from those in careerless occupations? How are they committed to work within this career channel? In attempting to answer these questions, the mechanisms of social inheritance may again play a part. One would expect them to contribute towards the creation and maintenance of a different type of relationship between these young people and their teachers than was the case for those pupils in the lower streams. The majority of young people in this channel in our sample (59 per cent) came from upper working class and lower middle class families. From these social origins one would expect the child to have acquired both elaborated and restricted codes,[13] and so to be sensitive to the communication system of the school. In addition, the children from this type of family are more likely to have acquired values and standards of conduct that exhibit a higher degree of congruence with those of their teachers.[14] Both of these factors associated with their social origins are likely to facilitate the child's integration into the school, enabling him to experience school life as one of personal development. This positive orientation of the child to the school and its teachers is reinforced by the formal organization of the school, with the rigid separation of these children into the higher or middle streams. For these children are systematically treated as superior to those in the lower streams. They are seen

13. B. Bernstein, *Class, Codes and Control*, Vol. I, Routledge and Kegan Paul, London, 1971.
14. J. W. B. Douglas, *The Home and the School*, MacGibbon and Kee, London, 1964.

as innately more intelligent, capable of benefiting from their education and frequently within the modern schools, the best resources of the school are mobilized to ensure that they do succeed.

Once again, the process of commitment to their future type of work begins to operate from the early stages of their school life. Through the process of allocation, the pupils are denied access to those educational positions that provide the opportunity of acquiring advanced and intermediate forms of certification that would ensure access to occupations that provide the chance of making a middle class career. They are already committed to working class occupations. Yet, although they are in positions that provide the possibility of acquiring elementary certification, this does not necessarily commit them to entering those occupations that provide for a working class career. They could, if they so wished, enter careerless occupations. What does function to commit them to occupations that provide for a working class career, is the acquisition of a specific type of self-image and orientation to work.

As regards their self-image, the process of allocation serves, as it does for those in the lower streams, to symbolize the pupils' 'inferiority' and 'failure' in relation to those who enter higher streams or grammar schools: an inferiority of which they are conscious. . . . However, while they see themselves as academically inferior to some, and hence not capable of effectively performing the tasks required of those who enter occupations that provide for a middle class career, their position within the school does symbolize their 'superiority' in relation to those in the lower streams. Unlike those in the lower channel, the process of allocation and the set of beliefs that legitimate it provide them with support for the development of their identity. . . . It is through the acquisition of this type of self-image that they become committed to enter occupations that provide for a working class career, for these are the only type of working class occupations that enable them to 'get on', to 'make something of themselves'. They learn to see these as desirable and those occupations that do not provide these chances as 'dead end jobs', inferior and unsuitable for themselves.

In addition to acquiring this type of self-image, their experience of school may also lead them to acquire a different type of orientation to work than is found among the careerless. For while these pupils obtain certain immediate rewards—from the prestige associated with their position in the school, and the sense of personal achievement they derive from it—they are also offered the chance of greater future rewards. The problems they face at school are not primarily those of relieving boredom, but those entailed in mastering academic and practical subjects in order that they may obtain the greater future rewards associated with a successful educational performance: namely educational certification and the chance of entering an occupation that provides a career. Throughout their school life they are systematically offered and pointed toward the promise of a greater reward in the short term future.

. . . In their last year, school never takes on the function of a custodial institution as it does for those in the lower streams. For those in the higher streams it is marked by a gradual realization that school has little more to offer that is relevant to their future employment. However, unlike those in careerless occupations, the end of their school life does not necessarily mark the end, for all of them, of their formal education, since their education and training may continue during the course of their apprenticeship.

On making the transition from school to work, these young people have already made a series of 'side bets' that commit them to skilled work. From their point of view, professional and managerial jobs are beyond their reach while semi-skilled and unskilled jobs are beneath them. What is of crucial importance to them is that their job should enable them to develop their skills further and in so doing secure the short term future rewards that they think are to be derived from 'having a trade in your hands'. What attracts some is the higher earnings that they can expect from their trade in the future, 'I could get more money in hosiery now, but when I've finished my time I can earn far more'; for others the security their trade offers, 'skilled men are always the last to go'; or the superior status of skilled work. What they regard as crucial is that their jobs should provide these opportunities and rewards for the sake of which they are willing to accept a low initial income. . . .

Having chosen this type of occupation, the young people are still faced with the problem of choosing a specific trade. This problem is frequently resolved by reference to the immediate rewards and satisfactions they derive from the activities involved. For example, one sheet metal worker took his job because, as he said, 'I like working with metal'; an apprentice electrician entered his trade because 'I was good at electrical wiring at school'; and many of those who enter the building trades do so because they want to work outside. Like those who enter careerless occupations, these young workers seek immediate rewards from their work, but only within the context of occupations that provide greater rewards in the short term future.

On entering their occupations these young workers make a further series of side bets that function to commit them to skilled work. In contrast to those who enter careerless occupations, who as we have seen are committed to their occupational channel rather than specific jobs within it, the situation for these young workers is different. For the side bets they make function to commit them to a specific trade. Formal commitments are made through the signing of indentures. Less formal commitments are made as they acquire specific skills that can only provide them with the rewards they seek through their membership of one occupational group. For some the prospects of future advancement also tie them to their occupation. . . .

In moving through their positions at work, the self-images and orientations transmitted at school are again reinforced. Their image of themselves as future skilled workers is confirmed by their acquisition of the appropriate skills. Once again they find themselves in a position in which the successful performance of their tasks offers not only immediate rewards but the promise of greater future rewards. They are regarded both by their employers and by other tradesmen as capable of further developing their cognitive and manipulative skills and are in a position that provides the necessary opportunity. From the point of view of the young workers, they are once again (as at school) in a position in which they are working for future rewards, although admittedly short-term future rewards.

Unlike those who entered careerless occupations these young workers accept the dominant belief that young people should make a career. Although, in contrast to those who enter occupations that provide the chance for making a middle class career, for the majority their career is a short but determinate one. They know with a fairly high degree of certainty that they will reach the position of skilled man—the height of their career. . . . In short, all these young workers have prospects, and are making a career, albeit within the confines of manual work. . . .

For these young people, moving through positions that provide the opportunity for the development of skills and offer the promise of future rewards for successful performance, work becomes meaningful not just as a source of immediate rewards, but primarily as a means of securing the short-term future rewards associated with the acquisition of membership of a trade. At least, in the early stages of their career, work is a means of making something of themselves. For them the consequences of a wrong decision at the point of entry into the labour market are potentially far more serious than would be the case for those entering careerless occupations.

In the course of this paper, I have attempted to show how the problem stated at the beginning could usefully be approached from two different yet complementary perspectives. I have tried to show how the different properties of the configurations young people form at school and work present them with different types of problems, different opportunities for the development of skills and different levels of reward. From the experiential perspective I suggested some of the ways in which this leads to the development of different frames of reference that commit young people to certain types of occupation, and by providing them with different self-images and orientations to work enable them to adjust to their positions at work. The analysis, given the present state of our knowledge in this field, is tentative. Only a mere outline of the dynamics of the process whereby the young people acquire different frames of reference has been attempted. A more substantive analysis would require further research into the way in which both teachers and pupils, supervisors and workers, experience their world and their interaction with each other. Equally important, it would require research into the properties of the configurations they form. However, tentative as the analysis is, it does provide a preliminary answer to the question of why young people should experience the transition between school and work as a relatively smooth process.

SECTION THREE
OCCUPATIONAL CATEGORIES AND CULTURES

INTRODUCTION   Graeme Salaman

In his classic article in this section, 'Work and the Self' Everett Hughes writes

> ... a man's work is one of the things by which he is judged, and
> certainly one of the more significant things by which he judges
> himself.

Later in the same article he remarks,

> ... a man's work is one of the more important parts of his social
> identity, of his self; indeed, of his fate in the one life he has to live,
> for there is something almost as irrevocable about choice of
> occupation as there is about choice of a mate.

Such a conviction of the personal significance of work underlies the choice of articles in this section.

But what does it mean to argue that work has implications for the identities of those concerned—for their 'selves'? A number of different possible interpretations are evident. Hughes himself has pointed out the significance of work or occupational *titles* for peoples' self-images, and he has usefully discussed the ways in which particular sorts of work activity, or particular positions within the division of labour, or organizational hierarchy, can involve people in identity problems or crises (given the values of the society in general). Hughes argues that under these circumstances people develop what he calls 'collective pretensions' which '... give their work, and consequently themselves, value in the eyes of each other and of outsiders'. In general his approach to the relationship between work and identity involves an attempt to '. . . understand the social and social-psychological arrangements and devices by which men make their work tolerable, or even glorious to themselves and others'. Hughes' interest in the relationship between work and identity is to explore the ploys and techniques whereby people try to protect themselves from potentially ego-damaging work activities or relationships.

For many writers the Hughesian directive to '. . . penetrate more deeply into the personal and social drama of work', leads them into aspects of 'the politics of work' (see Article I) in which Hughes himself, for all his seminal insights and suggestions, was relatively uninterested. Writers such as Mills, Fromm, and Berger take a wider interest to include a critical theory of the nature of work and society and the values which underlie and determine work events and experiences. Frequently such analyses of the meaning of work, or of the nature and implications of the ways of thinking and evaluating which characterize industrialization make use of, or are inspired by, the Marxist concept of alienation. This is well illustrated in Mills' famous study, *White Collar*, which is too well known to need inclusion in this volume but which requires some mention. Mills describes the essential features of white collar work and their implications for white-collar workers: '. . . they sell not only their time and energy but their personalities as well. They sell by the week or month their smiles and kindly gestures, and they must practice the prompt repression of resentment and aggression'.[1] The result of this sort of work is that workers are driven to find meaning in their out-of-work lives. As Mills puts it, in a memorable phrase:

> Each day men sell little pieces of themselves in order to try to buy them back each night and weekend with the coin of 'fun'. With amusement, with love, with movies and with vicarious intimacy, they pull themselves into some sort of whole again, and now they are different men.[2]

But Mills, and others, do not restrict their concern for 'the personal and social drama of work' to the meanings, satisfactions, dissatisfactions and frustrations people derive from their work, or the impact it has on their identities. They also consider the nature and implications of the sort of society within which such work occurs. And they ask, how do the values which evidently inspire the increasing mechanization, rationalization, automation, sub-division, standardization and control of work relate to the values of the society at large? Is it not inevitable that the 'rationalities' and values which are evident in the nature and design of work and jobs, and in organizational and

1. C. W. Mills, *White Collar*, Galaxy, New York, 1956, p. xvii.
2. *Ibid.*, p. 237.

industrial decision-making pervade the society as a whole? Mills makes the point that,

> ... rationality seems to have taken on a new form, to have its seat not in individual men, but in social institutions which by their bureaucratic planning and mathematical foresight usurp both freedom and rationality from the little individual men caught in them. The calculating hierarchies of department store and industrial corporation, of rationalized office and government bureau, lay out the gray ways and stereotype the permitted initiatives.[3]

But this rationality has pervasive societal effects.

It is not possible to isolate separately the ways men know, understand and evaluate the world, themselves and each other from the forms of knowledge and evaluation which lie behind, and are displayed in, forms of work, and work organization. The sort of knowledge and consciousness that enables people to be competent in every-day life (whether at work, or during out-of-work hours), consists of structures of definitions, 'facts', expectations and moralities which are inevitably influenced by the knowledge and criteria which lie behind industrial, organizational, events and decisions. As Berger *et al*. have argued methods of production and organization involve knowledge and ways of thinking and evaluating that are carried over into out-of-work life:

> ... elements of consciousness that are intrinsic to technological production are transposed to areas of social life that are not directly connected with such production (for example, problem-solving ingenuity) ... Everyday life in just about every one of its sectors is ongoingly bombarded, not only with material objects and processes derived from technological production but with clusters of consciousness originating with the latter.[4]

But if the Marxist concept of alienation can be seen to have inspired interest in and concern for the nature and implications of work activities, titles, relationships and experience and the knowledge and culture which lie behind, and are displayed in the design and organization of work tasks, the Marxist concept of class-consciousness is also highly pertinent to research in this area. Much work has been done on the relationship between work events and the development of class-conscious attitudes and behaviour—or of attitudes and perceptions which are regarded as being related to, or part of, radical class-consciousness. Much of this work, including the two articles in this section by Lockwood and Mackenzie, attempts to describe the features of work and community which are relevant to the development of those

3. *Ibid.*, p. xvii.
4. Peter Berger, Brigitte Berger and Hansfried Kellner, *The Homeless Mind*, Penguin, Harmondsworth, 1973, p. 42.

sorts of attitudes towards fellow workers and perceptions of the class structure of the society which are regarded as essential elements of radical class-consciousness. Obviously the relationship between work events and experiences and attitudes of solidarity and opposition has practical, political significance as well as sociological importance.

Of course there is a direct link between the meaning of work and the developments of class-conscious attitudes among those who share a similar employment situation, or who do the same work. It might after all be the case that people have developed orientations to work which lead them to value only such rewards as it offers and have become indifferent to its apparent deprivations. If this were true (and it seems most unlikely) then presumably this would have implications for the development, or absence, of class-conscious attitudes. (For a consideration of this and related arguments, see Mann, 1973;[5] for a useful discussion of the literature on orientations to work, see Fox, 1971[6]). Finally it should be noted that the difficulties of analysing the relationship between work experiences and events and class-consciousness (an objective which has motivated many British industrial sociologists) are compounded by virtue of the complexity of the relationship between perceptions of class structure, or orientations towards work and employers, and class-consciousness as defined by Marx.

The majority of the articles in this section are relevant to Hughes' interest in the 'personal and social drama of work' in that they are concerned with work as a source of meanings, cultures and attitudes, through one or other of the two approaches outlined above. Some of the articles deal, in general terms, with the relationship between work events and activities and ideas and world views, others concentrate on this relationship only with reference to potentially class-conscious attitudes.

Berger's article deals, at a very general level, with the meaning of work. He argues that the problematic meaning of work is a result of two developments: '. . . the extreme intensification of the division of labour occasioned by the ongoing Industrial Revolution; (and) ideologically, the secularization of the concept of vocation.' It will be clear that by focussing on these two developments Berger is following the preoccupation of the early theorists, (see Article 1).

Berger's analysis of the changes that follow these two developments includes consideration of the sorts of issues discussed earlier: the significance of work for individual's identities, and the link between

5. Michael Mann, *Consciousness and Action Among the Western Working Class*, Macmillan, London, 1973.
6. Alan Fox, *A Sociology of Work in Industry*, Collier-Macmillan, London, 1971.

work and out-of-work life. Like many others he relates meaningless work to '. . . the concentration of the individual's search for meaning and identity in the so-called private sphere.' One result of this is that the world of work is increasingly regarded as a mere *means* to some other (out-of-work) ends.

Mackenzie's paper is also concerned with the meaning of work, but from the point of view of an interest in the relationship between work and the development of attitudes or values which can be seen as class-conscious. As noted above this is an issue which many British and European sociologists have studied and researched. Mackenzie follows the conceptual delineation of relevant aspects of work propounded by David Lockwood in his classic, *The Blackcoated Worker*.[7] The basic problem is a simple one, as Mackenzie remarks: how is it that workers who appear to share the same class situation display differing class attitudes? The answer is of course that the gross term *class situation* needs to be broken down into its empirical constituents, which Lockwood suggests, can vary independently of each other. Mackenzie takes the discussion further by attempting to relate the Lockwood model to variations in social imagery—those perceptions and definitions of the societal class structure which are taken to underlie, and to constitute an element of, class-consciousness.

Bensman and Lilienfeld contribute to the concerns of this section through their interesting analysis of the relationship between work activities, skills and techniques and 'basic attitudes towards life'. This is an unusual and ambitious attempt to *explore* rather than to *assume* the mechanisms whereby work activities encourage certain world images. The authors complement the suggestions of Lockwood and Mackenzie by their analysis of the role of '. . . the craft itself in determining world images and occupational attitudes.'

These authors concentrate on the *occupational* basis of world images, rather than the *work* basis, that is, they use the concept occupation to draw attention to the way in which people who do the same work occasionally develop a self-consciousness of their shared occupational identity and culture, and of themselves as colleagues. Members of occupations, as these authors point out, develop jargons, and attempt to advance the standing of the occupation. The result of their emphasis on occupation is that they can argue that 'occupational dynamics can be totally different from class.'

A great deal of recent work on class imagery, and the relationship between work and social imagery has been inspired by Lockwood's famous paper, 'Sources of Variation in Working Class Images of Society which is included here. The most important feature

7. David Lockwood, The Blackcoated Worker, George Allen and Unwin, London, 1958.

of Lockwood's typology of types of worker is his contention that attitudes towards work and employer are strongly related to social imagery, and that both are a result of the 'industrial and community *milieux* of manual workers'. Although Lockwood's typology has, inevitably, given its level of generality, been modified by more recent research it remains an important and useful starting point for the analysis of work and class attitudes.

In an important sense the Hughes article supplies the overall theme for the section as a whole, as the earlier remarks suggested. This is not to say that Hughes' suggestions and insights exhaust all that can be said about the meaning of work (indeed it should be clear that his approach is, in our view, highly partial). Nevertheless, his article does set the scene for the sorts of discussions included in this section, although many of the authors pursue the meaning of work in directions in which Hughes himself showed little interest.

The last two articles by Nichols and Hollowell have been included here because, in the view of the editors, both supply rich and persuasive accounts of occupational and work experiences and events, and as such they contribute an empirical flavour to the proceedings. Nichols and Hollowell *get inside* the work situations they describe, and their accounts and analyses of the nature and implications of industrial employment (albeit for very different purposes) consider the 'meaning' of industrial employment in very specific and empirical ways. Their analyses of industrial accidents and the history of foot-plate men should be seen as valuable contributions to the debate about the class nature of work experiences and events.

11. THE HUMAN SHAPE OF WORK   Peter Berger

Work is one of the fundamental human categories. Man is the animal that fashioned tools and built a world. Man is thus the only animal that lives in two worlds, the natural one shared with all other inhabitants of the planet, and that other nature, a *nature artificielle* (as French anthropologists have called it), made by himself. Since it is this man-made second world that provides the context of any conduct properly to be recognized as human, the process by which at any rate the physical foundation of this world is constructed is of crucial human significance. This can be said quite apart from the question whether the symbolic edifice that necessarily overarches the human world should also be thought of as the result of work, mental work being then understood as a correlate or even derivative of physical work. To be human and to work appear as inextricably intertwined notions. To work means to modify the world as it is found. Only through such modification can the world be made into an arena for human conduct, human meanings, human society or, for that matter, human existence in any sense of the word. It is not surprising, then, that the great revolutions in the character of human work entailed transformations of human existence in its totality, from the so-called neolithic revolution on to the Industrial Revolution that is still transforming our own existence today. Nor is it surprising that work was imbued from earliest times with profound religious significance. If to work means to build a world, then it entails, in a religious perspective, a repetition or imitation of the divine acts by which the world was originally built—and perhaps even a competition with these divine acts, as the myth of Prometheus suggests. To work is no light matter. To work is to mime creation itself.

Work as mimesis of the gods is a long shot from the questions that in one way or another have revolved around the problem of the meaning of work. It is, therefore, of some importance to see that this problem is a peculiarly modern one, related, as we shall indicate in a moment, to specific structural and ideological developments in modern Western history. In most previous societies the problem hardly existed in this form. On the one hand, work was a religious duty, on the other hand, suffering understood to be part of man's fate. Thus, for example, the Hebrew word *avodah* means 'service'—both in the ordinary sense of work and in the religious sense of serving the divinity, that is, of worship. A similar combination of meanings probably underlies the Greek *leitourgia*. The Latin *labor*, on the

11. Reprinted with permission of Macmillan Publishing Co., Inc., New York, from *The Human Shape of Work*, by Peter L. Berger, Editor. Copyright © Peter L. Berger 1964. (pp. 211-22)

other hand, means both work and toil, in the general sense of suffering. And the latter implication is borne out even more sharply in the Latin derivatives rendered by 'travail' in English (French *travail*, Spanish *trabajo*), which probably come from the word *trepalium*, referring to an instrument of torture. There is little if any hint in all this of the questions we associate with work today.

To deal with 'the problem of work' is to deal with peculiarly modern phenomena. The focus of the 'problem' is the question of 'meaning'. Now, social phenomena are always 'meaningful', but in most cases these meanings are taken for granted, organized in institutions, and fully legitimated in the symbolic system of the society. That is, 'meaning' is not ordinarily a 'problem'. It *becomes* problematic as the result of specific transformations within the society, transformations that put in question the previous taken-for-granted institutionalizations and legitimations. It is, therefore, logical to ask what the transformations are that have made our particular 'problem' possible. It seems to us that two developments are of decisive importance in this connection—structurally, the extreme intensification of the division of labor occasioned by the ongoing Industrial Revolution; ideologically, the secularization of the concept of vocation. We shall briefly look at these two developments.

The division of labor is probably as old as human society itself, since the latter would hardly be possible without at least a measure of the former. With advances in the technology of labor, the division of labor naturally gained in complexity. The Industrial Revolution, however, with its proliferation of techniques and skills, led to an intensification in the division of labor unique in history. We are still in the midst of this process, with no sign of abatement. . . . Moreover, the Industrial Revolution has brought about an ever-increasing fragmentation of specific work processes, removing the worker further and further away from the product of his work. The classical case of this fragmentation is the assembly line. In the case of the automobile assembly line there is still knowledge, on the part of the worker, what the final product looks like. The present writer has known workers engaged in assembly-line work who did not even know what the product they were working on was actually designed for, except that it had something to do with parts of 'precision machinery'—for all they knew, the workers might have been working on a part destined to set off a hydrogen bomb. Nor, may it be added, were they particularly interested in the question. This fragmentation of work has not remained restricted to the manufacturing process, but increasingly affects white-collar occupations as well. Large offices are set up on principles quite similar to those of the assembly line, and for the same reasons. Even some of the so-called professions have been subjected to the impact of these forces— there exist today situations of assembly-line medicine, assembly-line law, and even assembly-line scientific research, with physicians, lawyers and scientists attached to a small fragment of the overall work process very much as the automobile worker is to 'his' place in the assembly line. Work under such circumstances need not be hard or painful (that would be nothing new), but the question of its meaning is apt to become conscious much more so than in situations where the worker related to the work process until the final product emerged.

As the result of technological progress, moreover, there are constant changes in the social organization of work. Certain occupational specialities become obsolescent, others appear *de novo*. We are today very familiar with the crises brought on by occupational obsolescence due to automation, with such crises having become more and more central in recent labor/management disputes in industry. And it requires little imagination to grasp the human tragedies involved in this (though even this amount of imagination is often lacking in public annoyance with certain labor unions for clinging to 'outdated' work rules—for while we have plenty of engineers to 'update' the work, we have not been very successful in developing ways of dealing with the 'outdated' workers). However, this is only part of the basic human problem, the external, or socio-economic, part. But there is also an internal, or sociopsychological, part of the problem. Precisely because work has been for so long a fundamental human category, any particular work has been not only a means of livelihood but also a source of self-identification. To take a drastic example, the Hindu artisan who prays to his tools not only expresses the religious significance of his work but also, at the same time, essentially defines himself in terms of this work. To put it simply, for most of history men have *been* what they *did*. This did not have to mean that they particularly *liked* what they did—the problem of 'job satisfaction' is as modern as that of the 'meaning of work'. To say 'I am a peasant' was, very probably, a far cry from pride, enthusiasm, or even contentment. Nevertheless, it provided a self-identification for the individual that was stable, consistent, and so recognized both by others and by himself. To put it simply again, work provided the individual with a firm profile. This is no longer the case with most work in industrial society. To say 'I am a railroad fireman' may be a source of pride, but the pride is as precarious as the occupational title. To say 'I am an electro-encephalograph technician' means nothing to most people to whom it is said. To say 'I am an addressograph operator' means nothing for a different reason, not because people do not understand what kind of work it entails, but because it is next to impossible to derive any sort of self-identification from such an occupation, not even the self-identification with an oppressed proletariat that sustain many workers in earlier phases of industrialism. Fragmented and ever-changing work thus tends to become divorced from those social relationships and events from which the individual derives his self-identification, and *ipso facto* begins to appear to him as problematic if not downright meaningless.

One consequence of this has been the concentration of the individual's search for meaning and identity in the so-called private sphere, also a peculiarly modern phenomenon, of which a little more in a moment. Another consequence, though, has been a wild scramble for status among a large number of occupations. Status and identity based on work have become fluid, insecure, and thereby subject to manipulation. If one can no longer humanly identify with one's work, in many cases, one can still 'project an image' and, if successful, reap from this various economic and social advantages. In other words, occupational status has become a subject of one-upmanship. Indeed, there are occupations that can exist only by virtue of such one-upmanship. The hospital orderly, whose lowly job in the hospital hierarchy includes the removal of the repulsive debris of medical activity, may describe himself as a 'cuspidorologist' and perhaps even get away with it, at least outside the hospital. What goes on under the heading of 'professionalization' in many instances is not far away from this pathetic confidence trick. Occupations not only become obsolete, but long before this may have to defend their reason of existence. Other occupations, just emerging out of limbo and already aspiring to the status of 'professions', have to be even more strident in their claims to life, respect, and a healthy slice of the economic pudding. Thus the occupational scene today is filled with a multitude of defense organizations and propaganda agencies, totally bewildering to the average citizen and often enough bewildering to the various official bodies called upon to licence, adjudicate, and supervise in this jungle of competing image projections. This situation not only raises questions about such older concepts as that of 'the dignity of work', but again evokes the specter of meaninglessness over the whole occupational scene.

One very important result of the Industrial Revolution, already alluded to, has been the crystallization of the so-called private sphere of life, a sociologically novel phenomenon located interstitially between the large public institutions. Although this private sphere is, of course, dependent on the public institutions (especially the economic and political ones), it provides for the individual a decisive alternative source of self-identification and personal meaning. This has important sociological and social-psychological consequences that we cannot pursue here. What interests us is that this private sphere is, almost by definition, segregated from the sphere of work. Indeed, it was the industrialization of work in the first place that made possible the emergence of this new area of social life. The typical and statistically normal state of affairs in an industrial society is that people do not work where they carry on their private lives. The two spheres are geographically and socially separate. And since it is in the latter that people typically and normally locate their essential identities, one can say even more simply that they do not live where they work. 'Real life' and one's 'authentic self' are supposed to be centered in the private sphere. Life at work thus tends to take on the character of pseudo-reality and pseudo-identity: 'I only work here, but if you want to know me as I really am, come to my home and meet my family'. In terms of institutions, the most important process involved in all this has been the segregation of the family from the world of work, and its transformation from an economically productive to an economically consumptive agency. And, of course, it is the family that, for most people in our society, is the principal focus of private life.

This, as it were, ontological devaluation of the world of work has had far-reaching consequences for its character, psychologically as well as morally. The old profile-giving capacity of work is replaced by a peculiar dichotomization of life. The private sphere, especially the family, becomes the expression of 'who one really is'. The sphere of work is conversely apprehended as the region in which one is 'not really oneself', or, to use a social-scientific term increasingly and significantly used in common speech, one in which one 'plays only a role'. . . . Private morality and public morality become quite different universes of discourse. One must beware here of quickly regarding this dual ethics in terms of 'hypocrisy'. Given the structural dichotomization referred to above, the dichotomization of ethical theory as well as moral practice is only 'realistic', that is, appropriate to the prevailing social reality.

We would contend that this metamorphosis of work in industrial society has fundamentally changed its human character. In older societies one could usually distinguish between 'noble' and 'ignoble' work. While our business executive is undoubtedly engaged in work deemed 'noble' by himself and by almost everyone else, and our apartment-building janitor is pretty firmly considered to be doing 'ignoble' work, the older simple distinction no longer holds in most cases. We would rather suggest a threefold division of work in terms of its human significance. First, there is work that still provides an occasion for primary self-identification and self-commitment of the individual—for his 'fulfilment', if one prefers. *Thirdly*, there is work that is apprehended as a direct threat to self-identification, an indignity, an oppression. And secondly, between these two poles, is work that is *neither* fulfilment *nor* oppression, a sort of gray, neutral region in which one neither rejoices nor suffers, but with which one puts up with more or less grace for the sake of other things that are supposed to be more important—these other things being typically connected with one's private life. As in any typology, there may be difficulties in clearly assigning specific work situations or occupations in terms of it. But in most cases, we should think, the decision is not hard. In the first category, of course, are to be placed most so-called professions and the upper-echelon positions in the various bureaucratic apparatuses. In the third category continue to remain many of the unskilled occupations 'in the basement' of the industrial system. And in between, in the second category, is to be found the bulk of both white-collar and blue-collar work.

For better or for worse (and, by most possible criteria, probably for better), the first and the third category have shrunk in favor of the second. This would seem to be an inevitable consequence of ongoing industrialization. Rationalization of work, bureaucratization of the administrative machinery, mass organization for mass production and mass consumption—these functional necessities of the industrial system must inevitably lead to a shrinkage of the first category of work. Only at the top and in certain special positions elsewhere is there much room left for work that involves the totality of the person. More commonly the entrepreneur is replaced by the bureaucrat, the individualistic professional by a team, and the craftsman by a machine. But at the same time that the demand for masters shrinks, so does the demand for slaves. Work becomes safer and cleaner, its administration more humane, its demands in terms of time and energy more lenient. If some people have less joy in work, most have less pain. Whatever one may think of this balance of the human accounts, it will be clear that the expanding area in the middle will generate its own problems, different and perhaps less harrowing than those of a previous generation, but pressing nonetheless. And among these problems that of the 'meaning' of work is central.

Our 'problem of work' must, then, be understood within a specific historical and thus relative frame of reference, against the background of specific structural processes of modern industrial society. In addition, however, there is an ideological development to be taken into consideration, namely, the secularization of the concept of vocation. We cannot here give a presentation of the theory of Max Weber on this subject, and must limit ourselves to the observation that this theory is crucial to an understanding of the ideological dimension of work in modern society. Weber showed convincingly how, especially through the agency of Protestantism, the medieval concept of religious vocation was transformed into the modern concept of secular work as a vocation, that is, as action requiring the individual's highest religious and ethical commitments. Even those critical of Weber's theory will concede that work in the beginnings of modern Western history has come to acquire a meaning quite different from the one it had in previous periods and in other civilizations—not only a religious duty to be faithfully performed, not only an activity endowed with weighty ethical pre- and pro-scriptions (such as, say, the *dharma* of Hindu caste)—but a 'calling', in the sense of demanding from the individual a total and passionate commitment, channeling his entire life for the achievement of high goals and thus bestowing high meaning on this life. Needless to say, this attitude toward work must be seen in relation to the immense energy that modern Western man has invested in economic and technological activity, an energy (what Weber called the power of 'inner-worldly asceticism') that lies at the mainspring of both modern capitalism and modern industrialism. Now, although few individuals today approach their vocation as a task undertaken 'to the greater glory of God', the conception of work as the bearer of high ethical and personal meanings has persisted. In other words, the concept of vocation persists in a secularized form, maximally in the continued notion that work will provide the ultimate 'fulfilment' of the individual's life, and minimally in the expectation that, in some shape or form, work will have some meaning for him personally.

If we now try to see the structural and the ideological developments together, we are confronted by a paradoxical and even ironic situation. The structural development, as we have tried to show, makes it more and more unlikely that the individual will be able to 'realize himself' in his work, forces him to look for such 'self-realization' elsewhere, changes work from the exercise of a 'calling' to the playing of a 'role'. At the same time, there persists an ideology of work that continues to present the individual with the expectation that he find his work 'meaningful' and that he find 'satisfaction' in it, an ideology that is institutionalized in the educational system (for instance, 'vocational counseling'), in the media of mass communication and, last but not least, in the various occupational and professional organizations. Contemporary society does little to prepare its members for 'meaningless' if painless pursuits. Rather, it inculcates in them the generalized expectation of an ever-fuller realization of 'meanings' in everything they do. It is unfortunate that this expectation must then be carried out into a world in which it has very little chance of being met. Indeed, on *a priori* sociological grounds, one may expect that the ideology of work will gradually adapt itself to its structural reality. Indeed, we would argue that the 'privatism' discussed above constitutes, at least in part, precisely such an ideological adaptation. However, as long as the old ideological expectation persists, our 'problem of work' will continue to be particularly sharp.

12. WORLD IMAGES AND THE WORLD OF WORK
Gavin Mackenzie

Since the emergence of sociology as a distinct discipline the study of class and class conflict has been at the forefront. Indeed, at least within the European brand of the subject it can be argued that the analysis of class structure represents *the* core of sociology's subject matter. And yet, despite this fact the *theory* of social class has progressed in a very uneven manner. Our knowledge of the ways in which economic inequalities are created, sustained and changed has increased dramatically, but at the same time, in contrast, our understanding of many of the facets of that inequality has progressed little. In particular, the *explanation* of interclass differences in values, ideologies and patterns of behaviour is without doubt the least-developed aspect of the theory of social class. Furthermore, such a situation is difficult to explain. For the two writers who have contributed most to our understanding of the economic bases of class structure also addressed themselves, albeit briefly and incompletely, to the problem of the explanation of class ideologies and, of course, class consciousness.

Marx and Weber were both well aware of the fact that the emergence and subsequent development of class consciousness—the process of a class *in* itself becoming a class *for* itself—could not be regarded as either inevitable or automatic. Rather it depended on a number of people who shared a similar 'relationship to the means of production' or 'position in the market' being placed in a social situation that *engendered* an awareness of class consciousness and a feeling of class solidarity. And for both writers the situation most conducive to the creation of such a consciousness was to be found within the 'capitalistic enterprize' itself, which concentrates in one place large numbers of people sharing a common class position, with common class interests and a common *and visible* class enemy.

As is well known, while sharing Weber's view of the importance of the large-scale enterprize in the shaping of working class consciousness, Marx went further: he saw that consciousness eventually leading to the 'revolutionary reconstruction of the society at large'. In bringing together wage labourers and thus increasing surplus, the capitalist at the same time most effectively sows the seeds of his own destruction:

> . . . with the development of industry the proletariat not only increases in number; it becomes concentrated in greater masses, its strength grows, and it feels that strength more. . . . The advance of industry, whose involuntary promoter is the bourgeoisie, replaces the isolation of the labourers, due to competition, by their revolutionary combination, due to association. The development of Modern Industry, therefore, cuts from under its feet the very foundation on which the bourgeoisie produces and appropriates products. What the bourgeoisie, therefore, produces, above all, is its own gravediggers. Its fall and the victory of the proletariat are equally inevitable.[1]

It is evident that for both Marx and Weber *work situation* assumes *the* vital role in the emergence and development of class ideology. And yet, as I have said, although their writings on class formation, on the role of productive property, on market situation and 'life chances' form the basis of contemporary theorizing on these aspects of class and class structure, the potential gains to be made from the theoretical development of their brief references to *work situation* have been largely neglected. I say 'largely neglected' because there have been one or two exceptions: within British sociology the most notable of these is the work of David Lockwood. Thus, in his classic study *The Blackcoated Worker* Lockwood set out to explain the 'false consciousness' of the clerical worker in British industry. In particular he was concerned to find out why a group of people ('proletarians in white collars') who in *economic* terms shared the same market situation as the majority of manual workers, nevertheless saw themselves as being in a different (superior) social class to the latter group. His answer was couched unambiguously in terms of the influence of the differing work situations of clerical and manual workers, for:

> Without doubt in modern industrial society the most important social conditions shaping the psychology of the individual are those arising out of the organization of production, administration and distribution. In other words, the 'work situation'.[2]

In this case Lockwood laid stress on the manner in which distinct patterns of *social relationships* were engendered by distinct work situations:

> For every employee is precipitated, by virtue of a given division of labour, into unavoidable relationships with other employees, supervisors, managers or customers. The work situation involves the separation and concentration of individuals, affords possibilities of identification with and alienation from others, and conditions feelings of isolation, antagonism and solidarity.[3]

1. K. Marx and F. Engels, *Manifesto of the Communist Party*, Foreign Languages Publishing House, Moscow, pp. 64 & 71. Although writing from a different sociological perspective, Durkheim made a remarkably similar observation: ' . . . small-scale industry, where work is less divided, displays a relative harmony between worker and employer. It is only in large-scale industry that these relations are in a sickly state.' Emile Durkheim, *The Division of Labour in Society*, Collier-Macmillan, London, 1933, p. 356.
2. David Lockwood, *The Blackcoated Worker*, George Allen and Unwin, London, 1958, p. 205.
3. *Ibid.*

Given the fact that one of the outstanding features of modern industry is the physical and social separation of those on the factory floor and those in 'the office' it is therefore not surprising that clerks do not identify with, or see themselves as sharing a working class situation with, manual workers. Rather, and as a result of the close contact they enjoy with managers and supervisors (engendered by the very nature of clerical tasks and thus the clerical work situation), it follows that blackcoated workers will see themselves as *bona fide* members of the middle class. To be sure, clerical workers exhibit a level and type of class consciousness distinct from that of manual workers, but as that consciousness has been created and sustained by a radically differing work situation from that experienced by the latter group its content cannot really be regarded as surprising. To ask whether class consciousness is 'false' or 'real' has therefore little meaning.

In *The Blackcoated Worker*, then, Lockwood was concerned with explaining a particular phenomenon, class consciousness, with reference to one aspect of work situation: the patterning of *social relationships*. Two years later, however, in discussing the 'new working class' he drew attention to the fact that there were many other facets of work situation that may be of importance in the explanation of the ways in which people develop images of the world and where they place themselves in that world.

> The size of factory, the organization of the work group, its relation to supervisors and management, the degree to which the worker has control over his work process, the extent to which the job facilitates or prevents communication between workers, the rigidity of the distinction between staff and workers, security of tenure, the progressiveness of earnings, and job discipline; these represent some of the points of reference for a construction of a typology of work relationships, without which no clear appreciation of class identification can be obtained.[4]

Nonetheless, despite this clear delineation of the task to be done, and despite Lockwood's clear demonstration of the power of work situation as an explanatory variable, to my knowledge no attempt has been made to construct such a typology of work situations and to link aspects of that typology to differences in social imagery. And again this is surprising. For there already exist two bodies of literature that should enable at least the first steps in the construction of such a typology to be taken. On the one hand there are a number of studies, primarily descriptive, and carried out in several countries, on social imagery or, more particularly, on images of class structure. On the other hand the last thirty years have seen an enormous amount of work done in the realm of industrial sociology, much of which can be used for the furtherance of our understanding of the dynamics of work situation.

4. David Lockwood, 'The "New Working Class"', *European Journal of Sociology*, 1, 1960, pp. 256–7.

Accordingly it is the task of the present article to bring together features or aspects of these two bodies of literature and thus to attempt to make some small contribution toward an understanding of this, the most neglected area of the theory of social class. Before I do this, however, several caveats must be made. First, the focus will be on only one aspect of class differences—that of class imagery.[5] This means that whole areas of class behaviour and ideology will be ignored. For example, little space will be devoted to discussion of the revolutionary potential of the British (or Western) working class. To anticipate somewhat, the fact that significant numbers of people have been found to view society in dichotomous terms—in terms of one class exploiting another—does not mean that we will be able to formulate a theory of class mobilization: *seeing* society as consisting of two opposed camps is not the same thing as *acting* to change that situation or indeed of even *wanting* to change that situation. Clearly images of class structure and action are related. But for the purposes of this article my concern is the modest one of the analysis of images only. Second, in no way can this analysis either of images of class structure or of components of work situation be regarded as complete: as has been made clear it can only be based on the existing literature, the context of which is at best piecemeal, at worst contradictory. Third, and linked to the previous point, discussion will be in terms of ideal types—sociological constructs. Thus no claim is being made that, for example, all middle-class people view social class in the same way or that the working class can be treated as an undifferentiated mass. Rather, the further ideal or polar types of work situation and class imagery can be developed, the better can actual variations from these types be understood. Finally, in adopting the standpoint that the social or class imagery prevalent among a group of individuals sharing a common class situation is constructed out of experiences in the work situation is not to claim that the latter is the *sole* basis of the 'social construction of reality'. The symbolic representations of inequality held by any individual will be a result of his experiences direct and indirect, in a number of groups and situations, both in the past and the present. In this particular case other sources of stimuli will obviously be various aspects of the structure of the local community, of the family, both nuclear and extended, as well as that of the market. And these will not exhaust the list. For the present, however, my contention is that work situation provides *the* most important set of conditions shaping the social imagery of industrial man: for it is at work that relations and experiences of superiority and inferiority, of solidarity and separateness, of frustration and achievement are most persuasive, most visible and therefore most influential.

5. In referring to 'class imagery' I am contending that individuals sharing a common-class situation will have similar *perceptions* of the way in which society is divided along class lines, i.e., they will have similar *beliefs* about the extent and nature of structured economic inequality. Furthermore I am contending that these differences in this general social imagery will be reflected in more specific differences in class values, attitudes and perspectives: for example, toward child rearing, the use of leisure time or political viewpoint. Both contentions are firmly rooted in the results of empirical research. See, amongst others, the studies referred to in footnote below.

A review of the research[6] that has been carried out on images of class suggests that such images are composed of a number of facets which can be assembled to form a total picture or *gestalt* of the structure of social inequality in a particular society. My strategy in the present article will be as follows. First I intend to look at some of these facets in detail and then to bring them together to form *two* ideal type images of society. Then I shall look at a number of aspects of work situation that theoretically can be associated with differing views on the various facets of class imagery. Finally I shall attempt to distil from these aspects of work situation, two ideal types that might be expected to be created and sustain the two ideal type images of society already constructed. It is worth reiterating that I regard this exercise as an extremely tentative one: I am attempting to set out the groundwork for the vast amount of research that needs to be done before we reach anything approaching a clear or complete understanding of either the various images of society adhered to by industrial man or the various bases of those images.

Perhaps the most fundamental aspect of any individual's image of class structure is the *number* of classes or strata that are visualized. And although the results of the various studies differ considerably in their detail, they do indicate clearly that the great majority of individuals adhere to one or other of two basic images of class society—dichotomous or hierarchical. In general, although this is by no means always the case, manual workers are more likely to see society as comprising only two groups or camps while non-manual workers view their world as containing three or more social classes, arranged in a hierarchy. Thus Hoggart and Popitz *et al* found a dichotomous view of society to be almost universal in the working-class group of whom they were writing:

> All the workers with whom we spoke . . . see society as a dichotomy—
> whether this is changeable or unchangeable, bridgeable or to be
> mediated by means of a 'partnership'. . . .[7]

In contrast, in my own research conducted in the United States and involving nearly 200 highly skilled craftsmen only 7 per cent saw society as comprising two groups. Instead the vast majority saw America as containing three strata. This was also the case amongst the managers I interviewed, although over a third said

---

6. The studies to which I shall refer are: O. A. Oeser and S. B. Hammond, *Social Structure and Personality in a City*, Routledge & Kegan Paul, London, 1954; Elizabeth Bott, *Family and Social Network*, Tavistock Publications, London, 1957; Alfred Willener, *Images de la société et classes sociales*, Staempfli and Cie., Berne, 1957; Richard Hoggart, *The Uses of Literacy*, Pelican Books, Harmondsworth, 1958; David Lockwood, 'The "New Working Class"', *European Journal of Sociology*, 1, 1960; H. Popitz, et al., *Das Gesellschaftsbild des Arbeiters*, Tübingen, 1957 (part of this work has been translated and can be found in Tom Burns (ed.) *Industrial Man*, Penguin, Harmondsworth, 1969); David Lockwood, 'Sources of Variation in Working Class Images of Society', *Sociological Review*, 14, 1966, pp. 249–67; John H. Goldthorpe, 'L'image des classes chez les travailleurs manuels aisés', *Revue Francaise de Sociologie*, 11, 1970, pp. 311–38; and Gavin MacKenzie, *The Aristocracy of Labour: the Position of Skilled Craftsmen in the American Class Structure*, Cambridge University Press, Cambridge, 1973. See also the brief discussion of the work of Hoggart, Willener and Popitz, et al., in Ralf Dahrendorf, *Class and Class Conflict in Industrial Society*, Routledge and Kegan Paul, London, 1959, pp. 280–89.
7. Tom Burns (ed.) *Industrial Man*, Penguin, Harmondsworth, 1969, p. 320.

they belonged to a society containing four, five or even six distinct classes.[8]

Following on from any discussion of the number of distinct groupings that any one individual might see in society it is important to ask in which of these groupings that individual places himself. Again, the available evidence suggests that such self-placement varies both in terms of the class situation of groups of individuals and in terms of whether they adopt a dichotomous or a hierarchical view of their society. Thus all of the workers in the German study referred to above saw themselves as occupying positions in the lower of the two classes in their society while in that same study (as well as the American one already mentioned and one conducted in England by Elizabeth Bott) people seeing three or more classes in their own society tended to place themselves somewhere in the middle—above their 'inferiors' and below their 'superiors':

> ... the white-collar man knows a 'top' that is above him, and a
> 'bottom' that is below him. He places himself in the middle, and
> develops a remarkably acute sense of distinction and of social
> gradations. One may assume, therefore, that he sees society not as a
> dichotomy like the industrial worker, but as a *hierarchy*.[9]

A third feature of class imagery is the perception of the relative sizes of the various social classes, in other words of the *shape* of the class structure. (By size is meant simply the proportion of the population in each of the groupings identified.) At present this is one of the facets of world images about which we know least and yet it is clearly of importance. It may mean something very different if an individual sees himself in the lower of two classes along with the majority of the population than if he claims membership in a class containing only a small proportion of his fellows. Nevertheless, despite the paucity of information on this aspect we do know that people see the various classes as being of differing sizes and, furthermore, that in general manual workers (but not those in positions of authority in industry) see their 'own' class as being the largest in the society, *whether or not they view that society as dichotomous or hierarchical*. This generous view of one's own class has been found by a number of researchers and indeed has been dubbed 'the expansion effect'.[10] It is perhaps not very difficult to understand: the majority of the individual's workmates, friends and acquaintances will be people in a similar class situation to himself. It is not therefore difficult to understand why his image of society will assign the majority of the population to his own grouping.

Fourth, it would seem that individuals differ in terms of whether they see classes as comprising *groups* or simply loose aggregates. Again this distinction can have important consequences, for example in the analysis of class conflict. Thus the stereotype of the 'traditional' or 'proletarian' worker depicts him as having a clear idea of membership in, and commitment to, a solidary *group*,

8. Gavin MacKenzie, *The Aristocracy of Labour: the Position of Skilled Craftsmen in the American Class Structure*, Cambridge University Press, Cambridge, 1973, pp. 116–18.
9. Quoted in Ralf Dahrendorf, *Class and Class Conflict in Industrial Society*, Routledge and Kegan Paul, London, 1959, p. 284.
10. O. A. Oeser and S. B. Hammond, *Social Structure and Personality in a City*, Routledge and Kegan Paul, London, 1954, pp. 281-3.

resulting in very firm notions, for example, of 'them' and 'us'. In contrast the recent research of Goldthorpe and Lockwood in this country has led them to suggest that we might be witnessing amongst certain categories of privatized workers:

> ... the emergence of some relatively new mode of social consciousness in which the salient social inequalities are not those expressed through actual relationships (but) those manifested in extrinsic, quantitative differences in wealth, income and consumption standards, understood as the attributes of individuals or aggregates.[11]

Furthermore this 'desocialized' image of class and class differences, found predominantly amongst highly paid car assembly line workers, Lockwood suggests is a direct consequence or reflection of:

> ... work attachments that are instrumental and of community relationships that are privatized. It is a model which is only possible when social relationships that might provide prototypical experiences for the construction of ideas of conflicting power classes, or of hierarchically interdependent status groups, are either absent or devoid of their significance. [In other words] ... the privatized worker finds himself in a work situation that is socially isolating and, to a large extent, socially meaningless; a situation in which the dominant relationship is the cash-nexus.[12]

This last quotation from Lockwood takes us to another important facet of class imagery which is the nature of the perceived *bases* of inequality. And again, this aspect is inseparable from other features of the total *gestalt*, for example, perception of conflict or ease of movement between classes (social mobility). The latter feature is of particular significance since the bases of the individual's 'explanation' of the underlying structure of social inequality tend to be one of two types—either relatively fixed attributes such as the possession of power or of the means of production; or relatively fluid categories that can presumably change relatively swiftly, such as 'style of life'. Within these two types, however, research shows there to be a good deal of variation. For example, Willener found a Swiss sample to be using six separate bases of differentiation: socio-economic categories, socio-occupational categories, inter-dependent dichotomy, class conflict (dichotomous), prestige strata and political groups.[13] In contrast, several studies, especially those concerned with a relatively homogeneous working-class sample, show high levels of congruence on the basis of inequality. And not surprisingly, the perceived root of inequality in such cases is often between those who have power and those who do not.

In general the existing studies of class imagery suggest that people who see power as the basis of class divisions also view the relations between classes as

11. John H. Goldthorpe, 'L'image des classes chez les travailleurs manuels aisés', *Revue Francaise de Sociologie*, 11, 1970, pp. 333–4.
12. David Lockwood, 'The "New Working Class" ', *European Journal of Sociology*, 1, 1960, pp. 248–59.
13. Alfred Willener, *Images de la société et classes sociales*, Staempfli and Cie., Berne, 1957, p. 153.

being one of endemic conflict. And perception of the type of relations that exist between classes is yet another important facet of images of inequality. The available evidence would suggest that people view this facet in at least three ways, all of which are implied in Willener's categories already outlined. Thus in addition to viewing the relationship as one of conflict there is the possibility of regarding classes as separate strata with no clear-cut type of relationship (simply a 'harmonious hierarchy') or regarding them as inter-dependent parts of a team or system (an integration model). The latter type of imagery is summed up in the words of an American electrician: 'If the boss doesn't make any money, you won't either, so you have to work together.'[14] Contrast this perspective with that of a German steel worker subscribing to a dichotomous image of society—capitalists and workers:

> Profits are raised through technical progress. The workers have always been exploited but the better the plant functions from a technical point of view, the greater the exploitation. One lot slices off the profits for themselves, the others can go on the dole if it doesn't suit them![15]

I have already made reference to the concept of social mobility and indeed perceptions of the relative 'openness' of the society represent yet another important aspect of class imagery, which again has implications for class behaviour. In this instance also, the scanty evidence available suggests that manual workers are more likely to view their class situation as relatively fixed while non-manual employees see the class structure as a ladder that an individual may climb up or down according to his own abilities and ambitions. In discussing this latter perspective Bott observes:

> It was assumed that individuals could move from one class to another without being traitors. . . . both men and women suggested that individuals bettered themselves by acquiring the education, occupation, sub-culture, and personal friendship of people in a superior class.[16]

Given that individuals visualize the class structure of their own society in radically differing ways, the fact that they may also have differing *evaluations* of such structures must come as no surprise. Again, the available evidence would suggest that these evaluations are patterned and differ from one class to another, most particularly in the extent to which the structured inequality that is visualized is regarded as being *fair* or *legitimate*. Thus of the affluent workers studied in this country by Goldthorpe and his colleagues a majority of people saw class differences as being necessary and therefore legitimate. Typical comments were: 'We need to have a pecking order.'; 'it wouldn't do if we were all on the same level; there'd be nothing to aim for.'; 'there has to be someone you can look up to, someone to take the lead.'[17] In fact 69 per cent of this sample of workers had

---

14. Gavin MacKenzie, *The Aristocracy of Labour: the Position of Skilled Craftsmen in the American Class Structure,* Cambridge University Press, Cambridge, 1973, p. 139.
15. Tom Burns (ed.), *Industrial Man,* Penguin, Harmondsworth, 1969, p. 314.
16. Elizabeth Bott, *Family and Social Network,* Tavistock, London, 1957, pp. 175–6.
17. John H. Goldthorpe, 'L'image des classes chez les travailleurs manuels aisés', *Revue Francaise de Sociologie,* 11, 1970, pp. 324–30.

similar views of the legitimacy of inequality and were thus quite prepared to accept the existing class structure as a permanent, just and necessary part of their everyday life. Such a perception, however, is usually seen to be the prerogative of non-manual workers rather than members of the working class. However, the description offered by Popitz *et al.* of the way in which a group of German steel workers evaluated the class structure is indicative at least of the stereotype of a working-class viewpoint:

> [Its] most important general features are the fundamental rejection of the present social conditions, the conviction that a change in these conditions is possible and necessary, and the belief in the mission of the working-class movement which is fulfilled in the preparation and execution of this change. It is obvious that compromise, as expressed in the philosophy of distributive justice and in the belief in the advancement of the present social order is no longer possible.[18]

It is the study conducted by Popitz and his colleagues that is the source of most of our information on the last facet of class imagery that I want to mention: whether or not, and in what ways, the class structure is seen as *changing*. In fact it is this single aspect of imagery that these researchers used as the basis for categorizing the six different perceptions of class adhered to by the workers they studied. These were: society as a static ordered structure; society as a progressive ordered structure; society as an unchangeable dichotomy (passively accepted); society as an unchangeable dichotomy (resented); society as a dichotomy—reform possible; society as a dichotomy—revolution necessary. The last two of these alternatives raise the possibility that the individual may, in addition to his perception of the existing class structure, have some notion of the type of society he would like to see it replaced by—perhaps a vision of the 'just' society or some other form of utopia. The form such an alternative society might take, could, of course, be visualized with varying degrees of precision. At the present time, however, this area of class imagery is that of our greatest ignorance: we know very little about how either manual or non-manual workers visualize change in the society of which they are a part.

These then are some of the components of class imagery that the existing research suggests to be important in the discussion of the ways in which people in different social classes view their world. In general, as I have indicated, the large part of that research shows there to be fundamental differences in the images of class structure adhered to by non-manual workers (the 'middle class') and manual workers (the 'working class'). Accordingly I have 'summarized' the findings of these various studies, *in very simple form*, and constructed stereotypes of middle and working-class images of society. The result is shown below in Figure 1. *It must however be reiterated that these stereotypes are ideal types and nothing more.* The existing literature on social class makes it clear that to talk about *the* working class or *the* middle class is sociologically naive. Lockwood has suggested, for example, that we should distinguish between at least three types of worker: the traditional worker of the 'proletarian' variety, the deferential worker

---

18. Tom Burns (ed.), *Industrial Man*, Penguin, Harmondsworth, 1969, p. 308.

and the 'privatized' worker,[19] while since at least the middle of the nineteenth century observers have been pointing to the gulf that exists between skilled and non-skilled manual workers. Similarly, few students of social class would claim that clerical workers and managerial and professional employees share identical class situations. Nonetheless, and despite the oversimplification involved, as a first step, and only as that, the construction of these two ideal types is both necessary and useful for the eventual understanding of the nature and bases of social imagery. And it is to the bases of that imagery that I now turn.

Figure 1   Images of class structure: ideal type constructs.

	1 Number of classes	2 Self-placement in class structure	3 Shape of class structure	4 Classes, groups or aggregates	5 Bases of class distinctions
Middle Class Imagery	Three or more	'Middle' or 'Upper-middle'	Probably a diamond, with large part of population in the middle classes	Groups or aggregates	Style of life, occupation, ability
Working Class Imagery	Two	'Working' or 'Lower'	A pyramid: upper class or 'them' at the apex	Cohesive groups	Wealth, Power, ownership of means of production

	6 Relations between classes	7 'Open' or 'Closed' society	8 Evaluation of class structure	9 Changes in class structure	10 Vision of alternative society
Middle Class Imagery	Interdependent; Leaders and led; harmonious	Open	Legitimate, just, fair	Ordered and progressive	No
Working Class Imagery	Conflict	Closed	Illegitimate, exploitative	Change possible only through revolution	Yes

In this final section I want to look briefly at the nature of some of the variations in work situation which theoretically can be expected to create and sustain some of these differences in class imagery. Again my remarks must be regarded as incomplete and provisional and again they are based on an analysis of an existing body of literature—this time in the area of industrial sociology. Examination of that literature suggests that there are at least five components of work situation which can be seen to influence social perspectives. These are: the nature of work tasks; the nature of authority relationships; the nature of peer relationships;

19. David Lockwood, 'Sources of Variation in Working Class Images of Society', *Sociological Review*, 14, 1966, pp. 249–67.

the value structure; and the presence or absence of avenues of mobility. During the discussion it will be readily apparent that all five components are conceptually distinct but empirically inseparable, and that they are influenced to a greater or lesser extent by the *size* of the plant or organization and the type of *production technology* employed.

Although the amount of variety *within* non-manual and manual work situations is extensive, we have seen that, in terms of class imagery the distinction between the two types of occupation is still a meaningful one. Furthermore, Popitz and his colleagues have argued forcefully that at the most general level simply working with one's hands gives rise to a particular type of consciousness not found amongst members of the non-manual middle class. Whereas:

> In short, offices are places with all the opportunities in the world for doing nothing [certainly not] *physical work*, i.e. those human activities which are 'work' in its most meaningful sense; *productive work*, i.e. direct value-creating achievement; *primary work* . . . It is, therefore, apparent that the physical nature of his work represents for the worker the possibility of differentiating himself from 'the others'. . . .[20]

More specifically, a good deal of evidence suggests that differences in the type of work task *within* both the manual and non-manual categories are also important in the explanation of social perspectives. Perhaps the most important feature of all is the extent to which work tasks are fragmented and routinized, affecting the extent to which they allow the worker freedom in and control over his activities. A further powerful factor is the degree to which the total labour force within a particular section or plant performs work of an essentially similar nature. Both aspects have been most extensively studied in relation to 'alienation' and 'job satisfaction'.[21] Without doubt the most influential of these studies is the work of Robert Blauner, who defines alienation as:

> . . . a general syndrome made up of a number of different objective conditions and subjective feeling-states which emerge from certain relations between workers and the socio-technical settings of employment.[22]

In fact Blauner delineates four 'subjective feeling-states' which go to make up the alienation syndrome—feelings of powerlessness, meaningless, social isolation and self-estrangement. He then goes on to hypothesize that the degree of alienation a worker will experience will depend crucially on the amount of *control* he is able to exercise over every aspect of his work tasks. To the extent that man is controlled rather than controlling, so far will he be alienated. Blauner goes on to test this hypothesis by studying the nature of work tasks and the levels of alienation in four differing factories in America: a printing shop, an

---

20. Tom Burns (ed.), *Industrial Man*, Penguin, Harmondsworth, 1969, pp. 322–3.
21. The word 'alienation' should be approached with great caution as it is used in a variety of ways. Perhaps the greatest distinction is between the philosophically oriented definition of the young Marx and that of American industrial sociology. For the purposes of this paper I am using Blauner's definition.
22. Robert Blauner, *Alienation and Freedom*, University of Chicago Press, Chicago, 1964, p. 15.

automobile factory, an automated chemical plant and a textile mill. Not surprisingly, he finds his hypothesis proved, with the highest levels of alienation existing in the automobile factory and the lowest in the print shop and chemical plant. The significance of these findings for the analysis of the bases of social imagery is self-evident.

Equally important are the results of research carried out in the United States by Melvin Kohn. This research was concerned primarily with linking the work situations of manual and non-manual occupations with the methods of child rearing adopted by parents in these two types of employment. Nevertheless it is crucial for our discussion because Kohn's central finding was that differences in techniques of child rearing revolved around differences in the value systems of the two classes. In particular he found manual workers to be committed to a value system stressing conformity to *external* authority while non-manual workers were far more concerned to exercise (and to see their children exercise) *self-direction*. And these differences in values were linked to three aspects of work situation—aspects which differ radically between manual and non-manual occupations. These are: the extent to which individuals are closely supervised at work (to be discussed separately); the degree to which work tasks allow for a variety of approaches; the extent to which work tasks require initiative, thought and independent judgement. As Kohn expresses it:

> The conformity of people at lower social class levels is in large measure a carry-over from the limitations of their occupational experiences. Men of higher class position, who have the opportunity to be self-directed in their work, want to be self-directed off the job, too, and come to think self-direction possible. Men of lower class position, who do not have the opportunity for self-direction in work, come to regard it a matter of necessity to conform to authority, both on and off the job. The job does mould the man—it can either enlarge his horizons or narrow them. The conformity of the lower social classes is only partly a result of their lack of education; it results also from the restrictive conditions of their jobs.[23]

Again, the implications for the discussion of images of structured inequality are clear.

As I have already indicated, this study by Kohn is also valuable as one of a number of pieces of research which indicate that the kind of authority relations in which an individual is implicated at work fundamentally affect his social imagery. Exposure to close or formal supervision sustains a dichotomous societal image of rulers and ruled, an image which the individual regards as legitimate and not susceptible to change. In addition there has been a good deal of other research into variations in the structure and quality of management-worker relations. The large part of that research has not focussed directly on class imagery but on various aspects of industrial behaviour, e.g. absenteeism, union membership and activity, labour turnover, strike activity and other forms of industrial conflict. Nonetheless I would suggest that many of the findings of that

23. Melvin Kohn, *Class and Conformity*, Dorsey Press, Homewood, Illinois, 1969, p. 188.

research can provide important clues to the nature of the relationship between class imagery and patterns of authority or 'style of supervision'. Perhaps most important is the fact that the distinction between impersonal, formal or bureaucratic forms of authority on the one hand and personal face-to-face ones on the other has important repercussions for many areas of industrial behaviour. Specifically, in those plants employing the former type of authority structure workers tend *not* to identify with either 'the firm' or with management while in those enterprizes utilizing the latter type of control a 'sense of group loyalty' is a common feature. Consequently in firms employing an impersonal bureaucratic form of control of the system of production there are higher levels of conflict, e.g. absenteeism, accident at work, 'alienation' and strikes. Furthermore, following Weber, most of the writers in this area have argued that there is a clear relationship between bureaucratic forms of control and *plant size*. It is quite simply impossible for management to treat a large work force in anything but an impersonal and formalized manner.

The fact that the kinds of management-worker relations engendered by large plants are associated with various kinds of industrial behaviour symptomatic of conflict provides a sound basis for suggesting that such authority relationships also give rise to a dichotomous view of society in which the relationship between the two classes is one of endemic conflict. Such a supposition is lent added weight by the findings of Lockwood's study of the 'false consciousness' of the blackcoated worker:

> The calculability, rationality and discipline of machine production call forth relations between management and worker that are specific and impersonal. . . . A social situation is created in which the worker's experience of the impersonality of the factory bureaucracy is widened and generalized into *a sense of class division*. . . . [Finally] the continuing physical and social division between clerks and manual workers has generally remained a barrier to the mutual identification of the two groups. *The sense of social distance between manual and non-manual workers may, in turn, be traced primarily to their relative proximity to administrative authority.*[24]

Authority relationships are not the only types of social interaction that might be important in the nurturing of class imagery. Of equal significance are relationships with peers. Indeed, it will be remembered that the physical concentration of an undifferentiated work force on a single factory floor was seen by Marx, Weber and Durkheim as perhaps *the* most important feature of work situation associated with the emergence and development of a working-class consciousness. Subsequent research bears them out. For the extent to which the structure of the work situation allows for the formation of cohesive work groups is again associated with the presence or absence of a wide variety of industrial behaviour. In particular if the manual or non-manual worker is placed in a work situation conducive to interaction with his fellow workers—such as the large office, the mine, the ship-building yard—then he will act *as a member of a group*. Presumably his perceptions will also be those of the group. However, the way in

24. David Lockwood, *The Blackcoated Worker*, Allen and Unwin, London, 1958, pp. 206–7, my italics.

which membership of a work group (of whatever size) affects perception of the world will depend upon two interrelated factors: first, the extent to which social divisions exist within the work force, and second, the extent to which other components of the work situation create and maintain particular forms of class imagery. The most obvious example of a division *within* the work force is the separation of non-skilled workers from skilled craftsmen. Thus, following an intensive study of a group of ship-building workers in the North East, Brown and Brannen commented:

> The craft group then can be seen both as a moral community and as an interest group. The members of the craft group have a sense of exclusive competence in the use of certain tools and techniques and a belief in their right to protect this area against the encroachments of other groups (i.e. semi-skilled and non-skilled workers).[25]

Studies demonstrating the influence of group membership on the individual worker's behaviour are numerous and can be traced back to the classic Hawthorne studies carried out in Chicago in the late 1920s. One of the main findings to come out of these studies was that if the work situation permitted it, informal groupings developed which, among other things, set and enforced group standards of *productivity*. In certain situations these standards were set very high so that individual workers had to work very hard and efficiently to reach them, while in other situations the standard set was artificially low. The latter was often the case where members of a group feared that if they produced more than a certain amount management might either reduce the piece rate or create redundancies.[26]

It would seem reasonable to suppose, therefore, that the possibility or otherwise of interaction with peers in the work situation will influence class imagery: for example being a member of a group may well be associated with a perception of the class structure which views classes as *groups* rather than *aggregates*. Whether or not group membership will be associated with a dichotomous or hierarchical class imagery, or an 'acceptance' or 'rejection' of the form taken by the class structure will vary according to, for instance, the presence or absence of structural divisions within the work force, the nature of authority relations, and so forth. The importance of relations with peers is probably that such relations are associated with the emergence of *common definitions* of a situation. The *content* of those definitions will be influenced more by the other components of work situation that are the subject of this section of the paper.

Two studies carried out by Aberle and Naegele, and Miller and Swanson, again into techniques of child rearing, provide important clues that the kind of *value system* operative in a work situation might directly influence the nature of class imagery. Thus Miller and Swanson have demonstrated a high degree of congruence between the values which govern the achievement of differing kinds of work tasks in the work situation (bureaucratic versus non-bureaucratic;

25. Richard Brown and Peter Brannen, 'Social Relations and Social Perspectives Amongst Shipbuilding Workers—A Preliminary Statement', *Sociology*, 4, 1970, p. 200.
26. F. J. Roethlisberger and W. G. Dickson, *Management and the Worker*, Harvard University Press, Cambridge, Mass., 1939.

specific versus diffuse) and the values guiding the bringing up of children. In fact they suggest that as the definitions of occupational roles are becoming more rigid and precise in industrial society (if this be the case) then so are the value systems which underlie the socialization process. In other words bureaucratic standards are spilling over from the work place into the home.[27]

Similarly after the analysis of the results of a study aimed at understanding the relationship between the occupational role of the *non-manual* male and his 'aims and concern in the socialization of his children', Aberle and Naegele conclude:

> ... all of the traits we have mentioned as matters of concern (e.g. being excessively passive) are—from the father's point of view— prognosticators, direct or indirect, of adult traits which will interfere with success in middle-class occupational life. The ideal-typical successful adult male in the middle-class occupational role should be responsible, show initiative, be competent, be aggressive, be capable of meeting competition. He should be emotionally stable and capable of self-restraint. These qualities are part of the value structure of the occupational world, they are involved in the role definitions of that world, and fathers' discussions of their own jobs show that these qualities have great significance for them.[28]

Again, it would seem reasonable to assume that the 'value structure of the occupational world' will also have a direct influence on images of inequality in the wider society, especially those aspects concerned with perceptions of the legitimacy of, and presence of conflict in, the class structure.

Finally, there is evidence to suggest that the existence of *avenues of mobility* within the work situation will also exert a crucial influence on social imagery. Such avenues might either be increasing financial rewards or they might involve occupational mobility. But in either case a situation in which there exists the possibility of promotion can theoretically be expected to create and maintain images of society which can be described as 'individualistic' rather than 'collectivistic', as hierarchical rather than dichotomous and as legitimate rather than illegitimate. In contrast, in a situation where the chances of promotion or advancement are slight (as, for example, is usually the case amongst manual workers) we might expect the kind of class imagery that I have labelled 'working class'. In fact evidence supportive of such an expectation is provided by a study conducted by Sykes in Scotland in the mid-1950s. Sykes was concerned with a comparison of the attitudes of clerical and manual workers towards three aspects of their working lives: promotion, trade unionism and the company and its management. At the start of the research he found that the 'one major factor' in which the situations of clerks and manual workers differed was in terms of the opportunities for promotion. However during the research a management trainee scheme was introduced which was seen as drastically reducing the chances of clerical workers to be promoted into management. The result was an

27. Daniel Miller and Guy Swanson, *The Changing American Parent*, Wiley, New York 1958.
28. David F. Aberle and Kaspar D. Naegele, 'Middle-class Fathers' Occupational Role and Attitudes Towards Children', *American Journal of Orthopsychiatry*, 22, 1952, p. 373.

equally drastic change on the part of the clerks in terms of their attitudes toward the trade-union movement. At the beginning of the project only four out of 96 clerks said that they approved of such organizations for non-manual workers. At the end of the research most of these 96 clerks had joined a union. Similar evidence pointing to a clear association between opportunities for promotion and attitudes toward the labour movement are found in the work of Mills and Lockwood.[29] And again, their implications for the development of a typology of work situations and class imagery are self-evident.

Figure 2   Ideal types of work situation conducive to 'Middle Class' and 'Working Class' social imagery.

Work Situation conducive to:	Work Tasks	Authority Relations	Peer-group relations	Value structure	Avenues of mobility	Production technology	Plant size
'Middle Class' Imagery	Non-manual; varied; creative	Controlling or personal, face-to-face	Little developed	Creativity stressed	Present	Either absent or highly specialized	Small
'Working Class' Imagery	Manual; fragmented; routinized; restrictive	Controlled; impersonal; bureaucratized	Solidary work group, physically concentrated	Conformity stressed	Absent	Mass production; assembly lines	Large

As in the case of my discussion of images of class I have brought together these various aspects of work situation to form two ideal types: one that I suggest would be conducive to the creation and maintenance of a 'working class' image of society, and one that would be expected to lead to the adoption of a 'middle-class' set of perceptions (See Figure 2). It should not need to be repeated that this typology is provisional and doubtless incomplete. Its potential value lies in the fact that, hopefully, it will generate other, more accurate typologies—typologies based upon research aimed specifically at an understanding of the relationship between work situation and class imagery. And the advance of our understanding of this relationship is, of course, inseparable from the advance of our understanding of what I began by referring to as 'the least developed aspect of the theory of social class': the *explanation* of class differences in values, ideologies and patterns of behaviour.

29. C. Wright Mills, *White Collar*, Oxford University Press, New York, 1956, and David Lockwood, *The Blackcoated Worker*, Allen and Unwin, London, 1958.

13. CRAFT AND CONSCIOUSNESS J.Bensman and R.Lilienfeld

The occupational attitude

We have attempted to show how 'world images' or basic attitudes toward life and the world have emerged from the occupational technique and methodology of the practitioners of a limited number of occupations and professions. We have argued that every occupation or profession develops and takes specific stands to the world as a result of its craft. This approach to knowledge, to attitudes, and even to character formation coexists with other aspects of occupations. The craft attitude is located, together with and inseparable from occupational interests, in the sense that such interests are claims for prestige, income, and power in the Marxian sense of the term. Occupational attitudes are also separate from, but co-exist with, world views that derive from the selected social experience that the practice of any occupation necessarily entails. While one can argue, with Marx, that one's social experience determines one's consciousness, a major component of that social experience is the specific things one does in one's occupational and professional practice. This includes the peculiar quality of the social relations involved in the practice of a profession, illustrated in the social roles of the psychoanalyst or artist and the intellectual as outsider or as adviser.

It also includes the nature of the materials with which an occupation works. Dealing with words, sounds, symbols, computers, and people all contribute to the technique which becomes generalized as a basis for an occupational attitude. The specialization in the handling of different materials creates habits of mind, attitudes, and loyalties which give each occupation its specific character, and which then go beyond that character.

The craft attitudes are also interlocked with interests and attitudes which are based on the historical success of the occupation in developing its professional acceptance and claims in the society at large. The occupational attitudes are linked to the success of the occupation, in establishing an occupational legitimacy for those members. This means that, depending on relative success, the development of an occupation results in attitudes of affirmation, denial, or defensiveness with respect to the society at large.

The sociology of knowledge is replete with studies and theories concerning the development of all the external aspects of occupational structures. We have chosen to concentrate on the effect of the craft itself in determining world images

---

13. Reprinted from *Craft and Consciousness* by J. Bensman and R. Lilienfeld by permission of John Wiley & Sons Inc., New York. Copyright © John Wiley & Sons 1973. (pp. 336-49)

and occupational attitudes. We have selected those occupations and professions which are peculiarly related to the development of world images and attitudes that historically have and can be disseminated to the society at large. We have focused on such 'occupations' as religions, philosophy, the arts, intellectual articulation, the university, and literature.

This focus may be due, in part, to the subjective biases on the part of the authors. It may be due, in part, to the fact that the attitudes and images developed in the selected occupations have consequences far greater than the numbers of persons involved, since these occupations are specialized in the articulation and dissemination of attitudes to wider publics, and therefore provide the raw materials out of which more generalized class, societal, and cultural images and ideologies emerge.

We are also aware that the attitudes and interests of members of other occupations who are less specialized in articulating and disseminating attitudes and images function as selective devices in the acceptance and rejection of images and attitudes created by the articulating occupations. We could have expanded our catalogue of occupations and professions to provide for an extended survey of occupational and professional image- and attitude-making activities.

There is no doubt in our minds that such occupations as medicine, architecture, teaching law, steamfitting, cobbling, taxicab driving, and ragpicking produce unique and peculiar combinations of attitudes appropriate to the craft as well as to the societal and social position, ideological and material interests, and commitment to the society at large. Every occupation, every skill at every substantive level produces such attitudes.

The task of articulating the effect of occupations on attitudes and images is as large as the number of occupations with all their subdivisions. In other work, we have attempted to describe some of these attitudes and the conditions out of which they emerge.

Occupation and 'class'

The peculiar unit of our analysis has been the occupation itself. Karl Marx and his disciples have attempted to broaden the conception of occupational attitudes and interests by focusing upon class, a concept initially based upon similarity of occupations with respect to ownership of capital.

Such a procedure is possible when the occupational structure of a society is relatively simple, in which different occupations are highly delineated and demarcated, and in which the ownership of the means of production and the distribution of rewards and benefits of the occupational system is simple and highly visible. Even when such conditions exist, the development of classes cannot be based on occupation alone. The conversion of occupational attitudes to class attitudes requires, under Marxian analysis, concerted activity by the ruling or favored classes to create, through the conditions of exploitation, a consciousness of a common fate by members of classes who, because of their conditions of exploitation within an economic system, only then become aware of their common destiny. But even these conditions are insufficient. The creation of class consciousness requires, as postulated by Marx, the development of communication among members of an occupation and among members of similar occupations. It is usually the role of members of totally alien occupational classes, the intellectuals, who construct ideologies which remind the members of occupations of their common fate, interest, and ideology.

Occupation by itself does not create class consciousness or class identities. In our chapter on class, we have shown that members of similar occupations can have different 'class perspectives' based on the differential fate of their occupation as it is related to its acceptance in the society at large. Occupation as craft creates, for any particular occupation, an attitude which is unique. One could further argue that even the occupational career of a particular practitioner will give him a different class perspective from that of his fellow practitioners. Class is something different from occupation if and when class emerges at all, and operates upon separate and often conflicting dynamics from that of occupation.

The autonomy of occupational attitudes

Occupational dynamics can be totally different from that of class. We hope we have demonstrated that once an occupation emerges, its technique, methodology, and craft develop a dynamic of their own. The practitioners of the craft become self-conscious in their methods, and attempt to develop these methods as an autonomous set of skills and basis for their identity. The rationalization of occupational methods becomes the major means by which crafts and craft attitudes emerge. Prestige and esteem and commitment to craftsmanship itself become the basis for attempts to develop new methods, new approaches, new technology, and new skills in the craft. These become separated from the function or contribution of the occupation to others or to society. Occupations, for instance, develop jargons which are incomprehensible to all but the insiders. At times such linguistic devices are 'functional' in the sense that they help protect the occupation from a scrutiny that might otherwise render the occupation suspect on the grounds that it does nothing but talk to itself. But if this is the case, then the disease and the cure are in the long run the same thing.

The very obscurity of occupations, however, provides the basis for new occupations which serve to explain, clarify, and often propagandize for occupations which would otherwise be meaningless. Thus, the journalist, the public relations man, and the intellectual all at times have functions of this nature.

The dynamics of craft attitudes

The focus on craft methodology serves to provide a dynamic for an occupation because every technique, craft, and starting assumption which becomes the basis for a method is necessarily limited. The concentration on technique results in an elaboration and development of these various limited sets of assumptions which may cause such a proliferation of methods, vocabulary, and products on such a narrow base that the work done tends to collapse under the weight of over-refinement, complexity, repetition, and sterility. It may also collapse under the weight of its incomprehensibility and uselessness, for any craft or occupation can easily go beyond the point of diminishing returns in the pursuit of elaborate techniques with limited goals. When a set of technical, aesthetic, or other limited assumptions are exhausted through overdevelopment, then it may be necessary for innovators to alter the initial assumptions, methodologies, and techniques, so that these new assumptions can provide the basis for new or different methods, contributions, and content of an occupation. But even here there are dangers. The development of new assumptions, methods, and techniques may become an aesthetic and a dynamic of a profession which has no other impulse to its development than change per se. The emphasis on such change produces a kind of meaninglessness which can be called pure occupational virtuosity. Solutions to such problems of meaninglessness can be found by either the return to earlier methodological and aesthetic assumptions, or through the borrowing of such assumptions from related fields. The method of returning to simpler and earlier assumptions means that the history of the occupation becomes the source for new methods and new assumptions. Thus, in every occupation there are periods of archaic revivalism. In music one can return to an interest in the Baroque, Medieval, or Renaissance styles, or to 'primitive' or ancient musical forms. Similar trends may be found in painting. In religion, the return not only to the primitive origins of one's own religion is a recurring phenomenon, but also the incorporation of the ideas and practices of alien religions is possible. In academic and intellectual spheres, the return to the classics is always a theme, and the discovery or rediscovery of neglected classics always adds to our knowledge of what the classics were. As a result, experimentalism in world images and attitudes includes experiment with what has been previously tried and at least temporarily rejected.

The borrowing of aesthetic assumptions

The borrowing of occupational attitudes and images consists of using the occupational attitudes of related fields and occupations as the basis for the development of new attitudes and assumptions within one's own field. There is a unity within the world of the arts, letters, sciences, which goes beyond occupational specialization and boundaries. Every innovation in aesthetic or methodological assumptions, whether appropriate or not, ultimately becomes applied to other fields if only as a means of escaping from the limits and overdevelopment of assumptions within any particular field. Thus, the Classic, Romantic, Gothic, and Baroque have meanings in literature, arts, letters, philosophy, and even the sciences. These meanings vary with medium since the materials out of which they are constructed in a particular field are so different.

Such borrowings take place at uneven rates, so that the borrowings in one medium may occur at a time when the style is virtually exhausted or has taken different shapes in another medium or locale. Impressionism in music, for instance, began to be heard long after Impressionism was exhausted as a creative force in painting and poetry.

There may occur borrowings not only from techniques and styles of another field but a leaning upon general intellectual currents which cut across all fields. We would venture that philosophy is extremely important as a channel of borrowing, while in the past both philosophy and literary criticism have been extremely important as major sources for borrowing across fields. At earlier stages religion may have been more important, while today it appears to have been eclipsed by science.

But even with these time lags and delays, the predisposition to borrow results in a ragged, straggling movement of ideas, assumptions, symbols, and forms of consciousness which move through a whole culture and society over relatively long periods of time, and which make it possible to characterize an age or a period.

These characteristics in the development of knowledge and cultural styles are products of the attempt to work out the methodological, aesthetic, and artistic assumptions of an occupation at a given time in its history and development. The borrowing from its own past and from other occupations are all products of the internal dynamics of an occupation. Because they have these aesthetic and methodological dynamics, they achieve some degree of autonomy from the marketplace, from the economic system, and from a 'class system' which in occupational terms often does not exist. It is possible to argue that at least in the area of intellectual and artistic creativity, in the area of the creation of world images, the development of ideas does not directly reflect the material interests of either classes or occupations. Ideas, aesthetic, artistic, and intellectual productions have, in this sphere, an autonomy of their own.

Occupational attitudes and the spirit of the times

The concern with method, technique, form, and style as central to the development of an occupation often leads to the criticism of the major fields of creativity that they are becoming technologically obscure, devoid of substance or content other than technique itself. Some critics argue that such preoccupation is either a reflection of the bureaucratic spirit of the times, or a spirit that is broader but includes the bureaucratic spirit of the times. Thus, formalism is seen as related to the development of late capitalism and of the 'value-neutrality' and the technocratic determinism associated with late capitalism. While such an argument may seem attractive, and combines with the emphasis on instrumental rationality associated with the market rationality of early capitalism, the bureaucratic mentality of late capitalism, and the technical, stylistic, and aesthetic rationality in cultural and aesthetic spheres, yet we would conclude that it is easy to establish the separateness and independence of these various phenomena. Preoccupation with intellectual, aesthetic, and artistic methodologies has occurred in all periods prior to the development of capitalism. Focus on substance and content has occurred long after the development of capitalism. Medieval theology and philosophy had all of the characteristics of a method-centered system of thought, at least by the time of St. Augustine. Poetry has gone through innumerable cycles of preoccupation with the formal aspects of style and the rebellion against its own formalism. Late medieval music prior to the appearance of Dunstable was characterized by the exhausting of a limited style. Late Renaissance music achieved extremely high levels of sterility and was replaced by simpler music which in turn developed its own forms of complexity, replaced in turn by other styles. In painting, mannerist styles have risen to dominance almost as a signal of the decline of a dominant style in which the concentration on technique was a symptom that painters in the dominant style had relatively little to say, except to extend, amplify, and caricature the style itself. Within painting, the rise and decline of mannerisms has been a recurrent phenomenon, each new style of mannerism being different from earlier ones.

We have indicated that the focus on method becomes part of a critical attitude in which the objectivity of method and style becomes the most teachable part of the art, and the discussion of style becomes most communicable by the medium of the printed, and later, with radio and television, of the spoken word, rather than the medium in which the work is originally done. Thus, criticism, and associated with it, the preoccupation with methods, is associated first with the rise of the large university, and secondly with journalism, and of course with literacy. Added to this is the abstracting and mathematizing approach of modern physics, with its implied devaluation of everyday appearances, and the need for a critical philosophy of knowledge. As a result, preoccupation with methods becomes an increasingly important phenomenon in the late nineteenth and twentieth centuries, while the growth of criticism and the preoccupation with the dissection of method and style begins much earlier.

Occupational elites

The concentration on method, technique, and style is a product and a cause of a methodological self-consciousness of the practitioners of a craft. Such self-consciousness goes far beyond craft or technique. The artist, the intellectual, the philosopher, or the scientist begins to define himself as a species apart from the normal run of mankind. He regards himself as the bearer of special values upon which he bases his craft. He becomes a spokesman for Art, Literature, Reason, Knowledge, Science, Philosophy, Religion, and so forth. The domain which he occupies takes on special value, and he becomes the basis for claims for priority of that value. The 'civilian' world becomes of secondary importance. As he defines his world of value as being of primary importance, he constructs a social world which intensifies the social, cultural, ideological, and aesthetic ambience of that world. He associates more and more with other practitioners of that world and of other worlds that are immediately relevant to each other in their joint hostility to outside worlds. Thus the world of the 'civilian', the layman, the 'feather merchant', becomes more and more removed, and is by and large conceived as a hostile world. The worlds of the arts, literature, etc., become more and more dense, not only in their aesthetic, symbolic, and technological systems, but also in their subgroups, cliques, schools, friends and enemies. These worlds can become the sum total of the worlds of experience for the practitioners.

At the same time, if the central world of the artistic or intellectual practitioner is to gain the ascendancy which is appropriate to its primary importance (where its primacy is attributed to it by its practitioners), then the practitioners must engage in a continuous ideological, cultural, and intellectual propaganda. As a result, the 'civilian' world, the lay world, is always the receiver of 'messages' and propaganda from these 'higher' worlds. The very practice of the craft, the art, music, literature, is a message. To the extent that the art portrays an image of life or a form of sensitivity that is meaningful or superior, these messages serve as propaganda for their creators. Since intellectual and artistic craftsmen possess skills in communication, their success has been far greater than one would expect, based either on their numbers or on the resources available to them. But such communication is not by itself adequate to achieve predominance, given the conviction that preoccupation with a single value entails. While intellectuals, artists, philosophers, etc., are specialists at communication, they do not usually control the media by which their messages are disseminated. If the craftsman desires to exert the influence appropriate to his self-esteem, and to achieve the benefits therefrom, he must find means of gratifying the expectations of others, of coming to terms with their demands. This entails the discovery of the symbols, aspirations, 'psychology' of an audience, whether that discovery is the product of the direct knowledge of the craftsman, or is mediated by publishers, impresarios, managers, researchers, or media specialists. To the extent that the intellectual or artistic craftsman accepts such definitions and tailors his work to them, he sacrifices the autonomy of his art. Though he may, within the framework of communicating at an expected level, develop high levels of virtuosity and technique, such virtuosity and technique are aimed at expressing the commonplaces already known to exist in the attitudes of his audience. A true genius in any field may create his own audience simply by defining his message and technique in his own terms, but in doing so he creates in the audience a response to his message and technique that did not exist before the existence of the message.

Occupational attitudes and the attitude of everyday life

Intellectuals may thus define images of experiences and worlds of experience for lay audiences, but they also incorporate into their work the 'attitudes of everyday life'. The process is not a simple exchange in attitudes. There is a tendency among some academicians and intellectuals concerned with the sociology of knowledge to see 'Culture', knowledge, and attitudes as direct reflections of attitudes of everyday life, which in turn are reflections of the direct, primary interaction of individuals and communities. Knowledge is seen as a higher synthesis of attitudes of everyday life. So far as we know historical societies, we can say that, to the contrary, the attitudes of everyday life are a simplified, vulgarized, de-intellectualized reflection of highly articulated systems of thought originally developed by intellectuals, and disseminated through the communication machinery of a society. In the process of dissemination and diffusion, the attitudes become simplified, and incorporated into the common sense of a populace that need not know of the origins and intellectual articulations on which the attitudes are based. The individual, in internalizing such attitudes, adopts them as a rhetoric and a medium for the expression of his actions and his presocial impulses. The attitude of everyday life does not emerge out of everyday experience in the sense that that everyday experience precludes direct and indirect contact with 'higher' intellectual production. To think of the dichotomy between the attitude of everyday life and these more elaborate intellectual attitudes is to think in terms of a Robinson Crusoe isolated from his society and recreating a social and intellectual world *de novo*. But even Robinson Crusoe created his world with attitudes derived from the England from which he departed. He could not erase from his consciousness the memories of the ideas and practices which had emerged in his past. The isolated individual, creating a world out of his own experience and his own social interaction, enters such social interaction and each new experience with attitudes that are a product of his previous social interactions and the interactions of all those with whom he has had interaction. Thus, the notion of an isolated individual is, to all intents and purposes, an impossibility. Theories based on the conception of the microscopic and formal processes of interaction of undifferentiated individuals, by their very preconceptions, make it impossible to determine the degree to which these situations are permeated with culture and attitudes which are predetermined by other attitudes developed at more complex levels. It is far easier to make assumptions concerning the autonomous creation of attitudes and cultures in primitive societies, since they do not have a written history. The absence of a written history makes it difficult to assess the role of intellectuals and other institutionalized cultural creators of attitudes of everyday life. It is easy to assume that primitive culture is simply a byproduct of the undifferentiated actions of individuals in a community. Paul Radin has demonstrated, to our minds quite conclusively, that primitive intellectuals, prophets, and priests have performed the same functions of creating new attitudes of everyday life which become the products of social interaction.

In the area of folk music and folk art, there is considerable literature which suggests that much of what is regarded as the naive, simple direct creation of indigenous folk culture is actually the borrowed culture of other civilizations, hymns, popular music, and in some cases highly sophisticated symphonic music.

If attitudes of everyday life are reflections of highly articulated systems of thought, then the creators and communicators of new systems of thought must present their production to lay audiences who have internalized and incorporated, often in 'non-systematic' ways, older products of the elaborate intellectual and communications machinery of the surrounding society. The process of internalization of such cultural and intellectual production is selective. Individuals incorporate such culture on the basis of their differential exposure to that culture, the affinity of old and new ideas, their position in a social structure, and the interests that emerge as a result of these various factors. Thus, the concept of the attitude of everyday life refers to a very complex phenomenon, a phenomenon that is not referable exclusively to the isolated social interaction of an individual or of an undifferentiated community.

The analysis of attitudes of everyday life must include not only these primary group relations but the whole complex of institutional machineries, social, and class structures, and the problems related to individuals and groups of individuals in highly developed cultures and societies. The original creators of the sociology of knowledge, Marx, Weber, Mannheim, and Veblen, were fully aware of such complexities. The more recent developments in the sociology of knowledge which reflect relatively simple models of 'symbolic interaction', interpersonal relations, ethnomethodology, and role theory are all primitive in comparison. Their selection of data does violence to the realities under consideration—they define that reality as that which is necessary to their methodological preconceptions, rather than what must be studied in order to make a satisfactory solution to the problems under consideration.

Responses to success

When responding to the taste of an existing audience, the craftsman may vulgarize his art. In responding only in terms of the technique and his artistic community, he may fail to communicate his message to any audience. When he creates his own audience, he may succeed in instilling the attitudes of his art in an audience of laymen. Artists and intellectuals create, define and redefine non-artistic and nonintellectual worlds. But audiences, in accepting the world so created, frequently misunderstand it, though their misunderstanding may be accompanied by 'appreciation' and plaudits. The artist or intellectual, in responding to his own success, may accept and internalize the misunderstanding that was the basis of the success.

In doing so, the artist becomes the victim of his own myth and his own success. He also becomes the victim of the audience he created. The acceptance of the craftsman by the public or the bureaucracies which transmit his message tends to transform it. At the same time, the acceptance of the craft by outside groups, institutions, or markets causes a growth in self-esteem by the practitioners of the craft. This causes the craftsman to raise his own demands and expectations with respect to the capabilities of the audience. In such cases the artist-intellectual-scientist, now a member of an elite, develops images of society whose dimensions are defined by his craft, and in which the structuring of society will be done by himself and his elite. Thus, acceptance of an elite by the society increases the demands of the elite on society.

The artist-intellectual-scientist then begins to construct images of a society which, if it is to reach the true potential given by the elite's values, must be reconstituted. Its reconstitution must inevitably place the particular elite at the head of the entire society. The philosopher becomes the philosopher-king. The scientist provides the laws and methods for the governing of society. The politically superior intellectual becomes one of the ruling class of a postulated new society. Psychologists imagine an order in which they produce a mentally healthy society. Managerial scientists run society at levels of managerial efficiency that are heretofore unimaginable. The claims of specialized elites upon the total society have at specific times been unlimited. Their success, even when the opportunities have been given them, has been less than optimal. As a matter of fact, they have everywhere failed in terms of their own claims, and most often have produced forms of barbarism and totalitarianism that have violated every form of idealism and self-righteousness that was the basis of their claims.

Such failures are perhaps inevitable. The very condition of acceptance of the newly ascendant elite by the society is that the craft of the artistic or intellectual or scientific elite be subordinated to the needs of older dominant groups in the society. Thus the more the demand for change, the less substance there is to the change. And the more 'radical' the demand, the less substance there is to the radicalism.

The radical intellectual

The same analysis applies to revolutionary intellectuals. Rejected by or alienated from a society, they construct ideologies, images of a more perfect society, and negative images of existing societies, as a means of expressing their alienation or rejection. Such images may remain at the symbolic level, and have little or no organizational consequences. When intellectuals enter active organizational struggles, the party and the sect become the medium that restructures the original message that may have been the basis for the revolutionary movement. The intellectual as party member must then discipline himself to the demands of the party, to its strategy and tactics, and thus limit that vision which may have been the intellectual basis of the movement. If he can enter an organization, he may succeed in rising to the top of a revolutionary movement. If he retains his original habits of mind and emphasis on craft or vision, he is likely to be purged. If he does limit himself, his 'art' becomes subordinated to the stereotypes of an official ideology, and he in effect commits intellectual or artistic or scientific suicide. The problems for the left or right intellectual, the prophet and the priest, are essentially the same. The lust for power and influence in establishments that exist or that hopefully may exist by replacing present establishments operates to destroy what is intrinsic to the basic attitudes of the creative 'crafts'.

The narrowing and extension of craft horizons

In periods when social crises are less than revolutionary in intensity, the development of artistic and intellectual autonomy and imperialism has opposite effects. Each craft develops its own focus on values, and each subgroup and clique develops subfoci. The world of intellectual production becomes a cacophony of voices. A society at large is presented with an infinity of worlds of values, each presented as an ultimate value, each capable of sustaining the life of its audiences. Audiences are presented with conflicting voices, without a hierarchy of values or guides to choice. Each individual is left to choose on the basis of criteria that may be personal, arbitrary, or random. In one respect this represents a maximum amount of freedom, in another respect it represents chaos.

One of the limitations of occupational attitudes as a means of viewing the world and as a means of governing the world is based on the narrowness of the vantage point from which the non-occupational world is seen. The artist may see only those aspects of the world that are relevant to art, and ignore all other aspects. The psychologist will see the world of habits, of mechanisms for the distribution of affect, of perceptual processes, etc., as the only relevant reality. Sociologists, as we have indicated, are likely to see the social content and processes as being dominant, and to ignore, or treat only as constraints, such factors as economic or technological processes and institutions. Even when they recognize such phenomena, they do so only as part of a stage on which they can perceive sociological dramas. Economists are 'guilty' of similar procedures. In part such procedures are absolutely necessary. The total world of experience is so broad and subject to an almost infinite variety of perspectives, that to analyze it requires a limitation of the perspectives used in the analysis. Thus some forms of 'reduction' are necessary and appropriate. But such reductions are merely methodological devices, self-imposed restrictions, which enable one to deal with the world in an orderly way. They enable the observer and analyst to concentrate his vision so that he can see more in a given direction than he would otherwise.

It is unfortunate that individuals who start their work with self-consciously created points of reference lose, in the process of doing the work, their awareness that they are viewing only a limited aspect of the world. When they do this, they are making a reduction of sorts—all phenomena are reduced to something that can be seen only from a very limited perspective. It is correct to criticize the materialist reduction, the psychological reduction, sociologism, logical, linguistic, and epistemological reductions, even reductions to the 'thing itself'. In the latter case the reduction consists of refusing to entertain alternative possibilities. This stricture does not apply to Edmund Husserl, for whom an unlimited horizon of further determinations was an essential aspect of any object of experience. The reproach is more applicable to studies which call themselves phenomenological, but which appear to be subjectivistic. No reduction is in itself 'incorrect' so long as the observer or analyst is aware that, in using a restricted perspective or method, he is describing a limited aspect of experience. If the observer or analyst maintains such awareness he is likely to ask: How much of the phenomenon that I wish to explain is explained by the use of the methods that I have employed? How much remains unexplained? What other perspectives, or 'reductions', need I employ in order to do justice to the phenomenon? If he asks such questions, he is more likely to employ a wide variety of perspectives or reductions. In fact he is likely to rotate perspectives as his mode of analysis, asking always how much is left unexplained by his use of various reductions. Since the world of experience is infinite, subject to an unlimited number of perspectives, there is little likelihood that one will be able to ascertain a true image or absolute knowledge of any one thing, but rather by the use of such methods, it would seem to us that the probability of error is diminished. Moreover, it might, by such efforts, be possible to achieve a truly humanistic image of the world, and to escape the blunders that often appear to be the hazards of occupational attitudes.

14. SOURCES OF VARIATION IN WORKING CLASS IMAGES OF SOCIETY David Lockwood

For the most part men visualize the class structure of their society from the vantage points of their own particular *milieux*, and their perceptions of the larger society will vary according to their experiences of social inequality in the smaller societies in which they live out their daily lives. This assumption that the individual's social consciousness is to a large extent influenced by his immediate social context has already proved its usefulness in the study of 'images of society' and it has been stated most clearly by Bott, who writes: 'People do have direct experience of distinctions of power and prestige in their places of work, among their colleagues, in schools, and in their relationships with friends, neighbours, and relatives. In other words, the ingredients, the raw materials, of class ideology are located in the individual's various primary social experiences, rather than in his position in a socio-economic category. The hypothesis advanced here is that when an individual talks about class he is trying to say something, in a symbolic form, about his experiences of power and prestige in his actual membership groups and social relationships both past and present.'[1] Working from very similar premises, several quite independent investigations have suggested that there seem to be two broad ways in which individuals conceptualize class structure: 'power' or 'conflict' or 'dichotomous' models on the one hand; and 'prestige' or 'status' or 'hierarchical' models on the other. Further it has been proposed that the social ideology of the working class tends to take the form of a power model whereas that of the middle class approximates the hierarchical model. Although some of these studies have noted variations in social imagery within the working class, they have concentrated chiefly on explaining the variations between the classes. Thus the power or dichotomous ideology of the working class and the hierarchical ideology of the middle class have been accounted for primarily in terms of differences in the industrial life chances and life experiences of manual and non-manual employees.

While the similarity of the findings of these various investigations is very striking, it is also quite clear from other studies that the industrial and community *milieux* of manual workers exhibit a very considerable diversity and it would be strange if there were no correspondingly marked variations in the images of society held by different sections of the working class. Indeed, on the

1. E. Bott, *Family and Social Network*, Tavistock, London, 1957, p. 163.

---

14. Reprinted from the *Sociological Review*, vol. 14; November 1966.(pp. 249-67)

basis of existing research, it is possible to delineate at least three different types of workers and to infer that the work and community relationships by which they are differentiated from one another may also generate very different forms of social consciousness. The three types are as follows: first, the traditional worker of the 'proletarian' variety whose image of society will take the form of a power model; secondly, the other variety of traditional worker, the 'deferential', whose perception of social inequality will be one of status hierarchy; and, thirdly, the 'privatized' worker, whose social consciousness will most nearly approximate what may be called a 'pecuniary' model of society.[2]

The 'traditional worker' is, of course, a sociological rather than an historical concept; a concept relating to workers who are located in particular kinds of work situations and community structures rather than one purporting to give a description of the working class as a whole at some particular point of time. Moreover, the concept encompasses not only the most radical and class conscious segment of the working class (the proletarian worker) but also its most socially acquiescent and conservative elements (the deferential worker). Yet, distinct as the two traditionalists are from one another in social and political outlook, they do share several characteristics which make them traditionalists and thus distinguish them from the privatized worker. It would seem best, then, to begin with an account of the work and community structures underlying proletarian and deferential traditionalism.

The most highly developed forms of proletarian traditionalism seem to be associated with industries such as mining, docking, and shipbuilding; industries which tend to concentrate workers together in solidary communities and to isolate them from the influences of the wider society.[3] Workers in such industries usually have a high degree of job involvement and strong attachments to primary work groups that possess a considerable autonomy from technical and supervisory constraints.[4] Pride in doing 'men's work' and a strong sense of shared occupational experiences make for feelings of fraternity and comradeship which are expressed through a distinctive occupational culture. These primary groups of workmates not only provide the elementary units of more extensive class loyalties but work associations also carry over into leisure activities, so that workers in these industries usually participate in what are called 'occupational communities'. Workmates are normally leisure-time companions, often neighbours, and not infrequently kinsmen. The existence of such closely-knit cliques of friends, workmates, neighbours and relatives is the hallmark of the traditional working class community. The values expressed through these social networks emphasize mutual aid in everyday life and the obligation to join in the gregarious pattern of leisure, which itself demands the expenditure of time, money and energy in a

2. See David Lockwood, 'The "New Working Class" ', *European Journal of Sociology*, Vol. I, No. 2, 1960 and J. H. Goldthorpe and David Lockwood, 'Affluence and the British Class Structure', *Sociological Review*, Vol. II, No. 2, 1963.
3. See C. Kerr and A. Siegel, 'The Inter-industry Propensity to Strike: An International Comparison' in A. Kornhauser, R. Dubin and A. M. Ross (eds.) *Industrial Conflict*, McGraw-Hill, London, 1954, and N. Dennis, F. Henriques and C. Slaughter, *Coal is our Life*, Tavistock, London, 1956.
4. R. Blauner, 'Work Satisfaction and Industrial Trends in Modern Society' in W. Galenson and S. M. Lipset (eds.) *Labour and Trade Unionism*, Wiley, New York, 1960.

public and present-oriented conviviality and eschews individual striving 'to be different'. As a form of social life, this communal sociability has a ritualistic quality, creating a high moral density and reinforcing sentiments of belonging-ness to a work-dominated collectivity. The isolated and endogamous nature of the community, its predominantly one-class population, and low rates of geographical and social mobility all tend to make it an inward-looking society and to accentuate the sense of cohesion that springs from shared work experiences.

Shaped by occupational solidarities and communal sociability the prole-tarian social consciousness is centred on an awareness of 'us' in contradistinction to 'them' who are not a part of 'us'. 'Them' are bosses, managers, white collar workers and, ultimately, the public authorities of the larger society. Yet even though these outsiders are remote from the community, their power to influence it is well understood; and those within the community are more conscious of this power because it comes from the outside. Hence the dominant model of society held by the proletarian traditionalist is most likely to be a dichotomous or two-valued power model. Thinking in terms of two classes standing in a relationship of opposition is a natural consequence of being a member of a closely integrated industrial community with well-defined boundaries and a distinctive style of life. It may well be, as Popitz has argued, that the propensity to hold a dichotomous social imagery is a general one among industrial workers in large establishments: certainly the social divisions of the workplace, the feeling of being subject to a distant and incomprehensible authority, and the inconsiderable chances of escaping from manual wage earning employment are all conducive to the formation of such an ideology.[5] But is it probable that this image of society is fully developed only among those workers whose sense of the industrial hiatus is strengthened by their awareness of forming a quite separate community? Moreover, to anticipate the subsequent discussion, it would seem that the tendency to adopt a power model of society is most evident among workers who have a high degree of job involvement and strong ties with their fellow workers. In other kinds of work situations, where these factors are absent, or nearly so, the whole significance of the workplace as a determinant of a dichotomous class ideology is correspondingly reduced.

Our knowledge of the second variety of traditional worker is rather skimpy and results mainly from the efforts that have been made to track down that elusive political animal, the 'deferential voter'.[6] It may be assumed, however, that the model of society held by the deferential worker is a prestige or hierarchi-cal, rather than a power or dichotomous model. In fact, given that people who think of social divisions in terms of status or prestige usually distinguish higher and lower strata as well as status equals, his model is likely to be at least a trichotomous one.[7] Further, the deferential worker does not identify himself with his superiors or strive to reach their status; he defers to them socially as well as politically. His recognition of authentic leadership is based on his belief

5. H. Popitz, H. P. Bahrdt, E. A. Jueres and H. Kesting, *Das Gesellschaftsbild des Arbeiters*, Tübingen, 1961.
6. E.g., S. H. Beer, *Modern British Politics*, Faber, London, 1965; R. Samuel, 'The Deference Voter', *New Left Review*, Jan.–Feb., 1960 and M. Abrams, 'Class and Politics', *Encounter*, October, 1961.
7. E. Bott, *Family and Social Network*, Tavistock, London, 1957, p. 176.

in the intrinsic qualities of an ascriptive elite who exercise leadership paternalistic-ally in the pursuit of 'national' as opposed to 'sectional' or 'class' interests. But how refined his image of the status hierarchy really is, or how exactly he perceives his own position in it, is not known. It is merely suggested that he has a con-ception of a higher and unapproachable status group of leaders, his 'betters', the people who 'know how to run things', those whose performance is guaranteed by 'breeding'; and that he himself claims to be nothing grander 'than working class'. However, given these elements, it is possible to go a little further and to draw the not unreasonable, but wholly speculative, conclusion that the deferential worker thinks in terms of at least a four-fold division of society. Since he thinks in terms of 'genuine' or 'natural' leaders in both a local and a national context, it is likely that he thinks also of 'spurious' leaders and by implication, of 'misguided' followers. Spurious leaders are those who aspire to leadership, and indeed from time to time acquire it, without possessing the requisite qualities. They may have achieved wealth, power and position, but they lack the hereditary or quasi-hereditary credentials which the deferential worker recognizes as the true marks of legitimacy. Misguided followers are those, broadly in the same layer of society as himself, who refuse to acknowledge the objects of his deference, and who aid and abet the spurious leaders in usurping authority. If the deferential worker has an image of society as a status hierarchy, then the existence of 'undeferential' workers is almost a necessary condition for the protection of his own sense of self-esteem. There are few instances of lower status groups who both accept the legitimacy of the status hierarchy and fail to discover groups with an even lower status than their own.

Whatever niceties of status differentiation enter into the ideology of the deferential traditionalist, it would seem that he does hold a hierarchical model of some kind, and it would seem worthwhile exploring the hypothesis that such a model of society will be the product of very special work and community relationships. Here, studies of the deferential voter do not take us very far. The findings that these voters are more likely than non-deferentials to be elderly, to be women, to have low incomes and to come from rural areas are demographic facts relating to the properties of individuals rather than facts relating to the properties of the social systems in which these individuals are located.[8] Nor is it to be assumed that all deferential voters will be deferential traditionalists. The latter, like proletarian traditionalists, must be thought of as an extreme type, characterized by a combination of social rôles which, taken together, are most likely to lead to a hierarchical social imagery.

The typical work rôle of the deferential traditionalist will be one that brings him into direct association with his employer or other middle class influentials and hinders him from forming strong attachments to workers in a similar market situation to his own. These work conditions are most clearly present in the sorts of occupations that are to be found in small towns and rural areas, although they are by no means entirely absent in larger urban centres. Workers in various kinds

---

8. M. Abrams, 'Class and Politics', *Encounter*, October, 1961, p. 42; R. Samuel, 'The Deference Voter', *New Left Review*, Jan.–Feb., 1960, p. 11 and R. T. McKenzie and A. Silver, 'Conservatism, Industrialism, and the Working Class Tory in England', *Transactions of the Fifth World Congress of Sociology*, Vol. III, Louvain, 1964, p. 199.

of service occupations, in non- or rather pre-industrial craft jobs, those working in small scale 'family enterprises', and in agricultural employment, are workers who are most exposed to paternalistic forms of industrial authority. The essence of this work situation is that relationship between employer and worker is personal and particularistic. The worker has an unique position in a functional job hierarchy and he is tied to his employer by a 'special relationship' between them and not only by considerations of economic gain.

In the making of the deferential traditionalist certain features of community life will also play an important part in fixing and sharpening the sense of hierarchy that he acquires in his rôle as worker. Small, relatively isolated and economically autonomous communities, particularly those with well-differentiated occupational structures and stable populations, provide the most favourable settings for the existence of 'local status systems'. The key characteristic of such systems is that the allocation of status takes place through 'interactional' rather than through 'attributional' mechanisms.[9] The boundaries of the several status groups making up the local system are maintained by various means of social acceptance and rejection in both formal and informal association. People do not judge one another from a distance and attribute status on the basis of a few, readily observable criteria, such as the amount of an individual's material possessions. Status groups or rather the cliques of which they are constituted, are membership as well as reference groups. Through close acquaintance, people have a detailed knowledge of each other's personal qualities and can apply relatively complex criteria in deciding who is worthy of membership of a particular status group. There is also widespread consensus about the rank order of status groups in the community, so that lower strata regard their lowly position less as an injustice than as a necessary, acceptable, and even desirable part in a natural system of inequality. Local status systems, therefore, operate to give the individual a very definite sense of position in a hierarchy of prestige, in which each 'knows his place' and recognizes the status prerogatives of those above and below him. For the deferential traditionalist, such a system of status has the function of placing his work orientations in a wider social context. The persons who exercise authority over him at his place of work may not be the same persons who stand at the apex of the local status system, but the structural principles of the two social orders are homological; and from neither set of relationships does he learn to question the appropriateness of his exchange of deference for paternalism.

Although in terms of social imagery and political outlook the proletarian and deferential traditionalists are far removed from one another, they nevertheless do have some characteristics in common. They are first of all traditionalists in the sense that both types are to be found in industries and communities which, to an ever increasing extent, are backwaters of national industrial and urban development. The sorts of industries which employ deferential and proletarian workers are declining relatively to more modern industries in which large batch or mass production techniques are more and more the major modes of production. Again, the small isolated country town, or the mining village, or the working class

9. M. Young and P. Willmott, *Family and Kinship in East London*, Routledge, London, 1957, pp. 134–5.

enclave, such as is represented by the dockworkers' community, are gradually becoming linked with, or absorbed into, larger urban concentrations and with an increased amount of voluntary and involuntary residential mobility of the labour force the close link between place of work and community is being broken down.

They are also traditionalists in the sense that their horizons of expectations do not extend much beyond the boundaries of the communities in which they live and of which they are, so to speak, 'founding members'. This again is largely a product of the social isolation and social stability of both the deferential and proletarian communities. Workers in such environments are as unlikely to change their patterns of consumption as they are their political loyalties, because in both cases they are encapsulated in social systems which provide them with few alternative conceptions of what is possible, desirable, and legitimate.

Finally, and perhaps most significantly, the work and community relationships of traditional workers involve them in mutually reinforcing systems of interpersonal influence. The effect of group membership on class ideology will, of course, vary depending on the type of traditional worker under consideration. In the case of the deferential worker, his rôle in a paternalistic authority structure at work and his position in a local status system in the community both predispose him to think of society in terms of hierarchy. In the case of the proletarian traditionalist, his membership of the work gang and his participation in the system of communal sociability lead to a conception of a 'class-divided' society. But although the effects of group membership are very different in the two cases, both the deferential and the proletarian traditionalists are highly integrated into their respective local societies; and this means that their attitudes and behaviour are to a large extent influenced and controlled by means of direct face-to-face encounters. In this way, they experience a sense of belonging to actual social groups which are marked off from other groups by boundaries that are maintained through social interaction. This consciousness of definite social placement in turn affects their perception of the class structure. Whether their models of society are basically hierarchical or basically dichotomous, the fact that traditional workers have a strong sense of group membership means that they will tend to see 'strata' or 'classes' as active social formations and not merely as amorphous aggregates of individuals. In this respect, the social consciousness of the traditional worker differs markedly from that of the privatized worker, whose model of society is shaped by work and community relationships which do not convey, to the same extent, an awareness of group affiliation.

The social environment of the privatized worker is conducive to the development of what may be called a 'pecuniary' model of society. The essential feature of this ideology is that class divisions are seen mainly in terms of differences in income and material possessions. Naturally, there will be few individuals who think of class divisions in purely pecuniary terms. But the social consciousness of many individuals in the 'new working class' may be closer to this pecuniary model of society than to either of the two types of social imagery previously discussed.[10] Basically, the pecuniary model of society is an ideological reflection

10. See J. H. Goldthorpe and D. Lockwood, 'Affluence and the British Class Structure', *Sociological Review*, Vol. II, No. 2, 1963, pp. 149–54.

of work attachments that are instrumental and of community relationships that are privatized.[11] It is a model which is only possible when social relationships that might provide prototypical experiences for the construction of ideas of conflicting power classes, or of hierarchically interdependent status groups, are either absent or devoid of their significance.

The work situation of the privatized worker is such that his involvement in the job and his attachments to the enterprize and to his fellow workers are slight. Numerous studies have provided us with the generalization that workers employed in large factories with mass-production technologies and doing jobs which are highly specialized, repetitive, and lacking in autonomy, are workers for whom, in Dubin's words, 'work and the workplace are not central life interests' and for whom work is viewed 'as a means to an end—a way of acquiring income for life in the community'.[12] Under these conditions, work is a deprivation which is performed mainly for extrinsic rewards; and 'money-mindedness', the calculative exchange of labour power for maximum pay, is the predominant motive for remaining in the job. Frequently isolated from their workmates by the constraints of technology, and seeking no close relationships in a work situation that is viewed in purely instrumental terms, such 'alienated' workers do not form cohesive groups inside the factory and they are not prone to form occupational communities outside the factory. Their main attitude to work is that of its being a necessary evil; and given this orientation they have no desire to carry over into their leisure time the atmosphere and associations of work.[13] In all these respects —the low involvement in the job itself, the lack of cohesive work groups, the absence of occupational communities—privatized workers differ significantly from the traditional worker, and more especially from the proletarian traditionalist. Relative to the latter, the privatized worker finds himself in a work situation that is socially isolating and, to a large extent, socially meaningless; a situation in which the dominant relationship is the cash-nexus. But, although he is 'alienated' labour, he is unlikely to possess a strongly developed class consciousness because his involvement in work is too low to allow for strong feelings of any kind, except perhaps the desire to escape from it altogether. He is neither deeply involved with his workmates nor deeply antagonistic to his employer; on the whole his attitude to both more nearly approximates one of indifference.

These tendencies of the work life are reinforced and accentuated by a certain form of community life which is increasingly representative of the new working class: namely, the social structure of the council, or the private, low-cost housing estate.[14] From the present point of view, the most salient feature of these estates is that they bring together a population of strangers, who have little in common, save that they have all experienced residential mobility and that most of them gain their livelihood from some kind of manual labour. In such communities,

11. R. Dubin, 'Industrial Workers' Worlds', *Social Problems*, Vol. 3, January, 1956, p. 135.
12. *Ibid.*
13. R. Blauner, 'Work Satisfaction and Industrial Trends in Modern Society' in W. Galenson and S. M. Lipset (eds.) *Labour and Trade Unionism*, Wiley, New York, 1960, p. 351.
14. See J. Klein, *Samples from English Culture*, Vol. II, Routledge, London, 1965, chapter 5.

social life is very different from the communal sociability of the traditional working-class community. Unrelated by the ascriptive ties of kinship, long-standing neighbourliness and shared work experiences, and lacking also the facility for readily creating middle-class patterns of sociability, workers on the estates tend to live a socially isolated, home-centred existence. Such conditions favour the emergence of attributional rather than interactional status systems. Whereas in the traditional proletarian community status is allocated or more precisely made indeterminate through the individual's participation in several overlapping cliques, the status order of the housing estate is based on conspicuous consumption, by means of which people judge their social standing relative to others without usually associating with them in formal or informal leisure-time activities. The low housing density of the estate, its lack of recreational amenities, the uprootedness of its inhabitants and their limited capacities for creating new styles of sociability produce a society in which residents are only superficially acquainted and associated with those who live around them. The attributional nature of the status ranking that arises from this situation in turn induces an acquisitiveness and a sensitivity to competitive consumption that are quite alien to the communal sociability of proletarian traditionalism.

The work and community settings just described are the breeding grounds of the privatized worker, and his socially isolated existence not only predisposes, but also enables, him to adopt a pecuniary model of class structure. In the first place, he is strongly motivated to view social relationships in pecuniary terms. Lacking close primary group ties inside and outside the work situation, at work he is wage-oriented and in the community consumption-oriented. Just as money wages become of salient importance in attaching him to his work rôle, so, too, consumer durables are of primary significance in mediating his status with his neighbours. This pattern of motivation is neither natural nor accidental. If the privatized worker is more of an economic man than the proletarian or the deferential traditionalist, it is because his environment conspires to make him so. Secondly, however, the work and community relationships that foster this pecuniary outlook are unlikely to give the individual a feeling of definite social location through membership of either a status group or a class fraternity. The privatized worker may be a trade unionist and he may live in a community where status is reckoned by material possessions; but from neither of these sources will he derive more than a rudimentary awareness of belonging to a cohesive group and hence of the social distance between such groups.

By contrast with the proletarian traditionalist, the privatized worker will tend to join and support his trade union for instrumental rather than class solidaristic reasons. Given his materialistic, home-centred aspirations, the trade union for him is less the symbolic expression of an affective attachment to a working class community than a utilitarian association for achieving his private goal of a rising standard of living. Lacking the class consciousness which the proletarian traditionalist acquires from his involvement in solidary work groups and communal sociability, the privatized worker expects his union to devote itself exclusively to bettering the economic position of his own job category rather than to dissipate any of its resources in pursuing the more distant political objective of changing the wider society. As far as he is concerned, the trade union is a 'service organization', not part of a social movement; and, far from his union membership providing him with a consciousness of class, his orientation to trade unionism reflects precisely his lack of such a sentiment.

By contrast with the deferential traditionalist, the privatized worker is unlikely to be made aware of a system of status groups arranged in a stable hierarchy of prestige. His neighbours on the estate are mostly manual wage-earners like himself, socially undistinguished from one another save by marginal differences in their ownership of consumer durables. This means that whatever status distinction arises from the competition to possess these goods is inherently unstable and too superficial to be the source of a sense of unbridgeable social distance. Moreover, in so far as status groups fail to coalesce, the pattern of sociability in the community will remain privatized and there will be small opportunity for the individual to experience personal acceptance by his status equals or personal rejection by his status superiors. Hence, in the typically attributional status system of the housing estate the worker will not learn to perceive status as a phenomenon that manifests itself in group relationships.

The daily social encounters of the privatized worker do not, therefore, lead him to think of a society divided up into either a hierarchy of status groups or an opposition of class. His model of society is one in which individuals are associated with, and dissociated from one another less by any type of social exchange than by the magnitude of their incomes and possessions.

Before going on to outline the elements of this pecuniary model of society, it may be useful to summarize the argument thus far by a table which differentiates proletarian, deferential, and privatized workers in terms of work and community variables. The meanings of the terms used to describe these variables should now be evident from the foregoing discussion.

WORK SITUATION

	Involvement in Job:	Interaction and Identification with Workmates:	Interaction and Identification with Employers:
Middle Class[15]	+	+	+
Deferential	+	—	+
Proletarian	+	+	—
Privatized	—	—	—

COMMUNITY STRUCTURE

	Interactional Status System:	Occupational Community:	Occupational Differentiation:
Middle Class	+	+	+
Deferential	+	—	+
Proletarian	+	+	—
Privatized	—	—	—

15. Since this paper concentrates on manual workers, only the briefest comments on the position of the middle-class employee are called for. Here 'middle class' refers

The social isolation of the privatized worker reflects itself in his ideology of a 'de-socialized' class structure. The single, overwhelmingly important and the most spontaneously conceived criterion of class division is money, and the possessions, both material and immaterial, that money can buy. From this point of view, for example, education is not thought of as a status-conferring characteristic, but rather simply as a good that money can buy and as a possession that enables one to earn more money. In general, power and status are not regarded as significant sources of class division or social hierarchy. Power is not understood as the power of one man over another, but rather as the power of a man to acquire things: as purchasing power. Status is not seen in terms of the association of status equals sharing a similar style of life. If status is thought of at all it is in terms of a standard of living, which all who have the means can readily acquire. It may not be easy to acquire the income requisite to a certain standard of living and hence qualify for membership in a more affluent class; but given the income there are no other barriers to mobility.

Within this pecuniary universe, the privatized worker tends to see himself as a member of a vast income class which contains virtually the great mass of the population. This class may be called 'the working class' or 'the middle class'. Whatever it is called, it is a collection of 'ordinary people' who 'work for a living' and those who belong to it include the majority of manual and non-manual

---

to the administrative, managerial, technical and professional white-collar group (i.e., excluding lower grade clerical employees, who in many respects are similar to the privatized worker, as well as entrepreneurs). This group is included in the paradigm partly because their presence gives it a certain pleasing symmetry: but also because the same variables that are used to differentiate the three types of manual worker would also appear to be relevant in analyzing the social situation of non-manual employees. From the paradigm, it can be seen why the white-collar employee is predisposed to hold a hierarchical model of society. What cannot be seen is why his hierarchical ideology differs from that of the deferential worker. This is because a variable relating to chances and expectations of upward mobility is not included in the table, which, since it was designed to show differences within the manual group, implicitly assigns a low constant value to this variable. It is also quite obvious from the work of Prandy that there is much more variation in the work situation of the white-collar employee than is suggested by the above scheme (see K. Prandy, *Professional Employees*, Faber, London, 1965). The characterization of the middle-class employee in terms of community variables is likewise undoubtedly something of an oversimplification. However, even as it stands, the following points can be made in defence of the present scheme. First, there is ample evidence that middle-class employees of the kind in question do find their work intrinsically more rewarding and are more highly involved in their jobs than most industrial workers. Secondly, because their working relationships usually bring them into close contact with higher management and administration as well as with small groups of workers of their own rank, they are likely to identify themselves with both 'the firm' and their colleagues. Thirdly, because of their high job involvement, they are likely to form occupational communities; and this tendency should be more pronounced the more they are geographically mobile and thus the more they are dependent on friendships acquired through their occupational roles. Fourthly, middle-class employees are likely to live in occupationally mixed communities. Simply because there are relatively so few men in the middle ranges of white-collar employment, it is almost inevitable that their neighbours will include small-scale entrepreneurs, independent professionals, lower-grade clerical and sales employees, and perhaps even highly paid manual workers. Finally, white-collar employees are likely to be involved in interactional status systems. Whether social visiting, or membership of and participation in voluntary associations is taken as a measure of communal (and hence status) interaction, the middle classes rank so much higher than the privatized working class that the difference is qualitative.

employees. They are united with one another, not by having exactly the same incomes, but by not having so much or so little income that their standard of living places them completely beyond the upper or lower horizons. A minority of persons in the society have either so much wealth or such an impoverished existence that they lie outside the central class. They are the very rich and the very poor. Since the main criterion of class membership is money, the lower and, especially, the upper limits of the central class are hard to define, and are consequently defined arbitrarily or regarded as indeterminate. In general the 'upper' or 'higher' or 'rich' class is not perceived as wielding power or deserving of respect. It is simply a vague category of 'all those up there' who have incomes and possessions and a standard of life that are completely beyond the bounds of possibility as far as the ordinary worker is concerned. The rich, however, are different from the rest only in the sense of Hemingway's rejoinder to Scott Fitzgerald: that they have much more money.

Finally, the central class with which the privatized worker identifies himself is seen as a relatively new phenomenon, brought about by the incorporation of the old middle class into the new 'working class', or, alternatively, by the incorporation of the old working class into the new 'middle class'. Whether the end result of the change is seen as a 'working class' or a 'middle class', its identity is basically an economic one; people are assigned to this central class because they have roughly similar levels of income and possessions. Because the convergence of the 'old' working and middle classes is seen in essentially economic terms, the designation of the new central class as 'middle' or 'working' would seem to be largely a matter of how the change is perceived as having taken place rather than an expression of status- or class-consciousness. Indeed, the logic of a purely pecuniary model of society leads to neither class consciousness nor status consciousness but to commodity consciousness. Class and status models entail a perception of social groups whose boundaries are identifiable by acts of power and deference. But the pecuniary universe is one in which inequalities are not expressed through social relationships at all. Income and possessions may be the marks of persons, but unlike power and status they do not involve persons in relationships of inequality with one another. Inequalities take on an extrinsic and quantitative, rather than an intrinsic and qualitative form. In fact, compared with power and prestige, money is not inherently a divider of persons at all; it is a common denominator, of which one may have more or less without its thereby necessarily making a difference to the kind of person one is.

In so far as the privatized worker thinks in terms of the pecuniary model, he has, of course, a somewhat distorted view of the class structure. All available evidence indicates that the amount of informal social interaction between the lower middle and upper working classes is very small and that, in this sense at least, class boundaries are still quite distinct. The privatized worker's idea of a vast central class, differentiated only by marginal differences in income and possessions, is not, therefore, an accurate sociological picture. At the same time, it must be noted that the boundary between the middle and working classes is probably maintained as much by work and residential segregation as by personal exclusion. Thus, from this point of view, the mechanisms of class dissociation operate in a way which is not entirely incompatible with an image of a 'de-socialized' class structure.

There is, finally, no suggestion that the pecuniary model of society is to be thought of as a direct product of working class affluence. The pecuniary model is an outcome of the social rather than the economic situation of the privatized worker; and he is only able to hold such a theory of society in so far as his social environment supports such an interpretation. His relative privatization, his lack of a sense of class cohesion and his isolation from any system of hierarchical social status are the conditions under which he can view his society simply in pecuniary terms.

A purely pecuniary ideology is, of course, just as much of a limiting case as a purely class or purely status model of society. But it may be that it is at least as relevant as the other two in understanding the social and political outlook of the increasingly large section of the working class that is emerging from traditionalism.

15. WORK AND THE SELF   Everett Hughes

There are societies in which custom or sanctioned rule determines what work a man of given status may do. In our society, at least one strong strain of ideology has it that a man may do any work which he is competent to do; or even that he has a right to the schooling and experience necessary to gain competence in any kind of work which he sets as the goal of his ambition. Equality of opportunity is, among us, stated very much in terms of the right to enter upon any occupation whatsoever. Although we do not practice this belief to the full, we are a people who cultivate ambition. A great deal of our ambition takes the form of getting training for kinds of work which carry more prestige than that which our fathers did. Thus a man's work is one of the things by which he is judged, and certainly one of the more significant things by which he judges himself.

Many people in our society work in named occupations. The names are a combination of price tag and calling card. One has only to hear casual conversation to sense how important these tags are. Hear a salesman, who has just been asked what he does, reply, 'I am in sales work,' or 'I am in promotional work', not 'I sell skillets'. Schoolteachers sometimes turn schoolteaching into educational work, and the disciplining of youngsters and chaperoning of parties into personnel work. Teaching Sunday School becomes religious education, and the YMCA Secretary is in 'group work'. Social scientists emphasize the science end of their name. These hedging statements in which people pick the most favorable of several possible names of their work imply an audience. And one of the most important things about any man is his audience, or his choice of the several available audiences to which he may address his claims to be someone of worth.

These remarks should be sufficient to call it to your attention that a man's work is one of the more important parts of his social identity, of his self; indeed, of his fate in the one life he has to live, for there is something almost as irrevocable about choice of occupation as there is about choice of a mate. And since the language about work is so loaded with value and prestige judgments, and with defensive choice of symbols, we should not be astonished that the concepts of social scientists who study work should carry a similar load, for the relation of social-science concepts to popular speech remains close in spite of our efforts to separate them. The difference is that while the value-weighting in popular speech is natural and proper, for concealment and ego-protection are of the essence of social intercourse—in scientific discourse the value-loaded concept may be a

15. 'Work and the Self' by Everett C. Hughes in *Social Psychology at the Cross-roads* by John H. Rohrer and Muzafer Sherif (eds). Copyright 1951 by Harper & Row, Publishers, Inc. Reprinted by permission of the publisher.

blinder. And part of the problem of method in the study of work behavior is that the people who have the most knowledge about a given occupation (let us say medicine), and from whom therefore the data for analysis must come, are the people in the occupation. They may combine in themselves a very sophisticated manipulative knowledge of the appropriate social relations, with a very strongly motivated suppression, and even repression, of the deeeper truths about these relationships, and, in occupations of higher status, with great verbal skill in keeping these relationships from coming up for thought and discussion by other people. This is done in part by the use of and insistence upon loaded value words where their work is discussed.

My own experience in study of occupations illustrates the point that concepts may be blinders. My first essay into the field was a study of the real estate agents in Chicago. These highly competitive men were just at that point in their journey toward respectability at which they wished to emphasize their conversion from business-minded suspicion of one another to the professional attitude of confidence in each other coupled with a demand for confidence from the public. I started the study with the idea of finding out an answer to this familiar question, 'Are these men professionals?' It was a false question, for the concept 'profession' in our society is not so much a descriptive term as one of value and prestige. It happens over and over that the people who practice an occupation attempt to revise the conceptions which their various publics have of the occupation and of the people in it. In so doing, they also attempt to revise their own conception of themselves and of their work. The model which these occupations set before themselves is that of the 'profession'; thus the term profession is a symbol for a desired conception of one's work and, hence, of one's self. The movement to 'professionalize' an occupation is thus collective mobility of some among the people in an occupation. One aim of the movement is to rid the occupation of people who are not mobile enough to go along with the changes.

There are two kinds of occupational mobility. One is individual. The individual makes the several choices, and achieves the skills which allow him to move to a certain position in the occupational, and thus—he hopes—in the social and economic hierarchy. His choice is limited by several conditions, among which is the social knowledge available to him at the time of crucial decision, a time which varies for the several kinds of work.

The other kind of occupational mobility is that of a group of people in an occupation, i.e., of the occupation itself. This has been important in our society with its great changes of technology, with its attendant proliferation of new occupations and of change in the techniques and social relations of old ones. Now it sometimes happens that by the time a person has the full social knowledge necessary to the smartest possible choice of occupations, he is already stuck with one and in one. How strongly this may affect the drive for professionalization of occupations, I don't know. I suspect that it is a motive. At any rate, it is common in our society for occupational groups to step their occupation up in the hierarchy by turning it into a profession. I will not here describe this process. Let me only indicate that in my own studies I passed from the false question 'Is this occupation a profession?' to the more fundamental one, 'What are the circumstances in which the people in an occupation attempt to turn it into a profession, and themselves into professional people?' and 'What are the steps by which they attempt to bring about identification with their valued model?'

Even with this new orientation the term profession acted as a blinder. For as I began to give courses and seminars on occupations, I used a whole set of concepts and headings which were prejudicial to full understanding of what work behavior and relations are. One of them was that of the 'code of ethics', which still tended to sort people into the good and the bad. It was not until I had occasion to undertake study of race relations in industry that I finally, I trust, got rid of this bias in the concepts which I used. Negro industrial workers, the chief objects of our study, performed the kinds of work which have least prestige and which make least pretension; yet it turned out that even in the lowest occupations people do develop collective pretensions to give their work, and consequently themselves, value in the eyes of each other and of outsiders.

It was from these people that we learned that a common dignifying rationalization of people in all positions of a work hierarchy except the very top one is, 'We in this position save the people in the next higher position above from their own mistakes'. The notion that one saves a person of more acknowledged skill, and certainly of more acknowledged prestige and power, than one's self from his mistakes appears to be peculiarly satisfying. Now there grow up in work organizations rules of mutual protection among the persons in a given category and rank, and across ranks and categories. If one uses the term 'code of ethics' he is likely not to see the true nature of these rules. These rules have of necessity to do with mistakes, for it is in the nature of work that people make mistakes. The question of how mistakes are handled is a much more penetrating one than any question which contains the concept 'professional ethics' as ordinarily conceived. For in finding out how mistakes are handled, one must get at the fundamental psychological and social devices by which people are able to carry on through time, to live with others and with themselves, knowing that what is daily routine for them in their occupational roles may be fateful for others, knowing that one's routine mistakes, even the mistakes by which one learns better, may touch other lives at crucial points. It is in part the problem of dealing routinely with what are the crises of others. The people in lower ranks are thus using a powerful psychological weapon when they rationalize their worth and indispensability as lying in their protection of people in higher ranks from their mistakes. I suppose it is almost a truism that the people who take the larger responsibilities must be people who can face making mistakes, while punctiliousness must remain in second place. But this is a matter which has not been very seriously taken into account, as far as I know, in studies of the social drama of work.

Of course, the rules which people make to govern their behavior at work cover other problems than that of mistakes. Essentially the rules classify people, for to define situations and the proper behavior in situations one has to assign roles to the people involved. Among the most important subject matter of rules is the setting up of criteria for recognizing a true fellow-worker, for determining who it is safe and maybe even necessary to initiate into the in-group of close equals, and who must be kept at some distance. This problem is apt to be obscured by the term 'colleagueship', which, although its etymology is perfect for the matter in hand, carries a certain notion of higher status, of respectability. (In pre-Hitler Germany the Social-Democratic workers called one another 'Comrade'. The Christian trade-unions insisted on the term 'Colleague'.)

Allow me to mention one other value-laden term which may act as a blinder in study of the social psychology of work, to wit, 'restriction of production'. This term contains a value assumption of another kind—namely, that there is someone who knows and has a right to determine the right amount of work for other people to do. If one does less, he is restricting production. Mayo[1] and others have done a good deal to analyze the phenomenon in question, but it was Max Weber[2] who—forty years ago—pointed to 'putting on the brakes', as an inevitable result of the wrestling match between a man and his employer over the price he must pay with his body for his wage. In short, he suggested that no man easily yields to another full control over the amount of effort he must daily exert. On the other hand, there is no more characteristically human phenomenon than determined and even heroic effort to do a task which one has taken as his own. I do not mean to make the absurd implication that there could be a situation in which every man would be his own and only taskmaster. But I think we might better understand the social interaction which determines the measure of effort if we keep ourselves free of terms which suggest that it is abnormal to do less than one is asked by some reasonable authority.

You will have doubtless got the impression that I am making the usual plea for a value-free science, that is, for neutrality. Such is not my intention. Our aim is to *penetrate more deeply* into the personal and social drama of work, to understand the social and social-psychological arrangements and devices by which men make their work tolerable, or even glorious to themselves and others. I believe that much of our terminology and hence, of our problem setting, has limited our field of perception by a certain pretentiousness and a certain value-loading. Specifically we need to rid ourselves of any concepts which keep us from seeing that the essential problems of men at work are the same whether they do their work in some famous laboratory or in the messiest vat room of a pickle factory. Until we can find a point of view and concepts which will enable us to make comparisons between the junk peddler and the professor without intent to debunk the one and patronize the other, we cannot do our best work in this field.

Perhaps there is as much to be learned about the high-prestige occupations by applying to them the concepts which naturally come to mind for study of people in the most lowly kinds of work as there is to be learned by applying to other occupations the conceptions developed in connection with the highly-valued professions. Furthermore, I have come to the conclusion that it is a fruitful thing to start study of any social phenomenon at the point of least prestige. For, since prestige is so much a matter of symbols, and even of pretensions—however well merited—there goes with prestige a tendency to preserve a front which hides the inside of things; a front of names, of indirection, of secrecy (much of it necessary secrecy). On the other hand, in things of less prestige, the core may be more easy of access.

In recent years a number of my students have studied some more or less lowly occupations: apartment-house janitors, junk men, boxers, jazz musicians,

1. Elton W. Mayo, *Human Problems of an Industrial Civilization*, Macmillan, New York, 1933.
2. Max Weber, 'Zur Psycholphysik de industriellen Arbeit' in *Gesammelte Aufsätze zur Soziologie und Sozialpolitik*, Tübingen, 1924, pp. 730–70.

osteopaths, pharmacists, etc. They have done so mainly because of their own connections with the occupations in question, and perhaps because of some problem of their own. At first, I thought of these studies as merely interesting and informative for what they would tell about people who do these humbler jobs, i.e., as American ethnology. I have now come to the belief that although the problems of people in these lines of work are as interesting and important as any other, their deeper value lies in the insights they yield about work behavior in any and all occupations. It is not that it puts one into the position to debunk the others, but simply that processes which are hidden in other occupations come more readily to view in these lowly ones. We may be here dealing with a fundamental matter of method in social science, that of finding the best possible laboratory for study of a given series of mechanisms.

Let me illustrate. The apartment-house janitor is a fellow who, in making his living, has to do a lot of other people's dirty work. This is patent. He could not hide it if he would. Now every occupation is not one but several activities; some of them are the 'dirty work' of that trade. It may be dirty in one of several ways. It may be simply physically disgusting. It may be a symbol of degradation, something that wounds one's dignity.

Finally, it may be dirty work in that it in some way goes counter to the more heroic of our moral conceptions. Dirty work of some kind is found in all occupations. It is hard to imagine an occupation in which one does not appear, in certain repeated contingencies, to be practically compelled to play a role of which he thinks he ought to be a little ashamed. Insofar as an occupation carries with it a self-conception, a notion of personal dignity, it is likely that at some point one will feel that he is having to do something that is *infra dignitatem*. Janitors turned out to be bitterly frank about their physically dirty work. When asked, 'What is the toughest part of your job', they answered almost to a man in the spirit of this quotation: 'Garbage. Often the stuff is sloppy and smelly. You know some fellows can't look at garbage if it's sloppy. I'm getting used to it now, but it almost killed me when I started'. Or as another put it, 'The toughest part? It's the messing up in front of the garbage incinerator. That's the most miserable thing there is on this job. The tenants don't co-operate—them bastards. You tell them today, and tomorrow there is the same mess over again by the incinerator'.

In the second quotation it becomes evident that the physical disgust of the janitor is not merely a thing between him and the garbage, but involves the tenant also. Now the tenant is the person who impinges most on the daily activity of the janitor. It is the tenant who interferes most with his own dignified ordering of his life and work. If it were not for a tenant who had broken a window, he could have got his regular Sunday cleaning done on time; if it were not for a tenant who had clogged a trap, he would not have been ignominiously called away from the head of his family table just when he was expansively offering his wife's critical relatives a second helping of porkchops, talking the while about the importance of his job. It is the tenant who causes the janitor's status pain. The physically disgusting part of the janitor's work is directly involved in his relations with other actors in his work drama.[3]

---

3. Ray Gold, 'Janitors vs. Tenants: A Status-income Dilemma', *The American Journal of Sociology*, Vol. LVII, March, 1952, pp. 487–93.

By a *contre coup*, it is by the garbage that the janitor judges, and, as it were, gets power over the tenants who high-hat him. Janitors know about hidden love-affairs by bits of torn-up letter paper; of impending financial disaster or of financial four-flushing by the presence of many unopened letters in the waste. Or they may stall off demands for immediate service by an unreasonable woman of whom they know from the garbage that she, as the janitors put it, 'has the rag on'. The garbage gives the janitor the makings of a kind of magical power over that pretentious villain, the tenant. I say a kind of magical power, for there appears to be no thought of betraying any individual and thus turning this knowledge into overt power. He protects the tenant, but, at least among Chicago janitors, it is not a loving protection.

Let your mind dwell on what one might hear from people in certain other occupations if they were to answer as frankly and bitterly as did the janitors. I do not say nor do I think that it would be a good thing for persons in all occupations to speak so freely on physical disgust as did these men. To do so, except in the most tightly closed circles, would create impossible situations. But we are likely to overlook the matter altogether in studying occupations where concealment is practiced, and thus get a false notion of the problems which have to be faced in such occupations, and of the possible psychological and social by-products of the solutions which are developed for the problem of disgust.

Now the delegation of dirty work to someone else is common among humans. Many cleanliness taboos, and perhaps even many moral scruples, depend for their practice upon success in delegating the tabooed activity to someone else. Delegation of dirty work is also a part of the process of occupational mobility. Yet there are kinds of work, some of them of very high prestige, in which such delegation is possible only to a limited extent. The dirty work may be an intimate part of the very activity which gives the occupation its charism, as is the case with the handling of the human body by the physician. In this case, I suppose the dirty work is somehow integrated into the whole, and into the prestige-bearing role of the person who does it. What role it plays in the drama of work relations in such a case is something to find out. The janitor, however, does not integrate his dirty work into any deeply satisfying definition of his role that might liquidate his antagonism to the people whose dirt he handles. Incidentally, we have found reason to believe that one of the deeper sources of antagonisms in hospitals is the belief of the people in the humblest jobs that the physician in charge calls upon them to do his dirty work in the name of the role of 'healing the sick', although none of the prestige and little of the money reward of that role reaches them. Thus we might conceive of a classification of occupations involving dirty work into those in which it is knit into some satisfying and prestige-giving definition of role and those in which it is not. I suppose we might think of another classification into those in which the dirty work seems somehow wilfully put upon one and those in which it is quite unconnected with any person involved in the work drama.

There is a feeling among prison guards and mental-hospital attendants that society at large and their superiors hypocritically put upon them dirty work which they, society, and the superiors in prison and hospital know is necessary but which they pretend is not necessary. Here it takes the form, in the minds of people in these two lowly occupations, of leaving them to cope for twenty-four hours, day in and day out, with inmates whom the public never has to see and whom the people at the head of the organization see only episodically. There is a whole series of problems here which cannot be solved by some miracle of changing the social selection of those who enter the job (which is the usual unrealistic solution for such cases).

And this brings us to the brief consideration of what one may call the social drama of work. Most kinds of work bring people together in definable roles; thus the janitor and the tenant, the doctor and the patient, the teacher and the pupil, the worker and his foreman, the prison guard and the prisoner, the musician and his listener. In many occupations there is some category of persons with whom the people at work regularly come into crucial contact. In some occupations the most crucial relations are those with one's fellow-workers. It is they who can do most to make life sweet or sour. Often, however, it is the people in some other position. And in many there is a category of persons who are the consumers of one's work or services. It is probable that the people in the occupation will have a chronic fight for status, for personal dignity with this group of consumers of their services. Part of the social psychological problem of the occupation is the maintenance of a certain freedom and social distance from these people most crucially and intimately concerned with one's work.

In a good deal of our talk about occupations we imply that the tension between the producer and consumer of services is somehow a matter of ill-will or misunderstandings which easily might be removed. It may be that it lies a good deal deeper than that. Often there is a certain ambivalence on the side of the producer, which may be illustrated by the case of the professional jazz-musicians. The musician wants jobs and an income. He also wants his music to be appreciated, but to have his living depend upon the appreciation does not entirely please him. For he likes to think himself and other musicians the best judges of his playing. To play what pleases the audience—the paying customers, who are not, in his opinion, good judges—is a source of annoyance. It is not merely that the listeners, having poor taste, demand that he play music which he does not think is the best he can do; even when they admire him for playing in his own sweet way, he doesn't like it, for then they are getting too close—they are impinging on his private world too much. The musicians accordingly use all sorts of little devices to keep a line drawn between themselves and the audience; such as turning the musicians' chairs, in a dance hall without platform, in such a way as to make something of a barrier.[4] It is characteristic of many occupations that the people in them, although convinced that they themselves are the best judges, not merely of their own competence but also of what is best for the people for whom they perform services, are required in some measure to yield judgment of what is wanted to these amateurs who receive the services. This is a problem not only among musicians, but in teaching, medicine, dentistry, the arts, and many other fields. It is a chronic source of ego-wound and possibly of antagonism.

Related to this is the problem of routine and emergency. In many occupations, the workers or practitioners (to use both a lower and a higher status term)

4. Howard S. Becker, 'The Professional Dance Musician and his Audience', *The American Journal of Sociology*, Vol. LVII, September, 1951, pp. 136–44.

deal routinely with what are emergencies to the people who receive their services. This is a source of chronic tension between the two. For the person with the crisis feels that the other is trying to belittle his trouble; he does not take it seriously enough. His very competence comes from having dealt with a thousand cases of what the client likes to consider his unique trouble. The worker thinks he knows from long experience that people exaggerate their troubles. He therefore builds up devices to protect himself, to stall people off. This is the function of the janitor's wife when a tenant phones an appeal or a demand for immediate attention to a leaky tap; it is also the function of the doctor's wife and even sometimes of the professor's wife. The physician plays one emergency off against the other; the reason he can't run right up to see Johnny who may have the measles is that he is, unfortunately, right at that moment treating a case of the black plague. Involved in this is something of the struggle mentioned above in various connections, the struggle to maintain some control over one's decisions of what work to do, and over the disposition of one's time and of one's routine of life. It would be interesting to know what the parish priest thinks to himself when he is called for the tenth time to give extreme unction to the sainted Mrs. O'Flaherty who hasn't committed a sin in years except that of being a nuisance to the priest, in her anxiety over dying in a state of sin. On Mrs. O'Flaherty's side there is the danger that she might die unshriven, and she has some occasion to fear that the people who shrive may not take her physical danger seriously and hence may not come quickly enough when at last her hour has come. There may indeed be in the minds of the receivers of emergency services a resentment that something so crucial to them can be a matter of a cooler and more objective attitude, even though they know perfectly well that such an attitude is necessary to competence, and though they could not stand it if the expert to whom they take their troubles were to show any signs of excitement.

16. THE SOCIOLOGY OF ACCIDENTS AND THE SOCIAL PRODUCTION OF INDUSTRIAL INJURY   Theo Nichols

'Not exciting, except by accident.' That's how *The Times*[1] summed up public opinion about safety and health at work on the publication of the Robens Report.[2] An unfortunate comment perhaps, but apt enough. For Chapter 1 of the Report begins: 'Every year something like 1,000 people are killed at their work in this country. Every year about half a million suffer injuries in varying degrees of severity.' Some authorities give considerably higher figures for industrial injuries,[3] and for deaths—over 2,000 a year being killed at work or dying of diseases contracted at work on one estimate.[4] However, aside from newsworthy events like the Flixborough explosion of 1974, safety is rarely an important public issue. Industry, on one account, spends a mere 0.05 per cent of its R & D budget on research into safety at work.[5] The fraction of energy expended by British sociologists is of a not dissimilar order.

Sociology, psychology and 'accidents'.

A strange situation this, that so many sociologists should find it important to study 'mortifications of self' as per Goffman and 'degradation ceremonies' as per Garfinkel (both usually *sans* blood and broken bones); that so few should concern themselves with mutilation at work; that, in sociology, 'dirty work' should have come to suggest something about 'deviance', not coal mining; that in the overwhelming number of cases, injury and ill health should simply not figure in the works of industrial sociologists. There are exceptions of course. Carson[6] has shed

1. *The Times*, 'Leader', July 20, 1972.
2. *Report of the Committee on Safety and Health at Work*, Cmnd. 5034, HMSO, London, 1972 (The Robens Report).
3. A. A. Beddoe, 'The Cost of Industrial Injuries' in W. Handley (ed.) *Industrial Safety Handbook*, McGraw Hill, London, 1970, p. 451. A former Royal Assurance Chief Accident Surveyor has estimated that 'about 30 million injuries occur annually which require first-aid or medical treatment or both, and absences from work if only for the length of the treatment'. (For a discussion of accident statistics see P. J. Shipp and A. S. Sutton, *A Study of the Statistics Relating to Safety and Health at Work*, Institute of Operational Research Committee on Safety and Health Research Paper, HMSO, London, 1972.
4. 'Safety in Industry Symposium', *British Clinical Journal*, July, 1973, pp. 4-13.
5. *Memorandum on the Recommendations of the Robens Committee on Safety and Health at Work*, Public Interest Research Centre Limited, London, 1972, p. 4.
6. W. G. Carson, 'White Collar Crime and the Enforcement of Factory Legislation', in W. G. Carson and P. Wiles (eds.) *Crime and Delinquency in Britain*, Martin Robinson, London, 1971.

16. Original article. Copyright © 1975 Holmes McDougall Ltd., Edinburgh. Theo Nichols is Lecturer in Sociology at the University of Bristol.

some light on the functioning of the Factory Inspectorate. Above all, Baldamus and his associates have made considerable quantitative researches into industrial accidents. Wrench,[7] for example, has made statistical studies of the relationship between piece working and accidents. It is even possible that Baldamus's work may have played some part in changing the definition and analysis of accidents used by the Factory Inspectorate itself. And since, as Baldamus[8] himself has noted, it does not happen very often that official administrative bodies are influenced by academic sociological research, the contribution that a very small number of sociologists have made to this area should not be underestimated.

By and large, though, it remains the case that sociologists have done remarkably little work on industrial injury. This is why it is unfortunate that one of Baldamus's distinctive contributions should have been the development of the category 'pseudo-accident'—this being an idea that could meet a ready welcome from those who are wont to claim that, today, people stay off work 'for nothing', and from those who are wont to make strident complaints about 'ghost accidents'. Of course Baldamus may have a good case for labelling a proportion of, say, backaches, as pseudo-*accidents*. After all, aches and sprains may not manifest themselves in the neat, time-specific way that is apt to characterize the breaking of bones and severing of limbs. However, pseudo-*accidents* are not necessarily synonymous with pseudo-*injuries* or pseudo-*ill health*—and the increasing official use of the category 'not truly accidental accident'[9] could well backfire in the faces of those (like Baldamus himself) who care about the health of people at work. Quite obviously, there are ghost accidents; in work as in war, some men injure themselves or claim to be injured when they are not. But those who complain loudest about such 'accidents' (and complaints that 'Lying Workers Cost Us Millions' are to be heard in some of the most 'responsible' quarters[10]) are generally less anxious to emphasize the extent to which workers— all too honest workers, insecure workers, and workers who are just hard up— '*save* us millions' by 'struggling on'. And this despite minor injuries, gradually deteriorating health, and even work-induced mental illness, none of which show up in the accident figures.

Baldamus's own theorizing about accidents, and in particular about 'pseudo accidents', derives from Merton's ideas about anomie.[11] So, in his view, accident absenteeism can be considered as a form of 'work retreatism'; as a form of 'illicit conduct' arising from 'an insoluble conflict between culturally prescribed goals and institutionalized norms'.[12] Put more bluntly (and just slightly differently)

7. J. Wrench, *Speed Accidents: A Study of the Relation Between Piecework and Industrial Accidents,* University of Birmingham, Faculty of Commerce and Social Science, Discussion Paper, Series E, No. 17, May, 1972.

8. W. Baldamus, *The Concept of Truly Accidental Accidents,* University of Birmingham, Faculty of Commerce and Social Science, Discussion Paper, Series E, No. 14, October, 1969.

9. *1968 Annual Report of H.M. Chief Inspector of Factories,* HMSO, London, Cmnd. 4146, September, 1969, p. xiii.

10. See the front-page story of *Safety and Rescue,* 'Ghost Accidents—Lying Workers Cost Us Millions' in James Tye and Kenneth Ullyett, *Safety—Uncensored,* Corgi Books, London, 1971, chapter 13.

11. R. K. Merton, *Social Theory and Social Structure,* The Free Press, Glencoe, 1957.

12. W. Baldamus, *The Consumption Imperative: Structural Change in Advanced Industrial Capitalism,* Inaugural Lecture, University of Birmingham, December, 1971, p. 12.

accident absenteeism could be held to indicate the increasing extent to which present-day workers are less willing than their fathers to put up with ill health and/or rotten jobs—not that this sort of language is found at all frequently in accident research. More to the point, it is rarely to be found in psychologically based accident researches. For, of all the social sciences, it is psychology that dominates research into industrial accidents, and, of all the researches conducted by social scientists, few can rival that essentially asocial and mechanistic approach of some research to be found in this field.

As one review of the safety-psychology literature points out:

> Accident research has in general been concentrated in two main areas. Firstly, accident statistics have been collected and the frequency of different types of accident have been correlated with individual attributes ... of the individual sustaining the accident. ... Secondly, the frequency of different types of accident has been correlated with a wide variety of what might be collectively termed environmental factors.[13]

Basically, therefore, the first area of research is about 'personal factors' and 'variables'—age, sex, state of health, intelligence, personality—and the second area is about yet other, 'environmental' factors—including 'such things as environmental temperature, social and psychological environment, number of hours worked, and ambient lighting'.

Sometimes, psycho-analytic theory figures on the 'personal' side of the equation, as in the early work of the Tavistock Institute.[14] Hill and Trist's pioneer work on accidents and other forms of absenteeism, for example, argues *inter alia* that accidents which involve being hit by falling objects 'belong psychologically to the world of paranoid phenomena'—but that an employee will not be so prone to feel himself attacked 'as his relation with his employing authority improves'! They also claim on the basis of their researches that 'certain characteristics begin to emerge of the individual who has many absences, including perhaps one or more accidents. He would seem to lack the ordinary capacity to internalize a good object, to be rather prone to paranoid hostility and apt to disown responsibility for what he does and remain ignorant of his own motivation. A bad relation with his own super-ego may easily be acted out in a bad relation with his employing authority, without insight on his part. One way of acting out such a bad relation is through a more or less violent break in the employment contract, the person leaving or—they add—'getting himself dismissed'.[15]

In the fully developed interactionist model, the tendency is for environmental factors to be conceptualized in a way that can only be likened to that of

13. J. G. Dunn, *Safety Psychology: A Review of the Literature*, A.P. Report 35, Applied Psychology Department, University of Aston, August, 1971, p. 7.
14. See J. M. M. Hill, 'A Note on Labour Turnover in an Iron and Steel Works', *Human Relations*, February, 1953; J. M. M. Hill and E. L. Trist, 'A Consideration of Industrial Accidents as a Means of Withdrawal from the Work Situation', *Human Relations*, November, 1953 and J. M. M. Hill and E. L. Trist, 'Changes in Accidents and Other Absences with Length of Service', *Human Relations*, May, 1955.
15. J. M. M. Hill and E. L. Trist, 'Changes in Accidents and Other Absences with Length of Service', *Human Relations*, May, 1955, pp. 145, 147.

cue sticks in the billiard game of life. The result of such theoretical sophistication, and the correlate of anything methodological apt to go with it, can be rather difficult to digest. Certainly, the numerous 'factors' around which the major reviews[16] of 'findings' are structured go a long way to bear out Dunn's comment that 'one of the greatest difficulties in understanding the basic causes of accidents has been the lack of a general theoretical and conceptual framework.' The way he himself reports some of the empirical work that has been done illustrates this point all the more vividly. A 'study by Slivnick et al., (1957)' he reports,

> investigated accidents in 147 factories, and accident frequency and severity with 75 variables. They too (this follows immediately on the report of a study of 12,060 employees which 'correlated accident frequency and severity with 40 variables') found a number of significant correlations:
> (a) accident frequency is associated with seasonal lay-off rates, poor attitude of co-workers towards producers, small plants, easy access to prostitutes, other plants about, frequent handling of heavy materials and blighted living conditions.
> (b) Accident severity is associated with non-egalitarian eating, national union strength, no stated penalty for tardiness, no employee profit-sharing plan, extreme work-place temperatures and 'dirty-sweaty' work.

A theoretical research on accidents must not, however, be dismissed out of hand, despite the nonsense to which it can lead. A study like the National Institute of Industrial Psychology's 2,000 Accidents[17] is still, for example, of potential value in pointing to possible causes of accidents, even if it is a-theoretical and largely confined to examining the causality or otherwise of a jumble of 'environmental and personal factors'. After all, the factors considered—'noise', 'sleeping, eating and tiredness', 'monotony', 'alcohol', 'bonus pay', 'supervision', 'propaganda', 'malingering', 'removal of guards' and others—could all be possible final causes. The problem with forensic analyses—those which seek to specify highly particular causal factors[18]—is certainly not that they are inherently useless. The problem is that they take so much for granted; that even when they are adequate at one level, at another level they can no more provide adequate accounts of industrial accidents than would highly specific analyses of road accidents, were these to ignore the massive significance of the motor car for our society and concentrate instead on the design of bumpers and door handles and the state of mind of jay walkers.

Seemingly commonsensical causal categories—'lack of attention', 'tiredness', 'failure of machinery', 'wilful breaking of safety rules', 'inadequate supervision', 'management at fault', 'workers at fault' and the Factory In-

---

16. See J. G. Dunn, *Safety Psychology: A Review of the Literature*, A.P. Report 35, Applied Psychology Department, University of Aston, August, 1971, and A. R. Hale and M. Hale, *A Review of the Industrial Accident Research Literature*, National Institute of Industrial Psychology Research Paper for the Committee on Safety and Health at Work, HMSO, London, 1972.

17. *2,000 Accidents: A Shop-floor Study of their Causes based on 42 Months' Continuous Observation*, National Institute of Industrial Psychology, London, 1971.

18. I am indebted to Pete Armstrong for suggesting the term 'forensic' for such analyses: see our joint work, T. Nichols and P. Armstrong, *Safety or Profit: Industrial Accidents and the Conventional Wisdom*, Falling Wall Press, Bristol, 1973.

spectorate's so-called 'Big-Four' causation groups—'Handling and Lifting', 'Machinery', 'Persons falling', 'Falling objects'—categories like these have their place. But they cannot, of themselves, make sense of how and why objects or men fall, of how or why men come to use machinery or handle materials in such a way that they are injured, of why management or men are at fault. This is why the dominant form of analysis that has been applied to injury at work needs to be set in the context of a fuller social analysis: an analysis, that is, that takes account of the way in which the situations in which accidents take place are structured.

In the recent past it has been somewhat fashionable to point out that statistics are socially produced. Nothing could underline the truth of this more than a critical assessment of those statistics that allegedly pertain to industrial accidents. For a start, accident figures do not relate to 'accidents' but to injuries. Then, of injuries, only those which lead to loss of work time of a certain duration in certain industries are notifiable to HM Inspectorates. And, of these, only a certain percentage are actually notified. Indeed, all this represents only one facet of the problem. The observation made by Baldamus and the Factory Inspectorate about the meaning of injury to those injured constitutes another. As HM Chief Inspector of Factories put it in his *1968 Annual Report*:

> Changing social conditions over the years have altered the meaning of the three day absence criterion of reportability . . . [so that] the fatality rate [in the mining industry] has been reduced since 1947 by two thirds, and the incidence rate of certain classes of serious accident by one third [whereas] during the same period the number of accidents causing disablement for more than three days has risen by over 70 per cent.[19]

But interesting and important in its way as the analysis of the social production of accident statistics may be, it would be most regrettable were this to be substituted for the analysis of the social production of injury. For the plain fact is that industrial injuries do not only occur in the *physical* context of inanimate machinery nor do they occur only in a *mental* and *moral* context inhabited by more or less 'apathetic' or 'guilty' *individuals*, be they managers or workers. Injuries at work occur in the context of *the social relations of production*. This is why it is often not at all easy to apportion personal blame and responsibility for accidents. True enough, when accidents are slotted into the Factory Inspectorate's gruesome categories—'Management only', 'Deceased only', 'Fellow Worker only', 'Management and Deceased jointly' and so on—most blame is usually laid at management's door.[20] But, in essentials, this sort of classification remains inadequate. It deflects attention from the extent to which injuries and fatalities take place in a particular mode of production, which is characterized by par-

19. *1968 Annual Report of H.M. Chief Inspector of Factories*, HMSO, London, Cmnd. 4146, September, 1969, pp. xii–xiii.
20. Not surprisingly. Of 290 fatal accidents reported in factory processes in 1973 (these being the latest figures available) the Factory Inspectorate claim there was a *breach of law* by the employer in 124 (43%) cases; there was also a breach of law in 127 (55%) out of the 230 deaths in construction. 70% of factory fatalities, according to the Chief Inspector, might have been prevented had 'reasonably practicable precautions' been taken by 'management and workpeople jointly'. *1973 Annual Report of H.M. Chief Inspector of Factories*, HMSO, London, Cmnd. 5708, 1974, pp. 96, 98, 100–1.

ticular social relations; one, moreover, in which sociologically, if not existentially, neither managers nor men are free agents. It is just because of this that the common allegation that workers are 'apathetic' about safety cannot be accepted at face value.[21] Again, it is because of this that managers who are decidedly schizophrenic about safety should not be considered psychologically ill (but more of this later).

To make it plain: because of limits in technical knowledge, there is a sense in which it is perfectly correct to say 'accidents will happen' (though how far those who design machines and lay-outs can put safety before profit is also pertinent here). Also, the 'forensic' approach can, in principle, yield important information. Also, it is quite plausible to regard some accident absenteeism (along with some sabotage, lateness, sickness and so on, as an index of disaffection with work, though to demonstrate this empirically is no easy matter. Also, no doubt some employers care little for safety and some men do pride themselves on the risks they take. But for all this, it has to be said that the literature on industrial accidents is still very short on the analysis of social process and of social structure.

One of the very few exceptions is the work of Eldridge and Kaye,[22] two authors who prepared a research paper for the Robens Committee on Safety and Health at Work. Their paper, which employed essentially Weberian categories of analysis, served to underline the complexity of social behaviour and went far beyond the mechanistic explanations of so much safety psychology—and seems to have been totally disregarded by the Robens Committee. There is no way of telling whether this was because of Robens' inability to cope with certain unpalatable truths. But as Eldridge and Kaye note:

> The implications are far reaching . . . as soon as we move away from explanations of a mechanistic nature.

And their exploration of possible connections between wages and accidents does point 'to the issue of control': to the issue of

> . . . who is controlling whom, how effectively and how far is the control system regarded as fair or legitimate?[23]

The social production of injury

Who is controlling whom? How effectively (or ineffectively)? And why? These, I think, are very useful questions to ask. Very useful questions to start by asking, too; for the structure of work relationships exists before the entry of any given worker into the factory. But let's be concrete about this word *structure*. Let's look at some common or garden accidents. In fact, let's put aside this word

21. For a critique of the Robens Report's extraordinary apathy theory, see T. Nichols and P. Armstrong, *Safety or Profit: Industrial Accidents and the Conventional Wisdom*, Falling Wall Press, Bristol, 1973, pp. 6–10. (The accidents reported below are drawn from this source.)
22. J. E. T. Eldridge and B. M. Kaye, *Wages and Accidents: An Exploratory Paper*, Committee on Safety and Health Research Paper, in *Onderneming en vakbeweging*, University of Rotterdam, 1973.
23. *Ibid.*, pp. 159, 169.

'accident' that the safety psychologists tie themselves in knots defining. Let us look instead at injuries: at what happened to four men who lost fingers and one who had his head smashed in.

Here's Fred's story—

> The hopper line's on a gradient, as you know, and it was a very poor gradient at the top and all the empty hoppers used to get stuck. Now it was a condoned thing—I mean foremen used to more or less tell you to do it—to go up with a fork-lift truck and push the hoppers down. It was the only way of getting them down to keep the job going. Well I got the fork-lift up there, the hopper started moving and the fork-lift went into the side of it. I got my finger jammed. I lost my finger.

A readily understandable, not unusual and seemingly straightforward accident.

This is what happened to Joe—

> The rollers stopped and we called out downstairs 'What's going on?' So Joe went to see to save time—but then they stopped the chute as well, see? So now the rollers down here won't start either. The shaker wouldn't start. But then the blokes up there started up the chute and it was all coming down again, see. So Joe climbed across the rollers and pushed the start button. And his finger caught in a roller like that you see. And as soon as the rollers started up he lost his footing and all his weight came down on the finger and he just dropped and pulled it off like that.

The chain of events is a bit more complicated this time, but again not an unusual sort of accident.

Now here's what happened to Dick—

> At that time they were on bonus and if you kept stopping the rollers the blokes on boxing-up started shouting. The foreman wanted to know what the hell was going on and unless the blokes did a reasonable tonnage they didn't get the bonus. Well there was a fault on the rollers. The boxes used to come down two or three heaped together and unless you was quick they'd drop off the end. Of course you kept having broken boxes on the floor and you were falling over them. Well he was running back to catch a box, see. And the one behind suddenly came down and he pushed it and he pushed his fingers underneath you see. Well all right. Fair enough he could have stopped the rollers. He could have let the box fall. He needn't have bothered with it. But he was trying to do his job properly.

Another finger gone. Again nothing difficult to understand, nothing unusual.

And the same with Harry, who was lucky he didn't come out of it with a fractured skull—

> Now and again we used to get a very bad hopper. They'd just come out of servicing, you know, and the brakes were bloody terrible. This particular day there's six of us trying to push one down. We kicked it, we pushed, we

cussed it, we done every bloody thing. So we called out for the heavy gang and said, 'Can you lot move this bloody thing for us?' They said, 'All right'—they'd see to it like. And I said to the chappy that's there, 'Come on, whilst they do that we should get on bloody loading.' Because they're on high rates and if you hang about too much—'What the bloody hell's wrong down there?', you know, 'What've you bloody stopped for?' So in we go. Press button A. Rollers running—no boxes. They weren't coming down. So he says, 'Stick your head out, have a look up them rollers,' he says. 'Ten to one you'll have a bloody pile-up.' So I did. And just then the bloody heavy gang jerks this hopper free and it hits up against the one we're loading and I was jammed in there.

And now for another finger, just another finger lost again in a readily understandable way. Jack describes what happened—

I put the next box in, ready to go, when this box starts tilting. The bottom of the box was travelling along but the top was stuck and it took the top of it right off. So I stopped the stapler and I pulled the box out. And when I looked there was a piece of box jammed in the cogs there. We tried two or three times to pull it free but it wouldn't come. And the fella I was working with says he's going to get a pair of pliers. Well while he was gone I caught hold of a piece of the box and managed to pull it up a little bit.

Now we've got a safety device on there. When the lid is off that stapler shouldn't run. And without thinking about this lid I thought if I can pull on that and start the machine and stop it straight away I should be able to. . . . Of course it shouldn't have run anyway. But it did. And it took my finger into the cogs. Well, as it turned out somebody'd jammed a piece of wood in the safety switch, so it'd run even with the lid open, see.

Four of the five accidents involved loss or damage to fingers. But over and above this obvious similarity these accidents had something much more fundamental in common. On closer inspection a pattern begins to emerge. It is a pattern repeated in all the other accidents heard of in this workshop, with the sole exception of a man who nodded off, being only narrowly saved from falling into the machinery. Moreover, it is a pattern which may fit equally well a large number of accidents in other factories.

As the men's accounts make clear, every one of the accidents was associated with some kind of fault in the production process.

Fred: It was a very poor gradient at the top and all the empty hoppers used to get stuck.
Joe: The rollers stopped.
Dick: Well there was a fault on the rollers. The boxes used to come down two or three heaped together.
Harry: This particular day there's six of us trying to push one down. We kicked it, we pushed, we cussed it, we done every bloody thing.
Jack: I put the next box in, ready to go when this box starts tilting.

In four instances production had actually ceased. In the other case (Dick's), a fault was developing which, at the least, threatened to add to the difficulties of normal working. Three of the accounts also indicate that the faults in question were by no means isolated events. In fact this was the case with all of them. Hoppers with tight brakes, gradients too shallow to enable men to roll them, jammed staplers and pile-ups on the rollers—all of these were well-known facts of life.

Since each of the accidents occurred in the context of a process failure the men could not have been working 'normally' when they were injured. What then were they doing?

> *Fred:* [going] up with a fork-lift truck and push[ing] the hoppers down. It was the only way of getting them down to keep the job going.
>
> *Joe:* We called out downstairs, 'What's going on?' So Joe went to see to save time.
>
> *Dick:* running back to catch a box.
>
> *Harry:* So he says, 'Stick your head out, have a look up them rollers,' he says. 'Ten to one you'll have a bloody pile-up.' So I did.
>
> *Jack:* I [was catching] hold of a piece of the box . . . to pull it up a little bit.

Fred, Joe and Jack were hurt whilst trying to rectify faults which had halted the process. Dick was trying to prevent a fault from developing, whilst Harry was trying to maintain the flow of production during a breakdown and was actually injured whilst investigating a further breakdown. All five were acting so as to maintain or restore production.

In four cases the actions of the injured men were in direct violation of the company's safety rules. There are rules against using fork-lift trucks to push the hoppers down, walking on the rollers, reaching inside the safety-guards to re-position boxes and leaning out of hoppers while other hoppers are being moved.

Jack's case is less clear-cut because it was not Jack himself who broke the rules. The danger arose because somebody else had jammed the safety switch. But why should this have been done? Jack's foreman gave the answer—'They were on high [output] rates', he said, 'and trying to make the job easier for themselves. They don't deserve any sympathy.' The manager said the same. This indeed was the reason. The men made the job unsafe to keep up with production, 'to get the job out'. They jammed the switch in order to make it easier to deal with the frequent failures of the stapler and so keep up production. Of all five cases, then, it can be said that the accidents occurred in dangerous situations which were created or entered into, not so much because of breakdowns in machinery—which after all could have been left idle—but because of the men's attempts to maintain or restore production.

In this factory, such failures in production were not unusual but neither was the use of 'illegal' methods of getting the job going again. Fred claimed—

> It was a condoned thing. I mean foremen used to more or less tell you to do it.

Joe's foreman confirmed—

> I've seen many, many people jump over the roller just as he did. This is the quick way of doing things.

And as men said of Dick's accident—

> It's just instinct. If you see a box twisting, it's moving, stop it. If the guards
> are up you can't just go and pull the guard off and grab the box—it'd be
> gone anyway.

True enough, Harry's accident was rather unusual in that two breaks in production occurred simultaneously, a hopper sticking on the line and the rollers
jamming at the same time; and of course for Jack the danger arose because of the
deliberate jamming of the safety switch. But in the latter case, as the men themselves privately admitted, the safety switch had been jammed for some time, and
not just before the accident. Nor was this the only time when one of these
switches was jammed. This in fact caused difficulties for Jack. From his point of
view the questions asked by the Factory Inspector posed a distinct threat to
worker solidarity—

> We had the Factory Inspector down here. That man came to my house and
> he said that he had proof that the stapling machines were checked on the
> previous shift and that also our shift fitter had checked the machines on our
> shift. He was more or less saying that one of our blokes had done it and I said
> 'No'. Because I'd heard in the messroom, off of one or two different people,
> that a piece of wood had been there for weeks before I'd had my accident.
> He wanted me to name who it was but I wouldn't.

The point is, though, that the dangerous working situation in which this accident
happened was not unique. Other men, knowingly or not, had worked the job with
the safety mechanism out of action.

As noted earlier, *there are* accidents which arise from unlikely and unique
causes, but if the ones described here are any guide this is not the general rule.
Moreover, in cases of this type the 'forensic approach' suffers from a built-in
inadequacy, for the unique and particular reasons why one man gets hurt are not
the main point. Much more important is the fact that dangerous situations are
created repeatedly. And given this it is much more useful to ask why so many
men jump over rollers or whatever, than to ask why one individual's finger gets
caught when he does so.

So, why did so many men jump over the rollers? Part of a possible answer
is contained in a remark quoted earlier—

> It's just instinct. If you see a box twisting, it's moving, stop it.

It is very difficult for a man to stand there and take no action while the job goes
wrong. In fact it requires a very high degree of alertness—an alertness which
takes the form of a keen desire on the man's part to put himself before the job
for every minute of the working day. To do this means standing outside the
rhythm of production: but this rhythm is the only thing that makes many jobs
tolerable at all. It is all the more difficult when a man knows that he could put
things right by taking a risk that his workmates take as a matter of course,
especially if he is also aware that, if such risks are not taken, it is he and his
workmates who will have to work harder to make up for lost production.

This goes some way towards explaining why it is that men regularly engage in dangerous practices. But there is another and more important reason, one that was associated with each of the accidents reported here: in every case there was pressure from foremen or fellow workers to keep production going. This is evident from the accounts already cited—

> *Fred:* Foremen used to more or less tell you to do it . . . to keep the job going.
> *Joe:* We called out downstairs 'What's going on?' So Joe went to see to save time.
> *Dick:* The foreman wanted to know what the hell was going on and unless the blokes did a reasonable tonnage they didn't get the bonus.
> *Harry:* If you hang about too much—'What the bloody hell's wrong down there,' you know, 'What've you stopped for?'

The situation is aptly summed up by a comment a fellow worker made about the role played by the foreman in Jack's case—

> If he hears them rollers stop he's out of that office like a shot.

Obviously foremen were a major source of this pressure—though, in cases like Dick's where bonus earnings were at issue, there was pressure from workmates as well. In the first four cases the injured men acted dangerously as a more or less direct response to pressure. And whilst Jack was the victim of somebody else's dangerous act (jamming a safety switch), that dangerous act was of course intended to make it easier and quicker to get back into production once the stapler had failed. The pressure to keep up production again coming from the foreman.

In every case, then, shortcutting and dangerous means of keeping the process going were a response to pressure from foremen or workmates to keep up production. Two questions arise here and it is worth a digression to answer them. The first is: why should there be any pressure from workmates?

Where a bonus system is in operation the reason is clear. These systems are essentially a managerial device for giving each man an interest in keeping production up and making sure others do so as well. But even where such a scheme is not in operation men may pressure each other to keep the job going, for breakdowns and delays may well involve them all in extra work. In reality, however, this kind of pressure is essentially a transmitted form of pressure from foremen and management. It only exists, as pressure, in so far as men accept management's right to manage and management's rationality. Men exert such pressure upon themselves and their workmates in anticipation of the demands they believe management would make upon them if they failed to do so. Demands which, in this factory, as in many others, workers are not sufficiently well organized to resist.

The second question is—why should there be pressure from foremen? After all, the foremen in this firm were trained in safety and the firm itself is in many ways deservedly reputed to be a progressive one. Its managers are safety conscious and nobody wants men injured. Not only is safety on the agenda of all joint consultation meetings but safety officers appear at such meetings, making stern-faced declarations to the effect that '80 per cent of accidents are due to human failure', publicly asserting 'Men must *not* do jobs without first making sure they have the correct protective clothing and equipment' and giving voice to the belief (as per Lord Robens) that 'the greatest problem we face is *apathy*.' As against all this though—and as against the safety posters and the safety leagues published in the works magazine—other facts stand out. Both foremen and workers know that whatever managers may say on the subject of safety, they are always interested in production as well: 'I've heard that this company likes their pound of flesh', said one new worker with grim, if unconscious, humour. To foremen as well as workers, then, safety is an issue about which managers are decidedly schizophrenic. The reason why the foremen are, in the words of a shop steward, too busy watching those traces (production graphs) is precisely that this is what they know management really wants. That's why they are 'out of that office like a shot' if production stops.

Both foremen and managers harangue and sometimes penalize their men after accidents have happened. But in the day-to-day conduct of his job the manager of this firm is carefully watching his graphs and figures. The primacy of production is so deeply ingrained in his thinking that he does not refer to accidents but to 'LTAs' (that is, lost-time accidents—in this firm officially recorded accidents which lead to the man not reporting for work the next day or the next shift). Indeed the primacy of production is so deeply ingrained in the thinking of these managers—who, remember, do claim to care about safety— that some of their actions, looked at from a distance, can only appear farcical and fraught with contradiction. It is difficult to describe their behaviour in any other terms when, in one not untypical incident, a manager walked past posters proclaiming 'SAFETY BEFORE PRODUCTION', went straight into a joint consultation meeting and said, 'Right gentlemen, I'll take business in the usual order: production first, then safety'. Moreover, it is important to note that when this happened it fitted so well with the way most workers and foremen expected managers to think that it didn't even jolt; not even when later in the same meeting the Safety Officer waxed furious with workers about accidents, pledged that management's motto really *was* 'Safety before Production' and confessed himself incredulous that most workers didn't believe him.

To sum up: each of these accidents occurred in the context of a process failure and whilst the men concerned were trying to maintain or restore production. In every case the dangerous situation was created in order to make it quicker and easier to do this. In every case the company's safety rules were broken. The process failures involved were not isolated events. Nor were the dangerous means used to deal with them. The men acted as they did in order to cope with the pressure from foremen and management to keep up production — the foremen themselves not going out of their way formally to acquaint themselves with how the men were coping. For them—the foremen, that is—it was safer that way. This pressure was continual, process failures were fairly frequent and so the shortcutting methods used to deal with them were repeatedly employed. They didn't drift into danger, they were pushed into it via a choice between working harder or taking risks. In each case it was only a matter of time before somebody's number came up.

Each of these men's injuries could be slotted into any one or more particular categories ('tiredness', 'carelessness', 'unguarded machine', 'worker at fault', 'foreman at fault', 'process breakdown'). But the strength of the forensic approach is also its weakness. It is all too easy, in seeking out final explanations for particular 'accidents', to overlook how accidents like these are structured into, and arise out of, the continuous pressure for production. Sometimes this pressure may be crudely expressed, sometimes it may express itself in more subtle forms. But when it exists, and when men lack effective control over their lives at work—when as commodities first and men second, they are 'just numbers really'—the odds are that it *will* be only a matter of time before somebody's number comes up.

17. THE REMARKABLY CONSTANT FORTUNES OF THE BRITISH RAILWAYS LOCOMOTIVEMAN   Peter Hollowell

Practical concern with occupations tends to produce an impression that all is forever a state of flux in this area of social life. The social-problem approach usual in social and economic administration, stressing, for example, industrial contraction or economic growth, unemployment or work satisfaction, or the consequences of professionalization or other changes in prestige, does seem to emphasize the occupational system as an intensely dynamic one. Nor can the vast array of evidence, on changes in the occupational structure, on technical progress in advanced industrial countries, and on the near continuous spawning of specialisms to cope with the administrative imperatives of welfare industrial societies, be held as supportive of any static model of the occupational sphere. In addition, the more popularly acceptable ideology, of general and progressive betterment, acts with particular strength in the economic sphere. We believe that the occupational system ought to be sufficiently dynamic to satisfy ever more of the needs of the community. To focus on the stable patterning of an occupation may seem strange in such a context but change is not to be understood before an effective analysis of persistence has been made.[1] A further benefit would be the testing of many of the above general views of the occupational system through a detailed case study.

Often men of experience hark back to a past, remembered as more congenial than the present, in a fashion considered almost mindless by a younger audience. A study of locomotivemen,[2] employed by British Railways during the mid 1960s, suggests that they too are not exempt from such wistful nostalgia. Some of the statements recorded about locomotivemen's contemporary status were mild enough:

> 'It's [his status] deteriorated, I would say, from what they tell me—before the war you only had to say you were a driver and it was as good as collateral—it seemed that he was somebody special but today he's just an ordinary fellow doing a job.'
> 'Yes—the job's been cheapened. I don't think the skill there is what it was.'

---

1. P. S. Cohen, *Modern Social Theory*, Heinemann, London, 1968, p. 174.
2. The research was financed by a grant from the Department of Scientific and Industrial Research. I am grateful for the constant enthusiasm and support given by Professor P. M. Worsley of Manchester University.

---

17. Original article. Copyright © 1975 Holmes McDougall Ltd., Edinburgh. Peter Hollowell is Lecturer in Sociology in the Department of Sociology and Social Administration, University of Southampton.

Other responses made by the engine drivers were so forceful that any nostalgia was all but obscured by bitterness about the present:

> 'We've been reduced to bare labouring, we are just bloody hand rags— we've got niggers on the job, Pakistanis, we carry the rest of the railway on our backs—the money a driver was on was four pounds ten shillings before the war—we were probably at the top of the wage scale. There was only printers above us. Now you find that the engine driver is more near the bottom than anywhere else now.'

The strength of conviction expressed in such views make them deserving of attention. Were there ever such halcyon days for footplatemen, and if so what forms did the benefits take and why were things so good?

The privileged position of locomotivemen featured in these dreams of the past seems not unlike the condition of labour aristocracy, often referred to by historians,[3] or invoked by socialist theoreticians to explain the absence of class consciousness in the British working class.[4] Labour aristocrats had a unique position in that they had a life style qualitatively far above that of the unskilled workers yet well below most of even the lowest-paid clerks in the nineteenth century. They were respectable artisans, yet in social terms a caste-like gulf existed between the labour aristocrats and even the lower levels of the middle classes—the lower-paid clerks. The difference was one of life style rather than income as the labour aristocrats formed the 10–15 per cent of the working class which was economically on a par with many, though by no means all, clerks.[5] At the other end of the stratum the difference between the aristocrats of labour and the less-skilled members of the working class was more formidable. For the labour aristocrats, the monetary rewards from their work could be up to twice as much as the unskilled beneath them and their consumption patterns reflected as much. In industry their crucial skills and union organization led to a separate existence for them. They were skilled men at the top of a hierarchy of less skilled. In spite of this, and their organization, their general life style in the work-place situation was qualitatively different from those immediately above them. The artisans had to organize to obtain conditions well below those of the clerks. Unlike the clerks they dominated a worker hierarchy, yet were a good deal further away from the central locus of authority. In as much as they remained firmly categorized as working class, labour aristocrats had a less obvious effect on the structure of social stratification in Britain than on the pattern of industrial relations.

3. E. J. Hobsbawm, 'The Labour Aristocracy in Nineteenth-Century Britain' in E. J. Hobsbawm *Labouring Men*, Weidenfeld and Nicholson, London, 1968 and A. Briggs, 'Social Background' in A. Flanders and H. A. Clegg (eds.) *The System of Industrial Relations in Great Britain*, Blackwell, Oxford, 1967.

4. Marx seemed willing to believe in the revolutionary potential of the English working class and to make excuses for its inactivity. (Marx to Engels, November 17, 1862; Marx to Engels, April 9, 1863; Marx to S. Meyer and A. Vogt, April 9, 1870.) England's 'bourgeois proletariat' had exasperated Engels at a much earlier stage (Engels to Marx, October 7th, 1858). For Lenin the imperialist stage of capitalism produced 'super-profits' which were partly used to buy off certain sections of the working class. V. I. Lenin, 'Imperialism and the Split in Socialism', *Collected Works*, Vol. 23, Lawrence and Wishart, 1965, p. 115, specifically mentions 'narrow craft unions'.

5. D. Lockwood, *The Blackcoated Worker*, Allen and Unwin, London, 1966, pp. 22–9, demonstrates the great range of incomes for clerks in the late nineteenth century.

Returning to the locomotivemen's statements about past circumstances of their occupational group, it might be thought that they seem similar in many ways to the so described aristocrats of labour. The claim of broad similarity can be pressed to a degree where the criteria for labour aristocracy could be used to assess the locomotivemen's position. Accepting this to be the case, it will be useful to consider separately the locomotive drivers' technical skills, their working conditions including their authority position, their monetary rewards, and their defensive organization. Doubtless the group's occupational strategy and industrial relations should also receive attention, but this area will be almost entirely omitted since the detail required would produce distortion in the presentation and weighting given to the first four factors. More importantly these latter categories seem less likely to offer effective indication of the occupational group's social and economic position than the others.

Technical skills

Though they had developed considerably in complexity and had been codified in detail, by 1960 the technical skills of locomotivemen had survived fundamentally unchanged for well over one hundred years. This is not surprising since the basic steam technology remained throughout this time, albeit with refinements.

Broad job categories within the grade of steam locomotiveman are cleaner, fireman, and driver. Two other distinctive statuses exist in the grade, that of passed cleaner and passed fireman. These classifications of activities represent in one respect, different sets of rights, in another respect, different levels of expectations or duties, and also thirdly, different claims to areas of skill. An experienced steam-locomotive driver occupies a status in which all the various claims to skills have been formally accepted.

The cleaner is the lowest status in the line of promotion to the footplate. Activities constituting this role are estimated from various writers on railway locomotivemen's careers.[6] A driver could graduate from the position of messenger, knocker up, or bar boy. When a boy was too big to get into the fire box of a locomotive he became a cleaner. Cleaning engines was a dirty job requiring only simple instruments and materials. Swabs, waste, tallow, and oil were used. By cleaning the engine the process of learning about its parts and how it worked was made much easier for the future driver. There was, even within the sub-grade of cleaner a recognized entitlement to different kinds of work. The junior cleaner got the dirtiest work and gradually moved on through the gearing to concentrate on a particular area such as framing, footplate, or tenders. Cleaners worked in squads so that this specialization and a seniority system were possible as also was discussion about engines and how they worked. Cleaners who showed themselves proficient in the relevant subjects were allowed to act as firemen ('passed cleaners') until they were formally registered as firemen.

6. See T. A. McCulloch, 'Working on the Railway' in J. Common (ed.) *Seven Shifts*, Secker and Warburg, London, 1938; W. Greenwood, *How the Other Man Lives*, Labour Book Service, London, (undated); N. McKillop, *How I became an Engine Driver*, Nelson, London, 1960; R. Bonnar, *Stewartie*, Lawrence and Wishart, London, 1964 and M. Reynolds, *Engine Driving Life*, Crosby Lockwood and Son, London, 1894.

Firing a locomotive was more than merely shovelling coal into a hole. Expectations implicit in the status of fireman suggest that it is a much more complex constellation of activities, which are described in some detail in the British Transport Commission's handbook for locomotivemen.[7] The fireman inspected the locomotive before use to see that it had been prepared satisfactorily. He was responsible for the tools and safety equipment on the locomotive. Firing itself was done in accordance with the weight of the train and the gradient of the track. Fireboxes were filled at intervals and coal was to be spread evenly over the box. Water levels had to receive the constant attention of the fireman. The boiler pressure gauge and water gauge were on his side of the footplate, though on some locomotives water gauges were on both sides. All told some fourteen levers, gauges, and valves were the concern of the fireman. While the locomotive was moving he was also required to keep an eye open for signals. Whenever the opportunity arose the fireman was supposed to busy himself tidying the footplate. This last activity would be justified in terms of its technical importance, in reduction of wear and tear in the machinery, as well as in terms of the moral worth of taking a pride in the job.

Almost all firemen would have driven a great deal before attaining the position of registered driver. There was a recognized system of allowing competent firemen to drive (as 'passed firemen') prior to their formal certification. The steam-locomotive driver's duty involved ascertaining that the locomotive was in safe and efficient working order. While actually working a train, the driver had to use the regulator, reversing gear, and brake, to give a smooth and economic run. All this had to be done within a time constraint as nearly every job required the train to be run to a known schedule. Unless he was directly relieved at the end of his shift, the driver always had to dispose of the locomotive systematically, identifying and reporting any defects, and finally to stable it securely. These activities meant that the driver had to be physically fit, mentally alert, and generally responsible in his disposition, since they involved the application of several widely differing types of knowledge in what was usually a very rapidly changing situation.

Authority position and working conditions

A registered driver was not simply someone who took responsibility for operating locomotives and working trains; his status ranked highest in the hierarchy of footplatemen. As well as possessing formally certificated attributes and abilities, he had followed a career, working his way through a series of positions, before arriving in the sought-after final status of driver. Even after the twenty-five years, which was the average time[8] taken for men to move from cleaner to registered driver, there was still more hierarchical progression to be achieved. There might be another fifteen to twenty years wait before getting the better work—the long

---

7. British Transport Commission, *Handbook for Railway System Locomotivemen*, 1957, pp. 23–33.
8. An inspection of the records at the locomotive shed in 1965 showed that men who had joined the railway service in the period 1916–20 had taken 300.52 months on average to become registered drivers.

mileage jobs. The visible allocation of these long mileage jobs to the top links, which were only reached after a great many years, reinforced the hierarchy by showing the benefits to those who had worked their way through it.

By the mid-nineteen-sixties this hierarchical element was attacked with increasing frequency by footplatemen themselves. In spite of a number of sound reasons for the criticism levelled at it, hierarchy, in principle and structure, was still firmly present at the shed, where this study was made in 1965, albeit in modified form. By this period the time investment required to obtain driver status had been considerably reduced. The twenty-five years spent moving from cleaner to driver by men joining the railway service between 1916 and 1920 had been reduced to less than sixteen years for those joining in the 1946–50 period. Since the market for railway transport had been efficiently reduced by the private motor-car and road haulage,[9] the rewards of hierarchy were, relatively speaking, not as great as previously. Additionally hierarchy was no longer generally as respected in the surrounding non-occupational culture in the nineteen sixties as it had been even ten years earlier. Nevertheless the relative scarcity of work for the railways did a considerable amount to bolster the traditional hierarchical principle, when the resultant insecurity caused individuals to invoke the seniority criterion as much, if not more, than ever. It must also be admitted that by the standards of the mid-nineteen-sixties, a period of more than fifteen years was a long time to be spent in reaching the key position. In relative terms it could quite reasonably be equated with the twenty-five-year investment of the 1916–20 recruits.

Nowhere was the authority phenomenon more clear than on the footplate. For as long as steam technology remained, the socio-technical system of the footplate would necessarily include a considerable element of authority in the driver-fireman relationship. The fireman was always in the position of servicing the driver directly, since it was he alone who provided the steam for the driver to use according to route and weight requirements. Thirty years or so previously, the system of control on the footplate had frequently been one best described as autocratically authoritarian. The driver's sanctions over the fireman were absolute in the sense that they could refuse to have men working for them, even if they were merely uncongenial in personality terms. To some extent this might have been justifiable on the grounds that extremely close co-operation was needed on the footplate, especially while working trains at speed. Certainly it seemed that it was always the case that the fireman adjusted his behaviour to meet the expectations of the driver, whether with reference to the work tasks, to social behaviour, or even to psychological disposition, rather than the other way round. According to one driver:

> 'Some of the drivers in my time were ignorant and arrogant. You (as a fireman) had to carry them about—they treated you like shit. If a driver

9. Official statistics show in terms of ton-miles of goods transported that after 1954 the railways lost their supremacy in freight transport to the roads. In 1962 the rail-ton-mileage was under half that for roads, By 1965 it was almost down to one-third of that for the roads. See *Annual Abstract of Statistics*, HMSO, London, 1965, No. 102, Table 228 and 1973, No. 110, Table 236.

said something you did it. If he didn't like you, you didn't go. If he wired you off in a disagreement you lost your job.'

Until about the middle nineteen fifties there were numerous drivers of this type at the shed. Even in 1965, at the time of this study, individuals pointed out the two remaining examples of the autocratic authoritarian driver or 'old bastards' as they were termed. One of these drivers was even at that time so exacting that not only firemen, but also other grades, were anxious when working with him. Fitting-staff, in particular, were on tenterhooks until he and his locomotive had left the shed.

Except for serving as a reference point the autocratic driver was an anachronism by the early sixties. He was a relic who generally had only a nuisance, or at least an inconvenience, value. The system could no longer be worked in this way. Nevertheless, authority was still very much in evidence on the footplate. It simply took on different forms during this period. At this stage the predominant and officially recommended type of authority was the paternalistic form in which the driver could reflect credit on himself by giving the fireman tactful and careful instruction. No doubt the paternalistic form of authority had been operated all along in parallel with the much-remembered autocratic form. It was certainly recalled by several drivers of considerable seniority. The point to emphasize is that it was still in operation in the mid-sixties, and with company backing, whereas after 1950 the autocratic pattern was resisted with increasing success by firemen, and attracted less and less official support as time went on.

While rank and authority over others were, perhaps, the most obvious signs of the locomotive driver's superior status, in that he had a kind of servant at his command to do the heavy physical work, one more condition of his working life is worth mentioning. The driver, as a skilled man with experience, nearly always knew precisely what he would be doing on arrival at work. His energies could not be enlisted at the simple whim of any other person. Not only were the range of activities expected of him limited, they were on most occasions specified in detail. Both these aspects, the hierarchical position with its built-in authority element, and the freedom from continuous domination by others while doing his job, were two highly significant elements of the locomotive driver's status, which were still much in evidence even as late as the mid-nineteen-sixties.

Monetary rewards

A high level of income has been seen as a necessary, though not a sufficient condition of labour aristocracy. The important analytic element drawn from the discussion on labour aristocracy, and used in this description, is the 'differential'. The term 'differential' refers to the differences between the income levels of the skilled workers and those in semi-skilled and unskilled positions in industry. It provides a consistent criterion for the assessment of the locomotive driver's position with reference to the monetary rewards for his distinctive technical skills and responsibilities.

Evidence suggests that, except for very short periods, the railway locomotive driver has generally been among the better-paid workers in Britain since the 1860s. Hobsbawm's summary indicates that some engine drivers were earning forty shillings or more in 1865.[10] By 1906 definite proportions of railway drivers are shown to be labour aristocrats, in that nearly 72 per cent earned forty or more shillings weekly, and almost 55 per cent earned forty-five shillings or more. The extent of the differential is clearly brought out by the information that in 1906 almost 50 per cent of male workers in the railway industry earned twenty-five shillings or less per week. How much the level of earnings of locomotivemen was above that of other workers is further substantiated in Hobsbawm's tables. Only five out of twenty-three industries had a labour-aristocrat percentage of 20 or more. The percentage of 'plebians' (workers earning twenty-five shillings or less) even in the nine industries with a high proportion of labour aristocrats ranged from a low 16 in printing to a substantial 40 per cent in the cotton industry.

Railway locomotive drivers were earning high wages relative to other workers during the first half of the twentieth century though the differential had narrowed between their earnings and those of the unskilled both in the railway industry and elsewhere.[11] Between 1880 and 1950 unskilled time wage rates rose from being between one-half to four-fifths of those of skilled workers. The unskilled worker on the railways, the example used in the survey by Knowles and Robertson is that of a goods porter, was in a particularly unfavourable condition, relative to his skilled colleague, the engine driver. From 1880 until just before World War I he had only 50 per cent of the time rate of the experienced loco-motiveman. In shipbuilding the unskilled had time wage rates of between 51–54 per cent of those for the skilled in the same period. For engineering the figure

Relative earnings of railway locomotive drivers, 1906–1960.[12]

Type of Worker	(Average Male Annual Earnings. £)				
	1906	1924	1935	1955	1960
Railway only					
Skilled : Locomotive Drivers	119	276	258	622	863
Semi-skilled : Firemen	71	199	203	507	712
Unskilled : Shedmen	57	147	146	452	616
All workers (weighted)					
Skilled	97	182	197	629	804
Semi-skilled	68	136	144	506	627
Unskilled	56	134	136	458	565

was around 60 per cent, while in building it was about 64 per cent. By 1950, when the time wage rates of the unskilled in building, shipbuilding and engineering had risen to more than 81 per cent of the skilled, the goods porter still had rather less than 78 per cent of the rate for the engine driver.

Not only did engine drivers do well relative to the unskilled in their own

10. E. J. Hobsbawm, 'The Labour Aristocracy in Nineteenth-Century Britain' in E. J. Hobsbawm *Labouring Men*, Weidenfeld and Nicholson, London, 1968, pp. 280–88.
11. K. G. Knowles and D. J. Robertson, *Differences Between the Wages of Skilled and Unskilled Workers. 1880–1950*, Bulletin of the Oxford Institute of Statistics, 1951, pp. 109–27.
12. Source: G. Routh, *Occupation and Pay in Great Britain 1906–60*, Cambridge University Press, NIESR, 1965.

industry, they also remained well above more general indices for the skilled worker until after the second world war. Their earnings are shown by Routh to be considerably greater than the average for skilled workers in general, both before and in the decade after the 1914–18 war. In 1906 the skilled worker achieved barely 82 per cent of the earnings of the engine driver. By 1924 the railway engineman's economic position had strengthened to the extent that the earnings of the skilled were down to 65.9 per cent of his own. The relative position of the skilled had begun to improve by 1935 when their average earnings were slightly more than three quarters (76.3) of those for the engine driver. After the 1939–45 war the skilled workers fared better. Their earnings situation relative to the railway engineman was reversed, in that in 1955 the earnings of skilled workers were 101.12 per cent of those of engine drivers on British railways. By 1960 the situation was again reversed. With the exception of 1955 it is clear enough that the railway locomotive driver was on an economic level which was generally well above average for even other skilled workers from the beginning of the century up to 1960. Even in relation to the skilled he was an aristocrat but in relation to the unskilled he was a 'super-aristocrat'.[13]

The defensive organization of the group

A group with a responsible and autonomous task activity, a status involving considerable authority over others, and a superior pay level, might also reasonably be expected to have a definite form of defensive organization. The origins, structure, and policy of the organization which protects the group is likely to reflect these other special features of the work situation. Locomotivemen's defensive organization is distinctive amongst the structures whose purpose is the representation of railwaymen, without being entirely separate. In the mid-1950s most locomotivemen belonged to a trade union. There are difficulties in estimating precise proportions of membership since the union figures suggest some over-reporting and multiple membership. However it is clear that the great majority (80 per cent) of footplatemen belonged to their own special union, the Associated Society of Locomotive Engineers and Firemen (ASLEF). At the same time, a substantial 20 per cent were members of the general railway union, the National Union of Railwaymen (NUR). Even in this case, the structure of the NUR did not involve a loss of identity for locomotive grade members.[14] Clerical staff had the opportunity of joining the third significant railway union, the Transport Salaried Staffs' Association (TSSA), which had over eighty thousand members in 1955. The distinctly sectionalist features of railway representational structure were thus present as strongly as ever during the middle and late 1950s. Since those near to authority, and even those actually having it, had themselves traditionally been organized in this way, this sectionalist structure was well institutionalized.

13. The term is from E. J. Hobsbawm, 'The Labour Aristocracy in Nineteenth-Century Britain' in E. J. Hobsbawm *Labouring Men*, Weidenfeld and Nicholson, London, 1968, p. 288.
14. P. S. Bagwell, *The Railwaymen*, Allen and Unwin, London, 1963, p. 336, suggests considerable distinctiveness for footplatemen within the NUR since within each of six electoral districts one of the four departments was for locomotive grades.

The historical circumstances of the origins of the footplatemen's union ASLEF were in themselves a reflection of the distinctiveness of the locomotive grades. Specialist organizations representing locomotivemen came into existence early on in the life of the railway industry. The Locomotive Steam Engine and Fireman's Friendly Society, which had been founded in 1839, showed capable organization of a strike in 1848. There were several factors in the failure of this strike, including the presence of railway company directors in Parliament, but Bagwell's case for the weakness of sectionalism seems convincing. Work had been carried on during the strike through guards riding on the footplate to provide some knowledge of the route.[15]

Another locomotivemen's society, founded in April 1866, the Engine Drivers and Firemen's United Society, had a broad list of aims, including a ten-hour day, overtime payments, payment for Sunday work, mileage limits, and wages negotiation on a company basis.[16] Five large companies agreed to the union demands but two others with capital problems held out with the result that the industrial action, a strike, led to the collapse of this union. The society was indecisive about calling a national strike and the striking enginemen on the North Eastern railway were replaced through the use of voluntary financial contributions by the shareholders. The struggle broke the financial structure of the union as well as the morale of its membership and nothing was heard of its activities after May 1867.

The Amalgamated Society of Railway Servants (ASRS) was an extremely respectable organization, with some of the appearances of the 'New Model' unions of the 1850s, including those of a friendly benefit society, which was formed in 1871. In the 1870s a general worsening of economic conditions made respectability and public relations ineffective weapons for improving the working conditions of railwaymen. The delay in establishing a protection fund, for reasons of respectability, until 1880 brought about the formal defection of the enginemen. The ASRS was considered by many footplatemen to be too weak to defend their interests partly because of the very considerable difficulties of organizing a great diversity of grades. The craft union had emerged by the beginning of 1880. ASLEF was to be a trade union sick and benefit society but a much greater emphasis than usual was put upon the protection of those who engaged in industrial action.

> Should it be deemed necessary, at any time, for any portion of the members to be withdrawn from their employment, such members to receive twelve shillings per week whilst out, and two shillings per week for each child under ten years of age. Any member being discharged for having taken an active part in any question relating to hours, or wages, or the well-being of his fellow workmen, to receive a lump sum of £100 and fifteen shillings per week whilst seeking re-employment. By doing this we hope to disarm that tyranny from which many have suffered.[17]

15. *Ibid.*, pp. 31–3.
16. *Ibid.*, pp. 38–43.
17. J. R. Raynes, *Engines and Men*, Goodall and Suddick, Leeds, 1921. p. 39.

Membership of ASLEF was expensive but the benefits were large. Supporters of 'all-grades' unionism denounced the move by the enginemen calling it 'very selfish', 'an act of folly to incur such expense', 'reprehensible and treacherous'.[18]

When ASLEF had been legally established a circular was issued indicating the craft nature of the union, which is still to this day the basis of its distinctive ideology.

> We ask you again, the Enginemen and Firemen of this great country, one and all to assist us in carrying out our programme by joining this Society. The Rules have been framed by Enginemen and Firemen especially for your interests, the Executive duties are performed by men of your own class, your officials are, and will continue to be, elected from amongst you. They are your servants. The General Secretary is an Engineman of long and practical experience, who knows full well the nature of your responsibility and anxious duties, and who has been elected by his fellow-men to take the management of their affairs.[19]

This circular made the point about the distinctive nature of the locomotive engineman's job and rammed it home by stressing the importance of being represented only by those who had themselves learned those same job activities in detail through experience. The issues and disputes over the engineman's job activity, as well as its accompanying financial rewards, would be put forward by men of his own kind who knew the responsibilities and problems which he faced.

By contrast with the restricted membership of ASLEF, the ASRS was in principle open to all grades of railway worker from the earliest days of its formation. In practice this was difficult to effect. A genuine all-grades movement was not established until the formation of the NUR in 1913 through the amalgamation of the ASRS with the General Railway Workers' Union (founded in 1889 with approximately 24,000 members on amalgamation) and the United Pointsmen and Signalmen's Society (4,101 members on amalgamation). Differences between the 'all-grades' and the sectionalist type of organization, established at the inception of railway unionism, were maintained and even intensified, as time went on. Although the two unions, NUR and ASLEF co-operated on many occasions over the years, on many others they were bitterly opposed to each other.

Nowhere are the features of locomotivemen's representative organization more clearly demonstrated than in the ASLEF strike of May 1955. This seventeen-day industrial action indicated the tenacity of ideology, policy, and social-action pattern generated and established during the early life of the locomotivemen's union. The outcome of this very expensive action was not satisfactory even for the drivers, who fared best of all. ASLEF's costs during the dispute were over three hundred and fifty thousand pounds, while in return for a maximum of three-shillings-a-week increase the average driver had sacrificed twenty-five pounds in wages.[20] ASLEF bravely explained the award as one which, though not meeting the Society's full demand maintained

---

18. *Ibid.*, pp. 40–1.
19. *Ibid.*, p. 44.
20. P. S. Bagwell, *The Railwaymen*, Allen and Unwin, London, 1963, p. 651.

> . . . the fundamental principle of relativity. Strike action was taken to defend that principle. It therefore ended in a *craftsmen's victory*.[21]

Successful outcome of the dispute for the locomotivemen is of less concern here than the fact that their distinctive job activities enabled the membership of ASLEF to believe in and pursue their right to rewards superior to those of other grades just as resolutely in the mid-1950s as they had done since the union's formation in 1879.

Conclusion

In this brief case study of the locomotiveman, it has been strongly argued that his occupational position, and his social situation more generally, was one of advantage. Even relative to other skilled workers this was so, while compared with the unskilled this superiority was so marked, in terms of pay, working conditions, and authority, as to be more appropriately called privilege. Although, as might be expected, there were changes during the span of well over a hundred years, what emerges is the consistent maintenance of a position of advantage by the occupational group. The constituent elements in the locomotiveman's privileged situation were integrated in the sense of being stably homologous to each other throughout this long period. A more detailed analysis than the one presented here would perhaps be able to show that relationships amongst the various elements acted as a frame of reference for locomotivemen, who saw them as standards on which to base industrial action. This might be one of several fruitful ways of explaining the remarkable stability of the railway locomotiveman's situation for such a considerable length of time.

Though this paper is not in anyway an explanation, but simply a description of a stable occupational situation, it should be viewed as useful evidence of persistence, as opposed to flux, in the occupational system. There is also one other sense in which the description can be put to immediate use. The bitterness expressed by many drivers and recorded in the 1966 survey undoubtedly reflected a disgust at a loss of desirable conditions, which were regarded as inherent to work on the railways. Even during the 1930s the security of most railwaymen was apparent, although recruitment and promotion almost ceased, while occupational demotion was not uncommon. Intensified market pressures from the mid-1950s onward, and the dramatic technological changes of the 1960s, no doubt by themselves did account for some of the resentment amongst locomotivemen encountered during the study. When market and technological elements are seen as an intrusion against such a striking occupational stability, then what has been mere description becomes a powerful explanatory variable.

---

21. These two quotations are from the Associated Society of Locomotive Engineers and Firemen, *Victory for a Principle. Differentials—A Craftsmen's Battle*, July, 1955. The italics are as in the pamphlet.

SECTION FOUR
THE POLITICS OF WORK AND OCCUPATION

INTRODUCTION   Geoff Esland

The readings in this section are concerned in various ways with the
political aspects of work organization and with the means by which
certain occupations come to assume and maintain positions of dominance
in society. Rather than attempt to provide a comprehensive coverage of
such occupations—traditionally regarded as the professions—we have
focused instead on those whose prime tasks could be described as the
provision of diagnosis and therapy—that is, the 'personal service'
occupations which have a social right to reshape or 'correct' other
people's psychological states and world views. They include both those
in the medical and educational services such as psychiatry, child
psychology and social work, and also those in industrial social science,
such as occupational psychology and personnel management. These
occupations are interesting not simply because they provide insight into
the production of knowledge and the legislation of everyday social
reality, but also because they collectively represent an economic and
political phenomenon which is of some importance in the operation of
advanced capitalism.

As Johnson has pointed out, most of the studies of professions have
focused primarily on intra-occupational matters and so-called
micro-processes.[1] While these are clearly important for understanding

1. T. Johnson, *Professions and Power*, Macmillan, London, 1972.

work experience and work consciousness, the intention here is to situate this perspective in a 'political economy' of professional development. Our argument is that professional practice—and particularly the production of knowledge—should be looked at in terms of the wider logics and relations of production and consumption in society. It could be argued, for instance, that the growth of corporate capitalism has been paralleled by, and is dependent on, the rationalization of professional training and membership. As Millerson's work has shown in some detail,[2] during the late nineteenth and early twentieth centuries all the major professions underwent substantial rationalization in organization, curricula, and the validation of expertise and qualification; the changes in the division of labour produced a new infrastructure of industrially oriented professions (for example, accountancy, architecture and the various forms of engineering). As Baritz's paper demonstrates, many of these were and continue to be harnessed to the new managerialism of business organization. In this sense, 'professionalism' can be viewed as a form of technological production. To this extent, and particularly in relation to the state, professions have become significant providers of legitimation for industrial and welfare organization. Furthermore, as a result of the increasing control by the state of industrial planning and social welfare, the dynamics of professionalism have been partly dictated by the administrative demands of government legislation—the setting up of the National Health Service is a well-documented example.[3] This has resulted in the creation of new levels of political activity in the relationships between professional associations and government.

The operation of professionalism can also be seen as crucial to the activities and world views of other occupational groups. As creators and purveyors of knowledge about the operation of industrial management, accountancy, company law, urban and industrial building, etc., professional workers have a major capacity—upheld in the rituals of certification and expertise—for defining the lives and activities of other workers.

Similarly, the development and use of the social services as a form of consumption has also become professionalized. One of the effective means by which occupations exert control is through their power to create and apply 'rational' procedures for the solution of organizational or individual problems. As a number of sociologists have remarked (see, for instance, Baritz) the procedures for testing, diagnosis and therapy have become established as a major cultural form in contemporary society.

2. G. Millerson, *The Qualifying Associations*, Routledge and Kegan Paul, London, 1964.
3. H. Eckstein, *Pressure Group Politics*, Allen and Unwin, London, 1960.

The bureaucratization of these occupations and their attendant ideologies has led to their becoming a major structural force. Not only have they become concretely institutionalized, but they have become creators and suppliers of knowledge which is used for various forms of human manipulation and management. Not only do their techniques impinge on and define areas of everyday experience, but their assumptions and categories are disseminated through the various agencies of the mass media thereby becoming part of the self-experience of an entire population. As Berger has said of the psychoanalytic movement:

> Psychoanalysis has become a cultural phenomenon, a way of understanding the nature of man and an ordering of human experience on the basis of this understanding. . . . Most importantly, everyday life, as expressed in the common speech has been invaded by the terminology and interpretive schemes of psychoanalysis.

These occupations have, therefore, become central to the maintenance of social order and the operation of power in society. Their members can be seen as being involved in defining and upholding the cognitive parameters within which a society's members find their sense of social reality, and because, too, they operate on the margins of human activity they have a major institutional significance for policing the line between normality and deviance. Their power lies in their mandate for defining the criteria for competence, adequacy and responsibility in society. In this sense, the 'people working' occupations are engaged in a highly political process.

It is this aspect of professionalism which forms a central element in Hughes's article 'Professions'. Although he does not take up an obviously political view of professional activity, he nevertheless considers some of the implications of professional members' control of the generation of their own knowledge. 'Every profession', he says, 'considers itself the proper body to set the terms in which some aspect of society, life or nature is to be thought of, and to define the general lines, or even the details of public policy concerning it'.

A related question which Hughes considers is the increasing bureaucratization of professional employment. Rather surprisingly, perhaps, he appears to take an optimistic view of the professional as employee in a large organization, suggesting that the apparent freedom allowed in private practice may be illusory. He argues that the greater opportunities for specialism and influence within large organizations may allow more job satisfaction than having to work on the problems of clients in a local community. This may be a reasonable picture of some private practice, but in putting this view, Hughes is tending to minimize the amount of control which organizations are able to exert over the kinds of problems which professional employees are permitted to work on.

A somewhat different view of the political aspects of work is provided in Pettigrew's study of the relationship between the computer programmers and systems analysts working for the same firm during the early period of computer technology. Pettigrew charts the various strategies which were used by the programmers in order to maximize their control not only of their work, but also of their deviant (in relation to the firm) style and philosophy of work. As the programmers were in conflict with the systems analysts as well as the company management, they engaged in several ploys designed to increase the mystification of programming, one of the most successful being to represent their work as an esoteric mathematical activity. They were also able to capitalize on the market factors which gave them high rates of pay, thereby exacerbating their relationships with other employees of comparable status within the firm. One interesting development, however, which Pettigrew brings out is that as computer technology advanced, the mathematical skills required for programming diminished, thus reducing the programmers' control of their work. Pettigrew's article is interesting for the way in which it combines analysis of an emerging occupation with the technological and political elements through which it had to find its identity.

Elliott's article is also concerned largely with intra-professional politics—in this case of medicine. He develops the notion that occupations consist of competing segments and ideologies built around what Bucher and Strauss have described as 'different conceptions of what constitutes the core—the most characteristic professional act'.[4] Elliott examines the different conceptions of cancer which arose in the work experiences of the radiotherapists and research scientists working in the same hospital. Although the focus of the study is on processes internal to the organization, it raises questions about the career and ideological structures of different workers in the health service. What is perhaps surprising is the considerable variation in the characterization of cancer between these two groups. Not only were there disagreements of a fundamental kind about the nature and cure of cancer but also of the kind of 'factual' presentation which should be made to the lay public. There are some similarities between Elliott's arguments and the view put forward by Freidson in *Profession of Medicine*[5] that types of illness are not simply representations of organic states, but that they are in every sense social constructions. Using a theoretical approach derived from the sociology of knowledge, Friedson

4. R. Bucher and A. L. Strauss, 'Professions in Process', *American Journal of Sociology*, January, 1961.
5. E. Freidson, *Profession of Medicine*, Dodd, Mead and Co., New York, 1970.

argues that patients' symptoms are referred to a typificatory system which carries with it a set of regimes and programmes of treatment. These programmes should be seen not simply as logical necessities for the patient but as responses to a range of contingencies in the doctor's career and culture.

In the articles by Ingleby and Berger, the focus shifts to the issues which were raised earlier in this introduction. Both writers are looking at the cultural, political and institutional significance of forms of applied psychology—Ingleby at child psychology, and Berger at psychoanalysis. Using a sociology of knowledge framework, Berger sets out as one of his basic propositions that 'Since human beings are apparently destined not only to experience but also to explain themselves, we may assume that every society provides a psychological model (in some cases possibly more than one) precisely for this purpose of self-explanation'. Through the progressive institutionalization of 'scientific' psychology during the previous hundred years, decisions relating to competence and social adequacy are now grounded in occupational ideologies and have become systematized as various forms of expert knowledge, one of the main elements of which is the belief in scientific 'objectivity'. Since a major ingredient in an occupation's claim to professional status lies in its ability to point to a substructure of theory, and preferably scientific theory, on which its practice can rest, the legitimacy of this kind of claim is difficult to question. As Taylor, Walton and Young put it in their chapter 'The Appeal of Positivism',

> The evocation of natural science presents the positivist with a powerful mode of argument. For the system of thought which produces miracles of technology and medicine is a prestigious banner under which to fight. It grants the positivist the gift of 'objectivity'; it bestows on his pronouncements the mantle of 'truth'; it endows his suggestions of therapy, however threatening to individual rights and dignity, with the air of the inevitable.[6]

One consequence of this process is that what are in effect highly political activities are rendered as the logical actions of a 'people caring' occupation concerned for the cure and well-being of others. As Ingleby argues in his article 'The Psychology of Child Psychology', the dominance of the scientific world view in psychology effectively depoliticizes its apparent purpose: 'that which is "scientific", by definition, does not depend for its authority on the political loyalties implicit in it . . . Psychology borrows habits of thought from natural science and applies them to the human sphere in a manner which is logically quite inappropriate but politically highly functional'.

6. I. Taylor, P. Walton and J. Young, *The New Criminology*, Routledge and Kegan Paul, London, 1973, p. 32.

The alienating qualities of the diagnostic and therapeutic processes can also be seen in the language and rituals of 'industrial relations'. Eldridge's article examines the ways in which the bargaining relationships between management and trade unions are based on a common allegiance to 'economism'. He suggests that any attempt to identify class-consciousness in workers has to take account of their socialization into the grammar of capitalism and particularly the institutionalized belief in pay differentials and the importance of work performance. Eldridge argues that the Marxist analysis of the cash nexus has to be seen in relation to the employment contract of workers and the wide variations in the market controls on work. The effect of both, according to Eldridge, is to increase the sectionalism of worker interests thereby diminishing the formation of consolidated class-consciousness.

One of the underlying themes of this collection of readings, as indeed it is of other parts of this Reader, is the dispossession of self which is entailed in the technocratic consciousness and its various bureaucratic forms. The emphasis in many of the articles is on the alienation which is induced through regarding individuals as mechanized units whether as performers of work or as patients in need of therapy. It would be a mistake, however, to regard the occupations themselves as originators of this process. As several of the readings have tried to show, they merely articulate the positivist ideology which has become the ideational and managerial adjunct of contemporary industrialization.

The point is brought out clearly in the final extract from Baritz's book *The Servants of Power*. Here Baritz is concerned to chart the increasing reliance placed by industrial management during the twentieth century on psychological techniques of personnel selection and the 'motivation' of workers. He suggests that

> By the middle of the twentieth century industrial social science has become one of the most pregnant of the many services available to America's managers in their struggle with costs and labour, government and the consuming public. . . . Demanding that the social scientists in their employ concentrate exclusively on the narrow problem of productivity and industrial loyalty, managers made of industrial social science a tool of industrial domination.

There is a good deal in Baritz's chapter which is reminiscent of C. Wright Mills's discussion in *White Collar* of the nature of contemporary power and bureaucracy in which he underlines the politics inherent in the a-political stance of 'scientific management'. Mills suggests that the use of social science in maximizing industrial productivity is expressive of a significant change in the nature of power and control in both industrial companies and society at large. He maintains that 'in the movement from authority to manipulation, power shifts from the visible to the invisible, from the known to the anonymous. And with rising material standards, exploitation becomes less material and more psychological.'[7]

Clearly in making occupations the central point of their analysis these readings do no more than touch on the wider question of the exercise of power in contemporary society. They do, however, point to some of the ways in which forms of domination have become embedded in the taken-for-granted routines and practices of work. The task for the sociological analysis of work is to show how these might be related to the political and economic structures of society.

7. C. W. Mills, *White Collar*, Oxford University Press, New York, 1951, p. 110.

18. PROFESSIONS   Everett Hughes

Professions are more numerous than ever before. Professional people are a larger proportion of the labor force. The professional attitude, or mood, is likewise more widespread; professional status, more sought after. These are components of the professional trend, a phenomenon of all the highly industrial and urban societies; a trend that apparently accompanies industrialization and urbanization irrespective of political ideologies and systems. The professional trend is loosely associated with the bureaucratic, although the queen of the professions, medicine, is the avowed enemy of bureaucracy, at least of bureaucracy in medicine when others than physicians have a hand in it.

A profession delivers esoteric services—advice or action or both—to individuals, organizations or government; to whole classes or groups of people or to the public at large. The action may be manual; the surgeon and the bishop lay on their hands, although in the one case manual skill is of the essence, while in the other it need not be great because the action is symbolic. (Yet some priests and religious healers become very effective in their manner of laying hands on the heads of people who seek confirmation or comfort.) Even when manual, the action—it is assumed or claimed—is determined by esoteric knowledge systematically formulated and applied to problems of a client. The services include advice. The person for or upon whom the esoteric service is performed, or the one who is thought to have the right or duty to act for him, is advised that the professional's action is necessary. Indeed, the professional in some cases refuses to act unless the client—individual or corporate—agrees to follow the advice given.

The nature of the knowledge, substantive or theoretical, on which advice and action are based is not always clear; it is often a mixture of several kinds of practical and theoretical knowledge. But it is part of the professional complex, and of the professional claim, that the practice should rest upon some branch of knowledge to which the professionals are privy by virtue of long study and by initiation and apprenticeship under masters already members of the profession.

The Oxford Shorter Dictionary tells us that the earliest meaning of the adjective 'professed' was this: 'That has taken the vows of a religious order'. By 1675, the word had been secularized thus: 'That professes to be duly qualified; professional'. 'Profession' originally meant the act or fact of professing. It has come to mean: 'The occupation which one professes to be skilled in and to follow. . . . A vocation in which professed knowledge of some branch of learning

---

18. Reprinted by permission of *Daedalus,* Journal of the American Academy of Arts and Sciences, Boston, Massachusetts. Fall, 1963, *The Professions.*

is used in its application to the affairs of others, or in the practice of an art based upon it. Applied specifically to the three learned professions of divinity, law and medicine; also the military profession.' From this follows later the adjective 'professional', with the meanings now familiar.

Professionals *profess*. They profess to know better than others the nature of certain matters, and to know better than their clients what ails them or their affairs. This is the essence of the professional idea and the professional claim. From it flow many consequences. The professionals claim the exclusive right to practice, as a vocation, the arts which they profess to know, and to give the kind of advice derived from their special lines of knowledge. This is the basis of the license, both in the narrow sense of legal permission and in the broader sense that the public allows those in a profession a certain leeway in their practice and perhaps in their very way of living and thinking. The professional is expected to think objectively and inquiringly about matters which may be, for laymen, subject to orthodoxy and sentiment which limit intellectual exploration. Further, a person, in his professional capacity, may be expected and required to think objectively about matters which he himself would find it painful to approach in that way when they affected him personally. This is why it is unfair to ask the physician to heal himself, the priest to shrive himself, or the teacher to be a perfect parent. A professional has a license to deviate from lay conduct in action and in very mode of thought with respect to the matter which he professes; it is an institutionalized deviation, in which there is a certain strain toward clear definition of situations and roles.

Since the professional does profess, he asks that he be trusted. The client is not a true judge of the value of the service he receives; furthermore, the problems and affairs of men are such that the best of professional advice and action will not always solve them. A central feature, then, of all professions, is the motto—not used in this form, so far as I know—*credat emptor*. Thus is the professional relation distinguished from that of those markets in which the rule is *caveat emptor*, although the latter is far from a universal rule even in exchange of goods. The client is to trust the professional; he must tell him all secrets which bear upon the affairs in hand. He must trust his judgment and skill. In return, the professional asks protection from any unfortunate consequences of his professional actions; he and his fellows make it very difficult for any one outside —even civil courts—to pass judgment upon one of their number. Only the professional can say when his colleague makes a mistake.

The mandate also flows from the claim to esoteric knowledge and high skill. Lawyers not only give advice to clients and plead their cases for them; they also develop a philosophy of law—of its nature and its functions, and of the proper way in which to administer justice. Physicians consider it their prerogative to define the nature of disease and of health, and to determine how medical services ought to be distributed and paid for. Social workers are not content to develop a technique of case work; they concern themselves with social legislation. Every profession considers itself the proper body to set the terms in which some aspect of society, life or nature is to be thought of, and to define the general lines, or even the details, of public policy concerning it. The mandate to do so is granted more fully to some professions than to others; in time of crisis it may be questioned even with regard to the most respected and powerful professions.

These characteristics and collective claims of a profession are dependent upon a close solidarity, upon its members constituting in some measure a group apart with an ethos of its own. This in turn implies deep and lifelong commitment. A man who leaves a profession, once he is fully trained, licensed and initiated, is something of a renegade in the eyes of his fellows; in the case of the priest, even in the eyes of laymen. It takes a rite of passage to get him in; another to read him out. If he takes French leave, he seems to belittle the profession and his former colleagues. To be sure, not all occupations called professions show these characteristics in full measure. But they constitute the highly valued professional syndrome as we know it. Professions come near the top of the prestige-ratings of occupations.

Many occupations, some new, some old, are endeavoring so to change their manner of work, their relations to clients and public, and the image which they have of themselves and others have of them, that they will merit and be granted professional standing. The new ones may arise from the development of some scientific or technological discovery which may be applied to the affairs of others. The people who 'process' data for analysis by computers are a recent example. Some of the specialties within medicine are due largely to the invention of some diagnostic instrument, or to an extension of biological or chemical knowledge. After the virus came the virologist, who works alongside the bacteriologist and the person who knows about fungi—together they are the microbiologists, who work with microscopes, and lately with the electronic one. Other new professions or specialties (and specialties follow much the same course of development as professions themselves) may arise from some change in society itself. As impersonal insurance replaced the older, more personal ways of spreading the risk of death, injury, illness, unemployment and loss of property, actuarial knowledge was of necessity developed, and a new profession arose. The professional social worker is a product of social changes. In an epoch of great technological and organizational change, new techniques and new social demands work in some sort of interaction to produce new esoteric occupations.

Perhaps the way to understand what professions mean in our society is to note the ways in which occupations try to change themselves or their image, or both, in the course of a movement to become 'professionalized' (a term here used to mean what happens to an occupation, but lately used to refer also to what happens to an individual in the course of training for his occupation). Courses and seminars entitled Professions, Occupations, or Sociology of Work—which I have been holding for more than twenty-five years—invariably attract many people from outside sociology. As often as not, they want to write a paper to prove that some occupation—their own—has become or is on the verge of becoming a true profession. The course gives them a set of criteria for their demonstration. Librarians, insurance salesmen, nurses, public relations people, YMCA secretaries, probation officers, personnel men, vocational guidance directors, city managers, hospital administrators, and even public health physicians have been among them.

These people are serious, often quite idealistic. The changes they want to bring about or to document are directed to the same *terminus ad quem*, but the starting points lie in different directions. The insurance salesmen try to free themselves of the business label; they are not selling, they are giving people expert and objective diagnosis of their risks and advising them as to the best manner of protecting themselves. They are distressed that the heads of families do not confide in them more fully. The librarians seek to make themselves experts on the effects of reading, on bibliography and reference, rather than merely custodians and distributors of books; in schools and colleges, librarians want status as members of the teaching staff. They insist that they are, or must become, jointly with social psychologists, investigators of communications. That is their science, or one of their sciences. People in business management work at developing a science of management which could presumably be applied to any organization, no matter what its purpose. The social workers earlier were at pains to prove that their work could not be done by amateurs, people who brought to their efforts naught but good will; it required, they said, training in casework, a technique based on accumulated knowledge and experience of human nature and its operation in various circumstances and crises. Their first goal was to establish the position of the professional and to separate it from the amateur friendly visitor or reformer. The nurse, whose occupation is old, seeks to upgrade her place in the medical system. Her work, she says, requires much more general education than formerly, and more special knowledge; as medicine advances, the physicians delegate more and more technical functions to the nurse, who delegates some of her simpler functions to practical nurses, aides and maids. The nurse wants a measure of independence, prestige and money in keeping with her enlarged functions, as she sees them. The YMCA secretary wants his occupation recognized not merely as that of offering young men from the country a pleasant road to Protestant righteousness in the city, but as a more universal one of dealing with groups of young people. All that is learned of adolescence, of behavior in small groups, of the nature and organization of community life is considered the intellectual base of his work. The vocational guidance people have trouble in bringing the teaching profession to recognize that theirs is a separate complex of skills, presumed to rest on psychology. The public health men have a double problem. They must convince other physicians that their work—which is generally not the diagnosing and treating of patients—is really medicine. They must also combat the belief of physicians that they should do for fees some of what the public health people do for a fixed salary.

In these examples appear the main themes of professionalization. Detachment is one of them; and that in the sense of having in a particular case no personal interest such as would influence one's action or advice, while being deeply interested in all cases of the kind. The deep interest in all cases is of the sort that leads one to pursue and systematize the pertinent knowledge. It leads to finding an intellectual base for the problems one handles, which, in turn, takes those problems out of their particular setting and makes them part of some more universal order. One aspect of a profession is a certain equilibrium between the universal and the particular. The priest who would fix his attention entirely on the universal aspects of religious behavior might find himself indifferent as to which religion he would attach himself to; and thus, a renegade and a heretic. Churches do not encourage such circulation of the elite. Great corporations, too, although they may seek men who know the science of management, want an executive's curiosity about and love of the universal aspects of human organization tempered with a certain loyalty and commitment to his employer. I suppose there may be a professional man so free-sweeping in his interests that he does not mind what client he serves and what aspects of the client's affairs he deals with. He would be a rarity—a rich outcast or a poor idealist.

The balance of the universal and the particular in a profession varies, but there is always some measure of both, with an appropriate equilibrium between detachment and interest. The balance between universal and particular is related to that between the theoretical and the practical. Branches of learning are not always very directly related to the ordinary business of life. If some occupations become professions by developing an intellectual interest, others do it by becoming more practical. A large number of chemists are now employed by industries. Psychologists are seeking and obtaining legislation giving them monopoly over the name and making it an offense for anyone to 'practice' psychology without it. Some sociologists, especially those who do research by the 'project' for 'clients', would do likewise. Perhaps one should distinguish between professions in essence, such as medicine or engineering, which pursue knowledge to improve practice; and professions by accident, such as, say, archaeology, where the practices are merely the means to increasing knowledge. In both cases, the people engaged may make their living by their activities. There appears to be a trend in certain fields of knowledge for this distinction to disappear and for the learned societies to become professional guilds concerned with problems of practice, employment, licensing and distribution of their services. Many learned societies show strain between the intellectuals and the professionalizers.

This strain, incidentally, is found in some degree in all professions. A physician may be too devoted to research; a lawyer too concerned with comparative law; a social worker overcurious about the roots of human behavior. In fact, inside most professions there develops a tacit division of labor between the more theoretical and the more practical; once in a while conflict breaks out over issues related to it. The professional schools may be accused of being too 'academic'; the academics accuse other practitioners of failure to be sufficiently intellectual.

Another set of themes in professionalizing movements has to do with a change of status of the occupation in relation to its own past, and to the other people—clients, public, other occupations—involved in its work drama. Changes sought are more independence, more recognition, a higher place, a cleaner distinction between those in the profession and those outside, and a larger measure of autonomy in choosing colleagues and successors. One necessary validation of such changes of status in our society is introduction of study for the profession in question into the universities. It may be as an undergraduate program, leading to a Bachelor's degree with a major in the theory and practice of the occupation. A large proportion of the university undergraduates in this country are in such professional courses. Other professions seek to have a Master's degree made the standard professional qualification; so it is in social work, hospital administration, business administration, laboratory technology, librarianship and many others. The Master's degree is also used as qualification for a professional or administrative elite in occupations for which the basic preparation is a Bachelor's degree. The PhD or some substitute, such as the Doctor of Education, is also used as qualification for higher administrative and teaching positions in professional agencies and schools.

The older professions, law and medicine, have long been established in the universities; at present in this country, they can keep their aspirants in college for four years and in professional school for three or four years after that. Indeed, so sure are they of their place that they tend to encourage undergraduates to pursue what lines of study they will, so long as their achievements are high. One way in which an occupation—or a college—can document its high status is by being able to take its pick of the young people about to enter the labor market, and then to keep them in school a long time before admitting them to the charmed circle.

Some combination of scholastic aptitude, ambition and financial means is required to accomplish this educational aim. The ambition must have been fostered in some social setting, generally in the middle class family, although occasionally in a working class family with the aid of a sponsoring schoolteacher who sets high. The financial means may come from the aspirant's family, a discounting in advance of the income to be made in the profession, or from an investment in talent by government, industry or the foundations. The latter is of increasing importance in allowing people to continue in higher professional training, especially for work thought to be of use to defense or related industrial development. It is probably effective only when reinforced by the expectation of good income and high prestige.

Not all occupations which aspire to professional standing can promise enough of either of these ingredients to get the most talented and then to keep them in school as long as do medicine, law and the sciences. Characteristically they seek to improve their position in both recruitment and the education system; in the earlier phases of their move toward professionalism, the people in an occupation may have to earn their way slowly and painfully to higher educa-tion, and the professional school may have difficulty in getting itself accepted in universities. It may take an operation bootstrap to get a corps of people in the occupation academically qualified to teach succeeding generations and grant them professional degrees.

This competition for status is accompanied by a trend toward prolonging the professional training at both ends: at the beginning by multiplying prerequisites for entry to professional school, at the finish by prolonging the course and the various apprentice or internship programs. This is held in check by the fact that many of the would-be professions cannot offer enough future income and prestige to get people early and keep them long in school. Parents of less income and education also press their children to seek security in known middle-level occupations. This pressure may also work against the movement to lift profes-sional requirements.

Old and new alike, the professions cherish their recruits once they get them. Having picked their candidates with great care, medical schools, for instance, gnash their teeth and tear their hair over a sheep lost from the fold. They wonder what they have done wrong to make the lamb stray. They make it clear to the professional recruit that he owes it to himself, the profession and the school to stick with his choice. Has it not been discovered by all the tests that this is the one right outlet for his talents? Is it not his duty to use his talents for his country in the best possible way? Have not the profession and the professional school made a great investment in him? Has he the right not to give full return on it?

The day has passed when the youngsters entering professional school are told to look well at their neighbors in the classroom, for few of them will be there next year. The theme is mutual commitment, reinforced by students' auxiliaries sponsored by the professional associations, and by the use of such terms as 'student-physician', which stress that the student is already in the professional family. One owes allegiance for life to a family.

Thus we have a high degree of competition among the professions for talent, combined with a great feeling of possessiveness over the recruits as soon as they have crossed the threshold. The professional student is, to some extent, already an organization man.

But that is not the only respect in which the modern professional is an organization man. Professions are more and more practiced in organizations. The *Freie Berufe* in Germany were considered free not merely because they were worthy of free men, but because those who followed them had no employer. Even the *freier Gelehrte*, or independent scholar, once he had acquired the right to teach, received his income in fees from his clients, the students. The university merely gave him his validation and his forum, as the court gives lawyers a playing field and a referee for their contest. The true professional, according to the traditional ideology of professions, is never hired. He is retained, engaged, consulted, etc., by some one who has need of his services. He, the professional, has or should have almost complete control over what he does for the client.

Especially in medicine, the protest against working in organizations and for salary is very strong. Yet in this country, more than in England, where there is a national plan of medical practice, physicians work in organizations. A decade ago it was reported that for every physician in the United States, there were between four and five people in the related or paramedical professions. There are more now; many people in the medical systems are in nonmedical work such as accounting, housekeeping, engineering and maintenance, and actuarial work for medical insurance schemes. An increasing proportion of physicians are in specialties; the specialist characteristically must work with other physicians. Some specialties never get the first call from an ailing patient; they are reached only after one or more referrals. Some specialties are, like pathology and anaesthesiology, practiced only in hospitals or clinics. All physicians now work at least a year for salary as interns; many work for a salary for several years as residents. In some specialties—those far from the first call of ailing people—work for an organization, possibly for salary, is the rule. An increasing number of lawyers work in large firms where duties and cases are assigned, not completely chosen by the individual practitioner himself. The firm operates as a referral system and allows the individual lawyer enough cases of one kind to permit him to specialize. Many lawyers have but one client, a company; and when there is but one client, it becomes in fact an employer.

Law and medicine—the models which other professions try to approximate —in spite of nourishing free practice of the individual for a number of clients with a minimum of institutional apparatus, are in fact far along the road to practice in complicated organizations which intervene in many ways between them and their clients. Engineers, applied scientists and people in most of the newer professions nearly all work in organizations with others of their own profession, and with many people of related occupations. Indeed, it becomes hard to say who is the client in many cases; in the case of medicine, is it the insurance company or the patient? In the school, is it the child, the parent, the community at large or some class of people within it? In social work, is it the agency—which pays—or the so-called client, who is worked upon not always of his own free will? It is characteristic of modern professions that they do work in such institutional settings, often with capital goods which they do not own and with a great variety of people. Professional ideology prefers a two-party arrangement; the professional and his client. It prefers the client who can speak for himself and pay for himself. This is not the prevailing arrangement, nor is it likely to be.

Thus arise a great number of problems for professions. The problem of finding a clientele becomes that of finding a place in a system of organizations. The problem of colleague relationships becomes that of determining who, in a complex organization of many professions, are indeed one's colleagues, and in what degree. The problem of freedom becomes one of distinguishing between one's obligations to the person, if it be such a case, on which one performs some action or to whom one gives some advice, and to one's employer or organization. For example, does the college physician report the secrets of his student-patient to the dean and, if so, in what situations? There is also a problem of authority; what orders does one accept from an employer, especially one who is not a member of one's own profession and whose interests may not always be those of the professional and his clients?

The other side of this coin is that the employer, even in business, finds himself dealing with an increasing number of professional (staff) people, who will not be ordered about as freely as line people. . . . As the professions become more organized, business organizations become more professionalized. The result is the development of new patterns of organization. If the professional man giving staff services to business or industry sets a certain pattern of freedom not common among the employees of business, he has also lost a certain kind of freedom which inhered in the private practice of professions for clients of whom enough were solvent to assure him a good income and a fitting style of life.

But it may be possible that under present conditions the private practitioner of a profession does not have so much freedom, or at least not the same kinds of freedom as his colleague working in some sort of larger organization. In theory, the private practitioner is free to move at will; in fact, it is very chancey for a man established in practice in a given community to move. Reputations among the common run of clients are local and may depend upon conformity with local customs and beliefs concerning nonprofessional matters. The man who works in an organization may develop a wider reputation, even a national one; he may improve his lot by moving from time to time. He may be freer of social pressures. The man who practices privately may, in fact, be the choreboy of his clients, doing only those things which they want in a hurry and which do not warrant the seeking out of a better known or more specialized practitioner, firm or other organization. He may thus have little or no choice of what kinds of work he will do. The man in the larger organization may apply himself to some line of work and become so proficient in it that he need not accept any work not to his taste. Perhaps the man in the organization may not pick his client, but he can often pick his problems. It may perhaps be that a few men at the very top of a profession can practice privately and as they wish, because of a great reputation throughout the profession and among sophisticated and affluent clients; while the bulk of people in private and 'solo' practice will be choreboys without much reputation among clients and without any among their more specialized colleagues.

In between these two extremes there may be—and I believe there are—a large and increasing number of competent people who work in organized settings. They will, in order to be successful, develop reputations among their colleagues and will be, in case the profession is such as to demand it, known as effective with clients. They will work out new systems of relationships, which may be much the same in business, government agencies, universities, hospitals and clinics, and other kinds of organizations; among the relationships to be worked out are those of the balance between obligations to one's professional colleagues, both in and out of one's present organization, and the organizations in which one works. New formulae of freedom and control will be worked out. The people in organizations will be—although in some sense bureaucrats—the innovators, the people who push back the frontiers of theoretical and practical knowledge related to their professions, who will invent new ways of bringing professional services to everyone, not merely to the solvent or sophisticated few. Indeed, I think it likely that the professional conscience, the superego, of many professions will be lodged in that segment of professionals who work in complicated settings, for they must, in order to survive, be sensitive to more problems and to a greater variety of points of view.

On the other hand, the professionals will become more sensitive to outside opinion; and, like other organized groups, they will hire public relations people to perform for them the esoteric service of creating a satisfactory public image in the press, on television and in the schools, where young people learn about the careers open to them. It is all a rather confusing prospect. The professions will, in any case, be a large and influential element in our future, and in that of all societies which go the road of industrialization and urbanization; the organizational structures in which they will work will very likely resemble one another, no matter what the prevailing political ideologies in various countries of the same degree of industrialization.

In the meantime, there are large parts of the world which are not far along this road. In some of them there is an oversupply of professional people and an undersupply, or some lack of balance in the supply, of related professions. A recent paper reports that whereas in this country there are several nurses for each physician, in India there are seven physicians for one nurse. Oversupply means, of course, only more than can be supported by an economy. Lack of demand may be due to lack of money or to lack of acceptance of the very definition of wants to which a profession caters. It is generally both money and sophistication which are lacking. What will be the course of the rise of demand for medicine, education, legal protection and social services in the now poor and non-industrial countries? It will not be the same course as in the older industrial countries, for the latter had no models to go by; people of the now developing countries know, or soon will know, that such personal services exist and are widely available in the older industrial economies. They will hardly pass through the same stages of professional practice, organization and distribution of services as we did.

Many of the institutions of a modern society depend upon an adequate supply of professionals who perform services for corporate bodies: people to plan and build water systems, communications, roads, industrial plants; people to train others in various trades and techniques and to organize public services. Professionals who do these things have, in the past, come to a new country from abroad as employees or representatives of colonial powers, business concerns or missionary agencies. They have not always sought native recruits or successors; nor have they always given full recognition to local colleagues where there have been some. We are evidently in a new situation with respect to the deploying of professional people over the world. It is not clear who will sponsor such a deployment, what sort of reception professionals from abroad will get in new nations, or how professionals from the highly urban and industrial countries will fit work abroad into their careers.

Again we face the problem of the relation of the particular, the culture-bound, aspect of professions to the universal aspect. The professional may learn some things that are universal in the physical, biological or social world. But around this core of universal knowledge there is likely to be a large body of practical knowledge which relates only to his own culture. The physician may recognize the rhythm of the beat of an East Indian woman's heart, yet lack the slightest knowledge of how to get her to accept his diagnosis of what ails her and his advice about how to live with it. Furthermore, the physician—or other professional—may have become so accustomed to his own society's particular way of practicing, of payment, of dividing labor with others that he will not and cannot adapt himself to these particularities of another society, especially a pre-industrial and not highly literate one. An interlude in another part of the world might interrupt the accumulation of reputation, seniority and money so essential to his career at home; whatever he might learn in practice of his profession abroad might or might not be applicable to his future work at home. While professions are, in some of their respects, universal, in others they are closely ethnocentric. In many professions, careers are contained within a single economy and society. One of the interesting developments of the future will be new patterns of international exchange of professional knowledge and professional institutions.

19. OCCUPATIONAL SPECIALIZATION AS AN EMERGENT PROCESS   Andrew M. Pettigrew

One of the areas of continuing interest for students of organizations has been the study of specialist groups. Much of this literature has focused on the attitudinal and value differences between executives and specialists. Scientists and engineers have been used most commonly as empirical examples. Conceptualization in this area has been beset by numerous analytical problems, not the least of which has been the attempt to impose the ideal-type construct of *profession* in an empirical area which has required a more sophisticated analytical model. Gouldner,[1] Kornhauser[2] and Hower and Orth[3] are representative of the group of authors who use either ideal-type constructs or dichotomies in their conceputalization of specialist groups.

Critics of the frameworks of professions versus organizations, or cosmos politans versus locals, have tended to do one of two things. One approach ha tried to deal with the complexities of the data by creating hybrid categories—e.g. local-cosmopolitan.[4] The second approach has avoided discussion of whether a particular group *is or is not* a profession by asking whether a group is *more or less* a profession.[5] This latter method of treating 'profession' as a variable rather than an ideal-type would seem to have some promise if there had been agreement on what criteria to use in answering the question 'more or less'. The writings of Hughes,[6] Wilensky[7] and Hall[8] suggest anything but agreement on the criteria of professionalism.

The preceding argument has suggested a certain amount of mismatch between theorizing about professions and empirical studies of scientists and

1. A. W. Gouldner, 'Cosmopolitans and Locals: Toward an Analysi,of Latent Social Roles', *Administrative Science Quarterly*, Vol. 2, December, 1957, pp. 281–306.
2. W. Kornhauser, *Scientists in Industry*, University of California Press, Berkeley, 1962.
3. R. M. Hower and C. D. Orth, *Managers and Scientists*, Harvard University Press, Cambridge, Mass., 1963.
4. B. G. Glaser, *Organizational Scientists: Their Professional Careers*, Bobbs-Merrill, New York, 1964.
5. H. M. Vollmer and D. L. Mills (eds.) *Professionalization*, Prentice-Hall, Englewood Cliffs, New Jersey, 1966.
6. E. C. Hughes, *Men and Their Work*, Free Press, New York, 1958.
7. H. Wilensky, 'Professionalization of Everyone', *American Journal of Sociology*, Vol. LXX, No. 2, September, 1964, pp. 137–58.
8. R. M. Hall, *Occupations and the Social Structure*, Prentice-Hall, Englewood Cliffs, New Jersey, 1969.

19. Extracts from 'Occupational Specialization as an Emergent Process' from the *Sociological Review*, vol. 21, no. 2, May 1973. (pp. 255-78)

engineers. Given this incongruity for groups like scientists, where there is at least an approximation towards professionalism along the dimensions of rôle preparation and public values and reference groups; the question is raised as to how appropriate this form of conceptualization is for much newer specialist groups such as operational researchers, programmers and systems analysts. Studies of operational researchers by Thomason and Stenner[9] and Pettigrew[10] found little evidence of professionalism using the criteria of standardized rôle preparation, coherent group values and membership of public reference groups. Recently papers by Sheldrake[11] have questioned the applicability of notions of professional or organizational affiliation to computer programmers. 'Organizational and technical programmers, as they have been identified in the Bureau, do not differ simply in terms of professional or organizational affiliations, local or cosmopolitan orientations, or any other single set of discriminating features. . . . Rather, a more complex combination of all these features constitutes the difference between the two groups.'[12]

Sheldrake's way of dealing with these 'more complex combinations' is to discount existing analytical models and rely on the grounded theory approach recommended by Glaser and Strauss.[13] This attempt to move beyond the rigidities of earlier conceptualizations in the area of professionalization is welcome, and certainly the use of emergent categories in the structuring of his material seems particularly appropriate for a relatively unresearched group like programmers. It is unfortunate, therefore, that Sheldrake's data were sufficiently strong only to produce an assumed continuum of orientation ranging from 'technical' to 'organizational'. . . .[14]

Sheldrake acknowledges the simplicity of his model and recognizes that the limitations of his data 'preclude a more sophisticated analysis'.[15] What he does not discuss in his critical review of the literature on technical specialists is that body of the literature which focuses on occupational specialization as an emergent process. The main thrust of the present argument is that a concern with the processual aspects of specialization may be a particularly valuable analytical strategy in the study of specialist groups such as programmers and systems analysts, neither of which falls neatly into either the structural or the attitudinal criteria of professionalism set out by Hall.[16]

9. G. F. Thomason and B. R. Stenner, 'Attitude, Value and Performance', paper read at the Annual Conference of the Operational Research Society, Reading University, September, 1966.

10. A. M. Pettigrew, *Inter-Group Conflict and Role Strain*, Unpublished thesis for the Diploma in Industrial Sociology, Dept. of Social Science, University of Liverpool, May, 1967.

11. P. F. Sheldrake, 'Attitudes to the Computer and its Uses', *Journal of Management Studies*, Vol. 8, No. 1, February, 1971, pp. 39–62 and 'Orientations towards Work among Computer Programmers', *Sociology*, Vol. 5, No. 2, May, 1971, pp. 209–24.

12. *Ibid.*

13. B. G. Glaser and A. L. Strauss, *The Discovery of Grounded Theory: Strategies for Qualitative Research*, Aldine, Chicago, 1967.

14. P. F. Sheldrake, 'Orientations towards Work among Computer Programmers', *Sociology*, Vol. 5, No. 2, May, 1971, p. 211.

15. *Ibid.*, p. 212.

16. R. M. Hall, *Occupations and the Social Structure*, Prentice-Hall, Englewood Cliffs, New Jersey, 1969.

Specialization as an emergent process

The distinctive contribution of the emergent approach to occupational specialization is its concern with relational analysis over time. The focus is on the development of interdependencies within a speciality and across specialities sharing a common task environment. The concern is with how a specialist group defines its task, how it protects its identity by the development of a system of values and generally how it links itself with the activities of interdependent specialities.

For the purposes of the present analysis it is assumed that the task environment shared by the developing specialities is poorly institutionalized. That is to say, the system of rôle relationships, norms and sanctions which regulate access to different positions and sets of activities lacks both clarity and consistency. In the absence of such clarity and consistency a process of rôle crystallization takes place.[17] Strauss and his colleagues[18] have described the strategic aspects of this crystallization as the 'negotiation order'. A related assumption is that at any point in time each of the linked specialities is likely to be at a different phase of development and engaging in tactics appropriate to its position.

The problems for a new speciality are particularly those associated with status and power. New specialist groups are likely to be seeking social accreditation. Deprived as they often are of the full measure of their expected status and function, new groups may take on expansionist policies. Since the expansion of one jurisdiction often means the diminution of another, this method of increasing status produces conflict.

As a defensive reaction, the more established group may accuse the expansionist one of incompetence and encroachment.[19] The older group may also attempt to invoke a set of fictions about itself to protect the core of its expertise. These fictions or myths, supported by intra-group solidarity, can provide the established group with a comforting self-image to help meet and adapt to pressures from outside. Myers[20] has noted this process amongst groups in the building industry struggling to protect their identity.

The process of the conflict between the rival groups may take the form of a set of boundary testing activities. As one group seeks power and the other survival, each will develop a set of stereotypes and misconceptions about the other. A group declining in status and power may seek to emphasize that part of the core of its expertise which still remains and which may not be covered by the activities of the expanding group. This may be interpreted as a threat by the newer group, who are likely to be defensive about their own history of inexpertise in this area. They in turn may retaliate by emphasizing their particular strength. In this way one group's defensive behaviour becomes another group's threat and the cycle of conflict continues.

Over time the development of this conflict may lead to further changes in occupational identities, values and allocation of activities between the specialist

17. S. N. Eisenstadt, *Essays in Comparative Institutions*, Wiley, New York, 1965.
18. A. Strauss, L. Schatzman, R. Bucher, D. Ehrlich and M. Sabshin, *Psychiatric Ideologies and Institutions*, Free Press, Glencoe, 1964.
19. W. J. Goode, 'Encroachment, Charlatanism and Emerging Professions: Psychology Sociology, and Medicine', *American Sociological Review*, Vol. 25, 1960, pp. 902–14.
20. R. C. Myers, 'Inter-Personal Relations in the Building Industry', *Applied Anthropology*, Spring, 1946.

groups. Systems of career progression may be altered: since individual careers are likely to be tied up with the fate of specialities, so career opportunities that were possible for one generation may not recur for subsequent generations.[21]

The preceding analysis has suggested that issues of conflict, status and power are likely to be highlighted by an analysis which focuses on the emergence of specialist groups. The object of this research is to demonstrate how a particular methodological strategy may be used to explore theoretical insights about specialization as an emergent process, using the development of the occupations of programmers and systems analysts as a case.

The study of the emergence of specialist groups requires some form of longitudinal research design. This may entail an historical study, sustained participation in the field over time, or a combination of both. Neither of these strategies are currently popular either generally in the social sciences or particularly in the study of organizations.

The present study used a multi-method strategy. Data were collected from a single firm, Brian Michaels, covering the period 1957–69. This involved sustained observation from 1966–69 and an historical study from 1957–66. . . .

In the period 1957–69, Brian Michaels made four computer purchase decisions. The object of this part of the research was to use each of the decisions as a way of highlighting the changes in the distribution of activities, status and power between the developing specialities of programming and systems analysis in Michaels. The focus on a sequence of decisions over time had a similar objective to Turner's analysis of social dramas over time, where the aim was to look at 'the contemporary stage of maturation or decay of the social structure.'[22]

Operationalizing changes in status and power over time

A major hypothesis of the study was that over time the programmers' status was declining because of the dual impact of technological change and the need for and rise of a new occupational group—systems analysts. It was also suspected that the Michaels programmers had not declined in status relative to the Michaels analysts as much as the trend in industry generally. The ready explanation for this seemed to be the success of the Michaels programmers' power maintenance strategies. Testing these suppositions required data in the following areas: first, some way of operationalizing status changes in Michaels over time; secondly, details of the technological changes and why they were affecting the occupational structure of the industry; and thirdly, data on the power strategies of the Michaels programmers and analysts.

Information on the changes in the distribution of activities between the Michaels programmers and analysts and conflicts associated with those changes were provided by interviewing past and present members of the Michaels com-

21. R. Bucher and A. Strauss, 'Professions in Process', *American Journal of Sociology*, Vol. LXVI, No. 4, January, 1961, pp. 325–34.
22. V. W. Turner, *Schism and Continuity in African Society*, Manchester University Press, Manchester, 1957, p. 93.

puter team. Following Dahl[23] and Mechanic,[24] 'power' was operationalized through the identification of power *resources* together with individual perceptions of how those resources were used. It was assumed that the use of power was dependent on access to and control over structurally endowed resources, together with their effective exploitation. The successful use of power requires skills and not just possessions. Material on the power strategies of the programmers and analysts was also provided by the lengthy open-ended history interviews. These interviews were checked internally for contradictions and externally by cross-interviewing and documentary sources. Since loss of key personnel and controlling recruitment and learning processes for an occupation may respectively diminish and protect a group's power, the company's personnel records were analysed for labour turnover and the experience-training of past and present computer staff.

The sample of systems analysts and programmers used for the set of history interviews was not ideal. Because of the incomplete nature of the Michaels personnel records it was found difficult to identify, let alone trace, the programmers and analysts who left Michaels between 1957 and 1966. Faced with this difficulty and the additional validity constraint of choosing informants whose status was such as to have equipped them with the requisite kind of information, a decision was made to satisfy the latter constraint first. Seven of the eight people who occupied managerial positions in the programming or analyst sections were traced and interviewed. Ten programmers were interviewed—all ten had been in Michaels in the 1957–61 period and six had also been there in the 1957–61 and 1962–66 periods. Nine analysts were interviewed, seven for the 1957–61 period and eight for the 1962–66 period. Since about twenty-four programmers and twelve analysts left Michaels between 1957–66, the above samples are small. Nevertheless, the writer's familiarity with the Michaels system which made it possible to choose 'critical' informants, together with the almost one hundred per cent. success in interviewing those informants, makes the writer confident about the internal validity of the data.

Historically, there has been great confusion and uncertainty regarding the interface between the systems analyst and programming functions. This is to be expected in occupations which have arisen quickly from a technology which itself is continually undergoing change. Today the professional computer journals on both sides of the Atlantic are dotted with papers setting down what the two occupations *ought* to be doing. Naturally enough, the articles appear somewhat partisan. Robinson,[25] for example, describes the systems analyst's rôle in such complete terms that all the programmer is left to do is code. While Constantine[26] is equally anxious that programmers should fight attempts to make them into 'clerical coders' when their skills qualify them for the title of 'software engineers'.

Stated simply, the main issue in the task environment of analysts and

23. R. A. Dahl, 'The Concept of Power', *Behavioural Science*, Vol. 2, July, 1957, pp. 201–18.
24. D. Mechanic, 'Sources of Power of Lower Participants in Complex Organizations', *Administrative Science Quarterly*, Vol. 7, No. 3, December, 1962, pp. 349–64.
25. F. Robinson, 'The Role of the Systems Analyst', *Data Processing*, Sept.–Oct., 1968, pp. 228–33.
26. L. L. Constantine, 'The Programming Profession, Programming Theory, and Programming Education', *Computers and Automation*, February, 1968, pp. 14–19.

programmers is how near the computer are the analysts going to get. The closer the analysts get, the more the programmer's role is diluted. While each party might have developed certain expectations about the nature of the interdepend-ence between the two groups, the exact nature of that interdependence is likely to vary from situation to situation. 'At each institutional locale . . . the jurisdic-tional areas of each specialist group have to be adjudicated and negotiated. The division of labour cannot be legislated; it must be worked out at each locale.'[27] Such negotiation is an ongoing process. Few specialities are stable entities with relatively fixed boundaries and tasks. The present concern is to show how the specialities of programming and systems analysis emerged in Brian Michaels.

Computer activities in Brian Michaels, 1957–61

In the following sections material will be presented on the emergence of the programming and systems analyst functions in Brian Michaels. The research material has been organized into two time periods, 1957–61 and 1962–66. The reasons for this relate to changes in computer technology which began to take effect not only in Michaels but amongst all computer users in the period 1961–62. These two years mark the approximate cut-off point between first and second generations of computer hardware and appreciable developments in computer software. Michaels purchased their second computer in 1962. As we shall see its introduction had a major impact on the distribution of activities between the Michaels programmers and analysts and ultimately on their relative status and power positions.

The arrival of programmers in Michaels in 1957 produced a culture shock of such magnitude that many Michaels employees have never got over the experience. The programmers have equally vivid memories. To them Michaels was an alien environment: they were concerned only with the immediate challenge of their work. One programmer commented:

> 'In the early days we motivated ourselves. Getting the job on the computer was everything. The integration of the department in the company was very small indeed. As a group we were very independent.'

In spite of their claims for back-room boy status, the programmers found they could not isolate themselves. In fact, their strange work time-table and casual dress attracted criticism. The computer operators were the first group to pick up this feeling. One operator, now a senior programmer, said:

> 'It started off with the operators, they were the first people in the company to work odd hours. They had beards, used to dress roughly and were going home at 8.30 in the morning when everybody else was arriving. One day one of the personnel people came up and told me off for wearing a roll collar sweater. He said to me, "You're supposed to be a young executive, you should dress accordingly".'

The programmers also disrupted the company rules about clocking on and off. This, together with the rewards their market position afforded them at such a

27. A. Strauss, et al., *Psychiatric Ideologies and Institutions*, Free Press, Glencoe, 1964, p. 5.

263

comparatively young age, created problems with the company status system. Since the personnel department had to deal with these issues, they were a focus of a lot of the programmers' discontent. The personnel department had a terrible reputation for being ruthless and inconsiderate. One senior programmer referred to them as the '*Gestapo*'.

The programmers were clearly a group apart from the rest of the company. They differed in education, values, work patterns, dress and rewards from the rest of the Michaels employees. The major source of employee anxiety about the programmers, however, was the fact that the programmers symbolized the computer and this was an object of fear and mistrust. One member of a computer user department, later to join the programming team, recalled:

> 'I was very loath to join the computer set-up at first. There was a great deal of anti-feeling towards the programmers which was heartily reciprocated. I remember Kahn, who was the head of a user department at that time, going into a tirade about computers when I had to see him as part of my induction course. He used to say, "These people coming into the business with the machine aren't going to tell me how to run my department." I had scars on my memory about computers before I even got near them.'

Faced with increasing hostility between the programmers and user departments, the company decided to set up an Organization and Methods Department. This department's role was to act as a link between the programmers and the user departments and generally to translate the company's needs into computer terms. Specifically, it was felt that the analysts could redefine the system of work in user departments, set it out in the form of flow charts and reports, and leave the programmers to translate these flow charts into a form acceptable to the computer. This was the first encroachment by the analysts on the programmers' task environment. At this time the programmers seemed little concerned. Their attitude was more a matter of, '*We* have the skills, *they* don't. What's all the fuss about?' One senior programmer commented:

> 'There was a bit of friction, but not because we couldn't talk each other's language. The only real friction came when what we wanted and what they wanted in systems terms differed. There were no real technical arguments because we were involved in the actual system design. They weren't in a position to argue over technical points anyway.'

The analysts saw things rather differently. They were made to feel inferior by what they considered arrogance by the programmers.

> 'They (the programmers) had a tremendously selfish attitude. Anybody who was not a programmer was less than human.'

The analysts found it very difficult to convince the programmers of the value of their approach. One said:

> 'The programmers wanted to go their way. They regarded our work as trivial and time wasting. They more or less dismissed our work.'

In spite of these differences, both groups talked of a distinct feeling of group solidarity. Much of this was due to high involvement in their work. In 1957–58 there were only about a dozen computers on order in Britain. Michaels purchased the first SE 100. The Michaels computer people felt like pioneers. They were. A programmer remarked:

> 'In the main relations between the programmers and analysts were very good. Morale was very high when we were really trying to get the system going. I can't remember a group with such high morale or of such high calibre since. They were the pioneers.'

One analyst, after accusing the programmers of arrogance, said:

> 'There were these differences but not enough to really divide us. There was an air of enthusiasm to get things through that meant there was no real split.'

Since both groups were relatively unestablished in Michaels, they also found unity in what was experienced as a common threat from outside. A senior programmer noted:

> 'As I've said we were very much a group. . . . Nobody else in the business was obviously backing computers. We were the only group interested in proving they were worthwhile. We were bound to be a close-knit group.'

Programmer—analyst relations in Michaels, 1962–66

By the end of 1961 the programming and analyst functions in Brian Michaels were fairly well established. Each group had begun to stake out claims to a share in the handling of computer activities and were defining their identities *vis-à-vis* those activities. Following Becker and Carper,[28] Strauss,[29] and Bucher,[30] occupational identity involves the following components:

1. A definition of the field with which the occupation is identified—its boundaries, its major body of knowledge and associated methods.

2. A mission which the field serves—the value system which justifies and sustains the occupation.

3. The activities which are proper to the field.

4. The relationships that should obtain both between members of the field, and with persons in other fields.

The programmers were rather surer of their occupational identity. In the particular locale of Brian Michaels, they had been the first to carve out their area of expertise. They were able to sustain this early definition of their proper field of activities because of their control over computer technology. The programmers' power was bolstered by a value system which defined issues in technical terms

28. H. S. Becker and J. W. Carper, 'The Development of Identification with an Occupation', *American Journal of Sociology*, Vol. LXI, No. 4, January, 1956, pp. 289–98.
29. G. Strauss, 'Work-Flow Frictions: Interfunctional Rivalry, and Professionalism: A Case Study of Purchasing Agents', *Human Organization*, Vol. 23, No. 2, Summer, 1964, pp. 137–49.
30. R. Bucher, 'Social Process and Power in a Medical School' in M. N. Zald (ed.) *Power in Organizations*, University of Vanderbilt Press, Nashville, Tennessee, 1970.

and required solutions of an equally technically specific nature. Designing and programming a computer system was a mathematical problem which, of course, could only be handled by trained mathematicians.

To the analysts, the Achilles heel of the programmers was their lack of knowledge of, and interest in, company business systems. This had implications at the system design and implementation phases of the computer system. The analysts, backed by the company management and the user departments, tried to define their proper field of activities in those two areas. By the end of 1961 they had been fairly successful at the implementation phase but had done no real work in system design. They too had a value system. As the weaker group, this was often phrased to differentiate themselves from the programmers *and* to explain what they had to offer. A quotation from an interview with one analyst offers a good example.

> The programming characters were completely different from us. They knew a lot about maths, and how to handle the first generation "beasts". They hadn't the faintest idea of the commercial work involved. There were the people who couldn't speak the commercial language and us who knew a bit about programming and local systems in detail. There was therefore a process of mutual education.'

In the period 1962–66, the analysts sought to expand, and the programmers to maintain, their sphere of activities. Issues surrounding 'the reality of inter-dependence' were expressed in conflicts over power. Changes in computer technology modified the relative status of the two groups. These changes in status fed back on to the power conflicts. The aim of this section is to describe and explain the determinants of these conflicts and to explore how and why the changes in the task environment of the two groups impinged on their relative status.

Early in 1962 Michaels ordered and received delivery of their second computer, the NTL 200. Although by present standards this second generation machine was not revolutionary in design, it was a considerable advance on the first generation SE 100 Michaels had bought in 1957. The NTL 200 was bought as an addition to rather than as a replacement for the SE 100.

It is important to recall that in 1957 there was no micro electronic circuitry, no instant computer packages and no computer languages. Computers were only just being used for commercial purposes. The companies that bought them committed themselves to a very risky experiment. The machines were slow, bulky, and unreliable. One programmer recalled:

> 'Compared with modern computers it (the SE 100) was a real chewing gum and string thing. The input and output facilities were terribly naive. But the thing worked because the system was designed to suit the hardware.'

The last sentence from the above quotation reveals why the programmers were able to control their joint task environment with the analysts on the SE 100. With the first generation machines the systems design and programmes had to be tied to the particular technical constraints imposed by the computer and its input and output facilities. Each type of computer had its own machine language. In this situation, those who had the appropriate technical skills controlled the computer. The programmers with their mathematical training had these skills. The internally recruited and commercially trained analysts did not.

However, with the arrival of the faster, more flexible, simpler to programme NTL 200, the high calibre mathematicians Michaels had employed to install the SE 100 no longer became strictly necessary. Less trained people would now do. In addition, now that the systems design was no longer so constrained by the intricacies of the computer hardware, greater attention could be paid in matching the user departments' requirements to the new system. Since the analysts' rôle at Michaels had been designed to translate more effectively the user departments' needs into computer terms, they now could take on a more assertive rôle in their dealings with the programmers. This is precisely what they did.

One analyst described the changes in relations between the two groups like this:

> 'Yes, we started to take the initiative in some areas. We produced specifications from which the programmers had to write their programmes. They had to write programmes for the jobs we told them to.'

My retort to this answer was, 'There was some move into programming activities then?' I received a reply which was suggestive of strategic behaviour.

> 'Yes. This was partly because we were involved in the decision to buy the NTL 200. It was a conscious move to get in on the specifications. The problems were in taking away some of the programmers' activities and finding the staff at our end who could do that work.'

A programmer had this to say about the new pattern of interdependence between the two groups:

> 'Once we had ordered the NTL we started to have a real relationship with the analysts for the first time, because somebody had to specify the job we were doing in detail. This is where the analysts came in.'

The analysts had made some appreciable inroads into the programmers' activities as they stood on the SE 100 installation. Table 1 offers a comparison.

Whereas the programmers had effectively controlled the first four phases on the SE 100, they now played only a minor part in phase two and a more extensive part in phase four. Later conflicts were in fact to centre around the system design and specification stage. For the time being, like the purchasing agents in Strauss's[31] study, the programmers were starting to realize some of the problems of being at the end point of a work flow.

> 'It's a farce; they sort out the general systems and leave us to sort out all the mess-ups. People see the mistakes at the programming stage though it may be a systems fault.'

Goode,[32] using data from psychologists, sociologists, and medical personnel, has

31. G. Strauss, 'Work-Flow Frictions: Interfunctional Rivalry, and Professionalism: A Case Study of Purchasing Agents', *Human Organization*, Vol. 23, No. 2, Summer, 1964, pp. 137–49.
32. W. J. Goode, 'Encroachment, Charlatanism and Emerging Professions: Psychology, Sociology, and Medicine', *American Sociological Review*, Vol. 25, pp. 902–14.

Table 1   Comparison of Activities by Programmers and Analysts from the SE 100 to the NTL 200 Computer Installations

Phases of a Computer Project	SE 100	NTL 200
1. Application selection	Company Board/ Programmers	Company Board/ Analysts
2. Feasibility study and proposal for new hardware	Programmers	Analysts/ Programmers
3. Data gathering and analysis	Programmers	Analysts
4. System design and specification	Programmers	Analysts/ Programmers
5. Programming	Programmers	Programmers
6. System testing	Programmers	Programmers/ Analysts
7. Change-over	Programmers/ Analysts	Analysts
8. Operation including system maintenance	Programmers/ Analysts	Programmers/ Analysts

noted that emerging occupational groups are frequently accused of encroachment and charlatanism. One very specific way of doing this is to question the emerging group's competence. The Michaels programmers were very free with these accusations:

> 'Some individuals weren't too bad, the trouble was they knew nothing about computers. Some of them had never even seen one never mind been on a course. This meant they couldn't ask the right questions; this used to annoy us.'

The analysts were well aware of the ill feeling:

> 'I suppose there was a bit of difficulty; you might call it resentment. The programmers had to argue that we didn't know what we were talking about when it came to computers.'

There are strong similarities between the developing pattern of computer group relations in Michaels and some of the experimental literature on inter-group conflict. Sherif, Harvey, White, Hood and Sherif,[33] note that in competitive situations each group begins to see the other as the enemy, rather than merely as a neutral object. Distortions of perception develop in which each group emphasizes its own strengths and the other group's weaknesses. Thus the programmers were 'superior mathematical geniuses who knew nothing except maths' or 'were the people who couldn't speak the commercial language while we knew a bit about

33. M. Sherif, O. J. Harvey, B. J. White, W. R. Hood and C. V. Sherif, *Inter-group Conflict and Co-operation: The Robbers Cave Experiment*, University of Oklahoma, Norman, Oklahoma, 1961.

programming and the local systems in detail.' While from the other side, 'the programmers felt in time they could easily do the analysts' jobs' and 'the analysts had no knowledge of the equipment they were trying to use.' In fact these attitudes do not have to be based on distorted perceptions. Largely because of the recruitment and training policies of Michaels, the programmers had very little knowledge of company systems and the analysts little experience with computer hardware.

Blake, Shepard and Mouton go a little further than this negative stereo-typing approach in suggesting that mutual negative attitudes and actions feed upon each other. 'The consequence of provocation tends to be counter provoca-tion. This, in turn, leads to the further intensification of conflict. The end result is erosion of mutual respect and confidence in the constructiveness of the other's intentions.'[34]

Thus, the programmer's likely reaction in a situation where the analyst points out his weaknesses, is to emphasize his strengths. This response is likely to be perceived by the analyst as an attack on his weak point, his lack of technical expertise. The result is that one group's defensive behaviour becomes the other group's threat. This feedback-cyclical process helps to compound the existing conflict behaviour.

Strategies of power acquisition and maintenance, 1957–64

POWER RELATIONS, 1957–61

In this period, role relationships were fairly stable and status and power differ-entials well defined. For reasons already discussed the senior programmers in Michaels were unquestionably in control of computer activities.

A major problem for a group generating power in interaction with others in its environment is to establish its legitimacy. The stability of a power base depends on its legitimacy. From the beginning the programmers failed to stabilize their power. In fact, they engendered collective disapproval and opposi-tion from many groups in Michaels. The programmers generated conflict with others because of their arrogance, and by the way they openly displayed their disdain for company rules. The programmers were aware of the effect their behaviour was having, yet they persisted. This was not an effective use of their resources.

> 'Mind you, the other staff in Michaels felt as if they had plenty to moan about. The programmers didn't just consider themselves to be different, they thought they were better than everybody else. People became aware of this attitude, they saw the programmers taking what they considered to be liberties. Coming in late, having afternoons off to play golf, going out drinking in the evening when they should have been operating the com-puter.'

34. R. R. Blake, H. A. Shepard and J. S. Mouton, *Managing Intergroup Conflict in Industry*, Gulf Publishing Company, Houston, Texas, 1964, p. 24.

Like the printers in Lipset's[35] study, the programmers were driven into a cohesive group partly by their out-of-the-ordinary work hours. There was also the challenging work and the hostility and suspicion they had to live with. They were a group by themselves—outsiders. In this situation, they behaved very similarly to the maintenance men in Crozier's[36] study. Both groups' power was contested. It was not a legitimate power. Their reactive strategy was to cultivate a cohesive, aggressive group spirit to keep opposing power seekers on the defensive and to shield their own power resources from unfriendly eyes.

An unintended consequence of this strategy was to generate still further discontent and opposition. It was above all the programmers' aggressive group solidarity which was sensed and despised by those closest to them.

POWER RELATIONS, 1962–64

In this period the programmers' power was further threatened by technological change and encroachment by the analysts on their task environment. The first blow they received, however, was the departure of virtually all the senior programmers who designed the system for the SE 100. In this situation the programmers had to develop additional methods to protect their power.

Power maintenance strategies under technological change

The impact of technological changes on the computer industry have been discussed. Attention has also been given to how technological changes can break up configurations of expected status characteristics by altering the occupations from which those status characteristics develop. A crucial related area which has not been dealt with, however, is the power maintenance strategies used by an occupational group faced with a technological change which is eating into the core of its expertise; its major power resource.

The literature dealing with active and reactive strategies under conditions of technological change is practically non-existent. E. P. Thompson,[37] however, deals with the impact of technical change on nineteenth century craftsmen. He argues that in the first half of the nineteenth century the skilled trades were like islands threatened on every side by technological innovation and by the inrush of unskilled or juvenile labour. Invention simultaneously devalued old skills and elevated new ones. In this situation 'the artisan was as much concerned with maintaining his status as against the unskilled man as he was in bringing pressure upon the employers.'[38] According to Thompson, the artisans used two protective strategies. First, they looked to their trade unions to protect the knowledge base of their skills through the apprenticeship system. Secondly, they became politically involved. Thompson argues that the political radicals of that period came from the ranks of the 'debased trades' and not the unskilled or semi-skilled who flocked into the cities from rural England.

35. S. M. Lipset, M. Trow and J. Coleman, *Union Democracy*, Free Press, Glencoe, 1956.
36. M. Crozier, *The Bureaucratic Phenomenon*, Tavistock, London, 1964.
37. E. P. Thompson, *The Making of the English Working Class*, Vintage Books, New York, 1966.
38. *Ibid.*, p. 244.

W. Fred Cottrell[39] discusses the 'big four' occupational groups in the American Railroad Industry. He was interested in what happened to these big four when diesel and electric locomotives were introduced. The pattern of dilution and elevation which occurred with the nineteenth century artisans was repeated here. The boiler makers declined and the auto-mechanics and electricians increased in power and status. The engine drivers were no longer required to have a 'strong back and weak mind'. A knowledge of auto-machinery was now a more critical job skill. The engine drivers used similar protective strategies to the artisans: through trade union activity they kept control of the recruitment and learning process of their trade.

The Michaels programmers did not have an interest group of the trade union or professional association variety to bargain for them. Nevertheless, in the 1962–66 period, a number of factors helped them to protect their power base and occupational identity, although the perceived strategic implications of these factors by others induced reactive strategies which further weakened the programmers' position. The programmers used four main strategies: norms which denied outsiders' competence; protective myths; norms of secrecy; and protection of their knowledge base through control over training and recruitment policies.

The Chief Programmer in the 1962–66 period was the most outspoken on the first protective strategy:

> 'We knew it would not work, people trying to tell programmers what to do —they knew nothing about computers. We objected to suggestions from people who didn't even know what they were talking about. This was particularly so with the Systems Manager who tried to dictate what we did.'

In a programmer group interview the following comment received wide acceptance:

> 'We hardly saw them until we moved into the new office and there hasn't been much since then and you could hardly say that's been much use. If you asked any of the analysts in the early days they knew nothing about the specifications. They used to write their reports after jobs had been put on. ... They kept on changing their ideas. ... The trouble was they didn't know what they wanted in the first place.'

The second mechanism, the generation of myths, is less easily characterized as a strategy in the Michaels case. Myers[40] has argued that myths are likely to appear when an occupational group is faced with change and is seeking to protect its power and identity. Smith prefers to use the term 'fiction' instead of myth. 'Every profession operates in terms of a basic set of fictions about itself. These provide the profession with a comforting self-image and some stereotypes to help meet and adapt to the varied and often drastic contingencies of everyday operation.'[41] This point has also been made in the anthropological literature on myth.

39. W. F. Cottrell, 'Social Groupings of Railroad Employees' in S. Nosow and W. H. Form (eds.) *Man, Work and Society*, Basic Books, New York, 1962.
40. R. C. Myers, 'Myth and Status Systems in Industry' in R. K. Merton, et al., *Reader in Bureaucracy*, Free Press, New York, 1952.
41. H. L. Smith, 'Contingencies of Professional Differentiation' in S. Nosow and W. H. Form (eds.) *Man, Work and Society*, Basic Books, New York, 1962, p. 223.

'If we view social relations through a longish period of time, we see how various parties and supporters operate and manipulate mystical beliefs of varied kinds to serve their interests.'[42]

It is possible that the widespread *belief* amongst the Michaels computer people that the early programmers were especially well qualified was such a protective myth. Clearly it was in the programmers' interests to stress both the special skills required to perform that task and that they possessed those skills in abundance, especially when that was no longer true. In fact there was never a time when all the programmers had first class honours degrees in mathematics. Taking 1957–61, the most likely period, of the nine programmers for whom records are available, one had a first class honours degree, four had upper seconds, two had thirds, one had a pass degree and the other had not completed his degree course.

Another myth the Chief Programmer liked to use was that programmers could not operate under time constraints.

'People are always pressing for things to be put on the machine, but it's difficult to forecast the time periods for doing anything. The computer either works or it doesn't, there are no 75 per cent correct answers.'

This is emphatically denied by one of the Chief Programmer's deputies:

'The Chief Programmer has always argued we cannot work under time constraints. This isn't true, it's just his way of giving himself plenty of room for manoeuvre.'

The third strategy used by the programmers, withholding information which might have reduced the uncertainty and/or mystique of their task, has been noted by several authors. Crozier discusses the maintenance workers' strategy: 'Their strategy is a very simple and rigorous one. It aims, first, to keep the area under their control, free from outside interference. . . . Maintenance and repair problems must be kept secret. No explanation is ever given. Production workers must not understand.'[43] The Industrial Relations Officers in Goldner's study augmented their power by keeping union/management agreements 'secret' or, failing this, making them vague. 'They continually stressed that a contract was not what it seemed and agreed to make it specific only under pressure.'[44] Similarly Thomas Scheff[45] argues that if physicians broke the trading agreements they had set up with ward attendants, the latter could sanction them by withholding information and co-operation.

The programmers who mentioned the withholding strategy were prepared to admit that it was deliberate, but not that it was a protective device.

'From their point of view, they (the analysts) thought of us being Bolshie.

42. M. Gluckman, *Politics, Law and Ritual in Tribal Society*, Aldine, Chicago, 1965, p. 235.
43. M. Crozier, *The Bureaucratic Phenomenon*, Tavistock, London, 1964, p. 153.
44. F. H. Goldner, 'The Division of Labour: Process and Power' in M. N. Zald (ed.) *Power in Organizations*, University of Vanderbilt Press, Nashville, Tennessee, 1970, p. 126.
45. T. J. Scheff, 'Control over Policy by Attendants in a Mental Hospital', *Journal of Health and Human Behaviour*, Summer, 1961, pp. 93–105.

"They were the fellows who won't tell us why we can't do things." But what was the point, they couldn't understand our language.'

The analysts were aware of the programmers' withholding strategy and the reasons why it was in the programmers' interests to be secretive:

'The explanations they gave were clipped. If you knew what they were talking about the explanation was satisfactory but if you didn't catch on first time, well that would be too bad. . . .'

What really infuriated the analysts was the realization that programmers' norms of secrecy were making them completely dependent on the programmers.

'The moment changes occurred in the team we found there was no record of what had been happening. We found we were becoming terribly reliant on the persons who did the programming. . . . In its worst light it seemed that the programmers were trying to openly manipulate the situation. It looked like their attitude was "I know what's going on, therefore I'm indispensable." That situation was clearly not tolerable.'

The continuing problem for the analysts was to reduce their dependency on the programmers. In alliance with a number of other interested parties, the analysts attempted to implement a number of acquisitive power strategies. These involved efforts to reduce their dependency on the programmers by generating other sources of computer expertise. There was also the structural change in which the cohesive programming group was split geographically into three sections. By creating the impression that these three sections were of different status, and reinforcing this with different salary scales, competitiveness was encouraged amongst the programmers. This, and the labour turnover which it helped to stimulate, weakened still further the programmers' ability to resist encroachment. With the loss of still more of the 'old guard' of programmers, the analysts attempted to take a more active rôle in the recruitment and socialization of new batches of programmers. By 1964, however, the programmers were still the only group in Michaels with unquestionable computer expertise. As long as they could prevent the routinization of the core of their expertise, the programmers could maintain a certain amount of their former power.

In 1964 and 1969, Michaels purchased two further computers. These decisions also became 'social dramas' in which the analysts and programmers continued to negotiate around their joint task environment. In this way the process of attainment, maintenance and dissolution of power continued.

Conclusion

The above analysis has followed Smith's[46] recommendation that the appropriate field of anthropological study should be a 'unit over time, not merely a unit at a particular point in time.' In this way structural regularities may be abstracted from the succession of relatively unique events 'to reveal the outlines of an order within processes of simultaneous continuity and change.'[47]

46. M. G. Smith, 'History and Social Anthropology', *Journal of the Royal Anthropological Institute*, Vol. 92, 1962, pp. 73–85.
47. *Ibid.*, p. 84.

The process under view has been the emergence of the occupational groups of programming and systems analysis. This process may be conceptualized as the negotiation of occupational identities. Such negotiations are likely to be both constrained by and to alter structural arrangements. While such processes are the driving force for the elaboration of social structures, they may also be limited at any point in time by pre-existing ideological and institutional constraints. For many established occupational groups these could be codes of professional ethics and lines of trade union demarcation. However, in this case we were not dealing with a highly institutionalized setting.

The social arena in which the Michaels programmers and analysts interacted was regarded as poorly institutionalized, in the sense that there was no clear-cut set of mutually acceptable expectations about how the division of duties should be allocated between the two groups. Each party had vague and often discrepant beliefs about how their task environment should be shared. Conflicts developed over each group's perception of the reality of their inter-dependence. Much of this conflict was expressed in attitudinal and value differences. There was also the issue of power. As the technological environment in which they operated changed, so the distribution of power resources between the two groups altered. Ultimately their relative status changed with the shifts in the balance of power. Neither party remained either completely content with the initial task interdependence or chose to remain inert as their resource base altered. The preceding analysis illustrates the use of power maintenance and acquisitive strategies by the two groups.

The data in the present study do not in themselves permit confident generalization. The hope is, however, that the framework of specialization as an emergent process may have general applicability in the analysis of those specialist groups which do not fall neatly into any of the existing constructs associated with the literature on professionalization. Strauss and his colleagues have already profitably explored the emergent qualities of specialist groups working within psychiatric institutions. The above form of conceptualization should go some way towards meeting Turner and Hodge's[48] request for a framework for the analysis of occupations, rather than of professional occupations alone. The hope is that further occupational studies incorporating a form of relational analysis over time will help focus attention on the social processes in and around conflict, status and power in organizations.

NB No discussion whatever of structure of hierarchical control in Co., mgt policy, ec priorities/constraints — or even what the Co. is + does.

48. C. Turner and M. N. Hodge, 'Occupations and Professions' in J. A. Jackson (ed.) *Professions and Professionalization*, Cambridge University Press, London, 1970.

20. PROFESSIONAL IDEOLOGY AND SOCIAL SITUATION
Philip Elliott

The concept of professional ideology has a basis in the everyday experience that members of the same occupational group tend to think and behave in characteristic ways. Occupational differentiation seems to be one of the important dimensions along which the commonsense beliefs studied by ethnomethodologists vary systematically. This paper sets out the complex set of ideas and beliefs about cancer treatment and cancer research which were held by doctors and scientists in a hospital and laboratory specializing in the treatment and study of the disease. The main aim of the paper is to show how these beliefs were related to the work situation of the two groups and also to their relationship with each other and with various groups of rôle others, some outside the organization itself.

Professional ideologies face both inward and outward; in Dibble's terms they are both 'parochial' and 'ecumenic'.[1] In their original insights on the subject both Sorokin and Whitehead stress the parochial aspect, the limited frame of reference through which the members of any profession approach their work and, by extension, wider issues in society.[2] The ecumenic aspect of a professional ideology, however, is founded on the particular interests of the group and on their need to address others with different, maybe competing, interests. Mannheim's attempt to extend Marx's concept of ideology to show that all knowledge and belief is related to the situation of its production, should not be allowed to obscure the various different mechanisms involved.[3] Professional ideologies result from the need to make sense of recurrent work problems and tasks within a particular organization and career setting and of the need to present the work to others in the community, to compete for attention, control and resources.

The use of the concept of professional ideology does not involve making claims or assumptions as to whether the actual beliefs included are true or false. There are points of conflict between the three broad ideologies held by the doctors and scientists in this study and points of difference over matters of fact. There is no intention of arbitrating between these different positions. The aim is to show how each is linked to the occupational situation of different groups. In this sense,

1. V. K. Dibble, 'Occupations and Ideologies', *American Journal of Sociology*, Vol. LXIII, 1962, pp. 220–41.
2. P. Sorokin, *Society, Culture and Personality*, Harper, New York, 1947 and A. N. Whitehead, *The Adventure of Ideas*, Penguin, Harmondsworth, 1942.
3. K. Mannheim, *Ideology and Utopia*, Routledge, London, 1936.

20. Extracts from 'Professional Ideology and Social Science' from the *Sociological Review*, vol. 21, no. 2, May 1973. (pp. 211-28)

each is a valid way for the individuals and groups themselves to view their situation. Two of the ideologies identified in the study, 'therapy' and 'basic science', appear to be founded mainly on the different work experience of the two professional groups and on their relationship with each other in the particular organization. These two (especially 'therapy') are more parochial than the third, 'early diagnosis', which is shared by some in both professional groups and which is consciously addressed to others outside the organization. Nevertheless, all three ideologies have both inward and outward looking aspects.

The data reported in this paper were collected as part of a study investigating how those working in cancer research and treatment would respond to a televison documentary through which their work would be communicated to the general public. The research was divided into a pre- and post-programme phase. At the first stage, tape recorded interviews were conducted with thirty-one out of the thirty-five scientists working in the laboratories and eighteen out of twenty radiotherapists. The interviews on which this paper draws were loosely structured to encourage each individual to report on his or her career, his work, his view of the work situation and organization, the cancer problem and the communication media. The television programme provided a useful stimulus and sounding board to reveal more general beliefs.

The research was carried out in the autumn of 1967 in a hospital specializing in radiotherapy and so, *de facto*, specializing in the treatment of cancer patients, and in an associated cancer research institute. The hospital and the institute have been situated in the same area of a large city since before the Second World War. Just before the present study was carried out, the research institute had moved into a new, purpose-built block of laboratories and offices alongside the hospital. The original study included members of two other occupational groups, technicians in the laboratories and nurses in the hospital, as well as the two discussed in this paper.

Of the three sets of beliefs which were sufficiently coherent and prevalent to be labelled ideologies, two reflected the difference between the two professional groups and one was common to both. Those in the hospital who held the 'therapy' ideology emphasized their immediate responsibility to find the best treatment for patients already admitted to hospital. The 'basic science' ideology embodied the scientists' belief that progress was only possible through fundamental research, tackling such basic questions as the nature of life itself. The 'early diagnosis' ideology stressed the immediate returns to be expected from increased public education and awareness and from the opportunities for earlier diagnosis which should follow. Following sections discuss how each ideology was related to the particular work experience of the two groups, to their relationship with each other within the organization and to the interests of rôle others inside and outside the organization.

The doctors and the 'therapy' ideology

The eleven consultant radiotherapists had reached what was, in formal terms, the peak status of their careers. In informal terms too, the hospital offered excellent facilities for the practice of radiotherapy and had a reputation for a high standard of treatment which was difficult to match in the British Isles. Only in a specialized hospital such as this could sufficient equipment and a sufficient number of cases be brought together to make the practice of radiotherapy really worthwhile. Turnover among the senior clinical staff was very low. Most of the junior doctors, however, looked on the hospital as only a temporary stage in the development of their careers. Only the few who had been there longest commented specifically on the hospital's reputation.

Radiotherapy is a specialized treatment suitable for a limited variety of cases. This means that there is an element of instability in its status as a medical specialism. There is always the possibility that it will be overtaken by a new treatment. The clinicians, unlike some in the laboratories, did not see this as a real problem at the present time. Instead, they stressed the empiric development of radiotherapy. It has gradually increased in scope and effectiveness. They felt confident that because radiotherapy had been shown to work, it would continue to work and work more effectively.

The clinicians were unanimous in stressing the importance of clinical research in their work. The only reservations were by those who felt that in a situation of heavy patient load and staff shortage this aspect of the work was likely to take second place behind the more routine cares of general patient management. But others regarded clinical research as an integral part of their normal work, especially given the empiric basis of radiotherapy. Eleven clinicians (eight consultants) felt that up to that time clinical, empirical research had led the way in improving the cure rate for malignant diseases. Five of these admitted that basic research might have a place in the long run, but they stressed that it was equivalent to a very long term investment.

> 'So far as I know very little has come out of the basic scientific research that has been of direct application to the clinical treatment of cancer. I hope this would not be true in the long run, but it looks like being the very long run because it's certainly true so far.' (Junior Clinician.)

The fact that basic scientists work mainly with cells and animals was frequently mentioned as a reason why clinical research was superior in producing results. An alternative view of the relationship between clinical and basic research is that they are both part of a continuous chain of discovery and application. This 'continuous process view', stressing the apparently logical sequence of discovery, testing, application and treatment change, was taken by six clinicians, of whom four were junior doctors. It appeared that those more firmly established and committed to radiotherapy were more likely to stress its empiricism and to value clinical rather than basic research. Only one doctor, who had had post graduate training in scientific research, held the same view as many of the scientists in the laboratories: that progress could only come through basic research.

The doctors' concern for the welfare of their individual patients also played an important part in developing a particularistic frame of reference. It was illustrated in the doctors' distrust of general cure rates.

> 'But it is so difficult to generalize, you can take anything, say lung cancer. I can say to you it's got a two per cent survival (rate), but if I say this to a mass audience this implies that the whole lot die, well they generally do but for the individual who comes along, he may well not have a two per cent chance, but a fifty per cent chance, or even an eight/twenty chance and you

can only tell him when you've got him as an individual. You can only begin to impress upon him what his chances are, when he's an individual.'
(Junior Clinician.)

The concern with each patient as an individual contributed to a distrust of research with cells and animals and to a distrust of media publicity aimed at mass audiences.

In sum, the two main factors underlying the set of beliefs labelled the 'therapy ideology' in the hospital were the nature of radiotherapy and the exigencies of patient care. Those holding most firmly to this ideology argued that their work involved the meticulous manipulation of treatment techniques for the individual patient. They placed little value on wider perspectives in treatment or research. But there were variations from this set of beliefs in the hospital, as well as another set with sufficient prevalence and coherence to warrant the label ideology. Such factors as past educational experience and current career position contributed to the specific view taken by any single doctor; as was shown most clearly in the different assessments made of clinical and basic research. Other more general occupational and organizational factors, however, lay behind the second general ideology of 'basic science'.

The scientists and the 'basic science' ideology

The majority of scientists, both senior and junior, had spent all their scientific careers in non-industrial scientific research institutes of one type or another. The one senior scientist who had spent a long period of his career in industry mentioned specifically that he felt this marked him off from his colleagues. Three of the senior scientists had qualified in medicine before embarking on their scientific careers.

The picture of a separate, non-industrial career pattern was confirmed by the scientists' feelings about other places to which they might be attracted to work. The older scientists were strongly committed to work at the laboratories because they felt they were too old to move now. The younger scientists expected to move about from institute to institute, but only one thought about going back to industry. The scientists were attached to their scientific work and the organization was a setting within which it could take place. The only exceptions to this general proposition were the six senior scientists who showed considerable attachment to the Radiation Chemistry Department, a sub-unit within the laboratories. This had developed from the discovery at the institute of a new and powerful research technique. Scientists, full-time and visitors, had been attracted to share in the technique and exploit its possibilities. Until the necessary machinery was installed in the new laboratory buildings, the radiation chemists had been forced to conduct their experiments on a hired machine some miles away in another area of the city. Their physical separation from the general laboratories, as well as the feeling of being part of the clearest scientific growth point in the laboratories at that time, seem to have contributed to the radiation chemists' strong attachment to their department.

The majority of the scientists had worked in the same field throughout their scientific careers, though this necessarily depends on how the scientific fields are themselves defined. The scientists themselves reported a common process of cumulative specialization, usually started by the subject for the PhD, or the first research appointment, or both. Just as in the hospital clinical careers appeared to be defined by specialization in radiotherapy, which then entailed a concern with cancer patients, so in the laboratories scientific careers were based on scientific specialities which had then led into the general cancer problem. The contingencies of a scientific career make it unlikely that a scientist will start research work with an over-riding vocation towards the cancer problem. Moreover, it was felt that such a vocation would not be helpful in actual scientific research. . . .

In other words, particularistic concern with the problems of cancer and cancer patients might well hinder the scientist from achieving the universalistic requirements of the scientific rôle. The state of scientific knowledge about cancer is itself an important reason why the choice between a cancer focus and a scientific focus is a somewhat unreal one for the scientists. . . .

These factors, the nature of the scientific career, the universalistic basis of the scientific rôle and the nature of the cancer problem itself, all contribute to the 'basic science' ideology current in the laboratories. This stressed that only basic research, aimed at investigating the processes of life itself, could be expected to lead to advances in cancer treatment.

The 'basic science' ideology is a way of relating scientific research to cancer even though the disease itself only provides limited guidelines.

> 'Some of the things we do are pretty remotely connected with cancer in a sense. . . . The connection is that almost any advance in the biological sciences is likely to be helpful to cancer research. I think it was Haddow who said that cancer research was all of biology.'

Several scientists stressed this point when asked whether they had, or the lay public would have any difficulty in linking their work to cancer as a disease. The 'basic science' ideology also implied a contrast between a real cure—a means of reversing the disease condition—which might be discovered through scientific research and current treatment techniques which were little more than different ways of excising diseased organs.

It was a common analogy for scientists to talk of research as a game which they wanted to keep on playing, with the implication that playing the game itself supplied the rules. The importance of this analogy showed most clearly in the claim made by the majority of scientists that they never were in the position of having to choose a new piece of work. Instead, they suggested, the next piece of work grew out of the one which had gone before, in a continuing stream. This contrasted with the scientists' beliefs about industry, where they thought financial considerations were of paramount importance. The 'basic science' ideology keeps the field of science wide open. The scientist is left to follow his nose as science itself directs.

Six scientists did mention that the need to make a contribution to the cancer problem was an important factor when faced with a choice between lines of research. The various triggering mechanisms provided within science itself—published papers, discussions with colleagues or new experimental techniques—

were all cited as possible stimuli which might provide the impetus for developing research in a particular direction. The 'continual development' view of research was part of the 'basic science' ideology underlining the importance of science itself in determining the nature of research work.

The 'basic science' ideology also included a particular view of the likely progress of scientific research towards a solution of the cancer problem. This view rejected the idea that there would be one dramatic 'break-through' to a solution. Clinicians and scientists alike pointed out that cancer is not the name of a single condition but is a generic term, rather like the word 'disease' itself. Such a complex problem can only be attacked at a really basic level—as some scientists put it, at the level of life itself.

Nevertheless there was one scientist, who had only recently come into the laboratories from a very different kind of work, who did subscribe to the 'lay' view of potential breakthrough.

> 'I don't think it will be all that long before the problem is solved. It could be today or it could be tomorrow—you never know when somebody will hit on something.'

The 'basic science' ideology was made up of a set of inter-related beliefs which were widely shared in the laboratories, though again it is important to emphasize that not everyone subscribed to each and every aspect of it.

Ideology and professional and organizational relationships

The two ideologies were founded on different work experiences but they also drew on the relationship between the two groups, reflecting their different interests. The research unit had been established on the same site as the hospital on the common-sense assumption that the theory of one would become the practice of the other. Physical proximity, however, was only part of the story. The difference in the type of work, discussed above, and problems of control and autonomy in the relationship between the two organizations, inhibited close relations. Problems of control included both the specific history of the way the research institute had developed as an independent unit and more general issues such as the medical profession's control over medical research and careers and the different methods of finance through which the two organizations were supported. Looked at in dynamic terms, the 'therapy' and 'basic science' ideologies supported a tendency towards separation and polarization between the two groups. The difference in the outlook and responsibilities of the two groups can be summarized as a contrast between the clinicians' particularistic responsibility for the individual patient and the scientists' universalistic responsibility for the advancement of knowledge. One way in which this difference is experienced is in the problems of applying research results, often discovered through animal experiments, to the treatment of human patients. One scientist elaborated the difficulties which beset any scientist trying to set up clinical trials for a new drug —'It's a case of "Well, we've tried everything else, we'll have to give them drugs" . . .' Another, who had qualified as a doctor, understood medical caution.

> 'The problem I find is that the clinician is basically not a scientist, that's without being rude. A good clinician should treat every individual patient

as an individual and give him the best treatment that's around. This means it's very difficult to make a scientific appraisal of a new line of treatment.'

Most scientists, unlike most of the doctors, felt that there was value in their current contacts with the hospital, most hoped for increased relations.

'Here on the doorstep you've got a factory of human material and you are not, so to speak, using it.'

A few scientists, however, were frankly sceptical of the value of struggling to improve relations with the clinical side so long as other channels, such as conferences and journals, remained open for the dissemination of research findings.

The difference between the aims of the two organizations was partly a result of the particular course of development followed by the laboratories.

'The problem (in maintaining a close relationship between the hospital and the laboratories) lies really in the direction in which both are going. The clinical situation is fixed by . . . looking after patients. It cannot move very far away from the normal stream. The labs can either support, be what you would call clinical support laboratories, doing work at the behest of the clinician or they can go fundamental. . . . It's easier to do that because they do not have to supply a patient load.' (Senior Clinician.)

The older clinicians and the older scientists who had been at the hospital longest generally described the growth of the laboratories as a development away from clinical support towards an independent scientific function. Some clinicians still seemed to think of the laboratories as 'their' service unit, but one which had got out of hand. One scientist made the point that the new laboratories would provide the research staff with a more secure base from which to meet the medical staff on equal terms. A few scientists scattered in small laboratory groups had been more dependent on the hospital. This relationship of dependence and the notion of clinical support imply clinical control over the direction of scientific activity. 'Going fundamental', as the clinician put it above, was an option which maximized scientific values and minimized clinical control.

Beyond the immediate setting there was also a more general problem of control; that exercised by the medical profession over career opportunities in medical research.

'I am not a medical graduate. In cancer research that is quite an important thing. They tend to hold the upper levels of administration and research. There is this sort of feeling between medics and non-medics in research. The non-medics who have graduated in the sciences feel they have a better training in research than the medical degree where research is regarded, not flippantly, but as rather less important. . . . You are usually applying for jobs administered by the hospital where I feel an M.D. makes a difference. Medical people tend to gather together. We feel we're kept out.'

Another area of friction between the two groups was more hypothetical than real in the immediate situation. Methods of finance were fixed and the hospital and the institute do not compete directly for the same resources. Nevertheless, both groups were dissatisfied with the methods through which they were financed. Most clinicians felt that cancer therapy was in some ways a poor relation beside cancer research. Some of the older clinicians resented the fact that the

National Health Service had removed the hospital's access to charitable monies. In contrast, basic research appeared to have funds readily available, and what is more it appeared to have acquired all the glamour. They felt that those suffering from cancer were largely ignored by a public which would rather not know.

The scientists were conscious of their dependence on public charity and many felt that this was a burden. . . .

The scientists were evenly divided on whether new money should go to research or the clinical side, suggesting a problem of rôle confidence. Senior scientists tended to stress the former priority, juniors the latter. The 'basic science' ideology provided one way of resolving the problem, especially for the seniors. . . .

The 'early diagnosis' ideology and organizational coalition

The third ideology current in the two organizations—'early' diagnosis—provided another way of resolving the dilemma. Some scientists adopted it, advocating education/prevention campaigns and diagnostic facilities as an immediate priority.

Compared with the other two ideologies, the third, 'early diagnosis', was more clearly directed towards the public and external constituents of the two organizations. 'Basic science' reflected the scientists' involvement in a wider scientific community as well as including a justification of the research to the lay public. It was also embodied in the official policy of the institute. But 'early diagnosis' was part of the official policy of both organizations. A Department of Social Medicine had been founded in the hospital to conduct lectures, classes and research about the disease among the general public. Both clinical and research staff gave lectures for the department and toured local Women's Institutes, British Empire Cancer Campaign collection groups and similar organizations. There were also formal attempts to put the message across to junior members of staff within the laboratories and the hospital.

This ideology stressed the impact which prevention, education and early diagnosis would have on the cure rate within the current state of medical and scientific knowledge. While the public believes all cancer is largely incurable, there is a tendency to try to put off finding out one has the disease. The result is to make the general prognosis worse than is necessary and so to reinforce cancer's reputation in a vicious circle. A belief in early diagnosis is widely shared by organizations and groups dealing publicly with the cancer problem. It provides all those working in the cancer field with the idea that there is something which can be done now.

In the hospital, the narrower 'therapy' ideology had been explicitly countered by the broader orientation embodied in 'early diagnosis'. Whereas the former concentrated on the skills and practice of work performance itself, the latter was concerned with the consequences of the exercise of the particular skill and expertise, in this case with the more widely defined cancer problem. Although the two orientations are not mutually exclusive, radiotherapy can be seen as a highly sophisticated set of technical skills or as the means of effecting a cure on a cancer patient. In the course of their career the clinicians become progressively committed to radiotherapy as an empirical technique. At the same time they are in continuous close contact with cancer patients. Once they have reached peak professional status with a post as consultant, they may find they have more scope for thinking of themselves as 'cancer workers' as well as 'radiotherapists'. There is an analogy here with the 'blocked spiralist' who takes on voluntary activities in the community once he reaches his peak career status at work.[4] Certainly the reputation of the hospital rests not just on the excellence of the treatment provided but also on the active policy which has been followed, to tackle the cancer problem on a broad front.

Altogether twelve doctors expressed the belief that earlier diagnosis, coupled with a general reduction in public fear, would contribute at once to a sharp improvement in the cure rate. This belief was generally coupled with an optimistic view of the present chances of a cure. This is not simply a matter of fact, as it might appear. If the general public are believed to have an irrational fear of cancer as a killer disease, then even quite a low cure rate is better than no cure rate at all. On the other hand, it is quite possible to make the opposite interpretation, as five doctors did. In comparison with other diseases, the cure rates for many types of cancer are low. They felt that the possibilities of improving the situation now, in the existing state of knowledge, were very limited. By extension, this led to a contradiction of the 'early diagnosis' ideology. One clinician was quite convinced that change in the cure rate would be crucial, not any extension of public information.

> 'I don't think that public education is a particularly good idea, in any form. It's only scratching the surface. The public will fear cancer until there is a cure. . . . I don't think there has been a change in the public attitude to cancer really since I've been here. I still, just as much as when I first came here, tell patients they have not got cancer.' (Senior Clinician.)

It could be argued that a belief in public ignorance was less important to the scientists than to the doctors, who were continually made aware of the limited effectiveness of current treatment through patient contact. At any rate the scientists put more qualifications on the image of a lay public completely ignorant and afraid. Some scientists went further, denying some of the central beliefs of the 'early diagnosis' ideology.

> 'I have become more pessimistic about cancer generally, since I worked here. I had the idea, maybe wrongly, pure ignorance but it was always being put out, that if you detected cancer early enough it would be cured. But since then I have discovered that this just isn't so. With some types it does apply but some are vicious and incurable.'

Another scientist commented 'If anyone I knew had (lung cancer) I would assume it's not going to be cured', and he went on to explain that the diagnostic techniques were not yet powerful enough to detect the cancer when there was a chance of being able to do anything about it.

But the 'early diagnosis' ideology was widely shared in the laboratories. It had a direct value to the scientists in that it offered quicker returns for public expenditure on cancer research than the long term investment of 'basic science'.

4. R. Frankenberg, *Communities in Britain*, Penguin, Harmondsworth, 1966.

At the same time, being a short term investment, it was not in direct conflict with basic science. To suggest that more could be done with the knowledge already gained was at least a partial answer to those who doubted whether all the effort expended on scientific research was really worthwhile. Many scientists with a complete intellectual belief in 'basic science' felt uneasy about the claims they were making on public charity when they could hold out no prospect of certain or quick returns.

The 'early diagnosis' ideology provided both groups with a public front to present to the outside world. In that world different groups of rôle others had greatest significance for the two professional groups. Analysing the doctors' and scientists' beliefs about publicity for their work showed that while the former thought in terms of 'patients', 'patients' relatives' and 'potential patients', the latter were more likely to think in general terms of 'science' and 'society'. In 'society' they were particularly conscious of one specific public, the administrators, collectors and donors in the various cancer charities. Most scientists felt that as the general public contributed, they had the right to know what was going on. But they did not expect this to be of great benefit to the public or themselves. Some also saw publicity in terms of the 'early diagnosis' ideology as part of the general fight against cancer. Another group were prepared to argue that knowledge itself was valuable regardless of any use to which it might be put.

Some doctors shared the hope that publicity could be used to further 'early diagnosis', but otherwise the doctors' views on publicity contrasted sharply with those of the scientists. The doctors' work with patients was a much more direct and forceful contact with a special section of the lay public than the scientists' general need for charitable support. The individual frame of reference which the doctors used in their work carried over into their view of the public and society so that, for example, they saw the mass television audience as made up of many individual potential patients. Several contrasted the individual relationships and feed-back which could be established through the lectures they carried out for the Department of Social Medicine, with the complete lack of contact between television and the mass audience. Some clinicians held that for this and other reasons the whole idea of publicity through a mass medium was wrong. There was fear that television presentation would confuse and mislead with distressing consequences for those already affected by the disease and harmful consequences for those who might be in the future. The features of television which made the doctors condemn it—the size and breadth of the audience, the natural viewing situation in the home, the use of modern technology—were precisely those about which the scientists were most enthusiastic.

The two groups' views on publicity also reflected the elements of conflict and friction between them. Some scientists saw the television programme as an opportunity to show the public what their job involved, an opportunity to put over the 'basic science' rather than the 'early diagnosis' ideology. . . .

The doctors were not enthusiastic about a scientific programme, however, and not just because it would lose an opportunity to put over the belief in 'early diagnosis'.

'I'd guess that what I would see would be pictures of test tubes, rabbits being injected and more stupid pictures of cell division done on a micro-scope. To the uninitiated (this) looks like a mass of jelly that's pulsating. This creates, I am sure, a frightening reaction in the *average patient*, and in the average non-medical person. (Emphasis added.) (Senior Clinician.)

Several doctors were prepared to argue that for this and other reasons, there should be no media publicity for cancer treatment or research. The scientists on the other hand reacted against such a suggestion as a threat of censorship. One scientist had no doubt that there was a general difference here between doctors and scientists.

'I don't really like the medical outlook in this country. The doctor won't tell you what pill he has given you or what is really wrong with you. There should be more openness. The attitude of the doctor is you shouldn't know, you wouldn't know, you wouldn't understand and I'm a clever man.'

As well as reflecting on the relationship between the two groups, the scientists' position that there should be 'no censorship' owed much to their own commitment to the advancement and dissemination of knowledge. . . .

This paper has presented the ideologies and the two groups as if each was a separate unit, but enough qualifications have been raised to show that there was some over-lap between the opinions of each group and a considerable range of difference within them. One important element of difference was between the senior members of each group and the juniors, more newly recruited. There was a tendency for the latter to continue to interpret their situation according to the understandings brought from their previous, lay or educational environment. Examples include the different views of basic and clinical research taken by junior and senior doctors and the different financial priorities emphasized by junior and senior scientists.

The focus on work and the work situation adopted in this paper is open to the criticism that it follows earlier studies in treating work as a bounded system.[5] Some external factors have been introduced as referents for the three ideologies. Apart from these the most important non-work area which appeared to be relevant to the study was the personal contact of individuals with cancer patients. But though these contacts were important in influencing the beliefs of individuals, they did not influence the three ideologies in any systematic way, nor did they lead to any broad alternative view.

The concerns which the two groups expressed within this particular organizational setting cannot be seen in isolation from wider professional and social systems. 'Basic science' for example is one way of resolving some of the dilemmas which face all those involved in the administration and pursuit of scientific research. It draws heavily on well-established claims to scientific autonomy. It is likely that in other organizations, just as in this case, it will be used in disputes over control. It also underlines the fact that the scientists had important reference points in the scientific community. They spent a good deal of time associating and communicating with colleagues through the media of conferences and journals. One pointed out that judging which course to take in

5. E.g., see S. Cunnison, *Wages and Work Allocation*, Tavistock, London, 1966.

future work was a problem of balancing likely success against importance. He produced a hierarchy of criteria which showed a mix between scientific and cancer goals.

'Well, if it leads to a cure or prevention, that's very important, Nobel Prize type importance. Then there are lesser degrees of importance. For example, you may make a real scientific advance which will lead to further developments, or it may be just a small extension of knowledge which does not change the structure of science but adds a little. That's nice but it is not really important.'

By contrast the 'therapy' ideology was less clearly related to any views more broadly held in the medical profession. This is partly because the medical profession does not serve as a continual focus of career attention to doctors in the way the scientific community does to scientists. In Gouldner's terms, doctors are more likely than scientists to become locals, committed and attached to their particular employment setting.[6] Nevertheless these particular doctors were cancer workers as well as medical specialists. As such they, like the scientists, were involved in another network of organizations and associations all of which tend to place great emphasis on aspects of the 'early diagnosis' ideology.

'Early diagnosis' reflects and reinforces a particular set of criteria for the allocation and use of resources in this country. Most of these are provided by charitable donation with some direct and indirect government aid. The other two ideologies both include different sets of criteria, one stressing scientific research, the other patients and treatment. One importance of these ideologies is the part they play in deciding the distribution of resources and reflecting the interests of those involved. Such disputes are carried on at higher levels than the intra-organizational on which this paper is focused. These include the administration of the various grant-giving bodies, as well as government departments and occasional political decisions. These ideologies and the particular organizational settings in which they are found draw on the intellectual traditions and patterns of economic and social organizations to be found in the society. At all levels they play a part in restraining and ordering processes of social change by structuring the way the issues are presented and relating them to these continuing patterns and traditions.

6. A. W. Gouldner, 'Cosmopolitans and Locals—Latent Social Roles', *Administrative Science Quarterly*, Vol. 3, 1958.

21. THE PSYCHOLOGY OF CHILD PSYCHOLOGY David Ingleby

When St John the Divine writes, 'I was in the Spirit on the Lord's day', he seems to be letting us know that 'being in the Spirit' was a necessary condition for having the revelation he proceeds to unfold. In this paper I want to suggest that (although we are not told this, but have to find out for ourselves) the revelations of child psychology also require that one be in a certain spirit before they become convincing; that they are as much products of the mentality which is brought to bear on the evidence as of the evidence itself.

The mentality we are talking about is not, as in St John's case, a transitory state of the individual; it is the shared corpus of concepts, attitudes and methods of inquiry into which the 'fully trained' psychologist has been initiated. . . .

I shall try first of all to elucidate this mentality, and then to demonstrate that it can only be understood in terms of its place in (to borrow Laing's useful definition) 'the *political* order . . . the ways persons exercise control and power over one another'.[1]

In other words, I want to consider this mentality not just as a set of ideas viewed apart, but as an ideology; the essential difference being that an ideological critique takes into account the interests which a particular mentality is defending. As Mannheim states:

> The concept 'ideology' reflects the one discovery which emerged from political conflict, namely, that ruling groups can in their thinking become so intensively interest-bound to a situation that they are simply no longer able to see certain facts which would undermine their sense of domination. There is implicit in the word 'ideology' the insight that in certain situations the collective unconscious of certain groups obscures the real condition of society both to itself and to others and thereby stabilises it.[2]

The 'psychology of child psychology' I am thus trying to sketch is an exercise quite different in spirit from child psychology itself; I shall be attempting to practise the kind of psychology which that profession does not apply, in

---

1. R. D. Laing, *The Politics of Experience*, Penguin, London, 1967, p. 107.
2. K. Mannheim, *Ideology and Utopia*, Routledge and Kegan Paul, London, 1936, p. 36.

---

21. Reprinted from *The Integration of a Child into a Social World* by M. P. M. Richards, Ed., by permission of Cambridge University Press, London. Copyright © 1974. (pp. 295-308)

order to show why it does not apply it. For—with a few deviant exceptions (e.g. Reich or Laing)—child psychology has not looked at its subject-matter in the light of the political system in which it is found: the political order is usually seen as a source of extraneous variance which must be partialled out of the data to make them truly 'psychological'. If this is how psychology is to be defined, indeed, then the present essay is not psychology at all: but its purpose is to demonstrate that the 'facts' produced by any psychology which attempts to ignore the political context of what it observes will be about as useful as, say, an analysis of a violin concerto which ignores what the orchestra is playing.

In an earlier paper[3] I collected some examples of the way in which the approach which has come to be regarded as 'scientific' psychology seemed to be shot through with ideological biases. In the light of these biases I went on to contend that the 'scientific' label is a device for throwing us, ideologically speaking, off the scent: for that which is 'scientific', by definition, does not depend for its authority on the political loyalties implicit in it. My contention was that the social function which determines the spirit of inquiry in psychology—whatever convictions psychologists may have about it—is the maintenance of the *status quo*: psychology borrows habits of thought from natural science and applies them to the human sphere in a manner which is logically quite inappropriate, but politically highly functional. This activity was referred to as 'reification', defined as 'the misrepresentation of praxis as process'—'praxis' being the type of activity which characterizes an agent, and has to be understood as projects or communications having meanings, and 'process' being the activity of things, which does not harbour meanings in the same sense, but can be completely understood in terms of its antecedent causes (the traditional scientific paradigm of explanation). The effect of the many reifications that occur in psychology is to dehumanise the individual in the same way that the political system dehumanises him, i.e. to represent as impersonal, thing-like processes those aspects of people which the political order itself needs to remove from their agency; either to eliminate them, as in the case of 'deviant' behaviour (and other attempts men make to build their own order of values and perceptions), or—by abolishing the very distinction between people and things—to facilitate the use of people as if they were things. Where reification assists in the elimination of deviance, it is also accompanied by a 'normative' component (for instance, in the 'disease model' of abnormal experience or behaviour): the logic of 'correct/incorrect' functioning is superimposed on the dimension 'socially desirable/undesirable', via the use of metaphorical dichotomies like sickness/health, disordered/well-ordered, adjusted/maladjusted, adaptive/maladaptive, and so on.

Thus, in the earlier paper, the ideological content of psychology was located in a single general concept—reification—instances of which were described in theories of intelligence, personality and learning, and in psychiatry. The issues have been greatly clarified for us since then by Harré and Secord's[4] analysis of the 'paradigm shift' which they claim to detect in the social sciences; their 'old' and

3. J. D. Ingleby, 'Ideology and the Human Sciences', *Human Context*, 2, 1970, pp. 159–80, reprinted in T. Pateman (ed.) *Counter Course*, Penguin, London, 1972.
4. R. Harré and P. F. Secord, *The Explanation of Social Behaviour*, Blackwell, Oxford, 1972.

'new' paradigms overlap to a large extent with my 'process/praxis' distinction, though—in line with the current paradigm of 'philosophy of science' itself—they do not dwell on the political significance of these modes of explanation. In this essay I wish to return to the same theme, by showing how child psychology has wished out of existence the all-important political context of childhood, and how it is obliged to do this by virtue of the social function of the 'people professions' to which it belongs.

To summarize, then: I start from the belief that practically every act in relation to a child, from the moment of his birth and even before, reflects constraints dictated by that child's place in the political system. (From this point of view, we might say that the whole field of child development ought properly to be regarded as the study of socialization.) In psychology, however, this determination is not simply ignored, but the evidence about it is suppressed by the very methodology of the profession. . . .

Now the most effective means which psychologists have devised for keeping the political context of childhood out of the picture was the creation of that venerable distinction between 'socialization' and the rest of development, and the relegation of ideology to the waste-paper basket of 'cultural variables', which are supposed to enter only into the learning of explicit moral principles, allegiances, and social concepts. Having thus disposed of political factors, psychologists have moved increasingly towards areas where these influences are regarded as minimal, and towards a methodology which does not cater for them. The hope appears to be that if child development is studied sufficiently early on and in a sufficiently 'biological' way—which means, in the main, using concepts and observational methods borrowed from the study of animals, whose politics are less of a problem —if this is done, a picture of the process can be built up which will hold good regardless of the structure of the society in which the child develops. . . . We shall see later, in fact, how usable conclusions may be drawn from such research only by the addition of unstated and untested assumptions. The political system is inextricably present in the most basic aspects of childrearing and in the process of conception and gestation as well: its influence is manifest in the whole environment in which the child undergoes the first stages of his life.

This is true, first, in a practical and material sense. For example, the extent to which a mother can *afford* to meet her child's demands—how much food and attention she can give and when, how much crying she can permit or tolerate —must be strongly influenced by her position in the system of production and consumption; so that even the simplest 'time-and-motion study' approach is portraying the results of a given political system. Here, in fact, it might make sense to 'partial out social class' in order to study the effects of such environmental variables in their own right. On a different level of analysis, however, the influence of the child's environment cannot be disentangled from the socio-economic determinants of that environment. I am referring to the moulding of a child's mentality which starts with the first interactions, and which is all the more potent for being unconscious as well as unspoken: that is, the formation of his ideas about his own needs and propensities, and the response to them that can be expected from the world around him—about what he may take, own, reject, give, do or say; all of which boil down to expectations derived from early experience.

These ideas are not so much expounded in the process of socialization as embodied and enacted in it.

Psychology does not, in fact, provide us with a very adequate way of describing and measuring what I have called here the child's 'mentality': the topic spreads out untidily under several headings—concept formation, construct theory, motivation, language learning, attachment theory, object relations, psychodynamics. However vague it seems one must remain about its definition, this seems to me no drawback in asserting that it must be to a large extent a product of the political system—the totality of power relations—that the child grows up in. This, of course, is a truism in Marx (cf. 1910, p. 119: 'The same men who establish social relations conformably with their material productivity, produce also the principles, the ideas, the categories, conformably with their social relations'):[5] but its application within the field of child psychology has been not only neglected, but quite strongly resisted.

Thus, the aim of studying the child as if he and his family were living on a desert island is a futile one: they aren't—and even if they were, they would probably still behave as though they weren't. From the start, the responses which the child receives to his demands and activities are shaped by the fact that both his 'input' and his 'output' are destined for the slots which the social system will provide for them. In the type of society most psychology is written about, these slots will be highly specific ones, requiring the individual to adapt his demands obediently to market conditions (cf. Jules Henry's (1966) 'virtuoso consumer'),[6] and to tailor his creative capacities to labour conditions, since—to the system that sustains him—his physical energy, sensory-motor skills, and imagination (should he be privileged enough to retain any) are all essentially *commodities*. Precisely how the prevailing relations of production and consumption will impinge on him will vary greatly with his class position, but it is those relations which are the most important factors in determining the mould in which 'socialization' casts him. . . .

The reluctance of child psychologists to think too hard about these questions is well demonstrated in the notion that the 'rules, proscriptions, values and modes of behaviour' which a child must acquire to become 'social' are those which his *parents* require him to absorb. In the sense that parents may have wishes for the child that reflect their identification with interest-groups outside the family, this is partly true: but on the obvious interpretation, this notion seems a straightforward reversion to the 'desert island' school of socialization. It turns a blind eye to the fact that parents are not simply acting in their own interests, or even in those of the child, in bringing him up: they are first and foremost *representatives* of a particular sector of a particular political system, and—ultimately—it is in the cause of the perpetuation of that system that efforts will be directed. This oversight achieves an important misrepresentation of the nature of parental authority. . . .

Both the psychologist's and the parent's pretence that primary socialization serves only the interests of the primary group provides a vital line of defence for

5. K. Marx, *The Poverty of Philosophy*, H. Quelch (trans.), Chicago, 1910, p. 119.
6. J. Henry, *Culture against Man*, Tavistock, London, 1966.

the interests it really serves. To modify the infant's propensities in such a way as to make coexistence with him possible will surely be agreed by everyone to be not only necessary but in the child's own interests. Hence—since no genuine conflict of interests exists—there can be no argument about whose side to take: we are all on the same side. Such a picture can only obscure the true reasons for 'failures of socialization'. If the parents fail to produce a child adapted and reconciled to his allotted place in society, then on this model something is wrong with either the child or his parents (cf. the 'breakdown of family life' which is sometimes blamed for black unrest): for Science has shown that under normal conditions of family rearing, people will grow up adapted. It does not take much thought to see that what is masquerading here as a biological discovery is, in fact, nothing but a political preference for the *status quo*. In reality, children may also fail to acquire the 'right' values because they recognize the conflict between them and their actual interests, or because the parents do not fulfil their parental function (political rather than biological) and impose them. There are plenty of circumstances in which a family that produced, say, draft-evaders or transgressors of the law of property would not be in any sense biologically malfunctioning.

Faced with such an argument, the psychologist is likely to admit that the ethic into which a child is socialized does, after all, contain certain norms which subsume even the interests of the family to the smooth running of society as a whole. It is traditional to assume, at this point, that stating the need for some kind of 'social contract' sanctions whatever notion of 'social' or 'anti-social' behaviour is current in the situation being observed. It is not the purpose of this article to dispute whether some rule-based social structure—i.e. a political order —is necessary: but the argument that *some* version of the 'reality principle' must be instilled into a child cannot be used to justify the imposition of whichever happens to be around at the time. Such a presumption can only be based on the belief that the prevailing political system is the only possible or desirable one: an illusion which psychologists are not alone in holding.

Yet mere ethnocentricity is too simple an explanation of why psychologists present a view of socialization which serves to protect the *status quo*. Their involvement with the power-structure within which they work has to be understood via a more careful examination of the exact role which they play in that structure: for this mentality does not arise in ivory towers. (Neither, one might add, does the so-called 'ivory-tower' mentality itself.) When we explore the channels through which psychological knowledge is made effective, we find first that those responsible for implementing it belong to what we might call the 'people professions'—those whose province is the regulation of human behaviour and the removal of 'social problems': that is, psychiatry, social work, the educational, penal and welfare systems. (I have deliberately avoided the widely used term 'helping professions' because I want to emphasize what the latter have in common with behaviour-regulating institutions such as the prison system, which nobody—as yet—speaks of as 'helping'.)

Now it is not within my competence or this paper's scope to offer a thorough analysis of the way these institutions work, but for the purposes of my argument several key features of them may be singled out; the point I want to make being that it is implicit in their role in the social system that their energies will be devoted to adapting men to that system, instead of helping to adapt the system to human needs. It is the job itself, rather than the people who do it or the theories they inherit, that is by nature conservative.

First, the 'people professions' are almost entirely financed and administered by public authorities. This is an inevitable—and in one obvious way, desirable—feature of a welfare system; but it does seem to have led to the consequence that the people the professions in practice cater to—who, incidentally, also represent for the most part the economically least privileged sector of society—have no say in the way they are organized, no access to their secrets, and no right to dispute their advice.

Secondly, their manner of functioning is primarily by way of 'confiscating' problems: either by institutionalizing problem individuals, or by defining their difficulties in a specialized language which purports to remove them from the layman's province—for instance, the jargon of clinical psychiatry, psychodynamics, or educational psychology. (Thus, there is more than a grain of truth in the vulgar criticism that psychology says what everybody knows in a language nobody understands.) This, again, stems from the concept of 'welfare services' as a system set up *alongside* existing society, rather than part of it, whose task is to repair the damage done to human beings by the way of life the social system entails for them: its function thus being inevitably corrective, rather than preventive.

Thirdly, in consequence of this, the social expertise of the people professions must stop short abruptly at a certain level of the power structure; and the contradictions which these limits give rise to are responsible for much of the anguish among workers in these professions—whether they realize it or not. The closer one works to the client, the more conspicuous the contradictions become. Consider, for example, the paradox of social workers and therapists who use 'object relations theory' to help their clients—an elaborate language for dealing with, among other things, the problems of having, getting, and giving, and the distinction between 'using' others as objects and relating to them as people. Their task is to raise their clients' consciousness of these issues, but somehow to stop short of the level where questions would start to arise about the same issues in relation to the larger structures of society. It is healthy for members of a family to become conscious of their envy, to resist being used, and so on—as long as they do it in the privacy of their own home; but what if they extend the process to their landlords, employers and rulers? One may make the same point by noting that the problems of having, getting, giving, and 'using' people are precisely what Marx wrote about (i.e. property, consumption, production and alienated labour); but no social worker is likely to be initiated into the analysis he offered.

In a sense, then (not a very nice one), the people professions treat their clients as if they were children, with very limited rights to knowledge about, and responsibility for, their own situations; but, of course, they are not children, and this state of affairs is not adequately explained by the nature of their problems. A certain degree of authority is proper to anyone in an advisory role, but the 'people professions' operate with a variety of paternalism that is quite incompatible with their claim to be 'helping people to lead better lives', and betrays the fact that their real duties lie altogether elsewhere. If such were really their aim, then we should expect their voice to be the most insistent in articulating and attacking the ways in which the political system itself systematically limits the quality of their clients' lives: moreover, it would be the latter to whom they would divulge their analyses of the situation, not to the others in authority over them. In practice, they apply their energies to ways of dealing with problems that offer the mini-mum disruption to the existing order—on peril of their jobs. For if the human wreckage produced by the way society is organized can be discreetly removed, processed, and returned in re-usable form by these social garbage-workers, then not only will the service avoid producing disruption itself: it will prevent the disturbance which might result if the evidence of the political system's failure to meet human needs were left in our midst.

These, then, are the trades to which psychology purveys the commodity of its knowledge, and to whose functions it thereby allies itself; just as the child's mentality is tailored to the social functions he will perform, so is that of the child psychologist. It is by virtue of the need to maintain the myth that the prevailing order is the only possible or desirable one that statements such as 'the child is born social' gain approval: Reich, Laing, Henry, Sartre, or Marcuse[7] can only offer the type of knowledge for which psychology—quite literally—has no use.

Here, then, we arrive back at the central theme of this paper: that how people are trained to act and think—whether they are children, parents, re-searchers, or practitioners with people—has to be understood in terms of their position in the political order: we cannot pretend any longer that it isn't there. Both science and the people professions still confuse themselves and the rest of society with a Victorian image of magnanimous neutrality—one which might, indeed, have had some relevance in the days when science was still within the technical and intellectual means of curious gentlefolk, and charitable activities were an individualistic free-for-all. Now, however, these activities have become industries, and those who staff these industries are a new proletariat, who (like the rest) must submit to being used in order to stay alive. We must therefore be extremely careful not to set up these mental and emotional workers as 'enemies of the people', as much so-called radical criticism tends to do: in reality, the scientist, psychiatrist or social worker (like the teacher, the policeman, or the parent) is as exploited as those whose exploitation he facilitates, as brainwashed as those he brainwashes. What species of prostitute is more pitiable than the person whose most highly developed thoughts and feelings are bought and put to uses he has no inkling of?

Finally, if it is true that the mentality informing most psychological research is inherently conservative, our most urgent task is to find a framework within which psychologists could work who do not share the conviction that the existing political order is the only possible or desirable one. My belief here is that a sufficiently thorough analysis of the existing framework will supply all the keys to the construction of a new one.

Following a line of thought suggested by Gabel (1970),[8] we may consider the problem as analogous to the psychotherapy of psychoses. The analogy runs as follows: Ideologies are epistemological structures whose intrinsic rigidities pre-

7. R. D. Laing, *The Politics of Experience*, Penguin, London, 1967; J. Henry, *Culture against Man*, Tavistock, London, 1966; J.-P. Sartre, Foreword to *The Traitor* by André Gorz, Calder, London, 1960 and H. Marcuse, *Eros and Civilization*, Beacon Press, Boston, 1955.
8. J. Gabel, *Sociologie de l'Aliénation*, Presses Universitaires de France, Paris, 1970.

clude the perception of certain areas of reality which must be concealed for the security of the existing power-structure; in the same way, it has been argued by those who have studied psychosis in its familial context, that psychotic thought-patterns represent attempts to embrace reality without betraying the power-structure of the relationships an individual is entangled in. (Mme Mannoni's therapy, in these terms, consists in telling her patients the truths which the family finds unspeakable, in order that their experience may make sense again.)[9] The limits a psychologist unwittingly imposes on his own awareness, by assimilating the 'spirit' of the profession, correspond to the paranoid individual's defences against reality-testing: any evidence which might threaten the overall picture is either systematically ignored or turned into evidence confirming it. And this is not to protect the psychologist's (or paranoiac's) own interests, but the interests of those who rely on his unawareness to maintain their own positions. Anyone who sets out to do therapy on such thought-structures must do so primarily by analysing their inherent contradictions. We must work in the same way as the therapist, who, for example, demonstrates to a person that their difficulty in finding a 'lovable' person to live with stems from their deeper need for the presence of an 'unlovable' person by contrast with whom *they* can feel lovable. The people professions have difficulty in 'helping people to lead better lives', and the human sciences in understanding man in his social matrix: both must be helped to see, for a start, the extent to which their role in society requires them to fail at these very tasks.

If, then, the object is to produce a psychology which is genuinely open to reality testing (which is, after all, what a 'scientific' psychology would be), what has to be done is to restore an open-mindedness to psychology which will allow the situations it studies to impress their own logic on the observer—rather than imposing on these situations the fetishized concepts which survived the test of ideological acceptability. This does not imply a return to some naïve theory of 'direct' perception, but ceasing to delimit in advance the concepts which will best serve to grasp a situation, and replacing the closed 'shop-talk' of psychologists with an open language that will admit all perceptions. This goal would seem to correspond to the phenomenologists' 'return to the things themselves'[10]: but if our earlier analysis is correct, this kind of objectivity cannot be achieved by intellectual thoroughness alone, but by withdrawal of one's allegiance to the interest groups defended by the existing framework. 'Divergent thinking' is not enough: in the human sciences, phenomenology is inescapably a political activity, in that it must involve the undermining of a major system of power and control—that is, intellectual orthodoxy.

In other words, the relationship of psychology to the 'people professions', and of these professions to the existing order, must change. I have tried to show that membership of the élite to which most of my readers will belong confers many powers, but entails—indeed, is conditional on—a systematic attenuation and distortion of one's awareness. To set right that 'false consciousness', it is not enough simply to set off in pursuit of a wider range of viewpoints—as if, by some

9. M. Mannoni, *The Child, his Illness, and the Family*, Tavistock, London, 1969.
10. M. Merleau-Ponty, *Phenomenology of Perception*, C. Smith (trans.), Routledge and Kegan Paul, London, 1962.

ingenious system of mirrors, one could see what the world would look like from a different position in the political order: one doesn't escape so easily from the bemusement of one's own mentality, from the habits of thought and perception laid down during the many years spent socializing into a class and a profession. The only way is to analyse just what this mentality is: and the shortest route to an understanding of it, as I have tried to show, is by discovering the power-structure it props up.

22. TOWARDS A SOCIOLOGICAL ANALYSIS OF PSYCHOANALYSIS   Peter Berger

Psychoanalysis has become a part of the American scene. It is taken for granted in a way probably unparalleled anywhere else in the world. This can be asserted without hesitation even if one means psychoanalysis in its narrower, proper sense, that is, as a form of psychotherapy practiced both within and beyond the medical establishment. But psychoanalysis in this narrower sense constitutes only the institutional core of a much broader phenomenon. Within this core we find the highly organized structures of psychoanalytically oriented psychiatry, with its networks of hospitals, research agencies and training centers, the various psychoanalytic associations (both those which deny and those which admit non-medical practice), and wide sectors of clinical psychology. The prestige and privilege of this institutional complex in America are already a remarkable matter, not least for the sociologist. Yet, if we take psychoanalysis in a more general sense, that is, as an assortment of ideas and activities derived in one way or another from the Freudian revolution in psychology, then we find ourselves confronted in this country with a social phenomenon of truly astounding scope.

Surrounding the institutional core of psychoanalysis there is a ring of satellite organizations and activities that may be called, loosely, the counseling and testing complex. Here we find entire professions, young in age and quite peculiar to this country, the most important among them being social casework, which only in America has taken on the character of a psychotherapeutic activity.[1] The counseling and testing complex, increasingly professionalized in its staff, extends into large areas of the total institutional structure of the society, its heaviest sedimentation being in the areas of welfare organization, both public and private, education, and personnel administration.[2] Yet even this much more extended perspective by no means exhausts our phenomenon. For we are not dealing only, or even primarily, with institutions and organizations. More importantly, psychoanalysis has become a cultural phenomenon, a way of understanding the nature of man and an ordering of human experience on the basis of this understanding. Psychoanalysis has given birth to a psychological model that has influenced society far beyond its own institutional core and the latter's fringe. American law, especially in such new branches as juvenile and domestic relations courts, but by

1. G. Hamilton, *Theory and Practice of Social Case Work*, Columbia University Press, New York, 1940.
2. M. Gross, *The Brain Watchers*, New American Library, New York, 1963.

---

22. Reprinted from *Social Research*, vol. 32, no. 1; Spring 1965. (pp. 26-41)

no means only there, is increasingly permeated with psychoanalytically derived conceptions.[3] American religion, both in its thought and in its institutional activities, has been deeply influenced by the same psychological model.[4] American literature, both 'high' and 'low', would be unthinkable today without it. The media of mass communication are filled with materials derived from the same source. Most importantly, everyday life, as expressed in the common speech, has been invaded by the terminology and interpretative schemes of psychoanalysis. Terms such as 'repression', 'frustration', 'needs' and 'rationalization', not to mention the key concept of 'unconscious', have become matter-of-course expressions in broad strata of the population. While we cannot be sure how far this linguistic usage is merely rhetorical and how far it has actually influenced the conduct it purports to describe, we are probably on safe ground if we assume that at least three areas of everyday life have been significantly affected by psychoanalytically derived ideas—sexuality, marriage and child-rearing. Both the so-called sexual revolution and the so-called family renascence in America have been accompanied by a flood of psychoanalytically inspired interpretations, which, by the nature of such processes, have increasingly become self-interpretations of those engaged in these activities. If we accept Robert Musil's observation that ninety per cent of human sex life consists of talk, then we may add that in America this has become more and more Freudian talk. And if we may believe John Rechy's novel, *City of Night*, even the young male prostitutes on Times Square worry about their narcissism.

A phenomenon of such magnitude becomes part of what Alfred Schutz has called the world-taken-for-granted, that is, it belongs to those assertions about the nature of reality that every sane person in a society believes as a matter of course. Only a madman would have denied the existence in medieval Europe of demoniacal possession; demoniacal possession was a self-evident fact of everyday life. Today, only a madman would assert this once self-evident fact as against, say, the germ theory of disease. Sane people in our society take the germ theory of disease for granted and act accordingly, although, naturally, most of them have to defer to experts for proof of this theory. It would seem that a number of root assertions of psychoanalysis have come to be taken for granted in a similar way. Thus, the questioning of the existence of the unconscious in a gathering of college-educated Americans is likely to be as much a self-certification of derangement as would be the questioning of the germ theory of disease. Insofar as college-educated Americans interpret themselves, they know themselves to be equipped with an unconscious as a sure fact of experience and, what is more, they also have quite specific notions as to how this appendage is furnished. For example, they are predisposed to admit the existence of unconscious guilt and to anticipate its eventual eruption. And only in America could James Baldwin have converted this predisposition into a political strategy.

Sociology, like psychoanalysis, occupies a fairly unique position in the American cultural situation. There is probably a common reason behind the cultural prominence of these two disciplines of collective introspection. Be this as it may, it would be very surprising if they had not influenced each other. As we

3. T. Szasz, *Law, Liberty and Psychiatry*, Macmillan, New York, 1963.
4. S. Klausner, *Psychiatry and Religion*, Free Press, New York, 1964.

know, the mutual influence has been massive.[5] There has been a strong socio-logical undercurrent in the development of psychoanalytic theory in this country, especially in the neo-Freudian schools, which have transformed the gloomy vision of the great Viennese pessimist into a bright, uplift and social-engineering-oriented program of secularized Methodism. The influence in the other direction has been no less remarkable, although American sociology is still probably less influenced by psychoanalytic theory than its sister discipline, cultural anthropo-logy. What is very interesting, however, is the range of this theoretical accultur-ation within the field of sociology. Although individual sociologists differ in their views concerning the feasibility of integrating psychoanalytic ideas with sociologi-cal theory, those who have a strongly positive opinion pretty much cover the spectrum of contemporary positions in the field. Thus Talcott Parsons[6] who has gone very far in incorporating psychoanalytic conceptions within his sociological system, shares this predilection with some of his sharpest critics. Whatever else may be in dispute between the currently dominant structural-functional school and its antagonists, the propriety of the sociological employment of psychoanaly-sis is not. Those sociologists who have kept aloof from psychoanalysis, for instance is not. Those sociologists who have kept aloof from psychoanalysis, for instance those who prefer to draw upon George Herbert Mead rather than Freud for the psychological underpinnings of their sociological work, have generally done so without directly questioning the validity of the interdisciplinary intermarriage.

If one is married, one may describe precisely this or that facet of the marriage partner's conduct, but the apprehension of the latter's total *gestalt* becomes ever more difficult. A similar difficulty of perception has been the result of the American liaison between psychoanalysis and sociology. Thus we have excellent analyses by sociologists of specific, partial aspects of the psychoanalytic phenomenon. There is a whole literature which concerns itself with various social dimensions of the psychotherapeutic enterprize. There are studies of the social distribution of various psychiatrically relevant conditions, intensive analyses of the social structure of the mental hospital (these investigations now adding up to a sort of sub-discipline within the sub-discipline of medical sociology), studies of attitudes towards various psychotherapeutic procedures in different social strata, and studies of the social processes going on in the course of psychotherapy. In recent years much of this work has been generously subsidized by the National Institute of Mental Health, as well as by private foundations. Far be it from us to disparage these studies, which have greatly enriched our knowledge of many facets of the phenomenon and in some cases have yielded insights of much wider theoretical import (as, for example, the work of August Hollingshead[7] and Erving Goffman.)[8] All the same, there remains an enormous gap when it comes to the sociological analysis of the phenomenon as a whole. Three recent attempts at such analysis which have achieved a measure of comprehensiveness are Richard

5. H. Ruitenbeek (ed.), *Psychoanalysis and Social Science*, Dutton and Co., New York, 1962.
6. T. Parsons, *The Social System*, Free Press, Glencoe, 1951.
7. A. Hollingshead and F. Redlich, *Social Class and Mental Illness*, Wiley, New York, 1958.
8. E. Goffman, *Asylums*, Doubleday-Anchor Books, Garden City, New York, 1961 and E. Goffman, *Stigma*, Prentice-Hall, Englewood Cliffs, New Jersey, 1963.

LaPiere's *The Freudian Ethic*[9], Eric Larrabee's *The Self-Conscious Society*[10] and Philip Rieff's *Freud—The Mind of the Moralist*.[11] LaPiere's work is burdened with a heavy political bias (because the author looks upon Freudianism as some sort of socialistic subversion of American free enterprize—hardly a helpful suggestion), Larrabee's does not go much beyond description, and Rieff's is in the main an exegetical enterprize, with some general observations on what its author calls 'the emergence of psychological man' in the concluding chapter.

Obviously, the present paper cannot even begin to fill this gap. What it does attempt, however, is to outline some of the presuppositions for the needed task of sociological analysis and to venture some very tentative hypotheses on the possible results of such an analysis. The first presuppositions are negative. It goes without saying that a sociological analysis will have to bracket, or avoid passing scientific judgment on, the practical utility of the various psychotherapeutic activities. The sociologist, qua sociologist, can be of no assistance to distressed individuals hesitating before the multiplicity of healing cults available on the market today, just as he can be of no assistance in the choice of the many religious or quasi-religious *Weltanschauungen* which are engaged in pluralistic competition in our society. In addition, a sociological analysis of our phenomenon will have to bracket the question of the scientific validity of the psychological model under scrutiny. This might be a task for sociological theory or social psychology, but it is an unnecessary burden for the study of the empirical phenomenon itself. The sociologist, qua sociologist, need not serve as arbiter among competing psychologies, just as, to return to the previous analogy, the sociologist of religion does not have to concern himself with the question of whether God exists. It should be strongly emphasized that this bracketing can occur even if the sociologist believes, as most American sociologists evidently do, that the psychoanalytic understanding of man is somehow true. Ideas do not succeed in history by virtue of their truth but by virtue of their relationship to specific social processes. This, as it were, root platitude of the sociology of knowledge makes it imperative that a phenomenon such as ours be investigated in an attitude of rigid abstinence from epistemological judgments about it.

The most important positive presupposition for such a sociological analysis is that it proceed within a frame of reference that is itself sociological. This means that sociological modes of analysis must be pushed to their own intrinsic limits and not be blocked by limits stipulated by another discipline. This procedure excludes the common practice of American sociologists of conceding extraterritorial preserves to the psychologists within the sociological universe of discourse (a courtesy, by the way, rarely reciprocated by the psychologists). Whatever may be the methodological merits of other disciplines, the sociologist cannot allow the scope of his work to be dictated by the latter. Thus, in different areas of investigation, the sociologist cannot allow the jurist or the theologian to put up 'no trespassing' signs on territory that, by the rules of his own game, is legitimate sociological hunting ground. In terms of the phenomenon that inter-

9. R. LaPiere, *The Freudian Ethic*, Duell, Sloan and Pierre, Inc., New York, 1959.
10. E. Larrabee, *The Self-Conscious Society*, Doubleday, Garden City, New York, 1960.
11. P. Rieff, *Freud—The Mind of the Moralist*, Doubleday-Anchor Books, Garden City, New York, 1961.

ests us here, the sociologist cannot concede to the psychologist exclusive rights to that vast area we commonly call psychological. It was precisely the great achievement of George Herbert Mead to show how the sociologist may enter this area without abandoning the presuppositions of his own discipline.

This is hardly the place to argue in what sense a sociological psychology may be constructed on the basis of Mead's work. Two crucial propositions of a sociological approach to psychological phenomena must, however, be explicated (in this context, of necessity, in an abbreviated and axiomatic fashion). The first proposition asserts that there is a dialectical relationship between social structure and psychological reality, the second that there is, similarly, a dialectical relationship between psychological reality and any prevailing psychological model. It must be emphasized that, in either proposition, psychological reality does not mean some givenness that may be uncovered or verified by scientific procedures of one kind or another. Psychological reality means the way in which human beings in a specific situation subjectively experience themselves. The dialectical relationship between psychological reality, in this sense, and social structure is already implied in the fundamental Meadian theory of the social genesis of the self. A particular social structure generates certain socialization processes that, in their turn, serve to shape certain socially recognized identities, with whatever psychological configuration (cognitive and emotive) appertains to each of these identities. In other words, society not only defines but shapes psychological reality. Just as a given psychological reality originates in specific social processes of identity production, so the continued existence and subjective plausibility of such a psychological reality depend upon specific social processes of identity confirmation. Self and society, as Mead understood, are inextricably interwoven entities. The relationship between the two, however, is a dialectical rather than a mechanistic one, because the self, once formed, is ready in its turn to react upon the society that shaped it. This understanding, which we would regard as fundamental to a sociological psychology, provides the sociologist with his logical starting point in the investigation of any psychological phenomenon—to wit, the analysis of the social structures of the situation in question.

The second proposition concerns the relationship of this psychological reality with whatever theories have been concocted to explain it. Since human beings are apparently destined not only to experience but also to explain themselves, we may assume that every society provides a psychological model (in some cases possibly more than one) precisely for this purpose of self-explanation. Such a psychological model may take any number of forms, from highly differentiated intellectual constructions to primitive myths. And once more we have here a dialectical relationship. The psychological reality produces the psychological model, insofar as the latter is an empirical description of the former. But the psychological reality is in turn produced by the psychological model, because the latter not only describes but defines the former, in that creative sense of definition intended in W. I. Thomas' famous statement that a situation defined as real in a society will be real in its consequences, that is, will become reality as subjectively experienced by the members of that society. Although we have jumped many steps of argumentation here, it may be clear that our second proposition follows of necessity from our first; both propositions spring from the same underlying understanding of the structuring of consciousness as a social process.

As far as the second proposition, an important one for our phenomenon, is concerned, it may at least partially be paraphrased by saying that psychological models operate in society as self-fulfilling prophecies.

The phenomenon that interests us here is a particular psychological model, acculturated and institutionalized in American society in particular ways. The sociological analysis must then revolve around the question of what social structures, with their appropriate psychological realities, this particular psychological model corresponds to (or, if one wishes to use a Weberian term, with what social structures this model may have an elective affinity). Before we turn to some hypothetical reflections on this question, however, it will be advisable to clarify the character of the psychological model a little further. Now, it must be emphasized very strongly that in the characterization to follow it is not our intention to reduce the various psychoanalytic theories to some sort of common denominator. Indeed, at this point we are not primarily interested in theories at all, but in the much broader socio-cultural configuration outlined in our opening remarks, a configuration that has its historical origin and its theoretical as well as institutional core in the psychoanalytical movement, but which is no longer co-extensive with this movement. The following, then, is an attempt to isolate some key propositions of a psychological model operative in the taken-for-granted world of everyday life in our society, a phenomenon that (perhaps *faute de mieux*) we would designate as psychologism.

Only a relatively small segment of the total self is present to consciousness. The unconscious is the matrix of decisive mental processes. The conscious self is moved out of these unknown depths into actions the true meaning of which it does not understand. Men are typically ignorant of their own motives and incapable of interpreting their own symbolizations. Specific and scientifically verifiable hermeneutic procedures have to be applied for such interpretation. Sexuality is a key area of human conduct. Childhood is the key phase of human biography. The on-going activity of the self may be understood in terms of the operation of scientifically ascertainable mechanisms, of which the two most important are repression and projection. Culture may be understood as the scene of interaction between unconscious motor forces and consciously established norms.

What structural developments have a bearing on the success of this psychological model in our society? In the argument to follow we are strongly indebted to Arnold Gehlen's[12] and Thomas Luckmann's[13] contributions to a social psychology of industrial society.

The fundamental structurizing force in modern society is industrialization. In rationalizing and fragmenting the processes of production industrialization has autonomized the economic area of the institutional fabric. This autonomous economic area has then become progressively segregated from the political institutions on the one hand and from the family on the other. The former segregation does not concern us here. The segregation between the economic complex and the family, however, is very relevant for our considerations, for it is closely connected with the emergence of a quite novel social phenomenon—the

12. A. Gehlen, *Die Seele im technischen Zeitalter*, Rowohlt., Hamburg, 1957.
13. T. Luckmann, *Das Problem der Religion in der modernen Gesellschaft*, Rombach, Freiburg, 1963.

sphere of the private. A modern industrial society permits the differentiation between public and private institutional spheres. What is essential for the psychological reality of such a society is that its members experience this dichotomization as a fundamental ordering principle of their everyday life. Identity itself then tends to be dichotomized, at the very least, in terms of a public and a private self. Identity, in this situation, is typically uncertain and unstable. In other words, the psychological concomitant of the structural patterns of industrial society is the widely recognized phenomenon of identity crisis. Or in even simpler words, individuals in this sort of society do not know for certain who they are, or more accurately, do not know to which of a number of selves which they experience they should assign priority status. Some individuals solve the problem by identifying themselves primarily in terms of their public selves. This solution, however, can be attractive only to those whose roles in the public sphere (usually this means occupational roles) allow such identification in the first place. Thus one might perhaps decide that one's real self is identical with one's role as a top business executive or as some kind of professional. This option is not very seductive for the great masses of people in the middle and lower echelons of the occupational system. The typical option for them has been to assign priority to their private selves, that is, to locate the 'real me' in the private sphere of life. Thus an individual may say, 'Don't judge me by what I do here—on Madison Avenue I only play a role—but come home with me to Darien and I'll show you who I *really* am.'

This privatization of identity has its ideological dimension and its psychological difficulties. If the 'real me' is to be located in the private sphere, then the activities of this sphere must be legitimated as decisive occasions for self-discovery. This legitimation is provided by interpreting sexuality and its solemnization in the family as precisely the crucial tests for the discovery (we would say, the definition) of identity. Expressions of this are the ideologies of sexualism and familism in our society, ideologies that are sometimes in competition (say, *Playboy* magazine against the *Ladies' Home Journal*) and sometimes merge into synthesis (the sensible-sex-for-young-couples constellation). The psychological difficulties stem from the innate paucity of firm social controls in the private sphere. The individual seeking to discover his supposedly real self in the private sphere must do so with only tenuous and (in terms of his total life) limited identity-confirming processes to assist him. There appears then the need for identity-maintenance agencies in the private sphere. The family is, of course, the principal agency for the definition and maintenance of private identity. However, for many reasons that cannot be developed here, the family alone is insufficient. Other social formations must fill this gap. These are the agencies designed to meet the psychological needs of the identity market. Variously organized, some of these agencies are old institutions transformed to fulfill new functions, such as the churches, while others are institutional novelties, such as the psychotherapeutic organizations that interest us here. All reflect the over-all character of the private identity market, that of a social sphere poor in control mechanisms (at least as compared with the sphere of public institutions) and permissive of a considerable measure of individual liberty. The various identity-marketing agencies thus tend to be voluntary, competitive and consumer-oriented, at least insofar as their activity is restricted to the private sphere.

If we now turn briefly to the public sphere, with its central economic and political institutions, we are confronted with yet another structural consequence of industrialization—the prevalence of bureaucratic forms of administration. As Max Weber showed long ago, bureaucracy is one of the main results of the profound rationalizations of society necessitated by modern industrial capitalism. Bureaucracy, however, is much more than a form of social organization. Bureaucracy also entails specific modes of human interaction. Broadly speaking, one may say that bureaucracy tends to control by manipulative skill rather than by outright coercion. The bureaucrat is thus not only a sociological but also a psychological type. The psychological reality brought about by bureaucratically administered institutions has been studied by a good number of recent sociologists, the concepts of some of them having actually gained broad popular familiarity; we need only mention David Riesman's 'other-directed character' and William Whyte's 'organization man' by way of illustration.

With this excursus of sociologizing behind us it is not difficult to return to the phenomenon that concerns us here. In view of the structural configuration and its psychological concomitants just outlined one would like to say, 'If Freud had not existed, he would have had to be invented.' Institutionalized psychologism, as derived directly or indirectly from the psychoanalytic movement, constitutes an admirably designed response to the needs of this particular sociohistorical situation. Unlike some other social entities involved in the modern identity crisis (such as the churches on the one hand and political fanaticisms on the other), institutionalized psychologism straddles the dividing line between the public and private spheres, thus occupying an unusually strategic position in our society. In the private sphere, it appears as one of the agencies supplying a population of anxious consumers with a variety of services for the construction, maintenance and repair of identities. In the public sphere, it lends itself with equal success to the different economic and political bureaucracies in need of non-violent techniques of social control. The same psychological practitioner (psychiatrist, clinical psychologist, psychiatric social worker, or what-have-you) can in one role assist the privatized suburbanite in the interior decorating of his sophisticated psyche, and in another role assist him (let us assume that he is an industrial relations director) in dealing more effectively with actual or potential troublemakers in the organization. If one may put it this way, institutionalized psychologism is in a probably unique position to commute along with its clientele. It is capable of doing just what institutionalized religion would like to do and is increasingly unable to do—to accompany the individual in both sectors of his dichotomized life. Thus the symbols of psychologism become over-arching collective representations in a truly Durkheimian sense—and that in a cultural context singularly impoverished when it comes to such integrating symbols.

Sociological analysis, however, can penetrate even further into the phenomenon, to wit, it can clarify the social roots of the psychological model itself. Thus we can now go back to our characterization of this model and ask how its central themes relate to the social situation in which the model has been so eminently successful. We would suggest, first of all, that a psychological model that has as its crucial concept a notion of the unconscious may be related to a social situation in which there is such complexity in the fabric of roles and institutions that the individual is no longer capable of perceiving his society in its totality. In other words, we would argue that the opaqueness of the psychological model reflects the opaqueness of the social structure as a whole. The individual in modern society is typically acting and being acted upon in situations the motor forces of which are incomprehensible to him. The lack of intelligibility of the decisive economic processes is paradigmatic in this connection. Society confronts the individual as mysterious power, or in other words, the individual is unconscious of the fundamental forces that shape his life. One's own and the others' motives, meanings and identities, insofar as they are comprehensible, appear as a narrow foreground of translucency, the background of which is provided by the massive structures of a social world that is opaque, immensely powerful and potentially sinister. The interpretation of one's own being in terms of the largely submerged Freudian iceberg is thus subjectively verified by one's ongoing experience of a society with these characteristics.

As the crucial psychologistic concept of the unconscious fits the social situation, so do the other themes used in our previous characterization of the model. The theme of sexuality fits the requirements of the social situation in which the essential self is located in the private sphere. In consequence, the identity-defining functions of contemporary sexual myths are legitimated by psychologism on various levels of intellectual sophistication. Again, the theme of childhood serves to establish the primacy of the private sphere in the hierarchy of self-definitions. This theme has been particularly significant in the psychologistic legitimation of contemporary familism, an ideology that interprets the family as the most 'healthy' locale of identity affirmation. The understanding of the self as an assemblage of psychological mechanisms allows the individual to deal with himself with the same technical, calculating and 'objective' attitude that is the attitude *par excellence* of industrial production. Indeed, the term 'productivity' has easily found its way from the language of the engineer to that of the psychologist. In consequence, psychologism furnishes the (*nota bene*) 'scientific' legitimation of both inter- and intra-personal manipulation. Furthermore, the interpretation of culture as a drama between individual 'needs' and social realities is a fairly accurate reflection of the ongoing balancing act between 'fulfilment' and 'frustration' in the everyday life of individuals in a high-level consumers' society. In consequence, psychologism again provides a 'scientific' legitimation to the adjustment technology without which such a society could hardly get along.

Finally, psychologism provides a peculiar combination of soberness and fantasy that would seem to correspond to profound aspirations of people living in a highly rationalized society. On the one hand, psychologism presents itself as a science and as a technique of rational control. On the other hand, however, psychologism makes possible once more the ancient fascination with mystery and magic. Indeed, one is tempted to speak here of a form of neo-mysticism. Once more the true self is to be discovered through a descent into the presumed depths of one's own being, and, even if the ultimate discovery is not that of the divine (at least not anywhere this side of Jungianism), it still has the old flavor of the *numinous*. Psychologism thus brings about a strange reversal of the disenchantment and demythologization of modern consciousness. The other world, which religion located in a transcendental reality, is now introjected within human consciousness itself. It becomes that other self (the more real, or the healthier, or the more mature self, or however it may be called by the different schools) which is the goal of the psychologistic quest.

Our considerations here have had to be distressingly abbreviated. And, we would emphasize once more, our argument has been tentative and hypothetical in its intention. Hopefully, though, we have been able to indicate the scope of the analytic task to be undertaken. Thomas Szasz, in his recent study of psychiatric influences on American law, has spoken of the emergence of the 'therapeutic state'. It may well be that the latter is but one aspect of the emergence of a 'psychological society'. It is all the more important that the full weight of sociological understanding be brought to bear on this monumental phenomenon.

23. INDUSTRIAL RELATIONS AND INDUSTRIAL CAPITALISM
J.E.T. Eldridge

Introduction

In this essay on the sociology of industrial relations I am going to explore two themes: the cash-nexus relationship and the incorporation thesis. This serves as a way of prising open a good deal of the literature on industrial relations in capitalist societies. It has been argued that a good deal of this literature is 'static' in that it only serves to supply an academic rationalization to the existing structure of industrial relations.[1] This is allegedly because it is dominated by systems analysis which stresses value consensus in industrial relations and in the wider society. It is certainly possible to find accounts of industrial relations which do appear to have a view of industrial-relations systems as containing self-correcting mechanisms making for the stability of the whole.[2]

Despite the demolition job on writers who adhere to systems analysis, one discovers that Allen's 'dynamic' analysis, which he identifies as historical materialism, stipulates among other things 'that a part cannot be understood without reference to the whole, that segments of systems cannot be analysed in isolation from each other or their environments'.[3] As a programmatic statement this seems reasonable enough, since it leaves open the question of the stability or instability of the systems being analysed. As it happens, the issues surrounding the instability of systems have not been entirely ignored, to which the recent debate on the degree of anomie in British industrial relations bear witness.[4]

As always the difficulty lies in putting flesh on the bones of programmatic statements. What concepts are to be employed, what theories formulated? Some of the problems encountered in the struggle to do this are reflected in the discussion that follows. How does one ground the surface phenomenon of industrial relations to give a coherent explanation of what is observed? How does one set 'events' in 'context'? The two themes which I have chosen to look at represent

1. V. L. Allen, *The Sociology of Industrial Relations*, Longman, London, 1971.
2. J. T. Dunlop, *Industrial Relations Systems*, Holt, London, 1958.
3. V. L. Allen, *The Sociology of Industrial Relations*, Longman, London, 1971, p. 9.
4. A. Flanders, *Management and the Unions*, Faber, London, 1970; J. E. T. Eldridge, *Sociology and Industrial Life*, Nelson, London, 1972; Goldthorpe, 'Social Inequality and Social Integration in Modern Britain' in D. Wedderburn (ed.) *Poverty, Inequality and Class Structure*, Cambridge University Press, Cambridge, 1974, pp. 217–38 and A. Fox, *Beyond Contract: Work Power and Trust Relations*, Faber, London, 1974.

a range of attempts to account for the form, character and changes of industrial relations in capitalist societies. A good deal of the literature constitutes a debate with Marx but the divisions of judgement are by no means to be classified as Marxist versus non-Marxist as we shall see.

Industrial relations and the cash nexus

In this section I want to discuss the concept of the cash nexus and what relevance it may have to questions of control and conflict in industrial relations. The point of departure is located in Marx's writings. In the *Communist Manifesto*[5] Marx analyses the breakdown of the feudal order and its guild system and seeks to account for the advent of capitalist society with its factory organization. He comments explicitly on the revolutionary part which the bourgeoisie played in this transforming process:

> The bourgeoisie, wherever it has got the upper hand, has put an end to all feudal, patriarchal, idyllic relations. It has pitilessly torn asunder the motley feudal ties that bound men to 'his natural superiors', and has left remaining no other nexus between man and man than naked self-interest, than callous 'cash payment'. It has drowned the most heavenly ecstasies of religious fervour, of chivalrous enthusiasm, of philistine sentimentalism, in the icy waters of capitalistic calculation. It has resolved personal worth into exchange value. . . .[6]

One paradox that is much discussed in Marx's writing is this. The bourgeoisie in capitalist society are immensely powerful. With single-minded energy they control the state and the economy and hence the industrial proletariat. Yet the system they seek to control is inherently unstable, so much so that ultimately they will be unable to control it:

> The bourgeoisie cannot exist without constantly revolutionizing the instruments of production, and thereby the relations of production, and with them the whole relations of society. Conservation of the old modes of production in unaltered form, was, on the contrary, the first condition of existence for all earlier industrial classes. Constant revolutionizing of production, uninterrupted disturbance of all social conditions, everlasting uncertainty and agitation distinguish the bourgeois epoch from all earlier ones. . . . All that is solid melts into the air, all that is holy is profaned, and man is at last compelled to face with sober senses, his real conditions of life and his relations with his kind.[7]

Marx's *Capital* is, in an important sense, a detailed exposition and analysis of the sources of instability entailed in a system of wage labour.[8] There is, for example, a critical distinction drawn between the social division of labour and the division

---

5. K. Marx, *Manifesto of the Communist Party* in D. Fernbach (ed.) *Karl Marx, The Revolutions of 1848*, Pelican, Harmondsworth, 1973, pp. 62–98.
6. *Ibid.*, p. 70.
7. *Ibid.*, pp. 70–71.
8. K. Marx, *Capital*, Allen and Unwin, London, 1957.

of labour in the workshop. The first is characterized by anarchy because it rests inexorably upon competition and is reflected in the fluctuation of market prices. The division of labour in the workshop is affected by this wider process and contributes to it. If one then looks at the first capitalist society, Britain, the intricate and considered discussion of such matters as the length of the working day, shift and relay systems, child labour, methods of wage payment, industrial legislation and the effects of machinery upon workers, one can see that Marx is actually attempting to chart out the dimensions of a struggle which is, in essence, over the buying and selling of labour power.

The underlying rationale for the buying of labour power is expressed in the idea that . . .

> . . . the value of labour power, and the value which labour power creates in the labour process, are two entirely different magnitudes; and this difference of the two values was what the capitalist had in mind when he was purchasing labour power.[9]

But can the capitalist live indefinitely on this basis of control through the appropriation of this surplus value created by labour? For Marx the despotism of the workplace could be a desperate reality to those exposed to its oppression. Indeed, part of his commentary is designed to depict the misery of living under a regimented factory system, subject to the overlooker's book of penalties and working like an automaton, as an appendage to a machine. As he contemplates the worst abuses of employer power over factory labour, moral indignation is interwoven into his sober economic and social analysis. The heat, the dust, the noise, the lack of light, air and personal safety in workshops overcrowded with machinery combine to assault the senses of the worker. Yet this powerlessness of labour in relation to the conditions of its existence was not the last word. Proletarian consciousness—the awareness of the nature of its own exploitation—would develop with revolutionary economic and political consequences. An understanding that the real relationship of the bourgeoisie with the wage labourer was embodied in the cash nexus was a critical factor in developing such consciousness. This prediction was, in Marx's view, bound up with the imminent laws of capitalist development relating to the social division of labour: the growth in the scale of capitalist undertakings involving, through competition, the expropriation of many capitalists by the few. It is this very process which creates a disciplined, united and organized proletariat, a revolutionary class:

> The monopoly of capital becomes a fetter upon the mode of production, which has sprung up and flourished along with, and under it. Centralization of the means of production and socialization of labour at last reach a point where they become incompatible with their capitalist integument. This integument is burst asunder. The knell of capitalist private property sounds. The expropriators are expropriated.[10]

What is of significance for our purposes is that industrial relations comes to be viewed as an arena in which the struggle for control over labour power is

9. *Ibid.*, p. 174.
10. *Ibid.*, p. 789.

played out. At the same time industrial relations may be reckoned as shifting in character with structural changes that occur in the social division of labour. A Marxist perspective might appear to suggest therefore that one should take readings of the industrial-relations temperature to measure the degree of revolutionary class consciousness. One might re-formulate this to ask how exposed is the cash-nexus relationship in a given situation, since Marx implies that a growing awareness of this relationship between capital and labour reveals a truth, the knowledge of which is a prelude to revolutionary change.

The problem I want to consider is this: what kind of temperature gauge is the cash-nexus relationship? In what sense does it or might it contain Marxist implications? For example, a number of studies of industrialization refer to the development of calculative economic behaviour among workers. Much of the comment on and interpretative analysis of machine breaking and resistance to technological change during the industrial revolution hinges around the question as to how far this behaviour was related to the perceived economic interests of the participants (including employers who were often ambivalent in their attitudes to change). Whether these activities were successful in accomplishing their aims is essentially a matter for historical inquiry. In any event, so far as the participants were concerned, such activities could affect the pace and timing of technological change and give them, as it were, some breathing space in their struggle for survival in the labour market.[11] There were, in addition, less dramatic forms of resistance that strongly suggested an economic motivation. The attempts made by factory owners and their overseers to control the work force entailed the struggle to impose a time discipline and to get the required amount of work out of the employees once they entered the factory. This struggle is reflected in the array of sanctions and rewards deployed by employers and the forms of resistance generated by workers against speed-ups, tight piece rates, unsatisfactory working hours and conditions. Some of this resistance might well have been undertaken on grounds of tradition. The attempt may have been made to maintain the status quo so far as possible, irrespective of possible future economic benefits accruing from adapting to change. But some behaviour was more calculative as E. P. Thompson points out:

> The first generation were taught by their masters the importance of time. The second generation founded their short-time committees in the ten-hour movement; the third generation struck for overtime or time and a half. They had captured the categories of their employers and learned to fight back within them. They had learned their lesson that time is money only too well.[12]

The time struggle is inextricably intermeshed with what has come to be termed the effort bargain.[13] What constitutes a fair day's work for a fair day's pay? To ask the question seriously leads to a probe into the nature of the

11. E. J. Hobsbawm, *Labouring Men*, Weidenfeld and Nicholson, New York, 1964 and M. I. Thomis, *The Town Labourer and the Industrial Revolution*, Batsford, London, 1974.
12. E. P. Thompson, 'Time, Work-Discipline and Industrial Capitalism', *Past and Present*, Vol. XXXVIII, 1967, p. 86.
13. H. Behrend, 'The Effort Bargain', *Industrial and Labour Relations Review*, Vol. X, 1957.

employment contract. Whether people are paid for the expenditure of physical or mental effort, to carry out instructions or to exercise responsibility, a principle of compensation is involved for the time spent in the employment of another and for the energy deployed in work. Some of the shopfloor studies undertaken by sociologists reveal the ways in which workers may operate the effort bargain in an endeavour to improve their terms of trade.[14]

I am suggesting that the cash-nexus proposition has close affinities with the effort-bargain concept. Certainly the awareness of the effort bargain serves to reveal the essentially economic nature of the employment contract. One way in which this awareness can develop has been traced out in Gouldner's fascinating studies *Wildcat Strike* and *Patterns of Industrial Bureaucracy*.[15] There we see the communal relations of an American gypsum mine corroded and subordinated to economic goals, as a result of the way in which management responded to the increasing competitiveness of the product market. The 'indulgency' pattern, whereby certain work practices and habits were tolerated as an expression of good will between management and men (and were supported by local community values), was replaced by a 'stringency' pattern in which the attempt was made to bring about worker compliance to imposed bureaucratic rules. The various worker responses to this new code included strikes, absenteeism and work-to-rules. The general point which emerged was that, while some workers hoped by their actions to bring about a return to the traditional situation, the dominant worker adjustment was in terms of a market orientation. If management focuses on costs, then labour will more consciously come to do so. As the language of the market is more explicitly spoken so the employment contract comes to be more closely geared to a consideration of market power by the bargainers.

Market power is a concept which can apply and be seen to operate at various levels: the individual worker, the work group, the factory work force, the skilled craftsman, the occupational group, the trade union and the professional association. In a diversity of ways the attempt may be made to discover, exercise, defend or improve market power by these various categories. Thus one observes attempts to control the supply of labour, resistance to technical changes and work practices held to be disadvantageous, output control and the withholding of labour. The accounts of trade-union history witness to the ways and circumstances in which these and other practices have taken place, sometimes as a substitute for negotiation and sometimes as a context-setting activity for bargaining. Likewise, the weapons of the employers are also recorded including hiring and firing practices and lock-outs in the struggle to determine the market price of labour.[16] However, the realization of market power does not necessarily have anything to do with a generalized or universal proletarian consciousness. Indeed, at the level of what the Americans call 'business unionism' this pre-occupation with the market price

14. D. Roy, 'Quota Restriction and Goldbricking in a Machine Shop', *American Journal of Sociology*, Vol. LVII, 1952 and T. Lupton, *On the Shop Floor*, Pergamon, London, 1963.
15. A. W. Gouldner, *Wildcat Strikes*, Routledge and Kegan Paul, London, 1955 and *Patterns of Industrial Bureaucracy*, Routledge and Kegan Paul, London, 1959.
16. S. Webb and B. Webb, *History of Trade Unionism*, London, 1894; H. A. Turner, *Trade Union Growth Structure and Policy*, Allen and Unwin, London, 1962 and T. Lane, *The Union Makes Us Strong*, Arrow Books, London, 1974.

for labour has been labelled as 'economism' by socialists echoing Lenin because it does not generate any political activity devoted to revolutionary change. It may rather inhibit such action.[17]

Market power is differentially distributed as between groups of employees. It is precisely this reality which undergirds discussions of wage and salary differentials. For example, recent British experience of the militancy of low-paid workers (especially in the public sector) and of professional groups such as teachers and doctors represent attempts to realize effective market power. The language deployed typically relates to arguments over parity, comparability and to restoring or improving one's place in the earnings-league table. What is of particular interest in recent British experience is the way in which white-collar workers and middle-class professional groupings have become more contract conscious.[18] This has meant that 'vocational' attitudes which have stressed the ethic of service have become subordinated to a more stringent scrutiny of the terms and conditions of work. So, for example, doctors in the National Health Service have come to treat hours of work as something that needs to be calculated and consciously related to remuneration. Rather than a fixed salary with a flexible interpretation of work load and working hours, the language of piece rates, time rates and overtime payments now comes into the reckoning. This concern with the economics of the employment contract can lead, not to greater egalitarianism within an occupation but to the stretching out of differentials. In teaching and in medicine the concept of career structure is applied in negotiations.

Once the cash nexus becomes of central concern the character of employer-employee relations is affected, whether or not Marx was correct in the inferences he drew from this fact. One more recent analysis of the matter that has certain affinities with Marx's treatment is found in Baldamus' *Efficiency and Effort*.[19] In a closely argued study, he considers the factors which serve to institutionalize effort values (and which are reflected in the terms of the effort bargain) and the sources of instability that may disrupt them. An increase in the available supply of labour and tougher competition in the product market, for example, will, Baldamus suggests, tend to lead to an attempt on the part of management to intensify effort controls. The converse of these conditions may lead to a more favourable effort bargain being struck by employees. For heuristic purposes Baldamus utilizes the notion of wage parity, as a hypothetical equilibrium between effort and pay on a given level of expectations. He then considers the likely consequences of shifts from that position in terms of the concept of wage disparity. The existence of wage disparity is treated by Baldamus as a central explanatory factor to account for industrial conflict in its range of manifestations.

The parties to the conflict may or may not be aware that wage disparity is the heart of the problem. Historically in industrial societies, Baldamus suggests, some wage disparity in favour of employers has been condoned by employees because of certain moral expectations attached to the idea of work as a duty. Where such work obligations are firmly institutionalized they are not experienced

---

17. V. Lenin, 'What is to be Done?' in *Collected Works*, Vol. V, Moscow, 1961.
18. G. S. Bain, *The Growth of White Collar Trade Unionism*, Oxford University Press, Oxford, 1972.
19. W. Baldamus, *Efficiency and Effort*, Tavistock, London, 1961.

as a contradiction to the principle of effort compensation. However, it is further suggested that the growth of large-scale organization is accompanied by processes that reveal the basis of the employment contract:

> For the very methods that are the main administrative instrument of effort intensification, such as payment by results, make the process of effort compensation and particularly, the relation of effort to earnings, more and more transparent. The growing pre-occupation with the administration of effort values may thus possibly reach a point where the normative aspects of industrial work are less concealed or taken for granted than at present. This would amount to a general drift in the institutional basis of employment from status to performance criteria. Unless a new pattern of social supports emerges the disruptive effects of industrial conflict can then no longer be absorbed, as they have been hitherto, by the employees' tacit acceptance of work obligations.[20]

It is precisely the shift from status to performance criteria that the comments made above concerning the new-found militancy of teachers and doctors serve to illustrate. It is a particularly significant example, however, because whereas the moral commitment to some industrial occupations may be somewhat limited in the first place, here we are dealing with the erosion of moral obligations which are traditionally embedded in the idea of vocation. What follows from this contract consciousness is that general goals such as 'the welfare of the patient' or 'the education of the young' become much more contingent commitments.

What this discussion of the role of the cash nexus suggests is that an awareness of this relationship clarifies the basis of the employment contract. This contributes to the instability of social relationships and reflects other changes taking place in the industrial and occupational systems. It is possible now to indicate how Weber's discussion of class and status relations can throw further light on the matter.[21] Weber, like Marx, treats class as an economic category. Ultimately class situation is defined as market situation:

> We may speak of a 'class' when (1) a number of people have in common a specific causal component of their life chances, in so far as (2) this component is represented exclusively by economic interests in the possession of goods and opportunities for income, and (3) is represented under the conditions of the commodity or labour markets.[22]

Class situation is contrasted with status situation—the formation of socially ranked groups, embodying distinctive life styles. Such groups are described by Weber as 'communities' and are able to control mechanisms admitting or excluding people into membership and seek to regulate behaviour according to the values it cherishes. The question Weber confronts is under what conditions the class relations become exposed to reveal basic structural antagonisms that lead to class-conscious action. His answer is explicit:

20. *Ibid.*, p. 112.
21. M. Weber, 'Class, Status and Party' in H. H. Gerth and C. W. Mills (trans. & eds.) *Max Weber*, Routledge and Kegan Paul, London, 1961.
22. *Ibid.*, p. 181.

> Every technological repercussion and economic transformation
> threatens stratification by status and pushes the class situation into the
> foreground. Epochs and countries in which the naked-class situation is
> of predominant significance are regularly the periods of technical and
> economic transformations.[23]

It is precisely at such times that a given distribution of property or structure of an economic order is no longer taken for granted. The 'life chances' of class groups which stem from these formations may be challenged. It is then, for example, that 'rational associations' established to prosecute class interests are likely to emerge, and trade unions are a classic case in point. But if class situations are strictly economic and are seen by Weber as related to the labour market, the commodities market and the capitalist enterprize in industrial societies, it is clear that the variations which may occur here will not necessarily line up with a portrayal of generalized proletarian action of a universal and revolutionary nature. Essentially it becomes an empirical question to discover how far, for example, the evolution of the industrial proletariat moves in the direction of increasing uniformity or heterogeneity. The occupational structure (not only factory work) the scale of industrial organization and the process of bureaucratization are all of relevance in that they affect the contours of the market situation and therefore the shape of class antagonisms.

The Weberian perspective does I think present something of a dilemma to Marxist analyses of the cash nexus. In Marxist terms, where there are internal variations in the market situation for different groups of wage labour 'rational associations' organized to protect and represent specific interest groups may be labelled sectionalist. The activities they pursue and the interest groups so constructed may even be cited as examples of 'false consciousness'. This indeed is one of the reasons why Marxists have frequently had ambivalent attitudes to such phenomena as craft unions and moreover, the general doubt that trade-union activity expresses an approach of mere economism, that may inhibit revolutionary consciousness is also expressed. The problem for the Marxist may be illustrated by reference to one or two recent studies and commentaries.

In his excellent study, *The First Shop Stewards' Movement*, Hinton[24] traces the pattern of growth and decline of the Workers' Committees and shop stewards' organizations in various parts of the UK from 1910 to the early 1920s. This was a time of highly-class-conscious activity, he argues, with explicit revolutionary intentions built into the movement. The key to success and failure was in an important sense located in the same phenomenon: craft consciousness.

> Craft work induced a pride and an independence which manifested
> itself in a tenacious resistance both to managerial encroachments in the
> workplace, and to the logic of bureaucratization both in industry and in
> the trade unions. . . . To the extent that the shop stewards' movement
> succeeded in taking the craftsmen beyond exclusiveness, it was able to
> release these traditions of craft control and of local autonomy from
> the narrow embrace of a defensive craft consciousness, to transform
> them into weapons of an ambitious class offensive.[25]

23. *Ibid.*, p. 194.
24. J. Hinton, *The First Shop Stewards' Movement*, Allen and Unwin, London, 1973.
25. *Ibid.*, p. 15.

It was in areas such as Glasgow, Sheffield and Manchester, where the craft traditions were most developed and, at the same time threatened by dilution, that the movement was strongest. The conflict between the antibureaucratic craft-control system and the pressures of capitalist rationality intensified as a result of the war was combined with revolutionary syndicalist doctrines. The ambiguity resided in the fact that the labour aristocracy was a vehicle for a revolutionary potential subversive to the capitalist order, but also held on to its sense of craft exclusiveness. Hinton concluded:

> Faced with the prospect of making a decisive challenge to the Government, the craftsmens' élan shrivelled into a conservative militancy, the defence of vested interest. But however subordinate the revolutionary possibilities, they had been there, and had been seen by the revolutionary movement to be there.[26]

The study then is partly a reflection on what might have been, but even more the way in which such movements provide a glimpse of what is possible in some revolutionary future when capitalist rationality is transcended. In a way this pays unconscious tribute to the strength of the Weberian perspective.

This last point can be further illustrated by Westergaard's instructive commentary on the cash-nexus proposition.[27] Westergaard suggests that a number of recent studies of British industrial relations, that emphasize the instrumental behaviour of workers as reflected in strike activities and work attitudes, are actually pointing to the exposure of the cash nexus.[28] This is most developed, he argues, in industries such as motor manufacture where variations in earnings and job security go hand in hand with high monetary expectations.

> If the wage packet is the only link that ties the worker to a grudging commitment to his work, to his bosses, and to society at large, that is a brittle strand, liable to wear thin or to snap when the dependability of earnings is threatened or pay rises fail to keep pace with rising demands.[29]

Moreover, in these circumstances,

> ... even industrial disputes formally confined to wages and immediately related questions seem likely to bring wider issues of control, authority and economic policy recurrently into focus.[30]

Westergaard is interested in the ways in which industrial conflict has been extended and deepened as class conflict in British society and in some respects he

26. *Ibid.*, p. 337.
27. J. Westergaard, 'The Re-discovery of the Cash-nexus' in R. Miliband and J. Saville (eds.) *Socialist Register, 1970*, Merlin Press, London, 1970 and 'Sociology: the Myth of Classlessness' in R. Blackburn (ed.) *Ideology in Social Science*, Fontana, London, 1972, pp. 119-63.
28. H. A. Turner, *Labour Relations in the Motor Industry*, Allen and Unwin, London, 1967; J. E. T. Eldridge, *Industrial Disputes*, Routledge and Kegan Paul, London, 1968 and T. Lane and K. Roberts, *Strike at Pilkingtons*, Fontana, London, 1971.
29. J. Westergaard, 'Sociology: The Myth of Classlessness' in R. Blackburn (ed.) *Ideology in Social Science*, Fontana, London, 1972, p. 162.
30. *Ibid.*, p. 162.

sees the breaking down of local community ties and of some occupational boundaries as a means of transcending particularistic and sectional solidarities. The possibility of a socialist transformation is thereby placed on the agenda but for all that the future remains open. Westergaard remains cautious about drawing any revolutionary conclusions as a necessary consequence of his analysis. Rather he seeks to underline the potential for social protest which changes in the economic and social structure of British society have made possible.

One final example of the continued relevance of Weber's approach to class analysis must suffice. I would refer here to Hyman's paper, *Industrial Conflict and the Political Economy*, which is a considered evaluation of contemporary British industrial relations from a Marxist standpoint.[31] Recent experience of industrial militancy in Britain, has, in his view, been sectional in character:

> While the size of wage demands in the last few years seems, by previous standards, remarkably ambitious, they appear far more modest when set against such factors as the rise in the cost of living (and in particular food prices), the effects of 'fiscal drag', and the 'poverty trap'.... Moreover, the focus in wage disputes is still the relative pay of different sections of workers—rather than the process of exploitation which affects all workers. Or again, many of the major struggles of recent years may be seen as a response to the initiatives of employers in seeking to curb public-sector pay rather than as a reflection of an autonomous eruption of worker militancy. And even the recent developments in the *methods* of industrial conflict—the wave of sit-ins, flying pickets, occasional mass solidarity action—need by no means imply that the traditionally restricted aims of trade unionists in conflict have been significantly transcended.[32]

While Hyman treats such collective action as a response to economic exploitation and the deprivation of control—which he sees as inherent in the institution of wage labour—he does not regard it as signifying or even by itself generating 'an explosion of consciousness' in the working class. From a Marxist standpoint he concludes that political education is required to be able to shift industrial conflict from its sectional basis to that of the working class as a whole.

> Effective intervention in the current industrial struggle necessitates an adequate general theory of capitalism and the transition to socialism; a theoretical analysis of the present disposition of the class struggle—the objectives of the ruling class, the role of the unions, and the state of working-class consciousness; and a set of strategies and tactics, of immediate and transitional demands, which are internally coherent and are explicitly related to the first two elements. In addition organizational recourses and ability are essential for the integration of theory and practice.[33]

As with Westergaard's discussion of the cash nexus, the question, what does the future hold, is hedged with uncertainty and unpredictability. The relevance

31. R. Hyman, 'Industrial Conflict and Political Economy' in R. Miliband and J. Saville (eds.) *Socialist Register, 1973*, Merlin Press, London, 1974.
32. *Ibid.*, p. 125.
33. *Ibid.*, p. 130.

of the cash nexus in helping us to appreciate some salient features of industrial relations and industrial conflict can scarcely be doubted, but the linkage with the immanent laws of capitalist development is, to say the least, not a straightforward matter.

Containment or encroachment? Some frayed edges of the incorporation thesis

There are many variations on the theme of incorporation and a range of judgements as to the desirability of the processes discerned. What does seem to be implied with greater or lesser degrees of firmness is the proposition that wage labour in Western societies has been contained by the capitalist system. This thesis does typically present itself as an alternative to the polarization thesis of class conflict. Indeed, it partly addresses itself to the question of why such revolutionary conflicts have not occurred. Commentators examine the ways in which civil and political rights are extended to all classes of the population in the nation-state; the bureaucratization of trade unions and the political parties; the institutionalization of collective bargaining; and the role of parliamentary government in canalizing political conflict. Strong and weak versions of this thesis exist among Marxists and non-Marxists and I want in this section to indicate some of the rough edges and ambiguities that need to be considered as they bear upon industrial relations.

Take first the issue of union bureaucratization. The consequences of this process since the writings of the Webbs and Michels have been associated with 'the iron law of oligarchy'.[34] This has pointed to the great difficulties which rank-and-file union members may encounter in seeking to exercise democratic control over their leaders. Michels developed this 'law' as a way of drawing attention to the fact that the democratic rhetoric associated with trade union and socialist party organization might not, for various structural and psychological reasons, accord with reality. He recognized that democratic ideals could and did challenge oligarchical rule and himself advocated the spread of education to reduce the power and information gap between leaders and led. A well-documented 'exception' to the law is a study of the International Typographical Association.[35] Other writers, notably Gouldner, have suggested that one can go further than this exception to the rule argument. He maintains that the iron law of oligarchy is not based on an irresistible argument. Rather it is a product of 'the pathos of pessimism':

> It is only in the light of such a pessimistic pathos that the defeat of democratic values can be assumed probable, while their victory is seen as a slender thing, delicately constituted and precariously balanced.[36]

The relation of leaders to led is manifestly a critical factor in any discussion

---

34. S. Webb and B. Webb, *Industrial Democracy*, London, 1911 and R. Michels, *Political Parties*, Collier, New York, 1962.
35. S. M. Lipset, et al., *Union Democracy*, Free Press, Glencoe, 1956.
36. A. W. Gouldner, 'Metaphysical Pathos and the Theory of Bureaucracy' in L. A. Coser and B. Rosenberg (eds.), *Sociological Theory*, Free Press, Glencoe, 1964, p. 507.

of union democracy and it is not difficult to see that education of union members can heighten an awareness of the significance of union rule books, of organization structure and of the mechanisms of policy implementation. There is also the question of what union leaders do, in particular how they behave in their dealings with business leaders and the state. The incorporation thesis sometimes seems to stress the corruptibility of union leaders and to suggest that this has facilitated the integration of the trade unions into the state. This formed part of Michel's own account. The matter cannot be reduced to psychological instances. That this is so may be illustrated in a number of ways.

Take, for example, Wright Mills' discussion of labour leaders in the USA. As he surveyed the complex interaction between union leaders, business corporations and the state, he concluded that the role of union leaders was not one of 'transcending' the existing capitalist and elitist social structure, but rather one of 'maximum accommodation'. Accordingly, union leaders are locked into a structural drift towards an elitist-dominated mass society. They are not fighting it but seeking to join it albeit on the most favourable terms for themselves and the unions they represent. Consequently:

> These unions are less levers for change of that general framework (of political economy) than they are instruments for more advantageous integration with it. The drift their actions implement in terms of the largest projections is a kind of 'procapitalist syndicalism from the top'. They seek, in the first instance, greater integration at the upper levels of the corporate economy rather than greater power at the lower levels of the work hierarchy, for, in brief, it is the unexpressed desire of American labour leaders to join with owners and managers in running the corporate enterprize system and influencing decisively the political economy as a whole.[37]

What is implied by this kind of analysis is that industrial relations must be understood in context and at the societal level this means considering them within the framework of political economy. What trade-union leaders do cannot simply be accounted for by reference to their personal ambitions or corruptibility. This treatment of incorporation in terms of structural drift finds some echo in Marcuse's work, notably *One Dimensional Man*.[38] More important in this connection is Miliband's *State in Capitalist Society*.[39] In the latter study we have a more explicit and worked-out extension of the Mills' thesis from American to other advanced capitalist societies. Miliband maintains that American trade-union leaders accept the capitalist order in theory and in practice. To that extent business unionism is scarcely a surprising phenomenon. In West European societies, on the other hand, trade-union leaders may be ideologically committed to a socialist order but in practice their behaviour is similar to their American counterparts. Assessing the nature of the collaboration between business, government and the trade unions, Miliband argues:

37. C. W. Mills, *Power, Politics and People*, Oxford University Press, New York, 1963, pp. 108–9.
38. H. Marcuse, *One Dimensional Man*, Routledge and Kegan Paul, London, 1964.
39. R. Miliband, *The State in Capitalist Society*, Weidenfeld and Nicholson, New York, 1969.

> Trade-union leaders have found it easy to believe that because they
> have been recognized as a necessary element in the operation of
> capitalism, they have also achieved parity with business in the
> determination of policy. In fact their incorporation into the official life
> of these countries has mainly served to saddle them with
> responsibilities which have further weakened their bargaining position,
> and which has helped to reduce their effectiveness.[40]

It is fair to add that Miliband does, elsewhere in his study, express the view that there are profoundly destabilizing forces at work in capitalist society and that ultimately the working class will no longer be incorporated but will acquire the faculty of ruling the nation. Nevertheless between then and now is a gap which he does not see easily bridged. Moreover, given the realities of state power and the divisions in the labour movement and the socialist parties, he envisages a movement towards more authoritarian forms of state control as a not unlikely outcome in liberal democratic societies.

The structural-drift argument has been referred to as an alternative to over-psychologistic explanations of union leadership. It is, however, not the only kind of structural explanation available and it will be helpful to set it against other perspectives. One well-known version of the incorporation thesis is located in Dahrendorf's *Class and Class Conflict in an Industrial Society*.[41] There, great emphasis is placed on the institutionalization of collective bargaining in 'post-capitalist' societies and in the separation of political from industrial conflict, which has served to insulate industrial conflict within the industrial system. The stability of industrial societies is thereby enhanced. This borrows a good deal in conception from the liberal pluralist analyses of Clark Kerr and his colleagues and in consequence has certain affinities with the 'end of ideology' interpretation of conflict in industrial societies.[42] There is, however, one important difference. Whereas in the systems analysis of the liberal-pluralist industrial conflict is seen as contained and controllable, for Dahrendorf the bureaucratization of trade unions is a process which may contain and pattern certain forms of conflict, but also may generate conflict, especially of an inter-union type:

> The fact that industrial conflict has become less violent and intense
> in the last century does not justify the inference that it will continue to
> do so. On the contrary, experience shows that in the history of specific
> conflicts more and less violent, more and less intense periods follow
> each other in unpredictable rhythms. It is certainly conceivable that the
> future has more intense and violent conflicts in store.[43]

There are, in addition, other dimensions to the issue of containing industrial conflict. The impact of inflation is a particularly important case in point. If one looks at Galbraith's study, *American Capitalism*,[44] one of the salient features of it

---

40. *Ibid.*, p. 161.
41. R. Dahrendorf, *Class and Class Conflict in an Industrial Society*, Routledge and Kegan Paul, London, 1959.
42. C. Kerr, et al., *Industrialism and Industrial Man*, Heinemann, London, 1962 and C. Kerr, *Labor and Management in Industrial Society*, Anchor, London, 1964.
43. R. Dahrendorf, *Class and Class Conflict in an Industrial Society*, Routledge and Kegan Paul, London, 1959, pp. 278-9.
44. J. K. Galbraith, *American Capitalism*, Penguin, Harmondsworth, 1963.

is that the thesis of 'countervailing power' is put forward partly as a tendency statement and partly as a policy prescription for managing capitalism. Galbraith sees countervailing power as a curb on economic power and sees the labour market as an important exemplar of this mechanism. He notes that in the USA industries which are dominated by large corporations, such as steel, automobiles and farm machinery, have been the breeding ground of strong unions. Where countervailing power is not, as it were, self-generating, Galbraith concludes that the state must assist. Such an intervention will serve to defuse more violent conflicts that otherwise might have splayed out into the political sphere. It is the existence and promotion of countervailing power that forms the keynote of Galbraith's response to the Marxist critique of monopoly capitalism:

> ... the Marxian attack has not been on capitalism but upon monopoly capitalism. The fact that the power of the genus of monopoly is ubiquitous has not been difficult to show. So long as competition remains the conservative's defence, the left is bound to have a near monopoly of the evidence and the logic.[45]

Yet the point is conceded by Galbraith that countervailing power as a mechanism ceases to operate when there is inflationary pressure on markets. Incorporation, by definition, becomes problematical in such circumstances.

A more recent study by Giddens, whilst different in many significant respects, comes up against the same obstacle.[46] Giddens argues that state socialism, as an alternative variant to liberal capitalism, has its best chance of coming into being when a society is at a relatively low level of economic development moving from feudalism to capitalism. If the revolutionary outcome does not occur at that stage then working-class protest is likely to be incorporated and institutionalized through the extension of political, industrial and legal rights to the whole population. For him, therefore, it is the presence of revolutionary class consciousness, rather than its absence, that requires explanation. Nevertheless, Giddens recognizes the contradictions that can occur in a managed mixed economy, especially in periods of growing inflation. The stability of liberal democratic societies which the process of incorporation brought about can become threatened and even fragile. This is because even if union leaders may seek with the government of the day and with employers to agree on the regulation of the economy (and that is not unconditional) it will be no easy coalition. Attempts to regulate wages and long-term contracts may well meet with rank-and-file resistance. The ability to carry their members with them can become an issue and, in consequence the credibility of their leadership. In such circumstances the likelihood of class conflict spilling over into the political arena is strong. This is directly contrary to a major tenet in the incorporation thesis, namely the institutional separation of industrial from political conflict. With continuing attempts to control incomes through statutory or voluntary incomes policies in capitalist societies has lent a certain artificiality to this notion for many years now. Further, if as a result of inflationary pressures liberal capitalist societies are unable to

45. *Ibid.*, 182–3.
46. A. Giddens, *The Class Structure of the Advanced Societies*, Hutchinson, London, 1973.

generate real wage increases, then movements for workers' control may be translated into political and economic action that has the effect of transcending capitalism.[47] This is, to say the least, a strong caveat to the incorporation thesis.

The incorporation thesis has always provided a challenge if not a threat to Marxist theories of class consciousness. A good summary of many of the Marxist and neo-Marxist responses to the thesis is found in Hyman.[48] It is not necessary to re-capitulate all the lines of the argument. Clearly, from a Marxist standpoint, incorporation has to be treated as a transient phenomenon. Certainly, Marx and Engels may be said to have revised their theory of class conflict. The polarization of classes based upon the increasing poverty and misery of the working class had to reckon with a British working class, which in their view was becoming more bourgeois. This, however, they anticipated would only be the case while Britain maintained a dominant position in the world economy. A commonly held derivative view is that at a later stage of capitalist development crises will occur leading to breakdown and the ultimate triumph of the proletarian revolution. Since the 1930s this view has not had much immediate evidence to feed upon. In the 1970s it has re-emerged in the wake of more general doubts as to the continuing validity of the Keynesian economic methods to serve as a basis for managing capitalist or neo-capitalist societies. This indeed serves as a basis for Glyn and Sutcliffe's critique, referred to above.

This dramatic prospect is not the only one which Marxists are able to call upon. In the event that capitalism does not break down as a result of recurring and intensifying crises, there remains what may be called the 'prosperity is not enough' motif. This really suggests that when all there is to be said about the economic and cultural subordination of the working class, the hegemony of the state, the benefits of economic growth albeit within a structure of social inequality, it will not be the last word. The relevant text here is Marx's *Grundrisse*.[49] The argument is that it is possible to portray capitalism in its most advanced forms, with the payment of 'surplus wages' to workers with the application of science to industry and the growth of automation, with even the decline of working-class occupations compared to middle-class occupations, and yet to envisage the transcendence of capitalist society. It is not proletarian revolution which must needs bring this about. The system, with all its incorporating tendencies, provides an arena in which the material forms of production come into conflict with the existing relations of production. The reason is that the system of production based upon the concept of exchange-value becomes thoroughly undermined. Through advanced technology, and automation, man stands at the side of the production process instead of being its chief actor and by the same token he comes to realize that this mastery over nature is not dependent upon the theft of labour-time (that is exploitation). What had been perceived by the capitalist as technological innovation brought into being in the service of profit has unintended consequences.

47. See also G. Hunnius, et al., (eds.), *Workers' Control*, Vintage, London, 1973 and A. Glyn and B. Sutcliffe, *British Workers and the Profit Squeeze*, Penguin, Harmondsworth, 1972.
48. R. Hyman, *Marxism and the Sociology of Trade Unions*, Pluto Press, London, 1973.
49. K. Marx, *Grundrisse*, Pelican, Harmondsworth, 1973. See also M. Nicolaus, 'The Unknown Marx' in R. Blackburn (ed.) *Ideology in Social Science*, Fontana, London, 1972, pp. 306-33.

> Productive forms and social relations ... appear. Forces of production
> and social relations—two different sides of the development of the
> social individual—appear to capital as mere means, and are merely
> means for it to produce on its limited foundation. In fact, however,
> they are the material conditions to blow this foundation sky-high.[50]

All this of course opens up questions concerned with the nature of class consciousness in advanced capitalist societies (sometimes labelled post-industrial) on which discussions of the 'new working class' and the 'new middle class' have focused.[51] In particular it raises questions as to what kind of collective control of such economies is possible and realistic. How far has any encroachment begun that tames the arbitrary power of capital and makes it more accountable to the community and to the producer? How far has the 'revolution' recurred behind the backs of those who proclaim the need for it? Or is it at least in progress?

It is possible to have a wooden, static view of the incorporation thesis, which is rather odd when one recalls that it is process that is being described not the end of history. Naturally it can lead to pessimism among those commentators who do not like what they see but cannot envisage any effective political change taking place. For example one of the problems encountered by those who see the work place as a battleground between labour and capital is: can the resistance to managerial prerogatives that one observes be transformed into anything other than guerilla warfare? This is something of a key question for those who look for political transformation as opposed to adjustments within the present system. It is posed by Beynon in his notable study *Working for Ford*.[52] He is impressed with the amount of time and energy spent by shop stewards in representing the interests of their members. Yet, as it seems to him they necessarily become absorbed in the day-to-day minutiae of negotiations. This leads to an ad hoc approach to the challenges of the day rather than a systematically developed policy of encroaching on managerial prerogatives. They have found themselves pushed into a position of trying to control the assembly line but have not set out to control the plant. Hence even 'factory consciousness' is a rather tender plant and talk of workers' control is little more than rhetoric.

This kind of argument involves a built in scepticism of union bureaucracy, of collective bargaining and of political activity within the Labour party. It is of interest to compare it with approaches that have a somewhat different emphasis, not least because they put the incorporation thesis in a somewhat ambiguous light.

There are approaches which, while recognizing the problem of bureaucratization for union and industrial democracy also point to the inroads that unions and union leaders can make on the running of capitalist society, which if not revolutionary certainly change its character in some important respects. Perhaps the most developed recent work on these lines is Banks' *Marxist Sociology in Action*.[53] Looking at the British industrial scene in historical per-

50. K. Marx, *Grundrisse*, Pelican, Harmondsworth, 1973, p. 706.
51. M. Mann, *Consciousness and Action Among the Western Working Class*, Macmillan, London, 1973.
52. H. Beynon, *Working for Ford*, EP Publishing, Wakefield, 1975.
53. J. A. Banks, *Marxist Sociology in Action*, Faber, London, 1970.

spective Banks points to the role that union leaders played in advocating and working for the public ownership of industry. The role of the union leadership in the case of both the mining and the iron and steel industries serve as examples and in so far as capitalist owners were removed from the ownership of strategic areas of industry, this can be defined as no small change. That state ownership can create other problems and certainly cannot be regarded as a recipe for industrial peace is not the point. The opposition to private ownership, although sometimes grounded in economic and technical considerations of efficiency, was typically rooted in moral objections. In an inquiry into the coal industry at the beginning of the century (the Foster Report) a representative of the Northumberland coal owners' association cross-examined a leader of the Northumberland miners. What possible difference could it make to the miner, he wondered, whether the profits of the industry were collected by the few or many, or by a neutral body like the State, so long as he got his fair share? 'Because he is now realizing that he is a citizen of the State,' replied Straker for the miners.[54]

Banks' argument, in the British context, puts a rather different slant on the incorporation thesis as compared to the approaches of Mills and Miliband discussed earlier. He stresses the idea of organization consciousness among trade-union leaders as a phenomenon that was in fact revolutionary in its consequences. The organizations which they lead have not so much been incorporated by capitalist society but have acted to change its texture in an anti-capitalist direction:

> The whole history of trade-union participation in British politics, both
> before 1926 and afterwards, is a history of the acceptance of the
> constitutional machinery with the express purpose of using it legally to
> improve the situation of the working class. In so far as deliberately, or
> willy-nilly, this has actually resulted in the piece-meal erosion of the
> capitalist system of exploitation, such participation is, of course,
> revolutionary in the present context.[55]

With this interpretation Banks takes over Lenin's concept of the vanguard of the proletariat and applies it to trade-union leaders, rather than to trained professional revolutionaries. Incidentally, on this reading it is the rank-and-file union member who is more open to Lenin's charge of economism and not the trade-union leader who has operated on an economic and a political front.

The pessimism of writers such as Beynon and to some extent Hyman can in part be explained by their scepticism if not cynicism with official union structures and the operation of collective bargaining. Consequently they see the rank and file as hemmed in and encapsulated even by their own union organizations. Banks' approach suggests a different perspective. So too does the approach of writers such as Hughes[56] who advocate the development of strategic collective bargaining. This is a view which seeks to link together a concern to articulate economic and social policies that not only recognize the realities of the concentration of capital and the role of multi-internationals in the economy, but also

54. C. Goodrich, *A Study in British Workshop Politics*, G. Bell & Son, London, 1920.
55. J. A. Banks, *Marxist Sociology in Action*, Faber, London, 1970, p. 111.
56. J. Hughes, 'Giant Firms and British Trade Union Response' in K. Coates, et al. (eds.) *Trade Union Register 1970*, Merlin Press, London, 1970.

to contain if not tame their power by making them accountable to the work-force and to the community. This is an approach which does not operate in either/or terms (either political action or industrial action; either rank-and-file action or collective bargaining) but is multi-faceted and is well summed-up in the following statement:

> It has to be a strategic objective of collective bargaining to enhance the elements of workers' control within the domain of the giant firm; at the same time pressure has to be directed through political channels and through the TUC, to ensure that statutory powers can also be directed at strengthening workers' rights in the giant combine, and to strengthen the community's right to ensure efficient operation and the minimization of market exploitation through monopoly power.[57]

It is precisely this kind of approach which Hughes sees as building a bridge between the day-to-day needs of trade-union bargaining and socialist demands of community control over the centres of industrial power.

Conclusion

Are there any general lessons which may be learned in the light of the above discussion from the standpoint of the sociology of industrial relations?

(1) In order to understand and evaluate what is being said, it is continually necessary to examine the assumptions that are made, the evidence they are based on, the concepts formulated to account for the underlying 'reality'. It is also important to try and see how these explanations are linked to policy recommendations or prescriptions as to what should be done.

(2) It is instructive to see when ideological closures operate. This may occur in some version of the 'end of ideology' thesis when it is tied to complacent notions of a system able to maintain itself and resolve tensions within it. Or it may occur in some Marxist accounts which favour mechanistic engineering metaphors of social change—for example, the transmission belts through which revolutionary consciousness is inevitably generated.

(3) Some ideological closures are more apparent than real (whether Marxist or non-Marxist) and this comes from a recognition of the complexities of analysis and consequent uncertainties as to what the future may hold. This does not lead to empty-minded speculation but to a disciplined awareness of alternative possibilities. For those who want to be involved in the action as well as to observe and explain it, it leads very naturally to discussions and proposals for strategy and tactics in industrial relations. In their judgement the future may not be wholly open, but it is open enough, containing within it a range of alternative possibilities, and is worth fighting for. A sociology of industrial relations need not therefore generate political somnolence.[58]

57. *Ibid.*, p. 72.
58. R. Hyman, *Strikes*, Fontana, London, 1972, Chapter 6.

(4) Analytically it would appear that a good deal of purchase can be obtained from considering industrial relations in relation to the notion of control. This is because it is a question that can be pursued at various levels (work group, factory bureaucracy, union, society) and the connection between these levels considered. If one seriously pursues the questions, who or what is being controlled to what purpose, to whose benefit and with what degree of effectiveness, then one can approach the study of industrial relations in a way that tries to confront the realities of power.

24. THE SERVANTS OF POWER L.Baritz

Henry Ford, II, 1946: 'If we can solve the problem of human relations in industrial production, we can make as much progress toward lower costs in the next 10 years as we made during the past quarter century through the development of the machinery of mass production'.[1] By the middle of the twentieth century, industrial social science had become one of the most pregnant of the many devices available to America's managers in their struggle with costs and labor, government and the consuming public. But, even then, industrial social science remained richer in its promise than in its accomplishments, impressive as these had been. It was often what social science *could* do in the next five, ten, or twenty years that justified to managers their current support of its practitioners. Thus far, social scientists had contributed to management a useful array of techniques, including testing, counseling, attitude research, and sociometry. All to the good, certainly; but much was left to do. And most of what was left, as Henry Ford correctly pointed out, was centered in the area of human relations. The reason that an understanding of human relations assumed such monumental proportions was that, in an age of governmental regulations and more powerful unions, costs continued to rise. American management came to believe in the importance of understanding human behavior because it became convinced that this was one sure way of improving its main weapon in the struggle for power, the profit margin.

The promise of industrial social science has not been a subject about which America's managers have had to guess. The industrial social scientists themselves have, throughout their professional history, made explicit their aspirations, their hopes for the future, and their unbounded faith in the centrality of their discipline to the problems of modern life. The history of this explication of faith began, appropriately enough, with Walter Dill Scott, who argued in 1911 that a knowledge of the laws of psychology would make it possible for the businessman to control and therefore raise the efficiency of every man in his employ, including his own. At about the same time, a lecturer at the University of Wisconsin's School of Commerce assured his students that a knowledge of psychology would increase their 'commercial proficiency by fifty per cent'. Workers, according to

1. Henry Ford II, 'Human Engineering Necessary for Further Mass Production Progress', *Automotive and Aviation Industries*, Vol. XCIV, January 15, 1946, p. 39.

24. Reprinted from *The Impact of Sociology* by J. Douglas, Ed., by permission of Plenum Publishing Corporation, New York. Copyright © 1970. (pp. 137-55).

Hugo Münsterberg's 1913 statement, would have their wages raised, their working hours reduced, mental depression and dissatisfaction with work eliminated, all through the application of psychology to industry. He assured Americans that a 'cultural gain . . . will come to the total economic life of the nation'. A knowledge of psychology, reported another psychologist, would provide the business executive with the skills needed to influence the behavior of his workers. Psychologist G. Stanley Hall went all out: 'Our task', he said, 'is nothing less than to rehumanize industry'.

During the 1920s and 1930s psychologists reported that 'the fate . . . of mankind' depended on the help they could give to managers. Indeed, according to James McKeen Cattell, the founder of the Psychological Corporation, 'The development of psychology as a science and its application to the control of human conduct . . . may in the course of the coming century be as significant for civilization as has been the industrial revolution.' Specific tasks were also outlined for the psychology of the future. For example, General Motors' sit-down strikes of 1937 could have been avoided through the use of psychology, said a psychologist. If psychologists were as effective in industry as they had been in education, said another, 'something akin to an industrial Utopia would arise'. Over and over again these men assured anyone who cared to listen that many of the world's problems would disappear if only executives would be more receptive to the advances of psychology.

Even problems of general moment were thought to be solvable through the work of industrial psychologists; the factory, said MIT psychologist Douglas McGregor,[2] 'is a microcosm in which we may well be able to find answers to some of the fundamental problems of modern society'. Industrial conflict would disappear, reported other psychologists, if their conclusions were implemented in industry. In fact, said still another, if psychology were more widely accepted by management, 'the advancement of our emotional, social, and economic life' would be more certain. '*Potentially the most important of sciences for the improvement of man and of his world-order*' is the way Robert M. Yerkes, a psychologist at Yale, described his discipline in 1946.[3]

Sociologists, too, tried to make clear what they could do if they were given the chance, though they were usually more restrained than the psychologists. They recognized that managers determined the kinds of opportunities the sociologists had, and hence, if the claims of sociology were frustrated, the managers themselves would be at fault. If all was in order, however, if managers cooperated, sociologists could 'provide useful analytical tools and profitable guides for activity'. Other sociologists believed that they could help managers 'think more effectively about their human problems'. Perhaps this was why one sociologist accepted employment with a petroleum company in 1943 to explain why the CIO was able to organize its men. Margaret Mead thought her colleagues could help make the anonymous industrial worker feel important. Focusing on the top echelon of the business hierarchy, some sociologists were dissatisfied with what they saw. A different type of social control was needed, and they believed

2. D. McGregor, 'Foreword', *Journal of Social Issues*, Vol. IV, No. 3, Summer, 1948.
3. R. H. Yerkes, 'Psychology in World Reconstruction', *Journal of Current Problems*, Vol. X, No. 1, Jan.–Feb., 1946.

that they were the men to point the way to the future. The powers of the sociological elite would be concentrated on the sub-elite of managers who needed to be led and 'clarified'. All that was needed was some cooperation from those who wielded managerial power.

It was precisely this need for managerial cooperation that made the social scientists' conception of what they could do in the future seem at best a trifle grandiose and at worst silly. As part of the bureaucratization of virtually every aspect of American life, most industrial social scientists labored in industry as technicians, not as scientists. Not professionally concerned with problems outside the delimited sphere which management had assigned to them, not daring to cross channels of communication and authority, they were hemmed in by the very organization charts which they had helped to contrive. And the usual industrial social scientist, because he accepted the norms of the elite dominant in his society was prevented from functioning critically, was compelled by his own ideology and the power of America's managers to supply the techniques helpful to managerial goals. In what should have been a healthful tension between mind and society, the industrial social scientist in serving the industrial elite had to abandon the wider obligations of the intellectual who is a servant of his own mind.

Casting his characteristically wide net, sociologist C. Wright Mills[4] pointed out that 'the intellectual is becoming a technician, an idea-man, rather than one who resists the environment, preserves the individual type, and defends himself from death-by-adaption'.[5] Unless psychologists raised their sights and became concerned with broader social problems, said another observer, they would not 'rise to the level of professional persons but will degenerate into mere technicians'.

The technician's role was literally forced upon industrial social scientists by the nature of their industrial positions. Hired by management to solve specific problems, they had to produce. The problem was best stated by two of the most astute psychologists of the 1920's: 'Research, to be successful, has to be carried out under the most favorable conditions, and only the business man himself can say whether these conditions shall be provided'.[6]

A few industrial social scientists learned that they could not even rely on the much touted practicality of business executives. One psychologist employed by an advertising agency said in 1955 that he 'had expected that the businessman would be hard headed and practical. . . . To my surprise and frustration', he went on, 'they have accepted an awful lot of research mish mush. . . . Hard headed businessmen hell!' Managers, however, have usually been sufficiently practical, from their own point of view, to realize that controls over research programs were necessary. Demanding that the social scientists in their employ concentrate exclusively on the narrow problems of productivity and industrial loyalty, managers made of industrial social science a tool of industrial domination. Some social scientists warned that this procedure would result in a 'distorted view of industry', but failed to see that this was precisely what sophisticated managers wanted.

4. C. W. Mills, *White Collar*, Galaxy Books, New York, 1953.
5. *Ibid.*, p. 157.
6. A. W. Kornhauser and F. A. Kingsbury, *Psychological Tests in Business*, University of Chicago Press, Chicago, 1924.

Even Elton Mayo, of Hawthorne fame, feared that the forced status of technician would seriously limit the effectiveness of industrial social scientists whose science would thereby be strangled. Because of the control of management over the nature and scope of their work, Mayo said, 'the interesting *aperçu*, the long chance, may not be followed: both alike must be denied in order that the (research) group may "land another job".' The long-range effects would be even worse, because the 'confusion of research with commercial huckstering can never prosper: the only effect is to disgust the intelligent youngster who is thus forced to abandon his quest for human enlightenment'.[7]

Management, in short, controlled the industrial social scientists in its employ. Managers did not make use of social science out of a sense of social responsibility, but out of a recognized need to attack age-old problems of costs and worker loyalty with new weapons designed to fit the needs and problems of the twentieth century. Thus the recent arguments that American industry has entered a new era of social obligations and responsibilities have missed the main point in the motivation of managers. When fulfilling putative social obligations became smart business, smart managers became socially conscious. Walter Reuther is characteristic of the small group that has refused to be seduced by the sophisticated rhetoric of managers, their spokesmen, and the articulate academicians who insist that the American business civilization is the best of all possible worlds. Trying to educate a congressional committee, Reuther said that his extensive experience with employers had taught him that 'the one sure way of making them (employers) socially responsible is to make them financially responsible for the social results of what they do or fail to do'.[8] Because of the general climate of opinion today, it is perhaps necessary to repeat what in previous years would have been a cliche unworthy of serious argument: managers as managers, are in business to make money. Only to the extent that industrial social scientists can help in the realization of this goal will management make use of them.

Managers are forced by the necessities of the business world to measure their personal success or failure by the yardstick of the balance sheet; they have occasionally made considerable effort to clarify the thinking of industrial social scientists who just might be of help in improving the financial condition of the firm and therefore improving the position of the manager. It will be recalled that one of the main obstacles to easy interchange between managers and social scientists had long been the managers' conviction that social scientists were ignorant about the nature and purposes of industry. To employ an expert who did not recognize either the values or necessities of business might prove dangerous. Articulating what many managers felt, an executive of a large utility company, for example, in 1951 laid down the law to social scientists specifying the attitudes business expected of them:

---

7. E. Mayo, quoted in F. J. Roethlisberger and W. J. Dickson, *Management and the Worker*, Harvard University Press, Cambridge, Mass., 1939, pp. XII–XIV.
8. W. Reuther, quoted in U.S. Congress, *Automation and Technological Change*, Hearings before Sub-committee on Economic Stabilization of the Joint Committee on the Economic Report, 84th Congress, 1st Session, October 14–28, Washington, D.C., 1955, p. 105.

First—a willingness to accept the notion that businessmen perform a useful function in society, and that their methods may be necessary to accomplish this function. . . .

Second—a willingness to accept the culture and conventions of business as necessary and desirable. . . .

Third—a willingness to obtain personal satisfaction from being a member of a winning team, perhaps an anonymous member.

Fourth—a willingness and ability to practice the good human relations principles that he knows.[9]

How unnecessary was this managerial fear of the industrial social scientist. The popular image of the impractical and absent-minded professor who was either a political liberal or perhaps even worse blurred the perception of the hard-headed managers of the business life of the nation. For, throughout their professional history, industrial social scientists, without prodding from anyone, have accepted the norms of America's managers. If this attitude had not tended to influence their work, it would deserve merely passing mention. But this commitment to management's goals, as opposed to the goals of other groups and classes in American society, did color their research and recommendations. These men have been committed to aims other than those of their professional but non-industrial colleagues. Though the generalization has weaknesses, it seems that making a contribution to knowledge has been the essential purpose of only a few industrial social scientists. Reducing the pressures of unionism while increasing the productivity of the labor force and thereby lowering costs have been among their most cherished goals, because these have been the goals which management has set for them.

Managers, of course, had the power to hire and fire social scientists. If a social scientist was to be kept on the payroll, he had to produce. The judge of whether he was producing was his boss. His boss was interested in the specific problems of the business including those that threatened managerial control. Thus industrial social scientists have usually been salaried men, doing what they were told to do and doing it well—and therefore endangering those other personal, group, class, and institutional interests which were opposed to the further domination by the modern corporation of the mood and direction of American life. Endangered most have been the millions of workers who have been forced or seduced into submission to the ministrations of industrial social scientists. For these men and women there has been little defense, because organized labor generally has been apathetic to the movement, and because, even had labor been more active, management has played the game from a dominant position. Recently, however, there have been a few hints indicating that organized labor is beginning to make use of social-science techniques itself. In any case, to date nothing seems to stand in the way of increased industrial exploitation of social science, and the industrial social scientists themselves have been especially willing.

The position these social scientists have taken regarding the ethics and politics of power obtrudes as a red thread in the otherwise pallid canvas on which

9. *Personnel Psychology*, 'Industry Appraises the Psychologist', Vol. IV, No. 1, Spring, 1951.

they have labored. From the pioneers in industrial psychology to the sophisticated human-relations experts of the 1950s, almost all industrial social scientists have either backed away from the political and ethical implications of their work or have faced these considerations from the point of view of management. Aptly, it was Hugo Münsterberg who first formulated the comfortable and self-castrating position that industrial psychologists should concern themselves with means only, not with goals, aims, or ends, which could and should be determined only by the industrial managers themselves. Scientific method was clearly on Münsterberg's side, for science cannot solve political problems, and psychology, he argued, was a science which must be impartial. Thus he insisted that his colleagues should not pander 'to selfish fancies of either side'—that is, capital or labor—but should remain detached and scientific observers of the industrial situation.[10] Other early leaders in the development of industrial psychology quickly picked up Münsterberg's cue and explicated his position: 'Psychology will always be limited by the fact that while it can determine the means to the end, it can have nothing to do with the determination of the end itself'.[11]

During the 1920s the political stance desirable for social scientists was made even more clear. Moving from the justification by objectivity to a recognition of the industrial facts of life, psychologists were told that 'business results are the main object'. Objectivity was lifeblood to a true science, but the industrial manager would instruct his hired specialists about those problems or subjects that required analysis. 'The pursuit and enlargement of psychological knowledge is merely a by-product of business efforts', psychologists were further cautioned. Confusion was compounded when, late in the decade, another industrial psychologist explained his position: workers who were justifiably dissatisfied were not fit subjects for psychological analysis because such a situation was an 'economic or ethical problem'.[12] The obverse held: where workers were treated fairly and still were dissatisfied, there was the spot for psychological inquiry.[13] The controlling question of who determined the justification of employee dissatisfaction was unanswered, as of course it had to be. Moving from the academic to the industrial world, it seemed relatively clear that managers would at least suggest where psychological analysis should occur, which is to say that the decision about the justification of employee satisfaction or dissatisfaction was one that management made. The social scientist applied his tools where he was told to apply them.

Of major importance in this subordination of industrial social science to the pleasure of management were the assumptions made by the Hawthorne researchers. Perhaps this was the area in which the work of Elton Mayo was the most significant. For Mayo, more than any other single individual, directed the course of industrial research—obliquely, to be sure, through the statement of his attitudes and assumptions, which proved so comfortable that many disciples made them their own.

10. H. Münsterberg, *Business Psychology*, Chicago, 1915.
11. H. L. Hollingworth and A. T. Poffenberger, *Applied Psychology*, Appleton, New York, 1917, p. 20.
12. H. E. Burtt, *Psychology and Industrial Efficiency*, Appleton, New York, 1923.
13. C. F. Hansen, 'Psychology in the Service of the Life Insurance Business', *Annals*, Vol. CX, November, 1923.

Mayo's unshakable conviction was that the managers of the United States comprised an elite which had the ability and therefore the right to rule the rest of the nation. He pointed out, for instance, that many of America's managers were remarkable men without prejudice.[14] According to one of his critics, Mayo believed that 'management is capable, trained, and objective. Management uses scientific knowledge, particularly engineering knowledge, for making decisions. Political issues are illusions created by evil men. Society's true problems are engineering problems.' With this frame of reference, Mayo throughout his inquiring and productive life ignored labor, power, and politics. Indeed, he ignored the dignity that is possible in the age of the machine, despite his contrary arguments idealizing what for him was the soothing past, the pre-industrial America. And in his myopia his colleagues and the larger movement of industrial human relations shared.

But the commitment of social science to management derived not alone from Mayo's assumptions about the nature of the industrial world and of American civilization. Quite as important were the implications of the substantive research done at the Hawthorne Works of the Western Electric Company. The counseling program developed there, for example, led most industrial social scientists to conclude that, because workers felt better after talking to a counselor, even to the point of commenting about improved pay rates which the company had not changed, most workers did not have compelling objective problems. Much of industrial unrest was simply a function of faulty perception and conceptualization on the part of labor. One counselor, also an industrial consultant, put it this way:

> At least half of the grievances of the average employee can be relieved merely by giving him an opportunity to 'talk them out.' It may not even be necessary to take any action on them. All that they require is a patient and courteous hearing supplemented when necessary by an explanation of *why* nothing can be done. . . . It is not always necessary to yield to the worker's requests in order to satisfy them.[15]

More and more industrial psychologists heeded the injunction of one of their colleagues who, in 1952, said that

> . . . the psychologist must reorient his thinking from what is good management of the individual to what is good personnel management and, ultimately, good business.[16]

The industrial social scientists' view of labor and unionism adds further depth to our understanding of their sweeping commitment to management. What kind of man is he who labors and why does he join a union? He is the kind of man, the early industrial psychologists agreed, who is stupid, overly emotional, class conscious, without recreational or aesthetic interests, insecure, and afraid of

14. E. Mayo, 'The Fifth Columnists of Business', *Harvard Business School Alumni Bulletin*, Vol. XVIII, Autumn, 1941.
15. R. N. McMurry, *Handling Personality Adjustment in Industry*, Harper, New York, 1944, pp. 13-4.
16. J. M. Gorsuch, 'Industrial Psychology's Growing Pains', *Personnel*, Vol. XXIX, part 2, Sept. 1952, p. 154.

responsibility. He is a man who, when banded together in a union with others of like sort, is to be distrusted and feared. This blue-collar man joins a union, psychologists and sociologists eventually postulated, because of a personality maladjustment, one that probably occurred early in life. The need for an equalization of power between labor and management, the need for economic sanctions, were not seen as the real reasons why men join unions. Rather, said psychologist Robert N. McMurry:

> The union also serves the worker in another way. Being somewhat authoritarian *it may tell him what to do. He no longer has to think for himself*. . . . Once he has been relieved of personal responsibility for his actions, *he is free to commit aggressions which his conscience would ordinarily hold in check*. When this is the case, his conscience will trouble him little, no matter how brutal and anti-social his behaviour may be.

Granting such premises, solely for the sake of discussion, one is forced to conclude with McMurry, whose position was rather typical, that

> "where management is fair and is alert to discover and remove sources of employee dissatisfaction, a union is not necessary." [17]

The social scientists' view of industrial conflict further illuminates their commitment to management. Throughout their professional history, the majority of industrial social scientists insisted that as soon as management took the trouble to study or to authorize studies of its workers, to learn their wants, instincts, desires, aspirations, and motivations, management would be able to do something about the demands of labor before such demands tied up the lifeline of industry and resulted in a strike. Understanding human relations, in short, was the only certain way to avoid conflict. Thus the demand of labor for wages was merely camouflage, argued the social scientists, masking more real and human needs of appreciation, understanding, and friendliness.

Because of his impact, Elton Mayo's formulations have always been important, and his statement of the problem of conflict was no exception. His early approach to conflict, and one that was to become rather representative of a large segment of industrial social science, was based on the postulate of the primacy of the individual in all social processes, including labor-management conflict. Before the Hawthorne researches broadened his vision, Mayo believed that ' "industrial unrest" has its source in obsessive preoccupation'. And again: 'There is a real identity between labor unrest and nervous breakdown.' [18] Conflict to Mayo was neither inevitable nor economic. It was a result of the maladjustment of a few men on the labor side of the picture. Even after Hawthorne forced Mayo to grow, he remained firm in his conviction that conflict was an evil, a symptom of the lack of social skills. Cooperation, for him, was symptomatic of health; and, since there was no alternative in the modern world, cooperation must mean

17. R. N. McMurry, *Handling Personality Adjustment in Industry*, Harper, New York, 1944, pp. 15, 17.
18. E. Mayo, 'The Irrational Factor in Human Behaviour', *Annals*, Vol. CX, November, 1923, p. 122.

obedience to managerial authority. Thus collective bargaining was not really co-operation, but merely a flimsy substitute for the real thing.

The nature of the social sciences in the twentieth century was, and is, such as to encourage the type of thinking of which Mayo is a good representative. His illusions of objectivity, lack of integrative theory, concern with what many have called the 'wrong problems', and, at least by implication, authoritarianism, virtually determined the types of errors he committed. Such errors are built into modern social science.

The problem of objectivity has proved to be especially troublesome to modern social scientists. During the depression of the 1930s for instance, some social scientists warned that a rigid insistence on objectivity would place power in the hands of partisans who would not trouble themselves with such matters. In other words, social scientists, by providing, without interpretation or advocacy, techniques and concepts useful to men engaged in struggles for power, became by default accessories to the power politics of American government and industry, while insisting that they were innocent of anything of the sort. The insistence on objectivity made an impartial *use* of their research findings virtually impossible.

Only after World War II did many social scientists, including Mayo, blame their difficulties on a lack of theory. But the more general belief that

> ... the chief impetus to the field of industrial sociology has come from observational studies in industry rather than inference from theoretical principles[19]

discouraged a concentrated effort to tie together the many dissociated studies with some kind of underlying theory. Data were piled on data; statistical analyses were pursued with increasing vigor.

Only rarely was any attempt made to explain, in a broader framework, the significance and relationships of psychological and sociological research.

> Lacking an objective scale of values, *said one industrial psychologist,* we have accumulated a vast body of data on what some of us suspect are either the wrong problems, or false or misstated questions, or altogether minor ones.[20]

In 1947 the criticism was fully developed:

> The human problems of industry and economic relationships lie at the very heart of the revolutionary upheavals of our century. One might except industrial psychologists to fired by the challenge of these issues. But most of us go on constructing aptitude tests instead—and determining which of two advertising slogans 'will sell more of our company's beauty cream'.[21]

19. W. E. Moore, 'Current Issues in Industrial Sociology', *American Sociological Review*, Vol. XII, No. 6, December, 1947, p. 651.
20. G. W. Hartmann, 'Summary for Psychologists' in G. W. Hartmann and T. Newcomb (eds.), *Industrial Conflict*, Dryden, New York, 1939.
21. A. W. Kornhauser, 'Industrial Psychology as Management Technique and as Social Science', *American Psychologist*, Vol. II, No. 7, July, 1947, p. 224.

This concentration on wrong or trivial problems was a result of the fact that social scientists, especially those who applied their science to the desires or needs of power groups, were not in command of their activities. They have not been, and are not, free agents. Clearly, however, industrial social scientists have not been forced to accept the assumptions, biases, and frames of reference of America's industrial elite. These specialists, like virtually every other group in American society, freely shared the assumptions of this elite. Most managers have had no trouble in getting social scientists to grant managerial premises because such premises have also been assumed by the social scientists. According to some analysts, this acceptance and sanction of America's power status by social scientists can most easily be explained by reference to the social scientists themselves. Said a sociologist, 'American social scientists have seldom, if ever, been politically engaged; the trend towards the technician's role has, by strengthening their a-political professional ideology, reduced, if that is possible, their political involvement, and often, by atrophy, their ability even to grasp political problems'. Hence industrial social scientists have had no qualms about serving 'the needs of the business side of the corporation as judged by the business manager'.[22] This another sociologist believed, made 'something less than a scientist' of any social scientist directly involved in the power relationships of the modern bureaucracies.[23]

The classic statement of the position of the industrial psychologist in relation to the powers for which he worked was made, in 1951, by the eminent industrial psychologist W. V. Bingham, who said that industrial psychology 'might be defined as psychology directed toward aims other than its own'.[24] Who, then, should set the aims for industrial psychologists? Obviously, managers would have no scruples against telling the social-science specialists on their payrolls how they should earn their money. With Bingham's definition in mind, most industrial social scientists did not hesitate to do what they were told. 'The result', reported one of *Fortune*'s editors, 'is not a science at all; it is a machine for the engineering of mediocrity. . . . Furthermore', he continued, 'it is profoundly authoritarian in its implications, for it subordinates the individual to the group. And the philosophy', he concluded, 'unfortunately, is contagious.'[25]

A handful of industrial social scientists bitterly complained of this willing acceptance by almost all of their colleagues of the control of their science and their research by the managers and spokesmen of that ubiquitous concentration of power: the modern corporation. The psychologist Arthur Kornhauser was one of the first, when in 1947 he called industrial psychology a management technique rather than a social science, and complained that 'psychological activities for industry . . . are characterized by the fact that business management constitutes a special interest group which manifests its special viewpoint in respect to research as in other matters. . . . Certain areas of research are tabu', he went on. 'Certain crucial variables must not be dealt with. We must avoid',

22. C. W. Mills, *White Collar*, Galaxy Books, New York, 1953, p. 82.
23. R. S. Lynd, *Knowledge for What?* Princeton University Press, Princeton, 1939, p. 178.
24. W. V. Bingham, 'Psychology as a Science, as a Technology, and as a Profession' in J. Elmgren and S. Rubenowitz (eds.) *Applied Psychology in Industrial and Social Life*, Göteborg, 1952, p. 24.
25. W. H. Whyte, *Is Anybody Listening?* Simon and Schuster, New York, 1952, p. 209.

he concluded, 'explicit analysis of the broad and basic problems of *power and authority* in economic life.' On rare occasions an industrial sociologist expressed similar attitudes. In the same year, for instance, Wilbert E. Moore,[26] then of Princeton, warned his audience of sociologists that the persistent managerial assumptions underlying so much of their work would reduce their profession to a refined type of scientific management dedicated to the exploitation of labor. But such expressions were unusual and not representative of the opinions of most industrial social scientists. Most of these specialists remained content to develop and refine further the techniques in which management expressed an interest, and either did not bother about or approved of the implications of their research.

Despite the avowed or implicit hostility of virtually all industrial social scientists to organized labor, union leaders traditionally have been either unaware of or indifferent to the work of these specialists. With time, however, at least since the Second World War, a few labor leaders have spoken against the entire social-science movement as it was then implemented in industry. No major union has, however, taken action on the national level to counteract this movement.

One labor leader has been especially troubled about the industrial use of social science; his formulation of the problem serves to highlight the basic difficulties of labor in a social-science world that is built on the assumptions of management. First of all, he wrote, social scientists so complicate the bargaining relationship that control is taken out of the hands of the inadequately informed workers and their representatives; experts are required to get through the maze of confusion, and democracy becomes impossible. 'The essence of unionism', he continued, 'is not higher wages, shorter hours or strikes—but self-government. If, as some unions apparently believe, higher benefits are the essential objective, then unionism becomes another, and more subtle, form of paternalism. . . . As for me', he concluded, 'I would prefer to receive lower benefits than to lose control of my bargaining relationship. Unfortunately, and this is the nub of the problem, many workers prefer higher benefits to democracy.' The issues at stake in this man's dilemma are profound, and the impotence of all unions, including his own, to resist, as well as the general apathy of other labor leaders, causes rot at the heart of American unionism. But the industrialist's keen awareness of the problems pushes him forward in his use of social scientists to complicate and confuse bargaining, to reduce grievances, and to squelch militant unionism.

A final question remains. What difference does it make if social scientists have found a place in industry and generally have shared the points of view of management? Are not social scientists an esoteric group of academicians with little or no contact with reality? What if they have been hostile to interests other than those that pay them?

The difference is great. Many managers have not hesitated to make explicit the point that their use of social scientists and their skills is for the purpose of human control. Through group conferences, management hopes to pressure the recalcitrant individual into conforming with his more right-thinking colleagues.

26. W. E. Moore, 'Current Issues in Industrial Sociology', *American Sociological Review*, Vol. XII, No. 6, December, 1947.

Cessna Aircraft and Atlantic Refining have furnished good examples of this approach. American Telephone & Telegraph has been convinced that it is possible through an understanding of motivation to 'influence' a given employee. The Life Insurance Sales Research Bureau said that 'in learning to shape people's feelings and control their morale, we shall be doing nothing more difficult than we have already done in learning how to fly. . . . We need not 'change human nature', we need only to learn to control and to use it'. General Foods took the position that 'leadership' and persuasion would prove most effective in directing the thinking and conduct of its workers. Other businessmen and social scientists have agreed that the main business of business is the control of human conduct.

A few social scientists were concerned, however, about the implications of their growing effectiveness with a science of behaviour. Would this not lead to the most insidious and relentless form of exploitation ever dreamed of? One industrial social scientists argued that control in a complex and interdependent society is inevitable:

> Society has always outlawed certain techniques for getting people to do what one wants them to do. As our understanding of behaviour becomes more and more refined, we will have to refine equally the moral judgment on the kinds of coercion—however subtle—that are approved and disapproved.[27]

Control, in other and more simple words, is a given; what needs to be changed is the system of morals that disapproves of control. Slim hope for the future, this. But *Business Week* has assured us that there is nothing to worry about.

> 'There's no sign', *reported this organ of business interests*, 'that the science of behaviour is getting ready to spawn some monster of human engineering, manipulating a population of puppets from behind the scenes.'[28]

Business Week is wrong. Social scientists by now have evolved a series of specific techniques whose results have delighted management. Especially through the use of group pressures has management shoved its people into line. Majority opinions, even when directly contrary to visual fact, sway the attitudes of others who would rather not trust their own eyes than suffer the stigma of being unusual. This social scientists have proved. 'If a manager's superior', said the personnel director of Continental Oil, 'has had difficulty in developing a co-operative attitude within that manager, the group technique can frequently help in developing the appropriate attitude'. Even *Business Week* was forced to admit that the pressures of the group on the individual members were so relentless that this was 'one good way to change what they (managers) want'. The Harwood Manufacturing Company and American Cyanamid both learned to lean heavily on group techniques to assure the continuation of management control.

27. M. Haire, 'Group Dynamics' in A. W. Kornhauser, et al. (eds.) *Industrial Conflict*, McGraw Hill, New York, 1954, pp. 384–5.
28. *Business Week*, 'People: What's Behind Their Choices—in Buying, in Working', August 14th, 1954, pp. 50–60.

Through motivation studies, through counceling, through selection devices calculated to hire only certain types of people, through attitude surveys, communication, role-playing, and all the rest in their bag of schemes, social scientists slowly moved toward a science of behaviour. Thus management was given a slick new approach to its problems on control. Authority gave way to manipulation, and workers could no longer be sure they were being exploited. Said C. Wright Mills:

> Many whips are inside men, who do not know how they got there, or indeed that they are there. In the the movement from authority to manipulation, power shifts from the visible to the invisible, from the known to the anonymous. And with rising material standards, exploitation becomes less material and more psychological.[29]

Many industrial social scientists have put themselves on auction. The power elites of America, especially the industrial elite, have bought their services —which, when applied to areas of relative power, have restricted the freedom of millions of workers. Time was when a man knew that his freedoms were curtailed. Social scientists, however, are to sophisticated for that. The fires of pressure and control on a man are now kindled in his own thinking. Control need no longer be imposed. It can be encouraged to come from within. Thus the faith that if 'people develop propaganditis' the effectiveness of control would be weakened[30] seems to miss the point. A major characteristic of twentieth-century manipulation has been that it blinds the victim to the fact of manipulation. Because so many industrial social scientists have been willing to serve power instead of mind, they have been themselves a case study in manipulation by consent.

Over the years, through hundreds and hundreds of experiments, social scientists have come close to a true science of behaviour. They are now begining to learn how to control conduct. Put this power—genuine, stark, irrevocable power—into the hands of America's managers, and the work that social scientists have done, and will do, assumes implications vaster and more fearful than anything previously hinted.

29. C. W. Mills, *White Collar*, Galaxy Books, New York, 1953, p. 110.
30. H. L. Wilensky, 'Human Relations in the Workplace', Industrial Relations Research Association, *Research in Industrial Human Relations*, Harper, New York, 1957, pp. 40–1.

INDEX